Cold War Orientalism

Cold War Orientalism

Asia in the Middlebrow Imagination,
1945–1961

Christina Klein

UNIVERSITY OF CALIFORNIA PRESS
Berkeley · Los Angeles · London

University of California Press
Berkeley and Los Angeles, California

University of California Press, Ltd.
London, England

© 2003 by the Regents of the University of California

An earlier version of chapter 4 was originally published in Christian G. Appy, ed., *Cold War Constructions: The Political Culture of United States Imperialism, 1945–1966* (Amherst: University of Massachusetts Press, 2000) as "Family Ties and Political Obligation: The Discourse of Adoption and the Cold War Commitment to Asia."

A version of chapter 5 will be published in David Engerman, Nils Gilman, Mark Haefele, and Michael Latham, eds., *Modernization, Development, and the Globalization of the Cold War* (Amherst: University of Massachusetts Press, 2003).

Library of Congress Cataloging-in-Publication Data
will be found at the end of this book.

Manufactured in the United States of America

12 11 10 09 08 07 06 05 04 03
10 9 8 7 6 5 4 3 2 1

The paper used in this publication meets the minimum requirements of ANSI/NISO Z39.48-1992 (R 1997) (*Permanence of Paper*).♾

For my mother
and
my father

What's the show about? Well, it's the story of the confrontation of the Far Eastern and American civilizations. . . . The usual thing you hear, you know, is East is East, and West is West, and all that nonsense. We show that East and West can get together with a little adjustment.

Richard Rodgers on *Flower Drum Song,*
quoted in *Newsweek,* 1958

Contents

Illustrations

Acknowledgments

I am grateful to the many friends, colleagues, and teachers who, know-ingly and unknowingly, helped bring this book into existence. My un-dergraduate teachers at Wesleyan—John Paoletti, Richard Slotkin, and Jeanine Basinger—endowed me with the basic tools I needed to get started. When I was at Yale, Jim Fisher, Dick Brodhead, Amy Kaplan, and above all Michael Denning gave generously of their enthusiasm and advice as the project took shape. I thank Debby Applegate, Jean-Christophe Agnew, Akira Iriye, David Engerman, Chris Appy, Stephen Sumida, Penny Von Eschen, Takashi Fujitani, Henry Jenkins, and Pete Donaldson for reading all or portions of the manuscript and sharing their helpful suggestions and insights. The comments by numerous anony-mous readers have made this a better book.

I am indebted to MIT for supporting this project with research funds and leave time, and to the Charles Warren Center for Studies in Ameri-can History at Harvard for a year-long fellowship. Dick Newman at Harvard's W. E. B. Du Bois Center, Tim Caton at Pearl S. Buck Interna-tional, John Juergensmeyer, and especially Bert Fink of the Rodgers and Hammerstein Organization gave me much-needed assistance at crucial moments. I am grateful to Toni Radler at the Christian Children's Fund for allowing me to reproduce their advertisements from the 1950s, even though they no longer reflect the current identity of the organization, which provides health benefits, education, and job opportunities for millions of families around the world. I benefited greatly from the first-rate research skills of Marin Boney, Wendy Wasserman, and Cotten Seiler.

Teachers, of course, come in all forms, and I have learned important lessons from people outside the classroom. My mother, Lola Klein, displayed a devious brilliance when she seduced me into becoming a professor by bringing home Lucian Pye's manuscripts on China, ostensibly for me to proofread but really to pique my jaded adolescent interest. My father, Peter Klein, offers material lessons in the rewards of hard work and frugality from which I benefit daily. My brothers, sisters, nieces, nephews, and in-laws—and especially my sister Beate—never let me forget that there are things more important than work. Kathy Newman reminds me in subtle ways that problems exist to be solved. My husband, Carlo Rotella, is a model of curiosity, patience, and wisdom— he has been the best teacher of all.

Introduction

On the evening of March 29, 1951, an expectant audience filled the seats of the St. James Theater in New York City for the opening of Rodgers and Hammerstein's newest musical, *The King and I*. As the show began, the audience settled in to enjoy the unfolding spectacle of Rodgers and Hammerstein's songs, Jerome Robbins's choreography, and Irene Sharaff's costumes. One scene in particular stood out for many viewers that first night, as it did for subsequent viewers of the 1956 film version. Set in the palace schoolroom, it presents Anna Leonowens as teacher to the King of Siam's numerous children and wives; a large map, ornately framed and free-standing, serves as the backdrop for the scene (Figure 1). The map is unfamiliar, however, and hard to decipher: the land mass that dominates it only vaguely resembles Asia. The King's head wife, acting as Anna's assistant, begins the geography lesson in a proudly nationalistic vein: she contrasts wealthy and powerful Siam, a large red area of the map onto which a fierce-looking military figure has been superimposed, with its weaker and poorer neighbor Burma, a smaller green area accompanied by a pathetic naked figure. Anna quickly takes over the lesson and, explaining that the map they have been using is outdated, pulls down a new map—"just arrived from England"—that completely covers the old one. This map, a Mercator projection, centers on Europe and depicts the world's countries in a size and relation that theater and movie audiences would instantly recognize. When Anna points out Siam, now quite small (Figure 2), the crown prince becomes out-

Figure 1. Anna (Deborah Kerr) and the old map of Siam in the film *The King and I*, 1956. (Museum of Modern Art/Film Stills Archive)

raged and refuses to accept his country's decentering and diminution; he relents only after Anna compares it to the even smaller England. At this point Anna introduces a song as a way of reinforcing her cartographic lesson. Seated in front of the map with the royal children ringed around her, she sings "Getting to Know You." The children and wives join in at the refrain, and they all sing together about the pleasures of transforming strangers into friends. At the song's conclusion, the opening-night audience at the St. James Theater broke out into spontaneous cheers and applause.[1]

The King and I belongs to a distinct cultural moment in which Americans turned their attention eastward. Between 1945 and 1961 American cultural producers churned out a steady stream of stories, fiction and nonfiction, that took Asia and the Pacific as their subject matter. Journalist John Hersey documented the dropping of the atomic bomb on Japan (*Hiroshima*), playwright John Patrick brought U.S.-occupied Okinawa into Broadway theaters (*Teahouse of the August Moon*), novelist James Michener probed the merits of the Korean War (*The Bridges at*

Figure 2. Anna (Deborah Kerr) locates Siam on the new map of the world in the film *The King and I*, 1956. (Photofest)

Toko-Ri), travel writer Lowell Thomas Jr. explored Tibet (*Out of This World: Across the Himalayas to Forbidden Tibet*), Hollywood director Richard Quine put contemporary Hong Kong onto movie screens (*The World of Suzy Wong*), and photographer Margaret Bourke-White framed views of India (*Halfway to Freedom*). Diplomat Chester Bowles (*Ambassador's Report*) and former first lady Eleanor Roosevelt (*India and the Awakening East*) described the political changes that were sweeping the region, while political observers such as David Bernstein traced the historical roots of these revolutionary transformations (*The Philippine Story*). Alan Watts (*Beat Zen, Square Zen, and Zen*) and Columbia University lecturer D. T. Suzuki popularized Zen Buddhism; Jack Kerouac (*The Dharma Bums*) and other Beat writers inflected it with a bohemian cachet. Motels, restaurants, and cocktail lounges surrounded their patrons in Polynesian chic, even as Chinese-born and Chinese American writers such as Lin Yutang (*Chinatown Family*) and Jade Snow Wong (*Fifth Chinese Daughter*) introduced readers to their fellow Americans of Asian heritage.[2]

Why did Asia and the Pacific hold such a fascination for so many Americans in the late 1940s and 1950s? Why did Americans want to produce and consume so many stories about this part of the world?

This interest was not wholly new, of course: Americans had been producing and consuming Asia symbolically for the previous century and a half. In the late eighteenth century wealthy Bostonians decorated their homes with Asian textiles, pottery, and objets d'art brought to them through the newly opened China trade. In the nineteenth century Emerson, Thoreau, and Whitman dipped into Hindu and Buddhist scriptures for literary inspiration, Herman Melville narrated his own and the nation's adventures in the Pacific, and Christian missionaries published firsthand accounts of life in China, Japan, and India. World's fairs brought millions of Americans, including architect Frank Lloyd Wright, face to face with Japanese, Chinese, and Filipino culture between 1876 and 1915. The modernist sensibilities of Ezra Pound, like those of Wright, found stimulation in Asia, and his poetry in the 1910s and 1920s, such as *Cathay* and *The Cantos,* displayed his immersion in Confucian aesthetics and philosophy. This cultural fascination with Asia increased during the 1930s and 1940s, as war in the Pacific turned from a possibility into a reality. In 1931 Pearl S. Buck published her novel *The Good Earth,* which became the most influential American representation of China: it sold more than two million copies, appeared on Broadway as a play, and attracted twenty-three million viewers in a 1937 movie version. During the war publisher Henry R. Luce used his *Time-Life* empire to disseminate positive stories about America's Chinese allies, even as propagandists in Washington and Hollywood depicted the Japanese as a faceless mass of subhuman enemies worthy of extermination. Low-brow mass culture had its own investment in Asian material, and the pulp novels and serial movies of the 1930s and 1940s were filled with the Oriental villainy and detective heroics of Fu Manchu, Ming the Merciless, Charlie Chan, and Mr. Moto. Postwar representations of Asia thus constitute a chapter within a much longer history.[3]

Part of the reason why Americans were especially interested in Asia after World War II was that the Cold War made Asia important to the United States in ways that it had not been before. Between 1945 and 1961 the United States expanded its political, military, and economic power in the region to an unprecedented degree, making its presence felt throughout the great arc that stretched from Korea in the north, down through the Chinese mainland and Taiwan, along the offshore island chains of Japan, the Philippines, and Indonesia, out into the Pacific, across the Southeast Asian peninsula, and up into the Indian subcontinent. Hundreds of thousands of Americans flowed into Asia during the 1940s and 1950s as soldiers, diplomats, foreign aid workers, missionaries, technicians, professors, students, businesspeople, and tourists. Never before had American influence reached so far and so wide into Asia and the Pacific. This expansion of U.S. power did not occur in a smooth and uncontested fashion, however. It coincided—and existed in tension with—the revolutionary process of decolonization. Inspired by Japan's wartime victories against the West, nationalists throughout Asia launched independence movements after the war that succeeded in driving out the colonial powers. The Philippines gained independence from the United States in 1946, India and Pakistan from Great Britain in 1947, Indonesia from the Dutch in 1949, and Vietnam, Laos, and Cambodia from the French in 1949 (nominally) and 1954 (actually). "Between 1945 and 1960," Geoffrey Barraclough has noted, "no less than forty countries with a population of eight hundred million—more than a quarter of the world's inhabitants—revolted against colonialism and won their independence. Never before in human history had so revolutionary a reversal occurred with such rapidity."[4]

This book is an attempt to explain the relationship between the expansion of U.S. power into Asia between 1945 and 1961 and the simultaneous proliferation of popular American representations of Asia. I take as my starting point the end of the Pacific war in 1945, when the United States began extending the position of political and military dominance achieved during the previous four years. The year 1945 makes a logical starting point for an investigation of the cultural sphere as well, because the end of the war also prompted changes in American attitudes towards Asia. I conclude at a point when this expansive material and symbolic investment in Asia and the Pacific began to narrow down. After 1961 the war in Vietnam increasingly consumed the attention of Washington's policymakers to the near exclusion of the rest of the region, while the domestic tumult unleashed by the civil rights movement, the urban crisis, and the antiwar movement absorbed the interest of the nation's artists and intellectuals. At the same time, race relations conceived in black-and-white terms nudged Asian Americans off the nation's cultural radar screen. As the Kennedy and Johnson administrations' obsession with Vietnam deepened, Asia gradually—and perhaps ironically—faded from the bestseller lists and the Broadway stages. American interest in Asia did not disappear in the 1960s and 1970s, of course, but it found expression in different social and cultural forms.

One of the ways in which I explore the relationship between postwar foreign policy and popular culture is by breaking down the sharp division that is often assumed to separate the material from the representational. The exercise of political, economic, and military power always depends upon the mechanisms of "culture," in the form of the creative use of language and the deployment of shared stories. Throughout this book I interpret political speeches, White House memos, National Security Council deliberations, foreign policy analyses, and State Department publications—as well as specific policies themselves—as rich texts worthy of cultural analysis. At the same time, works of culture are always embedded in concrete material and social relations. Following Raymond Williams, I believe they are most fully understood not as free-standing aesthetic objects, but as component pieces of larger cultural formations. In my interpretation of individual cultural texts I am interested in the intricacies of literary, cinematic, and theatrical form and how they work to create meaning. I am also interested, however, in the particularities of any given text's production, circulation, and reception. I explore how popular representations of Asia took shape in relation to specific cultural institutions, to the political commitments of their authors, to the legal structures regulating race and statehood, to the ebb and flow of social attitudes, and to the shifting political discourses and policies that defined Asia. Biographies matter here, as do conventions of genre, sales figures, foreign-language translations, theatrical casting practices, editorial assistance, advertisements, and reviews. In reading individual texts as part of a cultural formation, I explore how meanings do not reside exclusively within the texts themselves, but are also generated through their intersections with other meaning-making discourses and activities. A combined focus on these imaginative, social, and material processes, which, taken together, constitute a cultural formation, helps to bridge the gap that divides the realm of foreign policy from the realm of popular culture.[5]

As a second method of exploring the relationship between the material and the symbolic investment in Asia, I also investigate the cultural work that these texts performed. Working with a model of cultural hegemony, I explore the role that representations of Asia and the Pacific played in reinforcing the famed "Cold War consensus," the domestic hegemonic bloc that supported the postwar expansion of U.S. power around the world. The realm of culture, far from being wholly separate from the realm of politics, offers a privileged space in which politically salient meanings can be constructed and questioned, where social categories can be defined and delimited, where shared values can be affirmed and contested. Cultural texts perform a hegemonic function to the extent that they legitimate a given distribution of power, both within and beyond the borders of the nation. Education and participation play a crucial role in this process. The working of hegemony requires teaching the various members of a particular historical bloc, or alliance of social groups, how their interests intersect and why a certain arrangement of power serves their needs. It also requires creating opportunities for people to feel that they are taking an active part in building a viable social and political order. These processes of education and participation foster new loyalties and affiliations and thus help to secure new social and political alliances. Cultural hegemony also works by developing what Raymond Williams has called "structures of feeling." In a structure of feeling, the ideological principles that support a given arrangement of power are translated into regularized patterns of emotion and sentiment. A structure of feeling brings these principles to life in the form of affective relationships, real or imagined, which can be lived as everyday experience and consciousness.[6]

Much of the popular interest in Asia found expression within the cultural formation that sophisticated intellectuals of the 1940s and 1950s dismissed as middlebrow, and it is on that formation that this book focuses. It explores how middlebrow intellectuals, texts, and institutions tried to educate Americans about their evolving relationships with Asia, and how they created opportunities—real and symbolic—for their audiences to participate in the forging of these relationships. Middlebrow intellectuals often presented the Cold War as something that ordinary Americans could take part in, as a set of activities in which they could invest their emotional and intellectual energy. By foregrounding these processes of education and participation, the middlebrow cultural for-

mation imagined and facilitated the forging of a new set of affiliations—
nationally, among diverse social and political groups within the United
States, and transnationally, between the United States and the noncommunist parts of Asia. Middlebrow culture brought these alliances to life
by translating them into personal terms and imbuing them with sentiment, so that they became emotionally rich relationships that Americans
could inhabit imaginatively in their everyday lives.

This book devotes its attention both to cultural institutions, such as
Reader's Digest and the *Saturday Review* magazines, and to those individual works that reached the largest audiences, had the widest influence, and managed to retain a measure of their popularity over the
succeeding decades. The chapters that follow analyze William J. Lederer
and Eugene Burdick's novel about foreign aid in Southeast Asia, *The
Ugly American* (1958); Dr. Thomas A. Dooley's two nonfiction accounts of his experiences in Laos, *The Edge of Tomorrow* (1958) and
The Night They Burned the Mountain (1960); James A. Michener's collection of travel essays, *The Voice of Asia* (1951), and his novel *Hawaii*
(1959); and Rodgers and Hammerstein's trio of Oriental musicals, *South
Pacific* (1949), *The King and I* (1951), and *Flower Drum Song* (1958).
Extraordinarily popular and widely circulated, these are the bestsellers,
the book club main selections, the Academy Award winners, and the
Broadway record-breakers of their time—the greatest hits, as it were, of
the postwar fascination with Asia. In their themes, styles, and attitudes
they are also representative of the larger body of middlebrow texts produced about Asia during this period. Like the vast majority of middlebrow cultural productions, these texts explore the noncommunist parts
of Asia: mainland China, North Korea, and North Vietnam remain
largely beyond their purview. James Michener and Rodgers and Hammerstein receive particular attention because each of them produced a
sustained body of work about Asia and the Pacific—eleven books for
Michener, a trilogy of musicals for Rodgers and Hammerstein—and because each ultimately linked the American presence in Asia to the story
of Asian Americans at home. This is not an exhaustive study of all postwar images of Asia, but an argument for thinking about U.S. global expansion and the culture of the Cold War in new ways based on an in-
depth investigation of one particularly rich representational vein.

The texts that I explore do not exist in a cause-and-effect relationship
with the Cold War foreign policies pursued by Washington: they did not
simply reflect those policies, nor did they determine them. Rather, they
served as a cultural space in which the ideologies undergirding those

policies could be, at various moments, articulated, endorsed, questioned, softened, and mystified. Nor were the texts I examine unambiguous or internally coherent ideological broadsides. Instead, they provided an arena in which the multiple voices of allied, but still distinct, social groups could be heard. They served as a forum in which ideas associated with residual, emergent, and alternative models of international engagement could find expression alongside affirmations of the dominant ones of the Cold War. A genuine utopian impulse often resided within them and suggested the potential for challenging the global arrangements of power that Washington pursued.

The texts that I look at performed a certain kind of cultural work: they helped to construct a national identity for the United States as a global power. Although the United States had been a world economic power since the end of the nineteenth century, and a world political and military power since the end of World War I, not until after World War II did it displace Great Britain as the world's most powerful nation. Because this was a new role, and because it required repudiating a long-standing intellectual tradition (if not a political reality) of isolationism, this rise to power demanded a reworking of national self-definition. The task of national identity formation was complicated by the fact that this rise to global power took place at the very moment when nationalist leaders throughout Asia were in the process of throwing off Western domination. The political and cultural problem for Americans thus became, How can we define our nation as a nonimperial world power in the age of decolonization? This was also a problem of collective subject formation: How can we transform our sense of ourselves from narrow provincials into cosmopolitan citizens of the world who possess a global consciousness?

In grappling with these problems, middlebrow texts often continued patterns of representation that earlier generations of Americans and Europeans had developed. Sometimes they told the same stories: *The King and I,* for instance, was indirectly based on a pair of books that the real Anna Leonowens published in the 1870s; other times they recycled familiar images, tropes, characters, and attitudes. Yet these postwar texts also differed from their predecessors in significant ways. Some of these distinctive features can be seen by comparing postwar texts with those of the prewar period, such as *The Good Earth.* Buck set her novel about Chinese peasant life during an unspecified period in the nineteenth or early twentieth century and focused it exclusively on Chinese characters, whose daily life and routines she painted in minute, ethnographic detail.

Postwar representations of Asia, in contrast, tended to take the geopolitics of the Cold War as the ground for their narratives, either directly or implicitly. They often figured Asia as a contested terrain caught in the struggle between the United States and the Soviet Union, or explored the tensions between U.S. expansion and Asian decolonization. Even those texts set in the past and wrapped in an air of fantasy, such as *The King and I*, resonated self-consciously with contemporary political issues. Second, postwar texts tended not to focus exclusively on the people, histories, and cultures of Asia, as Buck did with China. Rather, their interest lay with the Americans (or, in the case of *The King and I*, Americanized Western characters) who lived, worked, and traveled in Asia. They devoted their energies to exploring how these Americans came to Asia, what they were doing there, and whether or not their presence was justified. Ultimately, these texts were not interested in Asia per se, but in America and its relationship to Asia.

A third, and most distinctive, feature of the postwar texts lies in their treatment of race and the ways they linked questions of race to U.S. expansion. Numerous cultural historians have shown how constructions of racial differences in the eighteenth and nineteenth centuries played an integral role in America's expansion across the continent and in its acquisition of a territorial empire. They have explored how the geographical extension of American power was enabled by the myth of the frontier, by popular narratives of savage war and Indian hating, and by domestic narratives that imagined expansion as a process of expelling racial Others from an ever-expanding nation figured as home. Edward Said made a related argument in his groundbreaking work *Orientalism* (1978), in which he proposed that European representations of the Middle East had enabled the exercise of European imperial power in that part of the world for centuries. Said defined Orientalism as a pervasive Western discourse about the East that found expression in everything from painting to literature to scholarly treatises. At the heart of Orientalism, he argued, lay an ideology of difference. Orientalism constructed the "East" and the "West" as internally coherent and mutually exclusive entities; it insisted that "there is an 'us' and a 'them,' each quite settled, clear, unassailably self-evident." Orientalism worked as an instrument of Western domination, according to Said, by defining the East in relation to the West through a series of oppositions, each of which located the East in a subordinate position. It presented the West as, for example, rational, progressive, adult, and masculine, and the East, in turn, as irrational, backward-looking, childish, and feminine. This binary logic constructed the East as an inferior racial Other to the West, and legitimated European imperialism by overdetermining the idea of Western superiority. Said extended his argument to encompass American culture as well, arguing that when the United States displaced France and Britain as global powers after World War II, it adopted their discourse of Orientalism as well.[7]

While many American representations of Asia produced before World War II fit comfortably within Said's model of Orientalism, many postwar representations of noncommunist Asia do not, although they do not contradict it entirely. The reason for this lies in the evolution of the American understanding of race. Scientific thinking about race began to change in the early twentieth century, when anthropologist Franz Boas moved away from the idea of immutable biological difference as a way to explain the diversity of the world's people and developed a more flexible model of cultural difference instead. A pluralistic model of society gradually followed from Boas's work: if intergroup differences resulted from relatively superficial cultural factors rather than essential biological ones, then these differences could be more easily accommodated within a relatively flexible social order. During World War II, when the United States fought against a Nazi regime espousing racial purity, the Boasian culture concept found wide acceptance. Washington defended democracy during the war as a universal political philosophy applicable to all peoples regardless of race, and by doing so it helped move into the mainstream the idea of America as a harmonious nation made up of people from diverse ethnic, racial, national, and religious backgrounds. After World War II, as Penny Von Eschen, Nikhil Singh, and Mary Dudziak have shown, Cold War ideologues mobilized this idea of a racially and ethnically diverse America in the service of U.S. global expansion. The United States thus became the only Western nation that sought to legitimate its world-ordering ambitions by championing the idea (if not always the practice) of racial equality. In contrast to nineteenth-century European imperial powers, the captains of America's postwar expansion explicitly denounced the idea of essential racial differences and hierarchies. They generated instead a wide-ranging discourse of racial tolerance and inclusion that served as the official ideology undergirding postwar expansion.[8]

Middlebrow intellectuals eagerly embraced these ideals of tolerance and inclusion, and largely framed their representations of noncommunist Asia within them. Let's return for a moment to the "Getting to Know You" scene in The King and I, and read it as a representative instance of a hegemonic middlebrow culture. At one level the scene produces a hierarchical relation between West and East: Anna is an adult who dispenses knowledge, and her students are ignorant children subordinate to her authority. When Anna replaces the old Siamese map with the new English one, she replaces the local and implicitly inferior knowledge of the Siamese with a metropolitan and implicitly superior knowledge derived from European models. In the best Orientalist fashion, she denies the Siamese the ability to represent themselves and insists that they can only truly know themselves through a Western and literally Eurocentric system of knowledge. But something else is going on here as well: Anna is more interested in forging connections between East and West than she is in demarcating racial and cultural differences. Anna introduces a new worldview that defines Siam—which has never been colonized by Europeans—not through its traditional enmity with neighboring Burma, but by its heretofore unrecognized geographical similarity to distant England. She presents a world in which East and West can be understood as related to one another outside the coercive ties of empire. A shared history of political independence, as well as small size, implicitly connects England and Siam. Anna animates this vision of interconnectedness by infusing it with emotion: as she sings "Getting to Know You," she translates the map's geography lesson into a playful song about the intimate bonds of friendship that can reach across national and cultural divides. More important, Anna opens up a way for the children to participate in the forging of these emotional—and international—ties when she invites them to sing along. These ties are thus not imposed on the children, but created by them through the pleasurable process of singing in unison. By the end of the number the hierarchical differences that structured the scene at the outset—teacher and students, adult and children, European and Asian, Western knowledge and local knowledge—are looser, although they do not disappear entirely. Anna and the children sit together on the floor, laughing and hugging each other: through the processes of education, participation, and the cultivation of emotions, they create a new community that includes Asians and Westerners.

I want to read Anna as an idealized self-representation of the middlebrow artists and intellectuals who form the subject of this book. In addition to inculcating the ideal of East-West friendship, Anna also teaches the children a new way of understanding their relation to the world: in changing maps, she replaces their national consciousness with a global one. Just as Anna directs her students' attention beyond the borders of Siam and Burma, so middlebrow intellectuals of the late 1940s and

1950s saw themselves as educating Americans about their changing relationship to the world at large. Like Anna, middlebrow novelists, travel writers, memoirists, editors, and lyricists used mapping as one of their preferred cultural strategies. Their texts are full of maps, both literal and figurative, of an Asia being transformed by hot and cold wars, nationalist revolutions, and shifting political alliances; in the context of the Cold War, these mappings of Asia implied new mappings of America as well. Middlebrow cultural producers sought to replace the old nationalist map that Americans carried in their minds, in which the United States filled the frame, with a new internationalist one, in which the United States and "free" Asia alike were embedded within a larger world system. Like Anna, they wanted to replace a national imaginary based on separation with a global imaginary based on connection. On stage, the British schoolteacher mediates between her students and this new representation of the world, managing the children's access to it, helping them to locate themselves within it, and explaining the laws according to which it works. The producers of middlebrow culture performed a similar function: they sought to situate their audience in relation to a world increasingly understood as interconnected, whose ligatures were defined by the logic of the Cold War. From this perspective, we can see that the true audience for Anna's global lesson is not the nineteenth-century Siamese children on stage, but the postwar American adults sitting behind them in the theater.

Also like Anna, middlebrow intellectuals repudiated imperialism as an acceptable model for East-West relations. Instead, they produced what Mary Louise Pratt has called "narratives of anti-conquest," which legitimated U.S. expansion while denying its coercive or imperial nature. Middlebrow intellectuals tended to denounce all forms of internationalism based on religious conversion, territorial appropriation, or the direct rule of one people by another. Instead they envisioned U.S. global expansion as taking place within a system of reciprocity. In their view, America did not pursue its naked self-interest through the coercion and subjugation of others, but engaged in exchanges that benefited all parties. In keeping with this view, middlebrow texts are full of exchanges between Americans and Asians: intellectual exchanges of conversation, economic exchanges of shopping, emotional exchanges of love, physical exchanges of tourism and immigration.[9]

These middlebrow narratives of anticonquest were often produced within a sentimental framework. "Sentimental" is often used as a pejorative term to denote a false or shallow emotionalism, but it is better understood as a name for a complex cultural mode. The sentimental reached its peak of cultural currency during the early nineteenth century, but its roots stretch back to the writings of Rousseau and Adam Smith, and its branches reach forward into the "Lifetime" movies of the present day. Postwar middlebrow texts, such as *The King and I*, can be seen as sentimental not because they tell a particular type of story, but because they tell a variety of stories in a particular way. The sentimental mode has a number of defining features that make it an ideal vehicle for narratives of anticonquest. First, sentimental narratives tend to focus not on the lone individual but on the "self-in-relation"; they uphold human connection as the highest ideal and emphasize the forging of bonds and the creation of solidarities among friends, family, and community. Second, a sentimental text explores how these bonds are forged across a divide of difference—of race, class, sex, nation, religion, and so on; the sentimental is thus a universalizing mode that imagines the possibility of transcending particularity by recognizing a common and shared humanity. Third, these sentimental human connections are characterized by reciprocity and exchange, often of a personal, intellectual, or material nature; the paired acts of giving and receiving serve as the mechanisms through which differences are bridged. Fourth, emotions serve as the means for achieving and maintaining this exchange; the sentimental mode values the intensity of the individual's felt experience, and holds up sympathy—the ability to feel what another person is feeling, especially his suffering—as the most prized. Finally, the violation of these affective bonds, through the loss of a member of the community or the rupture of communal ties, represents the greatest trauma within the sentimental universe.[10]

It is not surprising that middlebrow intellectuals would use the sentimental mode to think about questions of the Cold War and U.S. expansion: the sentimental has a long history within the United States, and the West more generally, as a politicized discourse. Because of its emphasis on recognizing the humanity of socially marginalized groups, sentimentalism in the nineteenth century underwrote a wide range of reform movements, including temperance, child protection, urban reform, prison reform, and, above all, abolitionism. The real Anna Leonowens, for instance, used the sentimental mode in her books to make a case for the abolition of slavery and the harem in nineteenth-century Siam. The power of sympathy could be a double-edged one, however: in forging emotionally satisfying bonds across the divides of difference and in providing access to another's subjectivity, the sentimental could serve as an instrument for exercising power. Pratt has argued that sentimental narratives of anticonquest facilitated the colonization of South America, while others have suggested that sentimentalism underwrote social control projects such as the education of Indians in the American West and served as an instrument of American colonialism in the Philippines. As a politicized discourse, then, the sentimental carried both a progressive and an expansionist legacy that postwar intellectuals could tap into.[11]

The pervasive sentimentalism of middlebrow depictions of Asia in the postwar period complicates their relation to Said's model of Orientalism. Their sentimental insistence on bridging differences, in combination with their liberal disavowals of racial hierarchy, suggests a need to extend the definition of Orientalism beyond the confines that Said first established for it. A number of scholars have begun this work. Lisa Lowe has shown that Orientalism is a heterogeneous rather than a monolithic discourse, and that it takes multiple and often contradictory forms. Melani McAlister, in turn, has argued that post–World War II American culture is better understood via a model of what she calls post-Orientalism. In her analysis of the relationship between expanding U.S. interests in the Middle East and popular media representations, she discovered that the meanings the Middle East has carried for Americans over the past fifty years have been "far more mobile, flexible, and rich than the Orientalism binary would allow." Instead of a consistent discourse of opposition, she found a complex cultural logic of American investment in, affiliation with, and appropriation of the Middle East for a diverse range of purposes. Instead of working to separate the United States from the Middle East, she suggests, American culture has struggled to bind them together in myriad ways that sometimes supported and sometimes challenged the expansion of U.S. power. The representations of Asia that I explore in the following chapters work in similarly complex ways, sometimes following Said's model of difference and hierarchy, and in other ways contradicting it.[12]

In *Culture and Imperialism* (1993), Said proposed some alternatives to Orientalism. He suggested that producers of knowledge could extricate themselves from Orientalist discourse, and the power relations it constructs, by acknowledging the inextricable "interdependence" of East and West, by recognizing the inescapably "hybrid" nature of all forms of culture, and by developing the ability to think "sympathetically"

about "others" rather than just about "us." Only by becoming aware of
the progressive "integration" of East and West that imperialism set in
motion, Said argued, can the imperialist logic of difference be undermined. In fact, however, the Cold War Orientalism produced by middlebrow intellectuals and policymaking elites deployed the very discursive
strategies that Said saw as oppositional. These texts narrated the knit-
ting of ties between the United States and noncommunist Asia, and were
infused with a structure of feeling that privileged precisely the values of
interdependence, sympathy, and hybridity. These narratives and structures of feeling, far from undermining the global assertion of U.S. power,
often supported it. The distinctive form of Orientalism that middlebrow
Americans produced and consumed during the early Cold War period
must be seen, then, as working through a logic of affiliation as well as
through one of difference.[13]

The ideal of U.S.-Asian integration functioned as one of the founda-
tional concepts of Cold War Orientalism. Revisionist historians of the
Cold War have begun to view the period between 1945 and 1991 not as
a unique historical era defined by the conflict between the United States
and the Soviet Union, but as a chapter in the ongoing process of globalization. From this perspective, the Cold War was as much about creating an economically, politically, and militarily integrated "free world,"
as it was about waging a war of attrition against the Soviets. Within the
United States, the concept of U.S.-Asian integration manifested itself in
the reform of U.S. immigration and naturalization laws in ways that
eased the entry of Asians into the United States and facilitated their naturalization as citizens, thereby opening up the way for the gradual integration of Asian Americans into the social and political mainstream. I
want to suggest that Cold War Orientalism had this dual concept of integration—international and domestic—embedded in its core. Together,
middlebrow intellectuals and Washington policymakers produced a sentimental discourse of integration that imagined the forging of bonds between Asians and Americans both at home and abroad.

Different kinds of expansion demand and produce different legitimating discourses. Because U.S. expansion into Asia was predicated on
the principle of international integration rather than on territorial imperialism, it demanded an ideology of global interdependence rather
than one of racial difference. The Cold War Orientalism generated by
middlebrow intellectuals articulated precisely such an ideology. In texts

such as *The King and I*'s "Getting to Know You," cultural producers imaginatively mapped a network of sentimental pathways between the United States and Asia that paralleled and reinforced the more material pathways along which America's economic, political, and military power flowed.

CHAPTER I

Sentimental Education

Creating a Global Imaginary of Integration

What we have to do is to convince not only their minds but
their hearts. What we need to do is to make the "cold war" a
"warm war" by infusing into it ideological principles to give
it meaning.

> Raymond A. Hare, acting assistant secretary
> of state for Near Eastern, South Asian and
> African Affairs, 1950

In June 1957 *Newsweek* published a special report on the spread of anti-
American attitudes around the world, and, like many publications on international affairs from the late 1940s and 1950s, it illustrated its story
with a map. Titled "Worldwide—The Feeling About Us" and spreading across two pages, the map depicts the northern hemisphere from Ice-
land in the West to Japan in the East (Figure 3). It represents the scope
of U.S. global expansion in an unusually forthright manner: eleven text-
filled balloons pinpoint the countries and regions where the U.S. had a
major military presence, and indicate the number of U.S. troops, government employees, and civilians stationed there. The balloons also summarize the "feeling" of local populations, suggesting the mix of good
will and hostility that U.S. expansion provoked. The map notes "minimum personal friction" between Americans and locals in Morocco,
"friendly" personal contacts in Great Britain, and "basically good" relations in France. The situation in Asia, however, was less positive: "local frictions" persisted in South Korea, collaboration with Formosa was
"endangered" by "increasing civilian-soldier irritations," relations were
"worsening" in Okinawa, and irritations were "growing" in Japan.
Even in the Philippines, a nation with which the U.S. enjoyed a "basically strong friendship," relations had been "hurt" by jurisdictional and

19

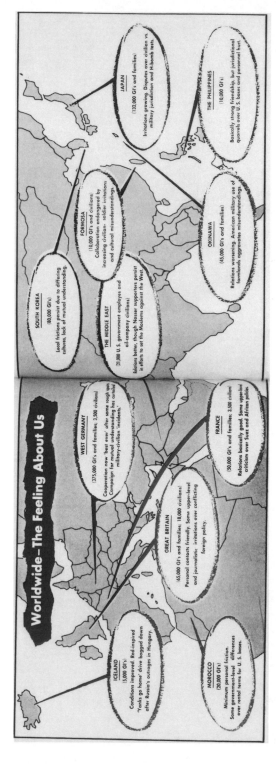

Figure 3. U.S. expansion and the feelings it provoked around the world. (*Newsweek* © 1957 Newsweek, Inc. All rights reserved. Reprinted by permission.)

personnel "quarrels." In calling attention to these frictions, the *Newsweek* map conveys some of the anxiety that the assertion of global power generated among Americans when they faced the contingent character of the U.S. presence abroad and the possibility of Asian opposition. The map offered the personalized language of feeling as the appropriate means for expressing that anxiety and for thinking about the dynamics of expansion and resistance.[1]

A few weeks after *Newsweek* published this map, Francis Wilcox, a mid-level State Department official, delivered a speech to an audience of educators in Philadelphia that recast the problem of foreign resistance to U.S. expansion into an issue of domestic pedagogy. Wilcox emphasized the profound effect that decolonization was having on the United States. He began by describing the rising influence of the new Asian and African nations and the accompanying shift in the Cold War from the military to the ideological plane. He explained that the Soviet Union, which in the late 1940s and early 1950s had "expanded its empire" into China, Korea, and Indochina through the use of force, was now turning to an "all-out war of ideas, ideologies, propaganda, and subversion" designed to win the allegiance of decolonizing peoples through peaceful means. Wilcox impressed upon his listeners that the U.S.-Soviet competition over the developing nations was creating an educational crisis among Americans, most of whom had been educated in what he called the pre–Pearl Harbor "isolationist era" and thus did not fully comprehend the importance of these new nations. He urged his audience of educators to help train the next generation of Americans for their "new role" of world leadership by teaching them about countries such as Indonesia, whose strategic location and vast natural resources made it valuable to both the Soviets and the U.S. Wilcox pointed out that in years to come an unprecedented number of Americans would spend a portion of their lives abroad as "soldiers, technicians, educators, government officials, business men and women, and tourists." In order for these people to do their jobs well and avoid generating "tensions" abroad, he explained, all Americans needed an "education for overseasmanship."[2]

This "education for overseasmanship," Wilcox implied, would not entail the learning of new information so much as the cultivation of new feelings. Wilcox did not suggest that Americans study Indonesian languages or history. Rather, he urged his audience to foster "closer economic, political, and cultural ties with the people of Asia and Africa" by training Americans in new attitudes. "We live in an interdependent world," Wilcox told his audience, and Americans had to learn to "understand the hopes and problems and attitudes of other people." Waging the Cold War in the decolonizing world, this State Department official explained, would require Americans to "cultivate the quality of empathy—the ability to put yourself in the other fellow's position and see things from his point of view." Only by learning new mental and emotional skills, he suggested, could Americans defeat the Soviet Union and secure the allegiance of the decolonizing world for themselves.[3]

For too long, diplomatic and cultural historians have taken the Truman Doctrine speech as the emblematic expression of Cold War ideology. Truman's 1947 address, in which he solicited Congressional support for a $400 million aid package to civil-war-torn Greece and Turkey, is often read as marking the start of the Cold War. In it the president cast the postwar situation as a worldwide struggle between "free peoples" who believed in "individual liberty" and "totalitarian regimes" that ruled through "terror and oppression." In a world structured by this Manichaean opposition, Truman declared, the United States must assume leadership of that half of the world that was "resisting attempted subjugation" by internal or external forces. The representative status accorded to Truman's speech has, however, obscured as much as it has revealed about the postwar era. Wilcox's 1957 speech in Philadelphia—a boilerplate address that reiterated the Eisenhower administration's key themes and concerns—deserves attention as an equally representative document, just as polemical and just as intent on rallying support for the Cold War, but one that expresses a different set of ideological principles.[4]

These two speeches should be seen in the context of the gearing up of a vast educational machinery designed to direct the attention of the American people to the world outside the nation's borders. As Wilcox indicated, the expansion of U.S. power around the globe depended upon the support and services of millions of ordinary Americans, acting as private citizens and as employees of the state, and it could not move forward if Americans continued to think in narrowly national and "isolationist" terms. In the view of political elites, the collective consciousness needed to be reshaped along internationalist lines. This internationalist education occurred in various places throughout the postwar social order, including grade schools, high schools, and universities. It also took place in less formal venues of education, such as the global imaginaries created by political elites and cultural producers.

The speeches by Wilcox and Truman are worth comparing in part because they express two distinct Cold War global imaginaries. A global imaginary is an ideological creation that maps the world conceptually and defines the primary relations among peoples, nations, and regions. As an imaginative, discursive construct, it represents the abstract entity of the "world" as a coherent, comprehensible whole and situates individual nations within that larger framework. It produces peoples, nations, and cultures not as isolated entities but as interconnected with one another. This is not to say that it works through deception or that it mystifies the real, material conditions of global relations. Rather, a global imaginary articulates the ways in which people imagine and live those relations. It creates an imaginary coherence out of the contradictions and disjunctures of real relations, and thereby provides a stable sense of individual and national identity. In reducing the infinite complexity of the world to comprehensible terms, it creates a common sense about how the world functions as a system and offers implicit instruction in how to maneuver within that system; it makes certain attitudes and behaviors easier to adopt than others.

Truman's 1947 speech articulated the relations between the United States, the Soviet Union, and the other nations of the world through what I am calling a *global imaginary of containment*. Wilcox's 1957 speech, in turn, articulated those same relations through a *global imaginary of integration*. These two global imaginaries were not invented by these individuals; they were collectively produced over the course of the late 1940s and 1950s by a broad array of political elites, journalists, academics, and cultural producers. These two global imaginaries educated Americans about the world and their role in it in very different ways. The global imaginary of containment offered a heroic model of education: it imagined the Cold War as a crusade against communism and invited the American people to join in. Much of the energy it generated, however, was directed inward and aimed at ferreting out enemies and subversives within the nation itself. The global imaginary of integration, in contrast, proposed a model of sentimental education. The State Department's "education for overseasmanship" encouraged Americans to "look outward." Directed to the world beyond the nation's borders, it represented the Cold War as an opportunity to forge intellectual and emotional bonds with the people of Asia and Africa. Only by creating such bonds, Wilcox suggested, could the economic, political, and military integration of the "free world" be achieved and sustained. When it did turn inward, the global imaginary of integration generated an inclusive rather than a policing energy.[5]

Most cultural histories of the Cold War take the foreign policy and ideology of containment as their foundation. I want to emphasize the discursive workings of integration instead. This chapter compares the global imaginaries of containment and integration, and explores the discursive and institutional means through which political elites undertook the sentimental education of the American people.

CONTAINMENT AND INTEGRATION AS IDEOLOGY AND FOREIGN POLICY

Containment and integration constituted the two ideological foundations of postwar foreign policy. Containment was a distinctly Cold War strategic ideology. Based on U.S. balance-of-power concerns vis-à-vis the Soviet Union, it posited a zero-sum conflict between Moscow, which it figured as aggressive and expansionist, and Washington, which it figured as defensive and peaceful. Containment held that, since cooperation with the Soviets was impossible and all communist governments were subservient to Moscow, the expansion of communism anywhere in the world posed a direct threat to the U.S. share of world power. George Kennan articulated its defining logic when he called for the "long-term, patient but firm and vigilant containment of Russian expansive tendencies" through the "adroit and vigilant application of counter-force at a series of constantly shifting geographical and political points." After the Truman Doctrine speech, containment became one central goal of postwar foreign policy.[6]

The ideology of integration, in contrast, originated in the nation's fundamental economic structures. Americans have always understood their democratic political freedoms to be inseparable from their economic ones. Since at least the early nineteenth century they have also believed that the nation's economy, in order to remain healthy, had continually to expand and integrate new markets and sources of raw materials. As the U.S. extended its reach, first westward and then into the Caribbean and the Pacific, it gradually created an economy that had a regional rather than merely a continental scope. This regional Pacific economy began to take shape early on, when the U.S. began trading with China in the 1780s and opened Japan up to Western trade in 1853. Seeking reliable stepping stones to these Asian markets, Washington acquired a territorial empire in the Pacific: it annexed the Midway Islands in 1867, Samoa in 1878, Hawaii, Guam, and the Philippines in 1898 (through the Spanish-American War), and Wake Island in 1899. Washington launched a policy of informal, or free trade, imperialism in 1899–1900 when it issued the "open door" notes to China and extended it in the 1920s under the rubric of "dollar diplomacy." World War II helped create a U.S. economy with a worldwide rather than merely regional reach and cemented the belief in the unity of economic and political freedoms. In the decades that followed, any restrictions on U.S. economic growth—such as those posed by communist governments—were seen as a threat to the nation's fundamental political structure and to what came to be called "the American way of life." At a time when the U.S. economy needed truly global access to markets and resources in order to sustain itself, the defense of the nation demanded securing that access through a variety of political and military means.

The ideology of integration took on a distinctive shape during the Cold War. Melvyn Leffler and Thomas McCormick have argued that the Cold War should be seen as a competition between the United States and the Soviets not just for strategic advantage, but also for exclusive access to the world's markets, industrial infrastructure, and natural resources. Washington concluded that the best way to guarantee its own access was by expanding the capitalist system of free trade on a global scale. As a result, it sought to create an internationally integrated free market economic order, in which each nation would have unrestricted access to the markets and raw materials of all the others, while capital, goods, and people would move freely across national borders. By giving up any efforts at economic self-sufficiency, individual nations would become dependent on each other for their prosperity and thus, Washington believed, much less likely to engage in activities that would lead to war. In practice, creating this economic order meant integrating the core industrial economies of the democratic West and Japan with the markets and resource-rich economies of the decolonizing periphery. Washington perceived any effort on the part of decolonizing nations to remain outside of this integrated system—by pursuing nationalist economic policies, for instance—as a threat to the economic and political stability of the capitalist "free world." The creation of this integrated global economy —and its preservation through political and military means—became, along with the containment of the Soviet Union, the other fundamental goal of postwar U.S. policymakers.[7]

Far from being opposed to each other, the containment of the Soviet Union and the integration of the capitalist "free world" are best understood as two sides of the same coin. The military alliances designed to contain Soviet expansion also facilitated economic integration among member nations, and the foreign aid programs designed to stimulate struggling economies served as channels for delivering military assis-

tance. Together the principles of containment and integration undergirded Washington's postwar foreign policy agenda and led to the creation of international financial institutions (International Monetary
Fund, World Bank), massive foreign aid projects (Marshall Plan), and
world-straddling political and military alliances (NATO, SEATO).

Washington pursued this double strategy of containment and integration throughout Asia in the late 1940s and 1950s. At the end of World
War II, the U.S. had preponderant power in the region (as it did in the
rest of the world), with troops spread throughout the Pacific and on the
Asian mainland. Washington undertook as its first major postwar project the occupation and reconstruction of Japan. Between 1945 and 1952
the U.S. promoted the democratization of Japan's political structure, restored its industrial economy, and ensured that it remained beyond Soviet reach; the peace and security treaties of 1951, which granted the U.S.
extensive military rights, cemented Japan's integration into the Western
political and economic system. In the late 1940s the U.S. intervened in
China's civil war, giving financial and military support to Chiang Kai-
shek's Kuomintang (Nationalist) government in its struggle against Mao
Zedong's communist forces; when Chiang fled to Taiwan in 1949, the
U.S. continued its support and refused to recognize the communist government on the mainland. When the Korean War broke out in 1950,
Washington rushed in thousands of troops to contain what it saw as a
Soviet-backed invasion of South Korea. In subsequent years, the U.S.
dispatched military advisors to and launched nation-building projects in
South Vietnam, exploded atomic bombs on the Bikini atoll, and sent
the Seventh Fleet to protect Taiwan from Chinese attack. It constructed
a network of military bases centered in the Philippines, Okinawa, and
South Korea, and crafted a web of political treaties that allied the U.S.
with South Korea, Japan, Taiwan, the Philippines, Thailand, South Vietnam, Laos, Cambodia, Malaya, and Pakistan. It increased its economic
presence by pouring in billions of dollars in foreign aid, exporting American goods, importing Asia's raw materials, and encouraging private cor-
porate expansion.

At the same time, however, forces across Asia, and especially the revolutionary independence movements, questioned and resisted this expansion of power. Washington had a mixed response to Asian decolonization. On the one hand, it was not unhappy to see the European empires
dissolved. Washington regarded these empires, which functioned as restricted trading blocs, as obstacles to economic integration and as incubators of communism and anti-Western revolution. On the other hand,

Washington recognized that Europe's economic and political stability often depended upon income generated in the colonies. Whether the United States supported or opposed a particular nationalist movement often depended on its relationship to communism. In Indonesia, for example, the U.S. initially endorsed Dutch efforts to reimpose colonial control at the end of the war, but in 1949 switched to support independence. A number of factors shaped this decision, but one of the most important was the staunch anticommunism of the Indonesian independence movement. Nationalist leaders had made clear their willingness to protect Western investments and preserve Western access to markets and resources after independence. In Indochina, in contrast, Washington sustained its support for the French war against the Vietnamese: unlike Indonesia's Sukarno, Ho Chi Minh was an avowed communist. To Washington, this meant that an independent Vietnam would inevitably ally itself with the Soviet Union, restrict Western access to markets and resources, and refuse integration into the international capitalist economy. Washington only endorsed nationalist movements, such as those in Indonesia and the Philippines, that promised to preserve Western access after independence. It was willing to abolish formal empire, as long as the relations of informal empire continued uninterrupted.[8]

Throughout the later 1940s and the 1950s, the United States suffered from what many Americans saw as major setbacks in Asia. Many in Washington took Mao's victory in China in 1949 as a devastating "loss" of 500 million friends and a dangerous shift in the world's balance of power, while the unsatisfying end to the Korean War in 1953 and the creation of a separate North Vietnam in 1954 seemed to portend the inexorable spread of communism. The birth of the nonaligned movement, the growth of nationalist sentiment, and the strengthening of anti-American attitudes challenged U.S. interests throughout the region. Over the course of the 1950s Indian intellectuals cast doubt on American claims to world leadership, North Vietnamese guerrillas killed American advisors, Japanese neutralists protested the extension of U.S. military rights, and Taiwanese civilians rioted against the extraterritorial powers of American military courts.

The result was that even as Washington extended its power in Asia, political elites often saw the U.S. as failing to achieve its goals there. Many Americans in the 1950s feared they were "losing" Asia just as they had "lost" China. This intense fear of loss fueled an almost obsessive public discourse that centered on securing the allegiance of decolonizing nations and binding them to America. Tension between the desire to integrate Asia and the fear of losing Asia permeated American thinking in the late 1940s and 1950s. It was one of the forces that drove foreign policymaking and spurred the flood of popular representations. It was this anxiety about Asia that *Newsweek* captured in its 1957 map, "Worldwide—The Feeling About Us" (Figure 3).

WINNING THE MINDS OF MEN

Although political elites crafted the foreign policies of containment and integration, they needed a broad base of public support in order to implement them successfully. The central task, as so many contemporary observers described it, became one of "winning the minds of men." The minds that needed to be won, however, belonged not only to people overseas, who might be tempted to choose communism over democratic capitalism, but to Americans as well, who might resist such an expansive—and expensive—foreign policy agenda. This meant that the waging of the Cold War was as much a domestic endeavor as a foreign one —and as much an educational endeavor as a political or military one. The American public needed to be schooled in internationalism: it needed to be persuaded to accept the nation's sustained engagement in world affairs, its participation in international organizations, and its long-range cooperation with other governments. Woodrow Wilson's failure to secure public support for his internationalist agenda after World War I, which many saw as paving the way for World War II, loomed large in the minds of policymakers, and they vowed not to repeat his mistakes.

Formidable obstacles hindered the winning of American minds. Weary from wartime sacrifice and eager to return to the work of family formation and homemaking, Americans often preferred to focus their attention on domestic political concerns. The very newness of containment and integration policies, which violated a long-standing tradition of avoiding permanent alliances outside the Western hemisphere, provoked public opposition, while the abstract nature of their objectives, in sharp contrast to the concrete goals of World War II, generated little enthusiasm. Fearing foreign economic competition, many Americans expressed skepticism about the value of free trade—a cornerstone of international economic integration— and wished to keep tariffs and trade barriers high. Underneath it all ran a lingering isolationist sentiment, which worried political leaders throughout the 1950s.[9]

In the late 1940s Truman's foreign policy agenda also faced serious opposition from the political right and left, each of which had its own vision of the kind of relationship that the United States should maintain with the rest of the world. The mid-term elections of 1946 delivered both houses of Congress to the Republican party, whose powerful right wing appeared bent on pursuing a neo-isolationist agenda. Senator Robert Taft of Ohio and his followers were economic nationalists who sought a self-sufficient U.S. economy and opposed Truman's policies of international economic and political integration. Traditionally known as isolationists, they were in fact only isolationist in regard to Europe, which they feared for its economic competition and disdained as morally corrupt. Fervently anticommunist, they desired a unilateralist foreign policy in which the U.S. acted alone, unimpeded by political and military alliances; they despised the United Nations as a precursor to world government. Bruce Cumings has identified "bulwarks" as the central metaphor of what I am calling this "right internationalism": barriers to prevent the spread of communism, to keep foreign goods out of the U.S., and to protect the moral rectitude of the American people.[10]

The Democratic left, in turn, made its bid for the direction of foreign policy in 1948, when Henry Wallace ran for president under the banner of the Progressive Party, a broad coalition of liberal groups endorsed by the American Communist Party. True internationalists, Wallace and his supporters were economic integrationists who advocated increased free trade and opposed Truman's policies of containing the Soviet Union. Heirs to Woodrow Wilson's idealistic global views and advocates of the United Nations, they rejected unilateralism in favor of a one-worldism that would knit the United States together with all other nations into a truly global system. Politically, they sought to extend Roosevelt's wartime alliances into the postwar period. Although opposed to communism, they did not believe that the Soviet Union needed to be ostracized from the international system; instead, they proposed enmeshing the Soviet Union with the U.S. and other capitalist democracies through a network of political and economic ties. The central metaphor, according to Cumings, of this "left-liberal internationalism" was the "open door": it sought a world in which obstacles to the free movement of goods, services, people, and ideas would be transcended.[11]

These competing internationalisms posed a problem for Truman, in part because each had ties to a broader social movement that had successfully embedded its particular global vision into a network of social institutions and cultural practices. The Protestant missionary movement, although not allied exclusively with the Republican party, provided right internationalism with a number of outspoken advocates and a steady stream of intellectual energy. Grounded in the universalist values of Christianity, missionaries had been powerful promoters of internationalist thinking since the nineteenth century. In general, they encouraged a U.S.-centered internationalism based on spreading American values and institutions and transforming other nations along American lines, initially through religious conversion and later by building schools, universities, and hospitals. With its network of congregations and settlements, the missionary movement also created a worldwide institutional infrastructure that enabled millions of Americans, especially in isolated Midwestern and rural communities, to understand themselves as participating in world affairs. These institutions enabled Americans to feel themselves bound to the people of Asia and Africa, despite the myriad differences that separated them, through ties of religion, money, and emotional investment.[12]

Missionaries in the nineteenth and early twentieth centuries also served as influential producers of knowledge about Asia. Prolific generators of newsletters, books, and photographs that circulated widely throughout American culture, missionaries effectively "produced" China, Japan, India, and other parts of Asia at a time when few Americans had such direct contact. At the same time, they also produced a particular identity for America. Missionaries played an instrumental role in creating the idea of a "special relationship" between the United States and China. A sentimentalized version of American exceptionalism, the "special relationship" defined America, in contrast to the European nations, as a non-imperial power that renounced military force in favor of economic access and political influence. It posited China as a nation of endless needs and America as its benefactor and protector, as well as a nurturer of democracy and modernizing reforms.[13]

Communism was the other great universalistic system of thought that offered Americans a way to feel themselves tied to the larger world. Richard Wright, in his contribution to the 1950 bestseller *The God That Failed,* explained the appeal that communist internationalism held in the 1930s. Like Christianity, it enabled the individual to transcend barriers of race and nation and discover a deep human connection. In joining the Communist Party, Wright argued, a black man became "one with all the members there, regardless of race or color"; he entered into an unparalleled state of "kinship" and "oneness" in which "his heart was theirs and their hearts were his." Communism appealed to Wright, as the missionary movement did to rural Americans, because it allowed him to participate in a worldwide moral struggle that bound him to millions of others despite differences of language, race, or geography. It likewise gave him an equivalent sense of global identification: "With the exception of the church and its myths and legends, there was no agency in the world so capable of making men feel the earth and the people upon it as the Communist Party." [14]

During the 1930s and 1940s, the Popular Front opened up this appealing form of left internationalism to thousands of Americans who did not think of themselves as communists. While not all left-liberal internationalists embraced the Popular Front, it did provide the political left with an institutional framework and a source of intellectual energy similar to what missionary culture provided for the political right. The Front functioned as a loose network of organizations—unions, cultural groups, refugee aid organizations, and adult education centers—that educated Americans about the world and provided an opportunity to participate in international politics. During the years when Washington retreated in the face of rising fascism, Popular Front groups promoted a politics of international solidarity, mobilizing Americans "to stand with the Spanish Republic besieged by fascist Franco, to support Ethiopia invaded by Mussolini, to defend China against Japan, and to aid the victims and refugees from Hitler's Third Reich." The popularity of the Front derived in part from its ability to tap into the reservoirs of Wilsonian internationalism that still existed and to create an institutional infrastructure in which a broad range of internationalists, from communists to liberals, could come together. Like the missionary movement, the Popular Front generated its own distinctive culture. Some of its representative works, such as Orson Welles's "voodoo" *Macbeth,* changed the way Americans imagined the world by telling international stories of antifascist and anti-imperial solidarity. Others, such Earl Robinson's musical anthem "Ballad for Americans," altered the ways Americans imagined the nation by redefining it as a multiracial, multinational entity. Perhaps the most distinctive characteristic of Popular Front culture was its aesthetic of social consciousness and political commitment, neatly captured by the book *Writers Take Sides,* in which noted authors expressed their support for the loyalists in the Spanish civil war. The Communist Party, with its motto "Art is a class weapon," had a tradition of valuing culture for its political utility. While the Popular Front deemphasized this idea of culture as a tool of social conflict and replaced it with the idea of culture as a means for uniting people, it continued to view culture as a medium of political expression and an arena for political activism.[15]

While the missionary movement and the Popular Front spoke to the general tendencies of right and left internationalism, they were not wholly homogenous or mutually exclusive groups. The missionary movement had its cosmopolitan side, its social gospel tradition had clear progressive tendencies, and some children of missionaries crossed over to embrace Popular Front ideas. At the same time, the Popular Front welcomed the support of missionaries when their interests converged, as they did on the issue of China in the 1930s. In 1939, for instance, former medical missionary and future right-wing Republican Congressman Walter Judd addressed the Fifth Congress of the American League against War and Fascism, a Popular Front organization.

The Truman administration, in order to secure passage of its ambitious Cold War foreign policy agenda, needed to forge a new historical bloc, a hegemonic alliance that would incorporate the divergent interests and constituencies of both left-liberal and right internationalism. In the late 1940s Truman did exactly that, crafting a synthesis—the famed "Cold War consensus"—that remained stable for decades. Truman's containment/integration model, which became the dominant form of postwar internationalism, combined the left-liberal ideal of international integration with the right's fierce opposition to communism. It thus retained these alternative internationalisms within itself as residual formations. It gave up the truly global scope of left-liberal internationalism's economic and political vision and with it the idea of enmeshing the Soviet Union in a "one world" framework. In its place, it created what Bruce Cumings has called a "second-best" internationalism, in which political and military bulwarks divided the world into a capitalist "free world" and a communist "bloc." Within that "free world," however, much of the left-liberal internationalist vision prevailed as nations around the world became economically and politically integrated via an open door economic system. This compromise satisfied the centers of both parties, enabling Truman to create an alliance that included Republicans such as John Foster Dulles and Arthur Vandenburg alongside the members of his own party.[16]

THE GLOBAL IMAGINARY OF CONTAINMENT

The Truman administration forged this Cold War historical bloc in large part by boosting anticommunism, and thus containment, to the status of national ideology. Beginning with the Truman Doctrine speech in 1947, the president spearheaded a campaign designed to sell his foreign

policy—and the idea of the Cold War more generally—by identifying communism abroad and at home as a threat to the nation that demanded an extraordinary response. Truman deployed anticommunism
as a political weapon against the competing alternatives of left and right
internationalism. His emphasis on anticommunism co-opted the right
by embracing one of the central tenets of its internationalist vision, while
bankrupting Taft's "isolationism" and unilateralism as responsible ap-
proaches to world affairs. It also undermined the left, enabling Truman
to weed out those members of his own party who advocated working
with the Soviet Union and to label their vision of internationalism as
potentially treasonous, as he did during the Henry Wallace campaign in
1948. Truman used anticommunism to delegitimize competing voices
on foreign policy and to ensure that there would be only one model of
internationalism circulating in the public sphere.[17]

This deployment of anticommunism helped forge the postwar hegemonic alliance by defining the boundaries of acceptable political debate
and by creating mechanisms for silencing those excluded from the alliance. Thousands of Americans, overwhelmingly on the left-liberal side
of the political spectrum, lost their jobs and had their reputations ru-
ined through what can be characterized as domestic containment programs. The Federal Employee Loyalty Program, which was launched
only days after the Truman Doctrine speech, purged suspected communists and sympathizers from the federal civil service and prompted
similar action at every level of government. Between 1948 and 1955 the
Attorney General's office and the House Committee on Un-American
Activities published long lists of allegedly subversive organizations, participation in any of which was grounds for suspicion, a hearing before a
loyalty board, and often dismissal from one's job. These actions quickly
winnowed the ranks of the Popular Front and decimated its institutional
infrastructure.[18]

Domestic containment fell particularly hard on those who held left-
liberal internationalist views on China. After the so-called "loss" of
China in 1949, the China Lobby moved into the political limelight. The
Lobby was an informal group of mostly right-internationalist politicians
and private citizens who had supported Chiang Kai-shek's Kuomintang
government during the civil war and continued to do so after he retreated to Taiwan. The Lobby publicly attacked a number of American
China experts who, having seen Mao's success in the civil war as all but
inevitable, had recommended that Washington prepare to work with the
new communist government. Starting with Senator Joseph McCarthy in

1950, the China Lobby and its supporters accused these scholars and foreign-service officials of working secretly to ensure Mao's victory. Years of accusations and investigations followed, and numerous China experts —including John Paton Davies, John Stewart Service, John Carter Vincent, O. Edmund Clubb, and Owen Lattimore—had their careers derailed, their reputations tarnished, and their access to the media restricted. The Institute of Pacific Relations, which in the 1930s and early 1940s had been the premier scholarly organization devoted to Asia, collapsed after the Senate Internal Security Subcommittee charged it in 1952 with being an "instrument of Communist policy, propaganda and military intelligence." [19]

The U.S. government also focused its coercive energies after 1949 on Chinese Americans as potential spies and subversives. Chinese family organizations sometimes ran afoul of the FBI for maintaining ties to similar organizations in communist China, while the Immigration and Naturalization Service used deceptive tactics to deport Chinese who it thought might be sympathetic to the mainland government. In 1956 federal agents swept through Chinatowns on the East and West coasts in an effort to track down suspected communists who it feared had entered the country illegally. Domestic containment policies revived latent "yellow peril" fears of a combined Chinese threat from both within and outside the nation.[20]

Containment worked as such a powerful hegemonic discourse because it created a global imaginary—a comprehensive way of understanding the world as a whole and America's role in it. The global imaginary of containment mapped the world in terms of Otherness and difference. It drew heavily on the right-internationalist vision of a world divided by bulwarks, as can be seen in James Burnham's map, "World Struggle," published in *Life* a few days after the Truman Doctrine speech (Figure 4). In keeping with its title, Burnham's map organizes the world around the principle of conflict. In contrast to a Mercator projection map, which separates the U.S. and Soviet Union with wide stretches of ocean, this map prioritizes the U.S.-Soviet relationship by centering on the North Pole and representing the adversaries in close physical proximity. A politically resonant color scheme visually emphasizes the boundaries that divide the two superpowers: Russia and its possessions are bright red, and the areas under its influence shaded pink; America and its possessions are white, and the areas under its influence shaded pale gray. A series of gestural arrows animate the "struggle" of the title by indicating the Soviet Union's aggressive and expansionist tendencies,

Figure 4. Mapping the Cold War—the global imaginary of containment.
(*Life*, March 31, 1947)

pointing to America's defensive commitments, and suggesting the places most likely to flare up into conflict. The map's bipolar structure reduces the developing regions of the world to a position of secondary importance: it literally marginalizes South America, Africa, and Asia by pushing them to the edges and cutting off portions of their landmasses. The global imaginary of containment, by mapping the world conceptually in terms of conflict, established a clear global identity and role for the U.S. It educated Americans at all levels of society about how the world worked and made it easier for them to endorse particular courses of action, such as the militarization of foreign policy and the creation of a national security state.[21]

The global imaginary of containment also translated anticommunism into a structure of feeling and a set of social and cultural practices that could be lived at the level of everyday life. Fear served as the emotional glue that held this imagined world together: fear of Soviet expansion abroad, of communist subversion at home, of nuclear war. The logic of containment rendered deviance in all its forms—sexual, political, behavioral—a source of anxiety and an object of investigation. The global imaginary of containment also opened up the Cold War to popular participation: ordinary Americans could take part in the "world struggle" by naming names, testifying before investigatory committees, enlisting their local community groups in the crusade, and keeping an eye on their neighbors and colleagues.

A number of social and cultural historians have characterized postwar America as dominated by what Alan Nadel has called "containment culture." Elaine Tyler May has described containment as the "overarching principle" that guided middle-class Americans into the fervent embrace of domesticity and traditional gender roles. Stephen Whitfield and Michael Rogin have traced the politics of anticommunism through popular film (On the Waterfront, My Son John, Kiss Me Deadly). Alan Nadel, finding the logic of containment embedded in texts as diverse as Catcher in the Rye, The Ten Commandments, and Pillow Talk, has argued that containment was "one of the most powerfully deployed national narratives in recorded history." Together, these scholars have seen containment as a force of restriction, intimidation, and suppression operating across the spectrum of American culture and society: it enforced "conformity" everywhere and led to the "containment of atomic secrets, of sexual license, of gender roles, of nuclear energy, and of artistic expression."[22]

Communist China figured prominently in the global imaginary and culture of containment. Resurrecting a long tradition of "yellow peril" imagery, the news media presented the Chinese under Mao as an inscrutable mass of political fanatics, a conformist colony of blue-suited ants. The unexpected and debilitating Chinese assault on U.S. forces during the Korean War brought forth dehumanizing descriptions of a "yellow tide" along with familiar commentaries on the Asian disregard for human life. In 1962 *The Manchurian Candidate* pulled together more than a decade of anti-Chinese discourse into one of the definitive works of Cold War filmmaking. Set in the aftermath of the Korean War, it imagined a complex communist plot to get a spineless, McCarthy-like senator elected president and thereby put his wife—a communist agent—into a position of power in the White House. The film linked the threat of Asian communism with that posed by changing gender roles by making its central villain a domineering wife and mother with grandiose political ambitions. The film presents the communist Chinese and North Koreans as devious foreign enemies who have learned how to insinuate themselves into the American political system, the American family, even the American mind: its most memorable scene presents a demonstration of Chinese "brainwashing" techniques on American soldiers who prove so defenseless against this mysterious Oriental knowledge that they kill one another without compunction. Brainwashed, these Americans become like Asians, like communists: passive, conformist, and obedient to authority. The film also links Asian enemies abroad with an Asian American threat within the nation: the Asian houseboy who seems so submissive and eager to please turns out to be a North Korean agent skilled in the deadly arts of hand-to-hand combat. According to *The Manchurian Candidate,* contact with Asians, either at home or abroad, could only weaken the nation. While American participation in the Korean War halted the spread of communism in northeast Asia, it also opened up a hole in the nation's defenses, allowing the Asian menace to invade and corrupt America. Asian-ness, it suggested, was something to be kept out of the United States at all costs.[23]

WHAT ARE WE FOR?

The Truman administration's campaign against domestic and international communism worked, and between 1947 and 1950 Congress endorsed the major foreign policy initiatives that established the foundations of the postwar world order. For all its rhetorical power, however, the global imaginary of containment had certain limitations as a means of defining America's identity as a global power in the era of decolonization. In fact, it gave rise to questions that proved difficult to answer. Many political elites saw anticommunism's negative formulation of American identity as an ideological weakness and regularly expressed a desire for a more positive one. Raymond Fosdick, Acheson's Far East consultant, gave this question its most common formulation in 1949: "It seems to me that too much thinking in the [State] Department is negative. . . . We are *against* communism, but what are we *for?*"[24]

The "What are we for?" question arose from anxiety over the perceived attractiveness of communism. Political elites sometimes stepped back from their public denunciations of the Soviet Union as a soul-killing bastion of enforced conformity and acknowledged communism's appeal. They recognized that to poor people struggling to improve their lives, communism's promise of economic equality and rapid development had a strong allure, while its idealistic vision of shared burdens and brotherhood held a deep spiritual attraction. Political elites feared that the U.S. could not compete with communism's vision of solidarity and a better world. In 1945 William Donovan, then director of the Office of Strategic Services and later ambassador to Thailand, expressed a commonly held view when he told Truman that the Soviets had "a strong drawing card in the proletarian philosophy of Communism," while the U.S. and its allies had "no political or social philosophy equally dynamic or alluring." The "What are we for?" question became even more urgent after 1954, when the vulgar anticommunism of McCarthyism had burned itself out. In a 1955 meeting with Eisenhower, T. S. Repplier, president of the Advertising Council, urged the president to find a way to compete with the universal appeal of communism:

> Briefly, it cannot be denied that in theory Communism is idealistic and moralistic. It promises help for the helpless, relief for the downtrodden. In short, it appeals profoundly to those with a sense of social justice; and as a result it has incredible ability to stir up quasi-religious fervor.
>
> I believe the United States will operate under a serious handicap until we can hold up for the world a counteracting inspirational concept. We cannot be merely against Communism; we suffer from the lack of a *positive* crusade. We need to focus on a moralistic idea with the power to stir men's imagination.[25]

When the members of the National Security Council sat down in 1950 to draft NSC 68, one of the basic blueprints of containment policy, they, too, grappled with the problem of how to translate the Cold War into an appealing structure of feeling based on something other than fear.

Robert Lovett, former undersecretary of state and later secretary of defense, insisted that "if we can sell every useless article known to man in large quantities, we should be able to sell our very fine story in larger quantities." But how to "sell" the "story" of containment's policies was precisely the problem, since emphasizing a military buildup and the conflict with the Soviets might backfire by raising fears of America becoming a "garrison state." One participant—the acting assistant secretary of state for Near Eastern, South Asian, and African Affairs—focused on the emotional needs of Americans. "What we have to do," he insisted, "is to convince not only their minds but their hearts. What we need to do is to make the 'cold war' a 'warm war' by infusing into it ideological principles to give it meaning." With this call to "warm" up the Cold War and to infuse it with "meaning" beyond anticommunism, the NSC articulated the need to reach Americans at the level of their "hearts." In the end, the members of the NSC did rely on anticommunism to sell Truman's agenda: NSC 68 is one of the core expressions of the global imaginary of containment. But the internal debate also marked a recognition that fear and the negative logic of anticommunism could not by themselves serve as the unifying concepts that the global expansion of American power demanded.[26]

The global imaginary of containment also offered little protection from the accusations of imperialism that dogged the U.S throughout the 1950s. Imperialism became a hotly contested term between the U.S. and the Soviets, as each side accused the other of pursuing imperialistic aims in the decolonizing world. As the U.S. replaced Britain as the world's most powerful country, it was often seen as taking on its imperial role as well. Asian and African nationalists regularly accused the U.S. of reintroducing Western colonial power under a new guise, a charge they substantiated by pointing to U.S. support for European colonial regimes and the proliferation of overseas U.S. military bases. Even U.S. allies shared this perspective at times: one American military advisor in South Vietnam identified "the continual task of assuring the Vietnamese that the United States is not a colonial power" as perhaps "the greatest single problem encountered" by the Military Assistance and Advisory Group. Washington was intensely aware of the need to deny the charge of imperialism and worked hard to identify the U.S. with the forces of independence. It produced reams of propaganda identifying the U.S. as the first postcolonial nation and publicized its support for Indian and Indonesian independence and its own voluntary decolonization of the Philippines in 1946.[27]

Imperialism in the 1950s was seen as inseparable from racism, and critics of the U.S. most often validated their accusations of imperialism by pointing out the unequal legal and social status—the internal colonization, as it were—of black Americans. The Soviet and Asian press paid close attention to race relations within the U.S.; State Department officials estimated that half of the Soviet's anti-American propaganda focused on racial issues. The world media gave prominent coverage to the lynching of Emmet Till in 1955, the expulsion of Autherine Lucy from the University of Alabama in 1956, the desegregation crisis in Little Rock in 1957, and other episodes of racial injustice. U.S. policymakers took these accusations seriously and worried that American racism was delegitimizing U.S. claims to world leadership in the eyes of Asians and Africans. Secretary of State Dean Acheson, who described the poor state of domestic race relations as the "Achilles' heel" of U.S. foreign relations, warned that discrimination caused significant "damage" to America's world standing and "jeopardize[d]" the strength of its alliances. A source of "constant embarrassment" abroad, it created a "formidable obstacle" to the achievement of Washington's goals. The members of the National Security Council also took accusations of imperialism into account when they formulated foreign policy. NSC 48, one of the key postwar policy directives on Asia, expressed concern that the achievement of U.S. goals in Asia was being hampered by "Asian resentments and suspicions of the West" and noted that the communists were succeeding in presenting themselves as the champions of "the national revolution against western imperialism." Questions of racism thus served to link the domestic American sphere with the sphere of foreign relations, proving their inseparability: how Americans dealt with the problem of race relations at home had a direct impact on their success in dealing with the decolonizing world abroad.[28]

Both the Truman and the Eisenhower administrations tried to minimize the deleterious effects of U.S. race relations on foreign policy. They feared that if Asian leaders came to see the U.S. as irredeemably racist, they would refuse to align themselves with Washington and would thus be "lost" to America. These foreign policy concerns prompted Truman to promote early civil rights legislation and support civil rights cases coming before the Supreme Court. Eisenhower, far less committed to the principle of racial equality, supported much weaker civil rights legislation and made known his unwillingness to intervene in what he saw as established social customs. Despite this uneven commitment to changing the institutional and legal structures that regulated race, both administrations regularly gave verbal support to the principles of racial tolerance and equality. They worked hard to manage the international perception, if not always the material conditions, of American race relations.[29]

As a result, antiracism occupied an ambiguous position in the ideological landscape of the Cold War. On the one hand, as one of the core principles of the Communist Party and the Popular Front, it was associated with an illegitimate form of internationalism and seen as an invitation to investigate. As the chairman of one loyalty board put it, "Of course the fact that a person believes in racial equality doesn't *prove* that he's a Communist, but it certainly does make you look twice, doesn't it?" On the other hand, professions of racial tolerance and inclusiveness became a staple of Cold War political rhetoric and appeared regularly in political speeches, policy documents, and newspaper editorials across the political spectrum. Antiracism thus became both a Cold War liability and a Cold War imperative, a mark of lingering leftist commitments and an integral component of the anticommunist program of winning the support of the decolonizing world.[30]

THE GLOBAL IMAGINARY OF INTEGRATION

Political elites tried to resolve some of the problems raised by the global imaginary of containment by shifting emphasis and defining the U.S. through its alliances rather than its enmities. By emphasizing the economic, political, and military integration of the noncommunist world, policymakers created another global imaginary that existed alongside that of containment as an alternative vision of how the world—or at least the "free world"—was organized.

Where the global imaginary of containment drew on the residual internationalism of the right, with its vision of bulwarks between nations and a mortal conflict between communism and capitalism, the global imaginary of integration drew on the residual internationalism of the left, which imagined the world in terms of open doors that superseded barriers and created pathways between nations. It constructed a world in which differences could be bridged and transcended. In the political rhetoric of integration, relationships of "cooperation" replaced those of conflict, "mutuality" replaced enmity, and "collective security," "common bonds," and "community" became the preferred terms for representing the relationship between the United States and the noncommunist world.[31]

Arthur Schlesinger Jr. articulated some of the key concepts of the global imaginary of integration. The young Harvard historian was an emblematic figure of the Cold War historical bloc. Untainted by any association with 1930s radicalism, he helped found the Americans for Democratic Action, a political group that enlisted the support of prominent New Deal figures such as Eleanor Roosevelt, defined itself in opposition to Henry Wallace's communist-supported Progressive Citizens of America, and pushed the Democratic party solidly into line behind Truman's foreign policies. With *The Vital Center,* published in 1949, Schlesinger produced a popular manifesto that explained and generated enthusiasm for Truman's model of internationalism. Excerpted in general-circulation magazines and widely reviewed, it was hailed by the *Saturday Review* for announcing "the spirit of a time to itself." [32]

Although Schlesinger devoted considerable attention in *The Vital Center* to laying out the rationales for containment, he also proposed to answer the "What are we for?" question by crafting a positive agenda for waging the Cold War. In doing so, he translated the ideology and foreign policies of international integration into a sentimental structure of feeling. At first this seems unlikely: Schlesinger explicitly condemned the "sentimentality" of the political left, embraced a Niebhurian realism which posited the inherent imperfection of man, and promoted a revivified masculinity of toughness that condemned the left for being "soft, not hard." Yet one cannot fully understand the broad impact that *The Vital Center* had without recognizing the ways that it tapped into this powerful strain of American cultural and political thought. Published in the same year that China was "lost" to America as both an ally and an object of sympathy, Schlesinger's book redirected Americans' sentimental impulses out to the decolonizing world in general.[33]

In keeping with the sentimental tradition, Schlesinger identified America's global problem as an excess of individualism and an insufficiency of bonding, and advocated its solution in terms of fostering a greater sense of the self-in-relation. Echoing Erich Fromm's *Escape from Freedom,* Schlesinger argued that industrial modernization had destroyed traditional social orders based on organic communities and personal ties, and replaced them with fragmented social orders, characterized by "frustration," "isolation," and "anxiety," in which individual responsibility had become overwhelming and freedom a "burden." Totalitarianism arose because it promised to alleviate this burden of freedom and to restore the bonds of community: to a people suffering from anomie, it offered "the security and comradeship of a crusading unit." If Americans hoped to prevent people around the world from choosing communism, Schlesinger insisted, they needed to match the appeal of totalitarianism by making "a positive and continuing commitment" to restoring a sense of "community." Americans must move away from their traditional conception of democracy, which tended toward a "sterile" and "arrogant" emphasis on individualism, and instead redefine it in terms of "solidarity with other human beings." [34]

Schlesinger grappled with the damning accusations of racism and imperialism by appropriating the ideal of antiracism from the political left and defining this community as a multiracial one. Acknowledging that the American Communist Party had made the "Negro problem" one of its highest priorities (although he insisted the effort was insincere), he called upon Americans to eradicate their collective "sin of racial prejudice." Like Secretary of State Dean Acheson, he linked the domestic and the foreign policy spheres: he argued that the U.S. was losing the Cold War in Asia and Africa in part because the Soviet Union, untainted by colonialism, could claim the banner of racial equality and contrast itself to the Western democracies, whose domestic societies and colonies had been characterized by "racial cruelties." Schlesinger attacked the persistence of American racism—"We have freed the slaves; but we have not freed Negroes, Jews and Asiatics of the stigmata of slavery"—and insisted that it undermined national security. The competition over the decolonizing world, Schlesinger argued, demanded that Americans "demonstrate a deep and effective concern with the racial inequalities within the United States" and "reform our own racial practices" by dismantling Jim Crow and repealing "such insulting symbols as the Oriental exclusion laws." This commitment to racial equality and civil rights had to go beyond laws, however, and become personally and deeply felt: all Americans had an obligation "to extirpate the prejudices of bigotry" not only "in our environment" but "above all, in ourselves." In Schlesinger's view, Americans would not be able to create a viable "free" community with the Asian and African peoples abroad until they created a multiracial community that included them at home. Like Popular Fronters, Schlesinger advocated a revised national identity that defined Americanness in multiracial and multi-ethnic terms. He suggested that integration, like containment, had to become a domestic as well as a foreign policy: waging the Cold War demanded not only the containment of American communists, sympathizers, and fellow travelers, but also the social integration of Asian and African and Jewish Americans. [35]

Schlesinger's sentimentalism allows us to see the extent to which the entire conceptualization of the Cold War as a problem of winning the allegiance of others was itself a sentimental formulation, grounded in the fear of loss and the desire for connection. Schlesinger and other creators of the global imaginary of integration managed the anxiety of the potential loss of Asia and the rest of the Third World by affirming America's need—and ability—to establish bonds of connection. As part of their effort to recover from the trauma of "losing" China, they focused on forging new and more secure ties to the decolonizing nations.

Eisenhower played a major role in constructing these bonds, both real and imagined, to the decolonizing world. The Truman administration had focused its attention on Europe, and by 1950 the political situation there had largely stabilized. After the Chinese and Korean crises of 1949–50, however, Asia increasingly moved to the forefront of foreign policy concerns. Eisenhower won the 1952 election not only by promising to end the Korean War, but also by supporting China Lobby accusations that the Democrats had underestimated the communist threat to Asia in general. By mid-decade, Asia had become a focal point of the Cold War: the French defeat at Dien Bien Phu in 1954 and the subsequent creation of Ho Chi Minh's communist government in North Vietnam made all of Southeast Asia appear vulnerable; the Bandung conference of Asian and African nations in 1955 testified to the growing economic and political nationalism in the decolonizing world; and Khrushchev was funneling Soviet support to independence movements throughout the periphery via his "peaceful coexistence" campaign. Eisenhower and Secretary of State Dulles, concerned that the decolonizing world was indeed turning toward the Soviet Union, stepped up their efforts at economic and political integration: they condemned expressions of Third World neutrality, expanded the alliance system to include virtually every non-neutral nation, increased foreign aid programs for nations willing to ally themselves with U.S. interests, initiated nation-building efforts in South Vietnam and elsewhere, and attempted to topple governments—successfully in Iran and Guatemala, unsuccessfully in Indonesia—that they saw as trying to limit their nation's engagement in the capitalist "free world" system.[36]

A State Department map of the world "United States Collective Defense Arrangements" visually expresses the global imaginary of "free world" integration (Figure 5). Published in 1955, a year after Dien Bien Phu, it offers a sharp counterpoint to *Life*'s 1947 map of "world struggle." The map centers on the United States and gives equal visual status to the northern and southern hemispheres. This map marginalizes the Soviet Union, pushing it to the edges of the frame and splitting it in two, thereby diminishing the importance of the U.S.-Soviet opposition.

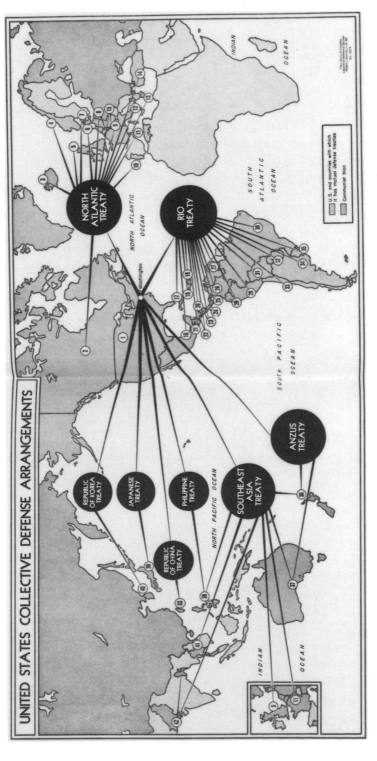

Figure 5. Mapping the Cold War—the global imaginary of integration. (*Department of State Bulletin*, March 21, 1955)

It assigns primary significance to the network of treaties that unites the U.S. with over forty countries in Europe, Asia, the Middle East, and Latin America. Eschewing a bipolar model, this map presents a world structured by a web of ties radiating out from Washington. The lines that link countries together, in contrast to the gestural arrows on the 1947 map, do not suggest aggression, conflict, or competition of any sort. Rather, their straightness and rootedness in the circles that identify the treaties suggest a stable international order built on the principle of U.S.-centered collectivity.[37]

Eisenhower worked hard to direct Americans' attention to the decolonizing world. He recognized that most Americans did not feel the same bond to the people of the periphery that they felt to Europeans, with whom they shared myriad ties of history and culture. Many Americans in fact believed that differences in race and culture made it unwise for the U.S. to involve itself too deeply in Asian affairs. In an effort to counter this view, U.S. policymakers tried to educate Americans about the bonds that already tied them to the decolonizing world and urged them to recognize that differences of language, religion, history, and race could be bridged. Francis Wilcox's call for a sentimental "education for overseasmanship" was part of this larger project of mapping the world in terms of emotional and intellectual affiliations, of teaching Americans to understand themselves not just as citizens of an autonomous nation but as participants in a world system that inextricably embedded them within a network of multinational ties. With speeches such as Wilcox's, the Eisenhower administration invited Americans to see—even as it discursively constructed—their connections with the people of Asia, Africa, and Latin America.[38]

Eisenhower tried to elevate free trade and economic integration to the level of national ideology, much as Truman had done with anticommunism and containment. He consistently emphasized the economic nature of the bonds that tied the U.S. to nations around the world. Throughout his two administrations, the president vigorously promoted a foreign economic policy based on reducing obstacles to trade, increasing overseas capital investment, and stimulating foreign economic growth with infusions of aid. Deeply concerned about maintaining access to the resources of the decolonizing world, he regularly publicized America's need for "continuously expanding world markets," and he defined the nation's fundamental interest as the ability "to trade freely, in spite of anything Russia may do, with those areas from which we obtain the raw materials that are vital to our economy."[39]

The president began this effort in his first inaugural address in 1953. Although he opened with the familiar language of containment—the "forces of good and evil are massed and armed and opposed as never before. . . . Freedom is pitted against slavery; light against dark"—he quickly moved beyond this conflictual imagery. Americans did not stand alone in their opposition to communism, he suggested, but were joined by the people of other nations: a "common dignity," he explained, united the "French soldier who dies in Indochina, the British soldier killed in Malaya, the American life given in Korea." Lest such phrasing imply merely an alliance among Western colonial powers, Eisenhower explicitly distanced the U.S. both from "imperialism" and from "any insinuation that one race or another . . . is in any sense inferior or expendable." His vision of international "unity" included the people of Asia and Latin America as well as those of Europe. Turning from military images to pastoral ones, he invoked "a common bond" that "binds the grower of rice in Burma and the planter of wheat in Iowa, the shepherd in southern Italy and the mountaineer in the Andes." Although Eisenhower understood this bond in ideological terms, as a shared "faith" in "freedom," he emphasized its economic nature as well. The pursuit of "economic solitude" by other nations would endanger the U.S. just as much as would the expansion of communism: "We need markets in the world for the surpluses of our farms and our factories," he explained to his listeners, as well as access to the "vital materials and products of distant lands." If Americans wanted to understand their new role in the postwar era, Eisenhower insisted, they needed to conceptualize the world not only in terms of conflict, but also in terms of this "basic law of interdependence." Eisenhower saw this interdependence—this inescapable interconnectedness—as the essence of the postwar world order, and he spent the next eight years trying to persuade the country to see it also.[40]

Eschewing containment's language of barriers, Eisenhower regularly used the language of transnational "flows" to illustrate this interdependence. Through free trade and private capital investment, Eisenhower assured Americans, the "flow" of U.S. dollars abroad would be matched by a corresponding "flow" of raw materials into the nation, and together they would unite the nations of the "free world" into a mutually beneficial union. Eisenhower and Dulles presented their goal as the eradication of "barriers to mutual trade," which would lead to the creation of "an international society in which men, goods, and ideas flow freely and without obstruction through a wide area." These intertwined concepts of flow and exchange emerged as central ideas during the Cold War.

They defined the "free world" as a place where people, commodities, resources, and the products of intellectual activity could move easily across
national boundaries, and distinguished it from the Soviet "bloc," where
all of these things were trapped behind iron and bamboo curtains. The
language of flow also suggested that the bonds of interdependence were
flexible, originating in multiple centers and moving in multiple directions. Although the United States benefited from these flows, their fluid
nature implied that the U.S. neither controlled them nor used them to
dominate others.[41]

Eisenhower also softened his economic language by translating the
principle of interdependence into the more emotionally resonant language of community. He and Dulles inverted Schlesinger's critique of
democracy's sterile individualism by characterizing the U.S. as the defender of community and then casting neutralist-minded Third World
nations as advocates of a dangerously excessive individualism. In one
1957 speech, for example, Dulles condemned "self-centered" decolonizing nations who "put what they deem their own national rights and
interests above the need of the whole society of nations," and contrasted
them with more collective-minded nations, such as the United States,
which "subordinate national interests to the interest of the world community." "Nations, like individuals," he insisted, "cannot live to themselves alone," and he warned against new nations that embrace "strident
and embittered nationalisms." The United States, he made clear, was
"unsympathetic to assertions of sovereignty which do not accept the
concept of social interdependence." Dulles's characterization of international "interdependence" as "social," however, barely masked the coercive nature of his threat to withdraw, or refuse to extend, the nation's
sympathy. Economic and political nationalism in the periphery posed a
risk to the international economic system that Dulles and Eisenhower
found unacceptable, and they attacked it as a threat to the bonds of
community.[42]

Developing nations were not the only ones who resisted the "basic law
of interdependence," however; they were joined by economic nationalists within the U.S. who feared the domestic effects of increased trade.
This tension came to a head on the issue of foreign aid. Eisenhower was
a fierce proponent of foreign aid, which he deemed the best mechanism
for integrating the decolonizing world: he saw it as a means to stimulate
struggling economies, open new markets, and increase the overall flow
of goods and resources. Neither Congress nor the public shared this enthusiasm, however, and foreign aid programs, especially those aimed at

Asia, quickly developed into the most contentious foreign policy issue of his presidency. Newspapers and magazines attacked foreign aid as wasteful and inefficient, while Congress fought and cut every aid allocation that the president requested. Eisenhower saw this resistance as evidence of the public's "abysmal ignorance" about the realities of economic interdependence, and he vowed to counter that ignorance with new forms of education.[43]

PEOPLE-TO-PEOPLE: CREATING A FEELING OF "WE"

The People-to-People program was one of the Eisenhower administration's efforts to cultivate public support for the foreign aid program and for Cold War internationalism in general. It was an attempt to make the idea of international interdependence come alive in the popular mind. The program's creators also saw it as a means to address some of the questions that had plagued policymakers since the outset of the Cold War: How can we "warm up" the Cold War in ways that will appeal to American "hearts"? How can we transform it into a positive crusade? How can we encourage Americans to abandon their lingering isolationism and learn to see themselves in relation to other peoples around the world? The People-to-People program served as a culminating point at which many of the ideological concerns of the early Cold War converged. Ultimately, the program was an effort to give the global imaginary of integration a material, institutional foundation.

The United States Information Agency (USIA) formulated the People-to-People program in 1955, and Eisenhower launched it in 1956. The program consisted of forty-two committees that arranged contacts between Americans and people around the world who shared a common interest. A quasi-public, quasi-private program, it was created, but not fully funded or administered, by the federal government; the committees served independently of one another under the leadership of private citizens who had been selected by the USIA Office of Private Cooperation. The People-to-People program functioned as an umbrella organization that promoted, coordinated, and raised the public profile of private efforts, some of which were already well established. As such, it both created something new and supplied a name for activities that had been taking place since the beginning of the Cold War.[44]

The program emerged out of Washington's postwar thinking about culture. American policymakers had long admired the Soviets for their skill at using culture for political ends and for their ability to mobilize

people through social organizations, and in the late 1940s they began to
emulate Soviet tactics. The result was the cultural Cold War, which the
U.S. waged with varying degrees of openness. Covertly, the CIA provided funds for cultural organizations, such as the Congress for Cultural
Freedom, that tried to wean Western European artists and intellectuals
away from Marxism. Overtly, Washington created a range of cultural
diplomacy programs that fostered intellectual linkages across national
borders and encouraged positive feelings toward the U.S. These programs introduced the world to abstract expressionist painting, sent African American jazz musicians on tour, and made American books available through USIA libraries. The People-to-People program emerged out
of this cultural diplomacy framework: it was aimed at an international
audience and designed to spread American culture, values, and ideas
overseas. It sought to counter Soviet propaganda by promoting face-to-
face contact between Americans and people in other countries and
thereby display what America was "really" like.[45]

   People-to-People had a double nature, however: it was also a domestic education program. Eisenhower administration officials had learned
the lesson that missionaries and Popular Fronters knew so well: that internationalist visions enjoyed popular support to the extent that they
could be embedded in social institutions and cultural practices. The
People-to-People program was designed to give Cold War internationalism a social and cultural foundation. It sought to enlist the public in
Washington's world-ordering project of "free world" integration by
turning it into a project in which ordinary Americans could feel a personal stake. At any given moment in 1955, approximately two million
Americans were living, working, or traveling abroad. While policymakers recognized this as global expansion in action and generally saw it in
positive terms, it also caused them anxiety. Eisenhower feared that since
most Americans did not fully comprehend the principles of U.S. foreign
policy, those who interacted with people abroad might inadvertently impede the achievement of U.S. goals by saying or doing inappropriate
things. The Eisenhower administration devised the People-to-People program as a means of what it called "orchestrating" this overseas flow of
Americans and coordinating it with the overall aims of U.S. foreign
policy. When Eisenhower invited prominent citizens to join People-to-
People, he emphasized the need to enlist ordinary Americans in the job
of waging the Cold War: "Our American ideology," he explained, will
only "win out in the great struggle" if it has "the active support" of "millions of individual Americans acting through person-to-person commu-

nication in foreign lands." Secretary of State Dulles agreed: according to
John Juergensmeyer, who studied the program in the late 1950s, Dulles
welcomed People-to-People as "a valuable device to create a sense of
public participation in the government's Cold War policies."[46]

The People-to-People program invested the quotidian culture and
daily practices of the American middle class with internationalist meaning. It established committees organized around the professions (bank-
ing), hobbies (stamp collecting), reading (books and magazines), and leisure (sports). The music committee facilitated Van Cliburn's entry into
the Moscow music festival, the hobbies committee sent gardening equip-
ment around the world, and the civic committee arranged sister-city affiliations. Although People-to-People coordinated fewer projects in Asia
than in some other parts of the "free world," it arranged numerous sister-city affiliations with Japan, sent books to the Philippines and magazines to India, Taiwan, and Cambodia, facilitated letter-writing campaigns by American schoolchildren, and sponsored English instruction
by U.S. military personnel stationed throughout the region. Some of
the most successful efforts focused on travel, orphaned children, and
medicine. The national cartoonist's committee produced a hundred-
page booklet instructing American tourists in how to behave abroad so
as to avoid generating ill-will toward the U.S. Members of the U.S. military stationed in Asia frequently supported orphanages, donating time
and money to help local children. Project HOPE was the most successful Asian endeavor: the medical committee refitted an eight-hundred-
bed Navy medical ship, staffed it with medical personnel, and sent it to
Southeast Asia as a floating clinic, hospital, and teaching center. The
project generated great publicity in the U.S. and in Asia, and galvanized
generous support from American corporations and individuals. Abbot
Washburn, the deputy director of the USIA and originator of the People-
to-People program, singled out Project HOPE as a domestic education
success: it "brought into active participation in foreign affairs thousands
of important people in American life" and generated "public support for
the overall Mutual Security Program," which was the administration's
main vehicle for foreign aid.[47]

As this linkage of People-to-People with foreign aid suggests, the Eisenhower administration understood the program as an adjunct to its
foreign economic policy. When the president first introduced the People-
to-People program in a 1956 commencement address at Baylor University, he framed it in terms of the economic integration of the noncommunist world. Eisenhower used the speech to reiterate his views on the

"economic interdependence of peoples" and the threat to world prosperity posed by the "intense nationalism" of some "new nations," who
felt such an "emotional urge for a completely independent existence"
that they constructed "barriers" and "obstacles" to the "flow of trade."
Such restrictions, he explained, inevitably depressed living standards
and created a breeding ground for communism. These barriers could
only be broken down through increased international "cooperation,"
and Eisenhower invited his audience of college seniors to facilitate this
cooperation by joining one of the voluntary associations that "promote
people-to-people contact around the world." Eisenhower thus rhetori-
cally opened up Cold War foreign policy to individual participation: he
suggested that ordinary Americans could foster the integration of the
decolonizing world into the capitalist world system by undertaking voluntary activities and forging personal relationships. This coordination
of the People-to-People program with the goal of international economic
integration occurred at the institutional level as well. The chairs and
board members of People-to-People committees often represented the
economic interests that had the most to gain from integration. The
board of directors of Project HOPE, for instance, consisted largely of
executives from pharmaceutical companies (Smith, Kline & French), international hotel chains (Hilton), the entertainment industry (the Motion Picture Association of America), international tourism companies
(American President Lines, Pan American Airways), and defense con-
tractors (General Dynamics).[48]

The People-to-People program helped construct the global imaginary
of integration by insisting that vast differences among peoples could be
bridged with relative ease. Eisenhower believed that the program would
enable people around the world to "leap governments" and "work out
not one method but thousands of methods" for learning about and forging ties with each other. In marked contrast to the global imaginary of
containment, with its focus on bulwarks and conflict, the People-to-
People program imagined a "free world" in which there existed no barriers—geographical, political, linguistic, religious—that ordinary citizens could not "leap." The program encouraged Americans to "reach
across the seas and national boundaries to their counterparts in other
lands," and it held out the promise that by doing so they could create
that sense of multiracial, multinational community that Schlesinger had
invoked.[49]

Eisenhower made the sentimental logic of the People-to-People program explicit in his speeches publicizing the program. In them he trans-

lated the "cold" principles of international capitalist economics into a "warm" and sentimental structure of feeling that could be inhabited at the level of everyday life. In Eisenhower's hands, the international arena became a domain of the personal, and economic integration became a question of understanding the feelings of other peoples around the world, rather than an expression of U.S. imperialism. Cooperation, he insisted, depended upon the realization that "every international problem is in reality a human one." Only through personal contacts could people come to understand that they were already "linked in partnership with hundreds of millions of like-minded people around the globe." Sympathy, the highest of sentimental values, had to form the sinews of this partnership. "People are what count," he insisted, and a "sympathetic understanding of the aspirations, the hopes and fears, the traditions and prides of other peoples and nations" was "essential to the promotion of mutual prosperity and peace." Eisenhower made sympathy —the ability to feel what another person feels, to share in his or her conditions and experiences—the defining feature of American globalism, and he commended those Americans who engaged in international communication that entailed "talking from the heart to the heart." Such "sympathetic understanding" was "a compulsory requirement on each of us if, as a people, we are to discharge our inescapable national responsibility to lead the world in the growth of freedom and of human dignity." One has the sense that Eisenhower believed that if he could stimulate the flow of feelings across national borders, he would also smooth the international flows of capital, manufactured goods, and raw materials.[50]

The People-to-People program offered a sentimental answer to the "What are we for?" question. In a 1959 book entitled *What We Are For*, Arthur Larson, a People-to-People official and former USIA director and speech writer for Eisenhower, grappled directly with the problem of defining America in an international context as something other than the opposite of communism. In the post-McCarthy era, he wrote, when "the dead weight of a decade of negativism is not easily thrown off," Americans needed to "discover and articulate clearly and affirmatively what we stand for and where we are going." Larson, like Eisenhower, made sympathy the defining characteristic of Cold War America. He determined that the key to America's relations with other peoples "lies in one word: 'identification,'" by which he meant "understanding the common principles that we believe in and that bind us together." The goal of such identification would be to create a "feeling, in relation to people of other countries, of 'we.' Not 'we' and 'they.'" If Americans "could once and for all become suffused with this concept of identification," then they could "create a people-to-people understanding between our own people and the people of countries now estranged from us." The People-to-People program encouraged Americans to enlarge their understanding of who constituted the "we" with whom they identified, and to redefine that "we" in international rather than merely local or national terms.[51]

The People-to-People program produced a national identity for the United States that differed radically from that produced by the global imaginary of containment. In this vision, America was less a free-standing, armed defender of the world and more a member of a community bound together through emotional bonds. One can read this assertion of an international "we" as a means of assuaging the anxiety that some Americans felt about U.S. expansion and the resistance it provoked, a way to stave off the dreaded loss of the Third World and to counterbalance containment's emphasis on fear of difference. It served as a way for Americans to affirm themselves as a global yet non-imperial power.

The People-to-People program, like the dual containment and integration foreign policy itself, carried within it the residual ideologies and cultural logics of both left-liberal and right internationalism. Although Eisenhower denied any desire to convert other countries to American ways, the People-to-People program was clearly indebted to the missionary tradition of internationalism. As a voluntary program run by private citizens, it looked back to the pre–World War II era when private and missionary organizations delivered most foreign aid. As had missionaries, the program implied that Americans and their allies abroad shared essentially identical interests, if not cultures, and it advocated personal contact and communication as the best way to spread American political values overseas. In its emphasis on ordinary Americans reaching out to help the less fortunate—by sending them American books, by teaching them to speak English—it continued the missionary legacy of individuals performing good works for the underprivileged.[52]

Perhaps more surprising, the People-to-People program also perpetuated elements of left-liberal internationalism. The program seems to have been part of Washington's effort to emulate Soviet cultural strategies. At the level of institutional organization, People-to-People echoed the Popular Front's structure of a loosely affiliated network of groups that promoted participation in international affairs. One can read the People-to-People committees, which were formed soon after the last updating of the attorney general's list of "subversive" organizations, as replacements for the Popular Front organizations that had been driven out of existence. Perhaps most important, the People-to-People program, like the Popular Front, appealed to Americans by saturating cultural forms and activities with political and specifically internationalist meaning. People-to-People officials privately acknowledged this debt to the Popular Front, and one internal memo appraising the organization's activities in 1959 traced the program's conceptual roots to the Kremlin:

> For a parallel or antecedent operation of this type, one must look more to the Soviet Union and Communist bloc, whose social and cultural organizations have been politically oriented and internationally active for a generation. The Communist world front movement of women's, youth, labor, writer's [sic], veterans and other social and professional organizations (once claiming more than 100 million members) germinated under the Comintern during the 1920's and blossomed during the 1930's and 1940's. At the end of the 1940's, however, it had become Stalin's political instrument.

People-to-People planners seemed to have imagined their program as taking over and redirecting the internationalist energies of the delegitimized Popular Front. The People-to-People program assured Americans that by sending their favorite books and records overseas and by sharing hobbies such as gardening, stamp collecting, and coin collecting, they could continue to stand, as they had in the 1930s, with people around the world who were resisting totalitarian domination. At the same time these positive activities also replaced the negative social practices, such as naming names, that domestic containment policies had encouraged and that faded away with the collapse of McCarthy.[53]

The dual nature of the People-to-People program meant that contemporaries saw it as simultaneously a failure and a success. When they evaluated it as a cultural diplomacy effort aimed at overseas audiences, observers often viewed it with contempt. The People-to-People Foundation, which sought to raise funds for individual committees, failed to generate any philanthropic enthusiasm and shut down after a year. Foreign affairs professionals, including members of the U.S. foreign service, by and large refused to support the program and rejected it as an "amateurish" approach to a complicated world which failed to consider the needs and problems of peoples overseas. One cultural affairs officer in Asia condemned the program for its superficiality and its American focus. Dismissing it as mere "lip service" and "slogans," he characterized the program as a bunch of Americans "running around with flags in both hands forgetting that other people have a story too." Another U.S.

official in Asia dismissed the program as an "appeal to walk around with a smiling facade and a mouth full of teeth showing," which the locals knew was "phony." Still others damned it as "superficial," "marginal," "unimportant," "meddlesome," and "too propagandistic." [54]

As a domestic education program designed to turn Americans' attention to international issues, however, contemporaries hailed it a success. In fact, foreign affairs professionals disliked the program precisely because it was so clearly designed for American participation rather than for overseas effectiveness. Ordinary Americans embraced the program with enthusiasm, and virtually every nationally organized group in the country included People-to-People efforts in its activities. Even the USIA officials in Asia who dismissed the program's impact there acknowledged that it had produced among ordinary Americans a greater awareness of Asia as a primary site of the Cold War. According to John Juergensmeyer, these officials identified "the increased American consciousness of foreign problems, particularly in Asia" as "one of the most valuable benefits" of the program. He also reported that U.S. officials overseas particularly praised the program for "increasing the political consciousness of American tourists." At a time when heated debates over foreign aid threatened to erode support for Eisenhower's foreign economic policy, the People-to-People program encouraged Americans to feel personally involved in the task of international integration. [55]

·   ·   ·   ·   ·

The immediate postwar period saw an extended effort to define the type of internationalism that Americans should embrace. As policymakers formulated a distinctly Cold War internationalism based on the twin pillars of containment and integration, they worked to disaffiliate the United States from those models of internationalism, such as colonialism, that were practiced by the declining European powers, and from the communist internationalism practiced by its adversary, the Soviet Union. At the same time, they worked to delegitimize alternative models of international engagement that had substantial domestic followings, such as the unilateralist right internationalism of the Republican party and the left internationalism of Henry Wallace and the Popular Front. Even as the Truman and Eisenhower administrations delegitimized these competing models, however, they appropriated some of their core concepts and their strategies of social motivation. This struggle to reshape and limit the ways Americans understood their relationship to the world was an integral part of winning popular support for Cold War foreign policies, and it took place in the sphere of culture as well as in the sphere of politics.

Near the end of his first year as secretary of state, John Foster Dulles delivered a speech, hosted by the New York *Herald Tribune*, on the need to secure public support for the waging of the Cold War. He explained that, with isolation no longer a viable option, the United States in recent years had to find a new way to be "part of the world." He contrasted the American "pattern for international living" with that of the Soviets: where the Soviet Union ruled its citizens and allies through "coercion," the United States, he explained, was a "society of consent" which achieved national and international unity through "the free acceptance of concepts which override differences." Ideas rather than brute force were what ultimately mattered, he suggested. Dulles explained that the working of this "system of consent" was "a slow business" requiring "persistence" and an "unwillingness to be discouraged." It depended upon a sustained effort to articulate and disseminate the "unifying principles" and "formulations" which, "like magnets, will draw together those who are apart." As secretary of state, Dulles argued, securing this consent and creating this unity among Americans and their allies was part of his job. He also suggested that the media had an important role to play, and he appealed to his audience of newspaper men and women to facilitate the workings of consent by "clarifying the issues" so that unity could be achieved.[56]

By and large, Dulles and other postwar political elites did secure public consent for the waging of the Cold War in Asia, at least through the mid-1960s. With varying degrees of enthusiasm Congress, and by extension the constituencies it represented, supported the range of foreign economic, political, and military policies—from alliances to free trade to outright war—that the Truman and Eisenhower administrations formulated for the decolonizing world. At the same time, however, that consent was never so solid that policymakers could take it for granted. The Korean War, while tolerated, never generated much popular enthusiasm; the actions against the governments of Iran, Guatemala, and Indonesia had to be undertaken covertly rather than in open public view; and political elites felt the need to hide the full extent of U.S. political and military involvement in South Vietnam, Laos, and Cambodia.

It is impossible, of course, to say definitively which of the innumerable factors in play at the time succeeded in securing public support for the policies of containment and integration. Was it the domestic containment policies that stifled dissent on foreign policy issues? A genuine fear of communism? A sense of personal participation in the nation's world-ordering ambitions? A state of political apathy that encouraged passivity in the face of foreign affairs? Most likely consent, or the limitation of dissent, was secured through some combination of these and myriad other factors. My goal is not to single out the global imaginary of integration as the decisive factor, but somewhat more modestly to make it visible as one of the key "unifying principles" that political elites put forth in their effort to "draw together" the American people in support of the Cold War.

I believe that the global imaginary of integration played a particularly important role in the "slow business" of securing consent for the Cold War because it animated that global project with a positive energy. It could serve as an effective "unifying principle" because, unlike the global imaginary of containment, it was grounded in the very idea of unification. Fredric Jameson has described the working of hegemony as a "strategy of rhetorical persuasion in which substantive incentives are offered for ideological adherence." In order to perform their ideological functions, hegemonic texts and practices must articulate a genuine utopian vision: "They cannot manipulate unless they offer some genuine shred of content as a fantasy bribe to the public about to be so manipulated." Invariably, for Jameson, this utopian quality lies in the "symbolic enactment of collective unity." The global imaginary of integration offered precisely this idealistic and compelling vision of U.S.-Asian collectivity. Endlessly reiterated in political discourse, the idea of integration took on a host of political, economic, and personal meanings that revolved around the process of forging bonds with others across a divide of difference. As a utopian ideal, it served as a discursive mechanism for constructing the Cold War as a concrete, positive project that ordinary Americans could own through their participation.[57]

This imaginative mapping of America's relation to the capitalist "free world"—and to Asia and the decolonizing world in particular—was shaped by a broad array of cultural figures, as well as by political elites. These middlebrow intellectuals, who form the subject of the following chapters, served as the cultural wing of the Cold War historical bloc. They acted, with varying degrees of intentionality, as the storytellers of Cold War internationalism. Like the producers of missionary and Popular Front culture before them, they brought to life the abstract principles of a particular form of internationalism by translating them into a concrete body of social practices, aesthetic philosophies, and cultural forms. In the process, they further worked out the synthesis of left and right internationalisms that the Truman and Eisenhower administrations had achieved at the level of political ideology and policy. Collectively, these middlebrow artists and intellectuals produced a sentimental culture of integration that coexisted with and counterbalanced the culture of containment.

Some of the most popular stories that these middlebrow intellectuals told imagined interdependence in terms of medicine, travel, and adoption, and offered the jungle doctor, the tourist, and the white mother of Asian children as emblematic figures who embodied the ideal of an internationalist America. It is thus not surprising that contemporaries counted the People-to-People efforts organized along these lines as among the program's most successful. The People-to-People program achieved its goals, to the extent that it did, because it drew on what were becoming established ways of thinking about America's relationship with the decolonizing world. The program was thus not a unique phenomenon, but part of a larger set of social practices and cultural narratives that were taking shape over the course of the late 1940s and 1950s.

The outward-looking sensibility of the People-to-People program infused the Cold War with an expansive, optimistic, open quality that contrasted sharply with the thematic of restriction and suppression that cultural historians of containment have explored. This popular internationalism carried a particular set of meanings in the 1950s. However, these meanings did not remain stable, and as domestic and international political conditions changed during the 1960s and 1970s, so did the meanings that these so-called citizen diplomacy programs carried. In the mid-1980s the Sister Cities program, which had originated as a People-to-People project, emerged as a central institutional framework for the grassroots political movement opposing Ronald Reagan's renewal of the Cold War in Central America. Political activists were looking for ways to express their anger at the U.S. funding of the Contras, the right-wing paramilitary movement dedicated to overthrowing Nicaragua's elected socialist government. At the same time, they wanted to avoid the politically marginalizing and negative logic of traditional peace movements, which simply declared their opposition to an existing set of policies. As a solution they adopted the positive discourse of the People-to-People program and began creating Sister City ties with Nicaragua. These initiatives appealed to people across the social spectrum who liked the idea of taking a positive action and who wanted to forge an alternative network of ties with people whom Washington was demonizing as threats to national security. The U.S.-Nicaragua Sister Cities movement spread quickly across the country as the Reagan administration stepped up its interventions in Central America: the ten programs that existed in 1985 doubled to twenty by 1986 and more than tripled to seventy-seven by 1987. Together they formed part of a network of organizations that offered an alternative source of news and education about events in Central America and sent money, food, medical supplies, and other forms of aid to people suffering the effects of U.S. foreign policy. Similar Sister City ties were established in the 1980s with other politically contested countries, including El Salvador, where the U.S. was backing right-wing elements in an ongoing civil war, and South Africa, where the U.S. supported the white minority apartheid government.[58]

Twenty years later, nongovernmental organizations that wanted to mobilize people against the corporate-led processes of globalization similarly appropriated People-to-People language. Global Exchange, for example, an organization that promoted itself as working for environmental, political, and social justice around the world, advertised its activities in left-liberal publications such as the *Nation* with the tag-line, "Building People-to-People Ties." I think that we can read these late– and post–Cold War projects as a return of the political repressed. They represent a resurgence of some of the residual left-liberal internationalisms that the People-to-People program had co-opted in the 1950s, but that it had also sustained in a submerged form. As a hegemonic project, the People-to-People program had embraced some of the Popular Front political ideals—international solidarity, popular participation in foreign affairs—and linked them up with a larger Cold War program of anticommunism and global capitalist integration. As the Cold War waned, however, that linkage was loosened, and the merged People-to-People/ Popular Front language became available for new political projects that contested, rather than supported, the global expansion of U.S. power and that imagined other forms of international integration.

CHAPTER 2

Reader's Digest, Saturday Review, and the Middlebrow Aesthetic of Commitment

What is important about Tom Dooley is that he tried to meet
the highest need of his age or any age, which is for a sense of
connection between man and man.

Norman Cousins, Saturday Review, 1961

In late January of 1961 Norman Cousins, editor of the *Saturday Review*,
sat inside St. Mary's Catholic Church in Vientiane, Laos. Cousins was
there to attend a requiem mass for Thomas A. Dooley, an American doctor who had been working in the jungles and villages of Laos since 1956
and who had just died of cancer at the age of thirty-four. As Cousins listened to the service, he gazed out the church door and contemplated the
country's civil war, a conflict that was threatening to spiral out of control and engulf all of Southeast Asia. In the most recent eruption of violence, in late December, General Phoumi Nosavan had attacked the neu-
tralist government of Souvanna Phouma and left the capital burned and
scarred, with 500 to 800 civilians dead. Both sides in the conflict, Cousins reported later, wore military uniforms supplied by the United States.[1]

As Washington contemplated its increasing involvement in Asian affairs, it worried about the kinds of people it was sending to work there.
In 1951 the National Security Council completed a report that reviewed
U.S. foreign policy objectives and problems in Asia. Its list of obstacles
to the achievement of U.S. goals included the usual Cold War suspects,
such as the Soviet Union, communist China, and the leaders of the noncommunist nations in Asia who lacked political skills and a sense of collective unity. The last item listed, however, stood out from the others:
"American Personnel in Asia." The National Security Council saw Amer-

icans themselves as one of the nation's problems in Asia. The achievement of U.S. objectives in Asia was "handicapped," the report stated, "by the lack of qualified and experienced personnel available to live and work in Asian countries." The pool of candidates who possessed the skills required to promote U.S. interests in Asia was, in Washington's eyes, simply too small. Americans' lack of knowledge about and experience in Asia was part of the obstacle, but not the whole of it: American attitudes mattered as well. Washington needed to take "utmost care" in selecting personnel who possessed a "temperament suitable for life in Asia and creditable to the United States Government." Above all, the people sent to Asia needed to avoid creating the impression that the U.S. wanted to "'colonize' or 'Americanize'" the countries in which they worked.[2]

Political observers agreed with this evaluation of the political danger posed by Americans' ignorance about the world at large. Historian Thomas A. Bailey, in a 1948 study of the impact of public opinion on foreign policy, lambasted the "huge mass of the educationally underprivileged" as a "great abscess on our body politic." Over the course of the late 1940s and throughout the 1950s, the leaders of public and private institutions tried to reduce this ignorance. The U.S. government promoted graduate-level international studies through a number of legislative acts, including the 1948 Smith-Mundt Act, the 1949 Point Four program, the 1949 Fulbright Act, and the 1951 Mutual Security Act. Area studies took off as an academic discipline between 1945 and 1952, largely due to the efforts of the Ford Foundation, which poured millions of dollars into funding graduate study. These efforts culminated in 1958 (with a little help from Sputnik) in the Higher Education Defense Act, which officially recognized the education of Americans as a factor in national security. However, a big gap existed between the calls to increase the knowledge of international affairs among the broad mass of Americans and the reality of foundation and government efforts, which funded relatively few students at colleges and universities.[3]

The policymakers and public intellectuals who called for mass education recognized that, if Americans were to be successfully enrolled in support of containment and integration policies, nontraditional forms of education had to be brought into the process. In a 1949 essay published by the Council on Foreign Relations, political scientist Martin Kriesberg urged social and cultural institutions to promote Truman's model of internationalism: "All the media of mass education, all the media of mass communication must be mobilized for the effort; the school, the college, the public forum, the press must all do their part." The National Security Council and members of the State Department also looked to the private sector for help in teaching the public about the Cold War in ways that would generate support for U.S. policies. One consultant to the NSC suggested that if the government created the "proper atmosphere," it could perhaps generate the "voluntary cooperation" of private citizens who would make the government's case before the public. Robert Lovett proposed that the government enlist the help of "a 'group of paraphrasers' "—by which he meant prominent and influential private citizens—"who could turn what it is we have to say to the American people into understandable terms for the average man on the street." [4]

This chapter explores how the education of Americans about Asia was understood in the late 1940s and 1950s as a distinctly cultural project. Middlebrow intellectuals, including the editors of *Reader's Digest* and the *Saturday Review,* took on the task of teaching Americans about their nation's new role in the decolonizing world. They acted as Washington's "paraphrasers," translating the principle of international integration into terms and forms of culture that were accessible to the man on the street. They did this in part by holding up as models certain types of characters—both real and fictional—whom they saw as possessing temperaments suitable for life in Asia and creditable to the United States. Tom Dooley was one of those characters. When they took on the job of public education, middlebrow artists, writers, and cultural brokers were not following a set of directives handed down to them from above. Rather, I want to suggest that they formed the intellectual wing of the postwar hegemonic bloc and as such they promoted political and ideological positions that harmonized with those held by political leaders. As a cultural formation, the middlebrow represented roughly the same alliance of social groups that comprised Truman's Cold War alliance. It worked out the same synthesis of the traditions of left and right internationalism and embodied the same political convergence toward a "vital center."

Reader's Digest and the *Saturday Review* proposed that cultural texts and institutions should promote international political engagement, and they offered themselves, in their capacity as cultural institutions, as vehicles for that engagement. This middlebrow work of mass education was cultural in another sense, as well, in that these intellectuals tried to inculcate in their audiences certain attitudes toward culture itself. They tried to teach Americans to embrace with enthusiasm rather than reject with fear the whole idea of cultural difference.

MIDDLEBROW AS A CULTURAL FORMATION

During the 1950s, *middlebrow* emerged as a preferred term to categorize the mainstream culture of the postwar era. It named the broad swath of culture directed toward an audience that rejected, on the one hand, the avant-garde intellectual movements, such as existentialism, that emanated from Paris, and on the other, the pulp culture of comic books and lewd paperbacks. Middlebrow was not just a cultural category, however, but also a cultural formation: a more or less self-conscious movement of artists, writers, and intellectuals who shared an aesthetic sensibility and were loosely connected through personal relationships and through an institutional infrastructure of magazines, publishing houses, book clubs, reviewers, and other organizations. Many of the middlebrow intellectuals who produced knowledge about Asia in the postwar period—including James Michener, Oscar Hammerstein II, William Lederer, Thomas Dooley, Norman Cousins, and DeWitt Wallace—knew each other personally, quoted each other in their writing, joined in each other's social and political causes, and sometimes even helped write each other's books.[5]

Historians have located the birth of the middlebrow in the 1920s, when booksellers began applying advanced marketing techniques to the selling of literature, and they have identified a number of defining characteristics. First, middlebrow had certain class connotations: it was the culture of a growing professional-managerial middle class whose members desired the cultural markers of their improved economic status. Its producers—often the children of immigrants on their way up the economic and social ladder—embraced the ideal of cultural populism, repackaging literature, classical music, and fine art to make them more accessible to mainstream audiences. Middlebrow thus offered its consumers the cultural capital that would make them feel more secure in their new class identity. Second, middlebrow had certain global implications: it was the culture of a nation that, after World War I, had a new awareness of itself as an international power and was eager to prove that it had "arrived" on the world stage culturally as well as politically. Middlebrow thus aimed at alleviating a national sense of provinciality. Third, middlebrow was deeply rooted in the principle of education. The purveyors of middlebrow culture promised their audience that if they read certain books and listened to certain radio shows, they could learn to understand the ideas and aesthetic forms that defined middle-class and international respectability. Unlike formal education, however, this

self-education need not be painful or time-consuming, but could be combined with entertainment in ways that made learning pleasurable. As
part of this pedagogical impulse, middlebrow promoters offered themselves as authoritative guides to twentieth-century modernity, promising
to lead their audience safely through the confusing new world of mass
consumer society. Fourth, and in keeping with its educational imperative, middlebrow was marked by a commitment to moral uplift, and it
retailed an optimistic attitude that all problems could be solved through
the application of time-tested principles. Underwriting all of these characteristics was a profound universalism: middlebrow affirmed what it
saw as the eternal, universal values that united all human beings across
time and space.[6]

Middlebrow culture can also be defined in terms of its sentimental
aesthetic. In her history of the Book-of-the-Month Club, Janice Radway
has argued that middlebrow's universalism and its pedagogical impulse
converged in a form of sentimental education. The club's institutional
and critical brokers promoted a literary style that Radway has characterized as "middlebrow personalism," in which large social, political, or
historical issues are explored through the experiences of a single individual. As part of this personalism, middlebrow texts strived to produce
an emotional and empathic response: they encouraged their readers to
feel intensely about other people. In doing so, Radway argues, they facilitated a "social habit of mind" in which the reader entered into a state
of identification and connection with a text's subject. By enabling this
imaginative communion, middlebrow texts facilitated the transgressing
of boundaries and the bridging of differences through the workings of
sympathy. Readers learned about the world beyond themselves by emotionally entering into a universe somehow foreign to their own. The de-
fenders of middlebrow understood this aesthetic as an alternative to the
reigning modernist one, that, in their eyes, produced primarily alienation, cynicism, and despair. Middlebrow purveyors kept an eye on the
social implications of culture: they believed that by enabling a sense of
imaginative community, their texts could encourage a sense of engagement and commitment with the world that had utopian possibilities.[7]

In the 1950s, the New York intellectuals brought middlebrow culture
into the forefront of intellectual debates. Leslie Fiedler attacked precisely this sentimental and universalizing quality in a 1955 article published in *Encounter*. Critiquing the class implications of its cultural style,
he argued that the typical middlebrow was a "sentimental egalitarian"
so committed to upward mobility and an all-embracing middle class

that he rejected genuine diversity in favor of the blandly uniform culture of "a truly classless society." Dwight Macdonald in a 1960 *Partisan Review* essay defined middlebrow as the corruption of turn-of-the-century modernism by mass consumer culture, and lambasted it as "the products of lapsed avant-gardists who know how to use the modern idiom in the service of the banal." The middlebrow had become, in Macdonald's eye, the dominant culture of postwar America: its "tepid ooze" was "spreading everywhere." [8]

The New York intellectuals condemned postwar middlebrow culture as, at root, a continuation of prewar Popular Front culture. Macdonald's preferred terms of condemnation—"liberalistic moralizing," "orgy of Americana," "folk-fakery," and "orotund sentimentalities"—had all been used to attack the Front's cultural style, while Fiedler's linkage between middlebrow's sentimental aesthetic and the desire for a "classless society" tarred it with the brush of communism. Robert Warshow charted a clear continuity between postwar middlebrow culture and the leftist culture of the 1930s when he declared that, despite the political demise of communists in the 1940s, Americans still inhabited "the intellectual climate that was first established by the Communist-liberal-New Deal movement of the 30's." Irving Howe and Lewis Coser extended the reach of the Popular Front well into the 1950s when they claimed that the "flavor" and "style" of contemporary mass culture—especially Hollywood social dramas, Broadway musicals, and historical novels— "is a heritage of the Popular Front." [9]

These attacks on middlebrow culture by the New York intellectuals must be understood within the context of postwar anxieties about mass culture and mass society. Many postwar critics, horrified by the political manipulation of the media by fascist and communist regimes of the 1930s–1940s, came to see mass culture and mass society as the foundations of totalitarianism. Their cultural critique derived from this fear of totalitarianism, and moved in two directions. In the first instance, the New York intellectuals sought to protect the realm of culture from corruption by insisting on a clear separation between art and politics. They tended to view forms of culture that retained any explicit social or political content as veering dangerously toward Stalinism. Instead, they championed a modernist high art that avoided explicit social or political engagement and that emphasized abstraction and formal innovations instead. Forced by the "difficulty" of such modernist art to make their own interpretations, critics believed, readers and viewers would retain their individuality and thus be less susceptible to mass control. At the same time, the New York critics also insisted that America possessed a clear cultural hierarchy, and they devoted much of their energy to marking the distinctions between the highbrow, the middlebrow, and the lowbrow. In doing so they sought to prove that the U.S. was not a standardized, conformist, mass society vulnerable to totalitarianism, but a pluralist, democratic society defined by politically healthy class and cultural differences. The highbrow condemnation of middlebrow arose from these two critical tenets. Middlebrow was suspect because it was a mass cultural form that engaged directly with social and political issues, and because its universalizing aesthetic threatened to obliterate meaningful class and cultural distinctions. The multiple critiques of middlebrow came together in the charge of sentimentality: to be sentimental was to be universal, to be accessible, to be popular, to value an emotional connection with others, to be persuasive, to be socially engaged.[10]

READER'S DIGEST AND THE SATURDAY REVIEW

The New York intellectuals seized upon the *Saturday Review* and *Reader's Digest* as middlebrow's fullest expression. Throughout his career Dwight Macdonald took an almost perverse glee in skewering the *Saturday Review*, branding its "*de jure* high seriousness and *de facto* low accommodation" as the "textbook example of middlebrow cultural journalism" and designating its editor, Norman Cousins, a "genteel, midcult entrepreneur." Irving Howe, when he argued in 1954 that middlebrow dominated the postwar cultural scene, offered by way of evidence that "the most powerful literary journal, read with admiration by many librarians and professors, remains the *Saturday Review*." Leslie Fiedler in turn linked the *Saturday Review* and *Reader's Digest* together and identified them as the aesthetic standards for middlebrows who wanted to defend "literature" from the corruption of lowbrow comic books and highbrow pornography.[11]

I want to read these two magazines as institutions that structured and organized the middlebrow as a formation. Other middlebrow magazines, such as Henry Luce's *Time* and *Life*, also dealt extensively with Asian affairs, especially during the 1930s and 1940s. *Reader's Digest* and the *Saturday Review*, however, serve as better windows onto the middlebrow formation as a whole. In their respective roles as a digest and a review, they made it their business to survey the broad terrains of fiction, nonfiction, theater, music, social criticism, and numerous other forms of culture. Their editors also played important roles as cultural brokers and gatekeepers and as such helped to define and maintain the fluid boundaries of the middlebrow as a cultural category. Each magazine also claimed for itself a unique cultural authority, either because of its unmatched circulation, as in the case of *Reader's Digest,* or because of its aura of cultural prestige, as in the case of the *Saturday Review.* I want to suggest that it was precisely the qualities that the New York intellectuals so despised in the middlebrow that made these magazines such powerful institutions of popular education.[12]

As all the magazine histories tell it, *Reader's Digest* was the brainchild of one man. DeWitt Wallace was born in 1889, the son of a Presbyterian preacher and professor of Greek and modern languages who went on to become president of Macalester College. Wallace hatched the idea for *Reader's Digest* while recovering from a shrapnel wound in France during World War I, and he and his wife, Lila Acheson Wallace, brought out the first issue in February 1922. The *Digest* began as just that, a digest of articles published in other magazines, and by implication it had no editorial position of its own. This began to change in the 1930s, when it started publishing original articles and planting articles in other magazines which it would then "reprint"; by the early 1950s, roughly 50 percent of its material had originated in *Digest* editorial offices.[13]

From his first issue, Wallace pursued an editorial philosophy that changed little over the decades: the presentation of "articles of lasting interest which will appeal to a large audience, articles that come within the range of interests, experience, and conversation of the average person." Wallace never wanted the *Digest* to serve as a news magazine, and he avoided publishing articles that would quickly become outdated. James Playsted Wood, the *Digest's* authorized historian, offers a succinct description of the magazine's editorial mission: "The Digest operates to reduce baffling complexities to understandable simplicities. It puts abstract problems into human terms and world concerns into a personal frame. The Digest makes at least some of life's confusions seem intelligible." True to the middlebrow mission, the *Digest* understood itself as a tool that would guide the average person through the confusions of the twentieth century by providing clarity and reassurance. As a result of this intimate and personal approach, the *Digest* appealed to readers at the level of feeling rather than intellect: "The Reader's Digest provokes an emotional as well as an intellectual response, more of an emotional than a cerebral response. The Digest is emotional. The Digest is sentimental." This sympathetic quality allowed readers to feel connected with the larger world in a familiar way: "The Digest offers the reader a simpler and homelier relationship to the world, and he is grateful." [14]

This formula brought the *Digest* instant and lasting success. Its circulation rose from 20,000 in 1926 to 1.5 million in 1935; during World War II it more than doubled, from 4 to 9 million; in 1951, domestic circulation stood at 9.5 million, international at 6 million. By 1967, the *Digest* was publishing thirty international editions in fourteen languages, and had 100 million readers every month, more than any other publication except the Bible. [15]

Public education figured prominently in the magazine's understanding of itself. Wood claims that "at heart [Wallace] has always been a teacher. There has been a strong didactic element in the Digest from the very first." The title page of Wallace's 1920 dummy proclaimed it "The Magazine of 100 Percent Educational *Interest*," and Wallace promised his targeted readers, who did not have the time or resources for formal education, that they could "acquire a broad understanding of the world —a liberal education" by reading the *Digest*. In both Wallace and the *Digest,* this educational drive was linked to an international perspective. Wallace's father had been a staunch internationalist who fought publicly for the League of Nations during the "isolationist" period after World War I, and in Wood's description Wallace "grew up in a household where the international viewpoint was part of the air he breathed." [16]

The *Digest*'s internationalism expressed itself most clearly in the form of international stories and international editions. The magazine published stories about Asia from the beginning: the first issue included a piece on the Philippines (then an American colony), entitled "The Philippines Inside and Out," and promised future articles providing "insights into Japanese life." In the first year it published thirty-eight stories with international settings, forty-four in the following year, and increasing numbers as it expanded. The international editions comprised the most overt form of Wallace's internationalism. From the early 1920s through the late 1930s, the magazine published exclusively within the United States. The *Digest* began looking beyond the borders of the nation when war threatened in Europe, and it expanded across the globe in step with U.S. government interests during and after World War II. [17]

Although the *Digest* never received direct subsidy from the government, its internationalism served official U.S. interests. Wallace himself felt that the *Digest*'s "over-all emphasis . . . has been a more or less conscious effort to promote a Better America . . . with a place for the United

States of increasing influence and respect in world affairs." It launched its British version, the first international edition, in 1938 and its Latin American version, the first foreign-language edition, in 1940. Both were started up in cooperation with the State Department in an effort to counter Axis propaganda and infiltration; Wallace, in announcing the Latin American edition, spoke of "the need for extending the interpretive influence of The Reader's Digest throughout those countries where a clear conception of the United States of today will promote an alliance of interests for the cause of peace tomorrow." The *Digest* launched the Portuguese/Brazilian and Swedish editions in 1942, and the Arabic-language edition in 1943, the latter two initiated at the urging of the Office of War Information. Throughout the war the *Digest* accompanied American troops around the world with four special editions published in the Mediterranean, Pacific, China-Burma-India, and European theaters, which eventually reached one of every seven Americans in uniform. The *Digest* inaugurated additional international editions after the war, as it entered countries devastated by fighting directly behind the U.S. army. It started the Japanese edition in 1946, the year after the U.S. began its military occupation, introduced the Italian edition in 1948, in response to fears that Italy would go communist, and initiated the Chinese-language edition, which circulated in Hong Kong, Taiwan, Malaysia, Thailand, and the Philippines, in 1964, the year the U.S. introduced ground troops into the Vietnam War. One roving editor—with not a little irony—put the magazine in a most exclusive pantheon: "The three great international institutions are the Catholic Church, the Communist Party and the Reader's Digest." [18]

This international orientation arose in part out of the *Digest*'s ties with the missionary movement. Lila Wallace, who, like her husband, was the child of a Presbyterian minister, had been a social worker with the YWCA and with the Presbyterian Board of Home Missions before marrying Wallace in 1922. Her brother, Dr. Barclay Acheson, was a trained Presbyterian minister who worked with the Near East Relief Fund and helped establish the American University in Beirut before becoming the *Digest*'s international ambassador. Numerous other employees had missionary origins, as well, which the *Digest* publicized in mini-biographies on the inside front cover. Ralph Henderson, Wallace's first employee, who went on to become business manager and senior editor, was born in the jungles of Burma to missionary parents and spent four years there teaching in mission schools with the American Baptist Foreign Mission Society. Roving editor William Hard grew up in India, the child of a Methodist missionary, and Stanley High served with Methodist missions in Europe and China after World War I. Senior editor Paul Palmer spent two childhood years in Korea, where his father worked as a doctor in a gold mine.[19]

Politically, the *Digest* allied itself with the Republican party. During the 1930s and 1940s it stood against Popular Front organizations and New Deal programs, while in the 1950s it found an easy harmony with the Eisenhower administration. For the 1952 election, the *Digest* loaned its subscription lists to Eisenhower's advisors to help them choose an effective campaign slogan, and over the course of his two administrations it published fifty-eight articles either written by or about members of his cabinet and staff, of which only eighteen were critical (many of these were about foreign aid). Its political positions matched those of the Republican administration: it promoted big business; opposed federal aid to education, highways, slum clearance, and urban renewal; gave weak support to the civil rights movement; fought Social Security and Medicare; and hammered away at federal waste and inefficiency, the mounting national debt, and uncontrolled spending. Overall, it favored less government and more private-sector problem solving. When Eisenhower left the White House, the *Digest* hired him as a writer for a rumored $25,000 an article.[20]

Reader's Digest carried the residual traces of right internationalism: it represented the right wing of the Cold War historical bloc and made anticommunism the core of its internationalist vision. The *Digest,* in the view of one observer, opened the Cold War in July 1943, with an extremely critical article about America's then-ally the Soviet Union, and it fanned the flames of domestic and international anticommunism throughout the postwar period by regularly publishing such red-baiting articles as Stanley High's "Methodism's Pink Fringe," Max Eastman's "Why We Must Outlaw the Communist Party!" and Whittaker Chambers's "I Was the Witness," as well as by condensing books like *Seeds of Treason: The Story of the Hiss-Chambers Case* by Ralph de Toledano and Victor Lasky. John Heidenry, author of a history of the magazine, charts how the *Digest* willingly served CIA and FBI interests throughout the late 1940s and 1950s, using its international editions, especially the Italian and the Latin American ones, to disseminate anticommunist propaganda and allowing J. Edgar Hoover, a regular contributor, to use "the Washington bureau much as if it were his own personal PR firm."[21]

Wallace made a point of hiring authors who had been on the political left in the 1920s and 1930s but had since made a rightward turn.

J. P. McEvoy had been known as "the young Debs" in his youth for his
espousal of socialism, William Hard had been a socialist-leaning muck-
raker for the *Nation* and the *New Republic,* Stanley High had been a top
speechwriter for FDR who turned against his former boss and went on
to write for Eisenhower, and Russian-born Eugene Lyons had worked
as an assistant director of Tass immediately following the Russian Revolution. The *Digest* also published the work of James Burnham, the former Trotskyite who swung to the far right, wrote the article which
accompanied *Life*'s 1947 "World Struggle" map, and worked as a consultant for the CIA.[22]

The *Digest* provided a home for what Hannah Arendt called "ex-
communists": people who had broken with the party but, as so-called
experts on totalitarianism, continued to hold on to communism as the
defining feature of their lives. Max Eastman was undoubtedly the most
prominent of these. Eastman had been editor of the communist journal
The Masses, a friend, biographer, and translator of Trotsky, and had
been tried twice on sedition charges. By 1940 he had broken with the
left and written his initial piece for the *Digest,* a first-person essay about
his mother, a Congregational minister. He went on to write a critique of
socialism, which the *Digest* titled "Socialism Does Not Gibe with Human Nature," that brought him denunciations from the *Socialist Call,
Partisan Review,* and the *Progressive,* as well as a permanent *Digest*
position as roving editor. In 1943 the *Digest* published his proto–Cold
War essay, "We Must Face the Facts about Russia." Eastman justified
his writing for the *Digest* in pedagogical terms: speaking of the satis-
faction of being able to bring his specialized political knowledge to the
attention of readers around the world, he said, "I have thought of it as
teaching, when writing for these millions. I *am* a teacher, and I love to
teach."[23]

The *Saturday Review of Literature* published its first issue on August 2, 1924, under the editorship of Henry Seidel Canby, a former professor of American literature at Yale. From its debut, two years after that
of *Reader's Digest,* the *Saturday Review* had ties with that bastion of
middlebrow culture, the Book-of-the-Month Club. Three of the *Review*'s
four editors worked for the Book-of-the-Month-Club, and during the
1930s Harry Scherman, founder and president of the club, helped keep
the *Review* afloat financially by letting it use the club's membership list
for a direct-mail promotion. Norman Cousins assumed the editorship
in 1940 at the age of thirty-five, after spending five years as critic and
editor at *Current History,* a journal of world affairs; he edited the *Re-*

view from 1940 through 1971, and again from 1973 through 1977. He guided the *Review* as a magazine of "literature and ideas" and followed Canby's original editorial policy of publishing reviews "directed to the broad spectrum of books, fiction and nonfiction, intended for the general reader." The *Saturday Review* shared with the *Reader's Digest* an optimistic editorial philosophy, and Cousins sought to distance the magazine from the more pessimistic strains of intellectual life, vowing that it would neither partake of the "bleakness of negative existentialism that emanated from France" after World War II, nor perpetuate the "debunking outlook of the Thirties." The *Saturday Review* flourished under his editorship, and circulation rose steadily, from 28,500 in 1940 to its peak of 650,000 in 1971. (The *Saturday Review* ceased publication in 1986.)[24]

Although the *Saturday Review*'s circulation was much smaller than that of *Reader's Digest,* it reached a more affluent and educated readership. In a 1965 study of weekly magazines, its audience led all others —including that of the *New Yorker*—in terms of income, education (52 percent were college graduates), professional and managerial jobs (46 percent), government jobs (16 percent), and book club membership (34 percent). A 1963 study showed that its readers also led in social consciousness, political activity, foreign travel, book purchases, and investments. A 1966 study showed that, in contrast, only 15 percent of *Reader's Digest* readers had graduated college, and only 10 percent held professional and technical jobs. In its analysis of "social position," which the study defined as a weighted index based on the head of household's occupation and education, the study found that less than 4 percent of *Reader's Digest* readers belonged to the "upper" class, while 20 percent of *Saturday Review* readers fell in that category; it classified 62 percent of *Reader's Digest* readers as "working class," a category to which only 28 percent of *Saturday Review* readers belonged.[25]

From the outset the *Saturday Review,* like *Reader's Digest* and in keeping with the middlebrow sensibility, conceived of itself as an instrument of public education. Henry Seidel Canby announced in his inaugural editorial that the *Saturday Review* would "be like a modern university where one seeks Principles, but also works in laboratories of immediate experience amidst the vivid confusion of experiment." Canby later described his editorial vision as "the Jeffersonian belief in the necessity of education for a successful democracy. I wanted to go in for adult education in the value of books. . . . I wanted criticism to be first of all a teaching job." Norman Cousins's own intellectual roots lay in the field of education—he had received a degree from Columbia University's Teachers College in 1933 and worked for two years as the education editor at the New York *Evening Post*—and he shared Canby's pedagogical vision of the magazine.[26]

Much of Cousins's educational impulse centered around internationalism, and he pushed the magazine and its readers to engage with global political issues. In the 1930s Cousins had flirted with Marxism, but an intellectual encounter with Gandhi turned his internationalist impulses away from an economic framework and toward a humanistic one. Like *Reader's Digest*'s international editions, Cousins's editorial philosophy developed out of World War II, which was just breaking out when he joined the staff. In an editorial written years later, he described how the fall of France in 1940 "had the effect of blasting us out of whatever ivory tower we may have been in" and making clear that there was a need for a literary magazine "that would see books not as ends in themselves but as part of an activist and political world." Regular contributor Joseph Wood Krutch described how the lingering Depression and the first rumblings of World War II brought an end to that "earlier, perhaps happier, day when purely literary matters had been clearly at the center of the responsible citizen's concern with the state of his civilization." In the postwar years "politics, economics, and foreign policy" began to capture an increasing share of the public's attention and "a different complex of subjects of dispute began to take precedence over purely literary matters, even in the minds of those who called themselves intellectuals." New questions arose that authors and critics alike had to address: "What ought we to do about the fact that we were now, fortunately or unfortunately, an indivisible part of a single human community? How should we use or not use the power which had made us the most powerful nation that had ever existed? What should we do about those inside and outside our own boundaries whom we could no longer call merely 'the lesser breeds without the law'?" For the editors it became "impossible to separate the discussion of literature from the discussion of these other matters," and so in 1952 the *Saturday Review of Literature* shortened its name to the *Saturday Review*—"not only of literature but of all the things with which literature itself was now, willy-nilly, concerned."[27]

Cousins saw international political affairs as among the most important matters that thinking people needed to concern themselves with, and throughout his editorship he sought to promote readers' knowledge of and participation in global affairs. The most significant change that Cousins made at the *Saturday Review* was to increase the nonliterary content of the magazine. Whereas the magazine devoted little editorial space to matters unconnected with literature prior to World War II, after the war nonliterary issues came to dominate. The 1935–36 issues had an even ratio of nonliterary to literary articles; in 1945, the ratio had become 36 nonliterary to 20 literary articles; by 1955 it was 67 to 32, and by 1965 it was 122 to 39. Many of these articles and editorials covered international issues, from wars and famines to foreign aid and travel.[28]

These pedagogical concerns came together in the *Saturday Review*'s calls for public education in internationalism. In the years immediately following the war, Cousins protested what he saw as a continuing isolationist sentiment. In a 1945 editorial he bemoaned that although "America has renounced isolation . . . officially," it was "doubtful whether America has ever been more isolationist than at this moment." He saw Americans as "isolationist in the vital sense, in the moral sense," in the "shocking failure thus far to accept responsibility for moral leadership that was laid at our door at the end of the war." The conversion to internationalism that Cousins sought was not happening automatically, and so, throughout the late 1940s and 1950s, the *Saturday Review* urged the education of Americans in order to make them responsible, engaged citizens of a new global order. Guest editor Harry J. Carman stressed the need for every person to develop a "world consciousness" and "an international as well as national point of view." For Cousins, the atomic bomb, and the apocalyptic destruction it threatened, made it imperative to "develop a world conscience" and to achieve a "transformation or adjustment from national man to world man."[29]

Where *Reader's Digest* marked the right wing of the Cold War hegemonic bloc, the *Saturday Review* anchored its cultural left wing. During the McCarthy years it criticized red-baiting attacks on schools, teachers, libraries, and overseas information centers, and protested the denial of civil rights to people of opposing political views. From the bombing of Hiroshima onward, Cousins protested the nuclear arms race, called for international control of atomic weaponry, and campaigned for a ban on nuclear testing. The magazine also provided a venue for Hannah Arendt's "former communists": writers and intellectuals who had distanced themselves from the Soviet Union and the Communist Party, yet still advocated left-liberal views. It published articles and reviews by journalist Harold Isaacs, agrarian land-reform expert Wolf Ladejinsky, and others, such as Robert Payne, whom it identified as "moderate Leftist[s]." While *Reader's Digest* employed Max Eastman as a staff writer, the *Sat-*

urday Review in 1958 gave a regular column to Granville Hicks, the former literary editor of the communist *New Masses*. At the same time, however, Cousins clearly distanced himself from the Popular Front. In 1949 he attended the Cultural and Scientific Conference for World Peace at the Waldorf-Astoria Hotel, which had been organized by a Popular Front organization as a last-gasp effort to preserve U.S.-Soviet wartime cooperation in the face of increasing Cold War antagonism. Two years after the Truman Doctrine, however, such left internationalism had become illegitimate: the New York intellectuals staged protests outside the hotel (and soon thereafter created the Congress for Cultural Freedom and the American Committee for Cultural Freedom), while inside, Cousins, at the request of the U.S. State Department, delivered a stinging attack on the conference organizers and the Communist Party.[30]

Cousins carried the residual traces of left-liberal internationalism, however, in his advocacy of world government. World government formed the core of Cousins's internationalism, providing the same organizing principle that anticommunism did for Wallace. The world government movement emerged out of the shock of the atomic bombings of Hiroshima and Nagasaki. Taking its slogan from Wendell Wilkie's 1943 internationalist bestseller, *One World,* and bolstered by the adoption of the United Nations charter, the movement resurrected the universalist ideals of Woodrow Wilson and the League of Nations: it called on nations to sacrifice some of their sovereignty and join a universal world government that had the power to create and enforce laws—including laws regulating war—that would be binding on all nations. Cousins became one of the movement's most influential supporters after publishing *Modern Man Is Obsolete* in 1945, and he joined, and later became president of, the United World Federalists when it was created in 1947. Cousins used the pages of the *Saturday Review* to voice his internationalist views, and in editorials, articles, and book reviews the magazine promoted the principles of world government and world law.[31]

The world government movement marked the left-most boundary of what was considered legitimate internationalism. Initially the movement had a broad appeal that cut across the political spectrum—even DeWitt Wallace supported it in 1945 and 1946—but as Cold War tensions increased and containment policies took hold, its universalist principles lost much of their attraction, and membership in the United World Federalists plummeted. After 1949 only diehards such as Cousins remained. Critics of the movement, including theologian Reinhold Niebhur, dismissed its adherents as naive idealists and dreamers who had not yet come to terms with the inherent corruptibility of mankind. Crucially, however, these critics did not attack World Federalists as communists or duped fellow travelers, thereby enabling them to retain a measure of legitimacy in the public arena. In *The Vital Center,* for instance, Arthur Schlesinger grudgingly tolerated world government as a "noble dream" that served to "distract men of good will" but that did not threaten America's free society.[32]

Both *Reader's Digest* and the *Saturday Review* pledged themselves to educating the public about Asia. Where middlebrow intellectuals in the 1920s had guided Americans through a new domestic social order of mass consumer culture, those of the late 1940s and 1950s guided their compatriots through a new international order of U.S. global expansion and Third World decolonization. Since 1945 each magazine had increasingly focused on Asia as a primary site of Cold War contestation and as the part of the world in which America's future would be determined. Already in 1948, the *Saturday Review* announced that it had become "evident that in the long run the battle between the Russian and the American ideologies will involve greater stakes and greater populations in Asia than in Europe"; by the early 1950s, it declared that America and Asia shared a "common destiny" and that events in Asia would determine the future of America. Both magazines produced an enormous amount of information about Asia—hundreds of articles, book reviews, first-person narratives, and condensed and excerpted books. In 1945 the *Saturday Review* exclaimed that "nothing like this flood of books on other countries has happened to American publishing before" and linked this phenomenon to America's new role in the world. In 1951 the *Saturday Review* published one of its many special issues on Asia and the Pacific; entitled "America and the Challenge of Asia," it included articles by prominent Asia specialists, reviews of ten new books on Asia, a list of forty-eight works published since 1949, and publishers' advertisements for eighty more. *Reader's Digest,* in turn, charted the evolution of the Cold War in Asia by publishing stories on different nations as they became seen as areas of contestation between the U.S. and the Soviets. Articles on China appeared frequently during the civil war years (1945–49), on Japan during the years of U.S. occupation (1945–52), on Korea during the Korean War (1950–53), and on Southeast Asia after 1950 when it appeared increasingly vulnerable to communist attack. Both magazines made Asia visible through a process of mapping, both literal and figurative, and kept their readers informed about the emergence of independent nations, shifting political boundaries, and

America's changing relations with new governments. Many of the movies, plays, novels, histories, and journalistic accounts about Asia produced during the late 1940s and 1950s found their way into these magazines, in the form of excerpts, reviews, advertisements, or shorter pieces by the same authors.[33]

As the magazines educated the public about Asia, they often staked out opposing positions on the issues that defined the poles of postwar internationalism. In the heated public debate that raged in the late 1940s and early 1950s over the Chinese civil war and who "lost" China, *Reader's Digest* gave voice to the representatives of right internationalism and served as an outlet for members of the China Lobby. It published articles by Republican Congressman Walter Judd, a former medical missionary in China, who charged that communists in the State Department were undermining Chiang Kai-shek's Kuomintang government. Other stories attacked China scholars such as Owen Lattimore, advocated the use of U.S. air power to retake mainland China, and proposed "unleashing Chiang" from his exile on Taiwan to help U.S. forces in Korea. Overall, the *Digest* participated enthusiastically in the post-1949 demonization of communist China. The *Saturday Review,* in contrast, covered the Chinese civil war from more of a left-liberal internationalist perspective. Cousins represented events in China within the context of rising Asian nationalism and legitimate demands for social and political change. Prior to 1949 the *Review* urged Washington to cease supporting Chiang's government, which it condemned as a corrupt, right-wing dictatorship; after Chiang's defeat, it rejected the idea that Washington had "lost" China—or that it had the power to determine China's fate one way or the other—and placed the blame for Mao's success on Chiang's unpopular and elitist government. It welcomed forthright admirers of Mao, such as journalists Edgar Snow and Anna Louise Strong, and published positive reviews of books by Owen Lattimore, whom it defended from red-baiting attacks. The magazines also staked out opposing positions in the debates over foreign aid. *Reader's Digest* emerged as one of the loudest and most insistent voices criticizing Eisenhower's foreign economic policy, while the *Saturday Review* supported economic aid and criticized what it depicted as Washington's overemphasis on military aid.

MIDDLEBROW UNIVERSALISM AND THE AESTHETIC
OF POLITICAL COMMITMENT

If the Cold War hegemonic bloc was not always uniform in its political views, it was in its fundamental goals: *Reader's Digest* and the *Saturday Review* came together in the effort to define a national identity for the United States as a global power in Asia. Despite their differences, the two magazines shared a set of keywords through which they defined America's relation to Asia. Recycling the language of the Truman Doctrine, the Marshall Plan, and innumerable State Department communiqués, they urged their readers to see themselves as bound to peoples beyond the borders of the nation in noncoercive, often personalized ways. In *Reader's Digest's* view, Americans had a "responsibility" in the question of whether China became democratic or totalitarian; they had to recognize their "obligations" to feed the hungry of the world. The *Saturday Review* shared this concern with responsibility and obligation, but more often explained America's role in the world in terms of "commitment." After the Korean War broke out, the *Saturday Review* urged Americans to extend their commitment to resist communism to the Middle East, Malaya, Burma, Indonesia, and Indochina. Cousins urged all the peoples of the world to make a "Grand Commitment" and fully "commit ourselves to each other." Most important, both magazines vigorously denied the idea of American imperialism. China Lobbyist John T. Flynn declared in *Reader's Digest* that, although Americans had been an imperialist power once in the Philippines, they had given it up forever: "We had the disease of imperialism. We didn't like it. Now we are immune." Both magazines echoed this view, in various formulations, throughout the postwar period.[34]

Reader's Digest and the *Saturday Review* also found common ground in their assertion of universalism, which was intimately bound up with their denial of imperialism. Popular discourse in the postwar period tended to treat imperialism as a material outgrowth of a misguided belief that Western and non-Western peoples were essentially different from each other. Middlebrow intellectuals, in contrast, embraced the Boasian culture concept: they tended to regard differences among the world's peoples as evidence of cultural variety within a larger human sameness, rather than as evidence of any one group's innate superiority or inferiority. Difference, understood now in cultural rather than biological terms, was not something to be feared but accommodated and even celebrated. This pluralistic universalism resonated with the political ideology of in-

ternational integration: like integration, which imagined a diversity of
nations subsumed under an overarching "free world" alliance, universalism embraced the richness of cultural differences as it subordinated
them to a larger human similarity. Humanistic universalism thus functioned as a central component of the global imaginary of integration—
it was yet another way of imagining the world as a diverse yet interconnected whole.[35]

Cousins regarded the embrace of this universalism as an unavoidable
requirement for Americans in the postwar period. In a typical *Saturday
Review* editorial from 1952, Cousins bemoaned the "miseducation" he
had received growing up, which taught him to focus on the differences
among people rather than similarities. Today, he explained, Americans
needed an "education against tribalism" that would teach them to "look
at someone anywhere in the world and be able to recognize the image of
himself." If Americans were to move out into the world, both physically
and imaginatively, they would need to embrace the idea of a single "human community" that was "greater than the separateness imposed by
nations, greater than the divergent faiths and allegiances or the depth
and color of varying cultures." Cousins assured his readers that if they
took this universalism to heart, they would be able to feel "at home anywhere in the world." [36]

Each magazine gave this universalism a different spin when applied
to questions of culture. For Cousins, "education for Western civilization
is not enough": he wanted his readers to welcome more of the world into
their homes. In his role as cultural broker he opened up a space within
the U.S. mainstream for Asian arts and literature. The *Saturday Review*
published articles and reviews about Buddhism, Hinduism, and Taoism,
introduced readers to the films of Akira Kurosawa and Satyajit Ray,
and celebrated the skills of Japan's Azuma Kabuki Dancers. It promoted
the work of Indian writers Rabindranath Tagore, R. K. Narayan, Ved
Mehta, Kamala Markandaya, and Ruth Prawer Jhabvala; of Chinese
writers Lau Shaw and Eileen Chang; of Japan's Yukio Mishima and the
Philippines' José Rizal. *Reader's Digest,* in contrast, understood cultural
universalism in more nationalistic terms as the global dissemination of
American stories, characters, ideas, and values. Until the mid-1960s, the
Digest's international editions carried only material that had been previously published in the American edition. The magazine interpreted its
high circulation rates abroad as evidence that this American material
captured a universal human perspective. As authorized historian James
Playsted Wood wrote in 1958, "At a stage in the world's history when it

is pleasant to have the point confirmed, the *Digest* seems to have proved once again that, despite geography and climate, differences in diet, politics, morals, and speech, people everywhere are much alike. They laugh at the same things. They feel pain when they are hurt. They share a common humanity." For the *Digest,* the differences among the world's people were not so deep that they could not be bridged by "Laughter Is the Best Medicine" and "I Am Joe's Liver." [37]

Both magazines, however, shared a belief that this universal humanism must have as its foundation an expansive sense of sympathy. The oneness of humanity would remain a cold abstraction, in their view, until Americans could feel themselves emotionally connected to people beyond the borders of the nation. Both magazines thus urged their readers to develop a particular emotional orientation towards non-Americans. Cousins exhorted Americans to "identify ourselves sympathetically— no, the word is not strong enough—identify ourselves *compassionately* with the mainstream of humanity." In his view, the ability to make global commitments depended upon this capacity to make emotional commitments. *Reader's Digest* echoed this view, and gave it a more instrumental twist, in a 1960 article by Dr. Charles Malik, former foreign minister of Lebanon and president of the U.N. General Assembly. Malik wrote that the West would not win the allegiance of Asia until "it rediscover[ed] and reaffirm[ed] what [was] genuinely human and universal in its own soul." In his view, "not until the businessman from Manchester or Detroit and the peasant from Iran or India can come together on a much deeper basis than the exchange of goods and money can the West really begin to have a chance in the ferocious competition going on at present for the heart and soul of Asia and Africa." Only an intimate and sympathetic bonding could nullify the differences of race and nation: "Only he, therefore, who feels with humanity, who is at one with all conditions of men, who is insufficient and incomplete without them, who is not protected and separated from them, can help them and lead them and love them and be loved by them." Waging the Cold War in the decolonizing world, he suggested, depended on the ability to overcome a sense of emotional separation from others.[38]

Reader's Digest and the *Saturday Review* were not satisfied with merely encouraging their readers to develop a sense of commitment to the rest of the world. They wanted their readers to take actual steps that showed they recognized the world's common humanity and were free of outmoded fears of foreigners. Both magazines facilitated their readers' active engagement in U.S.-Asian relations by creating opportunities for them to put the ideal of international commitment into practice. In 1957, for instance, *Reader's Digest* published an article that invited readers to cultivate mutual understanding between the U.S. and Japan. "America Seems Near to Me Now," a first-person story written by Mutsumi Kurahashi, told how a former GI had brought her family great peace of mind—and good feelings toward the United States—when he returned a diary taken from the body of her father, a Japanese soldier, as a battle-field souvenir in New Guinea. At end of the story, *Reader's Digest* urged its readers who had similar mementos to make "a generous gesture of international good will" and send them to *Reader's Digest* headquarters, which would forward them to Japanese families. Readers turned in one hundred thirty-seven mementos which, judging by the letters of appreciation written by the families who received them, brought America closer to many Japanese at a moment when anti-American sentiment was on the rise in Japan. By facilitating the return flow of these objects out of the U.S. and back to Japan, *Reader's Digest* reinvested them with new geopolitical meanings. It transformed items that had once served as symbols of wartime enmity into emblems of a secure postwar alliance.[39]

As this episode indicates, *Reader's Digest* promoted itself as an ideal medium though which Americans could participate in foreign affairs. The *Digest* presented itself as an active participant in the struggle against communism—a "weapon in the war for freedom." The magazine praised itself for inspiring American soldiers in Korea to keep fighting even as the war dragged on, for countering communist propaganda by representing America accurately abroad, and for offering Asians an alternative ideology to communism and neutralism. The *Digest* told its readers that they, too, could participate in this effort by sponsoring subscriptions to international editions for friends abroad. In this way, one self-advertisement proclaimed, "Every thoughtful American can establish a bond of friendship and understanding with individuals in other lands." If the reader had no acquaintances abroad, the *Digest* offered to select a recipient from its own files of public opinion-makers—"lists of teachers, doctors, journalists, and others, carefully gathered for this purpose"—whose minds the *Digest* thought most needed to be won for America. *Reader's Digest* promoted these subscriptions as a way for Americans "troubled by a sense of personal helplessness" to take action and help "stimulate in foreign lands a feeling of personal friendship and understanding" with the people of the United States. That the magazine kept such a file of overseas opinion-makers suggests the extent to which it saw itself as a counterpart to official U.S. propaganda efforts.[40]

The *Saturday Review* shared with *Reader's Digest* this drive to encourage a feeling of personal commitment to the world outside the United States. Cousins saw a pervasive sense of helplessness, brought on by bipolar tensions and the fear of nuclear war, as the biggest impediment to political engagement, and he organized several projects through which "disconnected" Americans could transcend their sense of helplessness. His most visible efforts consisted of a series of "partnerships" in which readers and editors worked together on an international humanitarian project. These partnerships included the moral adoptions campaign, through which readers financially supported hundreds of children orphaned at Hiroshima; the Hiroshima Maidens project, which brought adult female victims of the atomic bombing to the U.S. for plastic surgery; the Ravensbrueck Lapins project, which offered a similar service for Polish victims of Nazi medical experimentation; and support for Paul Brand's leprosy clinic in India. Like the *Reader's Digest* campaign to restore battlefield souvenirs to Japanese families, these partnerships had a sentimental quality: directed toward suffering women, children, and innocent victims, they recalled the nineteenth-century idea of the deserving poor; they often focused on restoring family feelings, and on correcting physical disfigurements that had led people to be expelled from what Cousins called the circle of "human sympathy and grace." [41]

Reader's Digest and the *Saturday Review* also supported Eisenhower's People-to-People initiative and adopted the program's rhetoric as their own. *Reader's Digest,* in keeping with its Republican belief in private solutions to public problems, supported the program with great enthusiasm. It financed an international competition to generate new People-to-People ideas and published articles promoting existing projects such as the sister-city exchanges. While the *Saturday Review* would support the publicly financed Peace Corps more vocally, Cousins endorsed the People-to-People program and promoted its efforts, especially the Project HOPE medical ship in Southeast Asia. [42]

The *Saturday Review* understood commitment as a cultural aesthetic as well as a social imperative. In his capacity as cultural arbiter, Cousins called upon writers to produce a politically engaged and globally aware literature. He rejected reigning modernist aesthetics that privileged formal experimentation at the expense of engagement with social and political issues, and he dismissed as "bankrupt" a realism that he saw as indulging in an adolescent fascination with the graphic and the prurient. Instead, he advocated a literature that would carry a "payload of social purpose" and cultivate in readers "a sense of personal commitment."

Although this call for commitment echoed the Popular Front's cultural style, editorialist Harrison Smith made clear that the *Review* had no desire to return to the literary standards of the 1930s, "when every novel was despised as worthless by a group of left-wing critics unless it was educationally and constructively proletarian and wearily depressing." Instead, Cousins urged writers to grapple with what he saw as the "fundamental" issue of postwar society: "the need for individual man to find a way of changing the general direction of his mind so that it turns primarily outward rather than inward." The middlebrow literature of commitment should encourage this outward turn by making the world beyond the nation's borders come alive. In 1947, the year the Truman Doctrine committed the United States to the defense of "free people" around the world, Smith urged writers to recognize that "there is a whole new world to explore, at home and abroad, and new men and women in it." The *Saturday Review* looked to literature to plot new ways of being in the world. Smith exhorted authors to accept their "responsibility" as "teachers of the great public" to write about the "daily existence of our envoys in Korea or Greece" and discover "what the leaders of our War or State Department have in store for us." In particular, he wanted writers to tell the story of international integration: "America as the head of a coalition of nations throughout the world, wherever Russian power has failed to establish itself, must have men who can explain and dramatize our position, not only to ourselves, but to our friends and to our antagonists where we can reach them." The *Saturday Review* called upon writers to map out the network of relations among nations that tied the postwar world together, to deal imaginatively with the new reality that "a riot in Bombay or a civil war in Mongolia will touch the nerve centers of Harlem or Washington." In keeping with its middlebrow mission, it asked them to represent this new global complexity, to make it knowable, to locate Americans within it, and to suggest the modes of behavior that they should adopt in order to manage it.[43]

As *Reader's Digest* and the *Saturday Review* promoted this middlebrow aesthetic of political commitment, they cultivated a genre of narrative that illustrated the underlying premises of the People-to-People program—long before the program itself existed. This genre, which included both nonfiction and fictional narratives, helped create the intellectual atmosphere out of which Eisenhower's program emerged and legitimated the program once it had been established. In fact, one can see the program itself as an effort to give this narrative form an institutional foundation. These people-to-people narratives, as I will call them, served as a cultural expression of the principle of international integration: they depicted politically engaged individuals communicating across racial and national boundaries, recognizing their shared interests, and working together to solve the root problems that provided a breeding ground for communism. The politically resonant ideals of responsibility, obligation, sympathy, and interdependence found full narrative expression in the people-to-people genre. These narratives centered around the creation of what People-to-People official Arthur Larson called an international sense of "we." The stories which the *Saturday Review* published chronicling its international partnerships, such as the moral adoptions campaign, were exemplary people-to-people narratives. *Reader's Digest* brought the genre to its fullest flowering and disseminated it around the world through its international editions. It published numerous articles about ordinary people who found ways to participate in international affairs and who did so with tolerance and affection for others: the Maryknoll priest in Hong Kong who invented a noodle machine to turn donated U.S. supplies into food that refugees from communist China would want to eat; the college student who arranged down-home tours of America for foreign visitors; the Nantucket husband and wife who helped a couple living on a South Pacific island to raise money by selling their handicrafts; the American businessman who traveled through Asia looking for and investing in men who wanted to start small businesses. Both *Reader's Digest* and the *Saturday Review* told the story of Jimmy Yen's mass education movement in China, Taiwan, and the Philippines, and acclaimed it as a model of Asians helping Asians.

THE UGLY AMERICAN AND DR. TOM DOOLEY

The people-to-people narrative reached its apex with the 1958 publication of *The Ugly American,* William J. Lederer and Eugene Burdick's quintessentially middlebrow novel about Americans living and working in Southeast Asia. Like the editors at *Reader's Digest* and the *Saturday Review,* Lederer and Burdick aspired not only to entertain their readers, but also to educate them about America's new role in Asia. In a 1957 letter to CIA agent Edward Lansdale, Lederer outlined his views, somewhat crudely, on the political necessity of public education. The "key to our Asia affairs is people," he wrote, "and, as there aren't enough geniuses to go around, we have to school, educate, enema, and beat the middle class intellectuals until they: (1) Know the area (before going).

(2) Know necessary techniques. (3) Know U.S. policy. (4) Glorify in having a tough job—not just look for a luxury vacation." With *The Ugly American* Lederer attempted to put this educational agenda into practice.[44]

Southeast Asia had become one of Washington's central concerns by the time Lederer and Burdick published their novel. In the late 1940s the United States began funneling millions of dollars to the French to finance their colonial war in Indochina. After the French defeat at Dien Bien Phu in 1954 and the signing of the Geneva Accords, which granted real independence to North and South Vietnam, Laos, and Cambodia, the U.S. took over the task of preventing Ho Chi Minh's forces from unifying Vietnam under a communist government. It increased its efforts to contain the spread of communism in the region and to integrate the newly independent nations into the capitalist "free-world" system. Washington began delivering military and economic aid to the South Vietnamese government of Ngo Dinh Diem and sending in military, technical, and economic advisors to help him run his government and build a viable army. By the late 1950s more than fifteen hundred Americans were stationed in South Vietnam; by 1961 the U.S. had poured in more than $1 billion of military and economic aid.[45]

During these same years the U.S. also began intervening in neighboring Laos, which had been granted independence on the condition that it remain neutral. The U.S. initially gave financial support to its moderately pro-Western government; when that government opened negotiations with the communist Pathet Lao, Washington encouraged a right-wing coup that installed a new government which then launched a military campaign against the communist insurgents. In 1960, this American-backed government was itself overthrown by a group of neutralists, who in turn secured U.S. support. By the end of that year North Vietnam and the Soviet Union were supplying aid to the anti-American forces, and what had been a relatively contained civil war seemed in danger of spinning out of control. Those Americans who thought about the situation in Laos saw it as far more serious than what was happening in Vietnam. In early 1961, Norman Cousins wrote two articles, one of which *Reader's Digest* reprinted, that chronicled the chaos in Laos and detailed America's involvement there. Cousins explained that since 1955, and in violation of the Geneva Accords, the U.S. had been paying the salaries of the entire Laotian army, training its officers, and supplying it with uniforms and arms; the U.S. had spent $325 million, all but 20 percent of it on the military. With the increasing shipments of arms by both China and the Soviet Union, Cousins wrote, Laos was threatening to turn into another Korea and destabilize all of Southeast Asia.[46]

William Lederer had intimate knowledge of U.S. political and military affairs in Southeast Asia. He joined the U.S. Navy in 1930, served in Asia during World War II, and stayed on after the war as an Asia specialist. From 1950 to 1958 he served as public information officer and special assistant to the U.S. commander-in-chief of the Pacific, a position which afforded him detailed knowledge of U.S. activities in the region. He was also closely affiliated with *Reader's Digest*. He began writing for the magazine in 1949, the year China became communist and the rest of Asia began looking increasingly vulnerable. He was hired as a part-time contributing editor in 1955, became a full-time Far East correspondent after leaving the Navy in 1958, and remained the *Digest*'s Asia liaison until 1963. During these years he wrote many of the magazine's more memorable people-to-people narratives. His coauthor, Eugene Burdick, who had also served in the Navy during World War II, taught political theory at the University of California, Berkeley, from 1950 to 1965.[47]

Burdick and Lederer wrote *The Ugly American* as an intervention in current U.S. foreign policies in Southeast Asia. Written as what Burdick called a "message book" and ostensibly "based on fact," it offered a scathing report on America's efforts to halt the spread of communism and an exposé of the failure of foreign aid programs. It purported to document the rampant incompetence of American diplomats, foreign aid officials, and civilians working in Vietnam, Burma, Cambodia, and the fictitious nation of Sarkhan. Even as it attacked foreign aid programs, however, it offered as the solution characters and practices that could have been drawn from the people-to-people narratives in the pages of *Reader's Digest* and the *Saturday Review*. The book aimed not to derail U.S. policies, but to suggest better ways to win Southeast Asians' allegiance and thus integrate the region more securely into the "free world."[48]

The Ugly American hit its mark: it became the most popular, influential, and controversial novel written in the 1950s about America's relations with Asia. *The Saturday Evening Post* serialized the novel in the fall of 1958, it was the Book-of-the-Month Club's main selection for October, and it spent seventy-eight weeks on the bestseller lists, eventually selling more than six million copies; in 1962 it was made into a movie starring Marlon Brando. Newspapers around the country explored the issues it raised, and magazines across the political spectrum, from *Reader's Digest* to the socialist monthly *Dissent,* published in-depth analyses, rebuttals, or confirmations of the authors' conclusions. The novel had a significant political impact as well. Eisenhower reportedly ordered a review of the foreign aid program after reading it, and the Senate debated its accusations throughout 1958 and 1959. Senator William J. Fulbright denounced the book's distortions and urged the State Department not to assist the production of the movie version. Senator John F. Kennedy, in turn, used it as fodder in his presidential campaign against the incumbent Republican administration, sending it to every member of the Senate, an act which the publisher publicized with an advertisement in the *New York Times*. The novel also reputedly served as the inspiration for the Peace Corps.[49]

Part of what made the novel both popular and open to charges of oversimplification was that it divided its characters into two neat camps of "ugly" and "non-ugly" Americans. Part of why it resonated so strongly with the people-to-people narratives was that it based this division on the characters' attitude toward cultural difference. The truly "ugly" Americans, primarily diplomats and high-level officials, are imperialistic characters who feel contempt for Asian people. Unable to appreciate anything unfamiliar, they adopt an air of racial superiority, refuse to learn local languages or participate in local customs, and live apart from the local citizenry in American-style compounds. All the while they support huge aid projects that waste millions of American tax dollars without improving the life of the common peasant. Because of their isolation from the world around them, they bungle their missions and cause America's influence in Asia to decline.

The "non-ugly" Americans are those who, although perhaps physically unattractive, like the engineer Homer Atkins, succeed in winning the friendship of Asians. They are able to embrace cultural differences and appreciate the common humanity that lies underneath. These ordinary Americans—an engineer, a housewife, a farmer, a priest—exemplify the people-to-people ideal: tolerant pluralists committed to self-education, they learn to speak local languages, eat local food, and live in local houses. Their curiosity about other cultures and their willingness to commit themselves to others make them effective agents of U.S. interests. Because they are willing to integrate themselves into local cultures, they are able to nudge the new nations of Asia into closer integration with the U.S. The "ugly" Americans are losing the Cold War in Asia because they think in terms of "we" and "they"; the "non-ugly" Americans, in contrast, can identify with Asian people and develop an expanded understanding of "we." Out of that "we" emerge the novel's successful development projects—a food-canning system, a bicycle-based water pump, a small newspaper—all of which meet local needs. Lederer and Burdick make the Cold War in Asia hinge on what they call "the sum of tiny things"—a love of Cambodian food, an interest in astrology, a knowledge of chickens. The novel endorses those Americans who are willing to learn about another culture's "tiny things"—who can understand how Vietnamese, Burmese, and Cambodian people think and who can adopt their point of view. A strategically deployed empathy, it suggests, is the quality that Americans most need to succeed in Asia.[50]

Lederer and Burdick try to solve imaginatively the "Problem of American Personnel in Asia" that so worried the National Security Council in 1951. Their "non-ugly" Americans stand as models of the kinds of people that Washington should send into Asia to pursue American interests and avoid the charge of imperialism. Lederer and Burdick go beyond simply offering their characters as models to be emulated, however. Like *Reader's Digest* and the *Saturday Review*, they want to prod their readers into a sense of participation in foreign affairs. To that end, the authors embed the ideal of political participation into the formal structure of the novel. They organize the novel as a kind of dossier, full of résumés, State Department cables, letters from foreign service recruits, and transcripts of interviews. In working their way through this primary "evidence," readers participate vicariously in the process of self-education that makes the "non-ugly" Americans so successful. They ostensibly learn how to distinguish a viable development project from a boondoggle and discover creative ways to integrate into Asian village life, should they ever be called upon to do so. The novel presents itself as a training manual for how to be a politically committed, global-minded, culturally tolerant American who can feel at home in Asia.

While *The Ugly American* provided the world with a phrase that captured the sense of the nation's failures in Asia, it also indirectly highlighted the work of Dr. Tom Dooley. Burdick and Lederer had used Dooley as a model for one of their characters, and in a 1959 *Life* magazine article they singled him out as one of the real-life "non-ugly Americans" who were trying to win Southeast Asia over to the side of the United States. Dooley, a young and handsome Catholic physician from St. Louis, had been working as a doctor in Southeast Asia since 1954. In 1956 he published *Deliver Us from Evil*, a nonfiction account of his experiences during the U.S.-Navy-led exodus of nine hundred thousand Catholic refugees from newly created communist North Vietnam to U.S.-backed South Vietnam. He wrote two other books—*The Edge of To-*

morrow (1958) and *The Night They Burned the Mountain* (1969)—
that chronicled his experiences setting up small hospitals in the villages
and jungles of Laos. In all three books Dooley presented himself as a
peaceful crusader against communism and an emissary of American values working on the front lines of the Cold War. Known to his Laotian
patients as "Dr. America," Dooley gave concrete form to the nation's
identity as a non-imperial power. He became a widely celebrated model
of the ideal American in Asia.[51]

As James Fisher has shown in his recent biography, Dooley was one
of the first people to introduce Americans, in a direct and lively manner,
to the nations of Southeast Asia in the years when the U.S. was stepping
up its political and military interventions there. In the process he became
a celebrity and something of a folk hero. Dooley's books sold extremely
well: *The Night They Burned the Mountain* spent twenty-one weeks on
the *New York Times* bestseller list in 1960, and reappeared there when
a combined version of all three of his books was published in 1961. The
United States Information Agency (USIA), as part of its cultural diplomacy efforts, arranged for *Deliver Us from Evil* and *The Edge of Tomorrow* to be distributed worldwide. Dooley lectured to enthusiastic
audiences around the country, appeared on the television show "This Is
Your Life" in 1959, and taped a radio show in Laos that was broadcast
weekly in St. Louis and heard in over twenty Midwestern states. A film
version of *Deliver Us from Evil,* starring Kirk Douglas as Dooley, was
even planned, although it never came to fruition. A charismatic speaker
and tireless self-promoter, the celebrated "jungle doctor" generated a
flood of media coverage and by 1960, according to a Gallup Poll, had
become one of the top ten most admired Americans.[52]

Dooley's public identity as a devout Catholic bringing elements of
Western civilization to non-Western, non-Christian people clearly drew
on the missionary tradition of internationalism. He presented himself
as a deeply spiritual figure who gave inordinately of himself, sacrificed
for others, and sought only nonmaterial rewards. At the same time, he
worked important modifications upon the missionary tradition. By the
1950s, the figure of the conversion-seeking missionary had lost much of
its cultural legitimacy and was increasingly seen as an outmoded figure of
cultural intolerance, if not outright racism. Dooley vehemently rejected
the missionary label for himself and in fact condemned missionaries for
their role as the advance agents of Western imperialism. His narratives
turn away from religious conversions and present a gradual process of
modernization and development instead.[53]

Dooley's broad appeal derived in part from the way he synthesized this residual missionary internationalism with left-liberal internationalism. Dooley was funded in Laos and promoted at home by the International Rescue Committee (IRC), an organization which Fisher has shown had its roots in the socialist antifascist politics of the 1930s and provided a base for the noncommunist left in the late 1940s and 1950s. The IRC promoted Dooley, as Fisher argues, as an emblem of a culturally tolerant and pluralistic form of anticommunist internationalism— an alternative to the rabidly intolerant anticommunism of such Catholics as Senator Joseph McCarthy and Cardinal Spellman. It did so as an attempt to resuscitate political tolerance at home in the wake of the ravages of McCarthyism. Dooley's synthesis of left and right also appealed to cultural Cold Warriors in the CIA, which coordinated and indirectly funded his activities in Southeast Asia. CIA agent Edward Lansdale discovered Dooley and created him as a public figure in 1954. Lansdale was coordinating the exodus of North Vietnamese Catholic refugees when he encountered the young Navy officer and became impressed by his charisma and public articulateness. From that point on, Fisher suggests, Dooley became a public relations agent—albeit an unwitting one—for the CIA. His first book, *Deliver Us from Evil,* was a carefully orchestrated piece of propaganda designed to sell the fledgling government of Ngo Dinh Diem to Americans skeptical of his democratic intentions, and his later books helped keep attention focused on the communist threat to Laos and Southeast Asia more generally.[54]

Like many people-to-people narratives, Dooley's two books set in Laos are sentimental narratives. Where *The Ugly American*'s sentimentalism resides in its emphasis on the possibility of finding a cultural common ground that unites Americans and Southeast Asians, Dooley's sentimentalism revolves around his emphasis on the shared experience of suffering. In the foreword to *The Edge of Tomorrow,* Dooley explains that his book "is not a document of figures and facts, nor is it to be taken as a historical narrative. It is not a generalization, nor is it fiction." Instead of presenting a detached overview of a politically volatile nation, he offers instead an intimate account of individuals forging bonds with each other: "It is a true story of six Americans who formed a fellowship with the people of Laos, and indeed with many other people throughout the world." Dooley uses the body in pain as his medium for forging this international connection. The narrative traces Dooley's membership in what he calls, after Albert Schweitzer, the "Fellowship of Pain," and it extends that fellowship out to millions of readers by inviting them to share in the pain of others. Dooley's narratives revolve around moments in which he encounters Laotian bodies in pain—bodies that have been burned, infected, mauled by animals, and misshapen by disease—and he describes these bodies in great detail. These descriptions come alive in numerous photographs, which show the reader what scabies, malnutrition, hare lips, and withered limbs look like. Dooley does not treat these bodies with clinical detachment; rather, he personalizes each of his patients by telling their unique story, situating them within a family and a community, and bringing them to life as individuals. In doing so, Dooley uses the figure of the body in pain to stimulate and mobilize an outward-looking attitude in his readers and facilitate a sense of personal connection to the people of Laos.[55]

Dooley's compassion for his patients becomes a model for the reader, and the intensity of his feelings becomes a conduit through which the reader's feelings can likewise flow. The episodic structure of the narrative revolves around moments in which Dooley and his American assistants bridge the divide between themselves and the Laotians with "kindness," "love," and "gentleness." Insisting that Americans would gain more allies in the world if they "emphasized the connections that exist between people" rather than the differences, Dooley declares his intention to teach Americans that they could "span the gap between nations with a bridge whose fibers are woven of compassion." The numerous before-and-after photographs of his patients display the physical rewards of Dooley's "love." What Dooley offers his reader is intimacy with Asians: social intimacy with them as a people and a culture, physical intimacy with their bodies through medical practice, and emotional intimacy with their feelings of suffering and joy.[56]

Dooley's description of his work as teaching Americans how to bridge the gap between themselves and the people of Asia captures one of the essential features of the people-to-people narrative and of middlebrow representation of Asia more generally. Dooley's stories involve a double narrative move. Initially, they construct a gap—a hierarchical difference—between Laotians and Americans. Many of Dooley's Laotians, like so many Asians in the history of Western representations, are dirty, sick, tradition-bound, and passive; the reader often encounters them as they lie on the ground. Dooley and his American assistants, in contrast, are healthy, active, and physically upright bearers of modern science who dress in neat clothes despite the jungle heat and rain. After constructing this gap, however, Dooley ostentatiously moves to bridge it: he reaches across the boundaries of difference he has himself constructed by extending his sympathy, compassion, and feeling. It is precisely this double move of constructing and crossing boundaries that gives these texts their emotional power. If the gap had not been constructed as so wide, its bridging would not be so thrilling. This double move performs the important cultural work of teaching Americans that such boundaries can be crossed and that it feels good to do so.

This double move also plays an important part in Dooley's construction of himself, and by extension America, as respectful of difference. Dooley repeatedly professes his regard for Laotian culture, and he displays his respect by cooperating with local healers and participating in traditional ceremonies. These exhibitions of cultural tolerance go hand in hand with his explicit repudiations of racism—"Differences of race and culture are not accurate measurements of superiority or inferiority" —and the disavowal of any desire to Americanize the Laotians. Dooley instead celebrates "diversity" and urges his readers to recognize the "distinct accomplishments of the Irish, the French, the Asian, the Negro." By extolling "difference" as something "obvious and pleasing" to him rather than as an excuse for domination, Dooley distinguishes himself, and by extension America, from the former colonial rulers of Laos, the French. This embrace of cultural difference serves an additional ideological function, as well: for Dooley, "uniformity is something to be abhorred" because it is the quality valued by communists who seek to impose social and ideological conformity through force.[57]

Dooley's expressions of cultural tolerance find physical manifestation in the homes that he constructs. Dooley represents his presence in Laos as a domestic project of homemaking. In both *The Edge of Tomorrow* and *The Night They Burned the Mountain* he devotes a good deal of energy to describing how he set up his various homes and hospitals, and he lavishes attention on the domestic details of furniture, decor, meals, plumbing, and daily routines. These representations of housekeeping are crucial to the ideological work of the narratives: they figure the American presence in Southeast Asia in domestic, and thus feminized, terms, rather than in political or military ones, and thus serve to deflect the charge of imperialism. Dooley's homes function as microcosms of the American presence in Southeast Asia—they give concrete form to the ideology of integration. Dooley takes care to present his homes as integrated into the local community; they are not the walled-in enclaves of Lederer and Burdick's "ugly Americans," whose very architecture proclaims a belief in impassable boundaries between Americans and Asians. Dooley expresses pride in the fact that his house in Vang Vieng is not only "functional" and "clean" but also "in keeping with the rest of the village": "No one could ever say that the men of Operation Laos lived apart from the natives in an air-conditioned 'American compound'" (Figure 6). The house resonates with two national landscapes and cultures: made out of bamboo and standing on stilts, the house proclaims its location in a Laotian village; at the same time, its wide front porch and flying American flag suggest a small-town American bungalow. The house in Nam Tha is a similarly hybrid space in which American and Laotian elements intermingle easily. Dooley and his American assistants live in the house with their four Laotian helpers, a telegraph operator and his family, and a pair of schoolteachers. No boundaries subdivide the house into American and Laotian spaces, either physical or social: "We did not close any part of the house off; doors were always open and Pavie, the teachers, and just about anyone who wished to could meander in and out of our living room." Dooley presents his multiracial, multinational homes not as imperial domains for the inculcation and policing of hierarchies, but rather as spaces in which differences could be acknowledged and then incorporated into an overarching whole. "Having a coolie, a cook, a houseboy, interpreters and other servants in Laos is a different thing than it is in America. We considered these people an integral part of our team, not employees. They dined with us, bathed with us, swam with us, worked with us, and came out on night-calls with us." Dooley proclaims the existence of a "team," defined by its commitment to helping others and by the physical intimacies of daily life, that overrides the superficial social differences of being a "coolie" or a "houseboy."[58]

Dooley's houses must be read in a national, as well as an international, context. He went out of his way to distinguish his Laotian homes from the types of domestic spaces—and relations—that were being defined within the U.S. as typical and normal. In the opening pages of *The Edge of Tomorrow*, Dooley explains his presence in Laos as a refusal to "settle down" into the upper-middle-class familial life that was expected of him, with " a home, a wife, kids, a nice medical practice, maybe a few fine hunting horses." Dooley presents this refusal as a choice of service to others over comfort for himself. What he does not mention is that he is an active homosexual and could never fit comfortably into that domestic situation. Dooley's Laotian homes must be seen in relation to what Barbara Ehrenreich has called the postwar "flight from commitment," in which middle-class American men sought to flee the narrowing-down of their social identities into the limited roles of husbands,

Figure 6. Tom Dooley's "non-ugly American" house in Vang Vieng, Laos:
"No one could ever say that the men of Operation Laos lived apart from the
natives in an air-conditioned 'American compound.'" (photo: Erica Anderson)

fathers, and breadwinners. Dooley's Laotian homes were, with a few exceptions, exclusively masculine spaces, occupied only by Dooley and his
American and Laotian assistants, some of whom had left wives and children behind in order to join him. As such they were as much refuges
from the compulsory heterosexuality of 1950s America as they were expressions of internationalist national identity.[59]

Dooley successfully escaped his heterosexual and middle-class commitments at home by embracing a political commitment to Southeast

Asia in their stead. Like many other Westerners who had traveled to the East over the years, Dooley found in Laos a freedom from the social rules that constrained him at home. Dooley's Asian homes existed on a continuum with those other homes on the American mainland—the playboy apartment, the Beat pad—from which women had been effectively banished, and as such they served to link the national and the international spheres of postwar American life. Dooley shows how the energy of a personal flight out of America could, with careful management, be turned into a form of national service.

Both *Reader's Digest* and the *Saturday Review* saw Dooley as embodying the middlebrow aesthetic and practice of commitment that they worked so hard to promote. *Reader's Digest,* in fact, played a crucial role in bringing Dooley into the public arena. Acting in his capacity as contributing editor and Asia liaison for the magazine, William Lederer —who was friends with Edward Lansdale, the CIA agent who discovered Dooley—shepherded *Deliver Us from Evil* into existence and brokered a relationship between Dooley and *Reader's Digest* that continued until Dooley's death. Lederer first met Dooley in Haiphong, North Vietnam in 1955 when, as a Navy public information officer, he too was involved in the relocation of North Vietnamese refugees. Lederer encouraged Dooley to write about his experiences and offered his own account of the U.S.-assisted exodus—a classic people-to-people narrative that *Reader's Digest* published in 1955 under the title "They'll Remember the Bayfield"—as a model. Lederer worked closely with Dooley as he wrote his account, reading and commenting upon chapters which Dooley sent him; after a draft of the book was complete, Lederer and Dooley spent two weeks holed up together in Hawaii polishing the manuscript. Lederer brought the manuscript to DeWitt Wallace, who assigned it to a senior editor for further polishing, excerpted it in *Reader's Digest,* arranged for its simultaneous publication by Farrar, Straus and Cudahy, and published a condensed book version. *Reader's Digest* went on to condense Dooley's subsequent two books, publish additional articles about him, and solicit funds for MEDICO, the voluntary organization that Dooley cofounded to bring American medical teams to the developing world.[60]

The *Saturday Review* was slower to pick up on the Dooley phenomenon, but it came to share *Reader's Digest*'s enthusiasm. In 1960 the magazine published an effusive review of *The Night They Burned the Mountain* that captured his status as a "living legend" whom "everyone knows" and whose admirers "must number in the millions." The reviewer praised his work and his decision to stay in Laos even after being diagnosed with cancer, and concluded by predicting his canonization, noting that Dooley "is the stuff from which saints are made." In 1961, after Dooley had died, Cousins wrote an adulatory editorial memorializing him and his work. Cousins saw Dooley not just as a noble individual but as a model for all Americans: giving Dooley his highest compliments, Cousins praised him as "one of the most useful teachers of his time." Dooley exemplified for Cousins precisely the universalist values that the *Saturday Review* upheld: "He tried to meet the highest need of his age or any age, which is for a sense of connection between man and man." Cousins saw him as a moral activist and a promoter of humanitarian participation: Dooley "had a big idea and knew how to bring it to life," and in doing so he "made it possible for many thousands of people to be rescued from the cynicism and dry-eyed attitude that regards service in the cause of man as mawkish ostentation." Cousins himself joined Dooley's efforts and served on the board of directors of MEDICO.[61]

Although Dooley figured prominently in the pages of *Reader's Digest* and the *Saturday Review,* he was far from a unique figure: both magazines published countless articles, reviews, and editorials about medical missionaries and jungle doctors. Missionary stories formed a prominent subset of people-to-people narratives in *Reader's Digest,* and among these the "medical missionary" was the most privileged. *Reader's Digest* published numerous stories about Christian missionaries who healed the sick in the Solomon Islands, New Guinea, and India and brought the miracles of Western medicine to isolated peoples. The *Saturday Review* also promoted medical narratives, although it tended to deemphasize the missionary angle in favor of the secular "jungle doctor" narratives, which it codified into a literary subgenre by reviewing and linking together fictional, nonfictional, and autobiographical accounts. Dr. Albert Schweitzer, the most famous of all postwar jungle doctors, appeared regularly in both magazines. *Reader's Digest* played a key role in introducing Schweitzer to Americans in the mid-1940s, and the *Saturday Review* published numerous articles written by Schweitzer, as well as reviews of the many books and movies about him produced during the 1950s. Cousins himself wrote a book about Schweitzer in 1960.[62]

The medical missionary and jungle doctor narratives proliferated in the pages of *Reader's Digest* and the *Saturday Review* in part because they satisfied a number of pressing cultural and ideological needs. While the jungle doctor did not originate in the postwar period—the World

War II account of "Burma surgeon" Dr. Gordon Seagrave, for instance, found a wide audience in 1943—the Cold War gave the jungle doctor a new life. As a cultural figure, the jungle doctor animated the discourses of both anticommunism and international integration. Medical discourse figured prominently throughout the late 1940s and 1950s as a vehicle for representing the conflict between the United States and the Soviets. George Kennan, in his 1946 "long telegram" from Moscow, described "world Communism" as "like [a] malignant parasite which feeds only on diseased tissue." In response, he urged, the United States had no choice but to adopt the role of world doctor: "We must study [communism] with [the] same courage, detachment, objectivity and [the] same determination not to be emotionally provoked or unseated by it, with which [a] doctor studies [an] unruly and unreasonable individual." This same discourse circulated throughout the popular media as well. *Reader's Digest* described postwar Germany as a "cancerous growth" festering with the "virus of Communism," and warned against the threat to China from the "totalitarian infection spreading from Russia." Disease also served as a metaphor for the underdevelopment that made communism an attractive alternative. In a 1947 *Saturday Review* editorial expressing skepticism about extending Truman's containment doctrine into India and China, where legitimate grievances bred an intense desire for change, Harrison Smith wrote that the "wound will become infected and will spread through the bodies of these nations and in the end the Russians or their satellites will march in just the same." Modern medicine and improved health, in turn, became a metaphor for the "freedom" America offered to Asia: a 1951 article in *Reader's Digest,* for instance, described the "complete medical revolution" that had taken place in Japan under the U.S. occupation, which had made Japan not only the "healthiest" nation in Asia but also one whose citizens fully realized that the "people of America are their friends." [63]

· · · · ·

Dooley concluded *The Edge of Tomorrow* by quoting a list of ten points that Americans should bear in mind when they think about Asia. Originally written by William D. Patterson for the *Saturday Review* and reprinted in the frontispiece of James Michener's 1951 book *The Voice of Asia,* this list informs us that most people in Asia are poor, hungry, and illiterate; they know nothing of democracy and civil liberties and have never seen a doctor. At the same time, they are determined to change their lives: distrustful of "people with white skins" and skeptical of Western claims to "free enterprise," they have vowed "never again to be ruled by foreigners." Dooley remarked that although he had first read these sentences years ago, he was discovering that they applied to his experiences in Laos with "astonishing accuracy." No longer mere words, they had taken on "a muscle and flesh, a hue and tone." Dooley expresses here one of the central aspirations of postwar middlebrow culture. *Reader's Digest* and the *Saturday Review,* along with the people-to-people narratives they published and promoted, aimed to give "muscle and flesh" to the abstractions of the Cold War. They tried to bring the issue of international integration to life and to construct a global version of American national identity by crafting emblematic characters who showed that Americans could live and work in Asia successfully.[64]

These narratives, and the larger middlebrow aesthetic of commitment to which they belong, demonstrate the continued vitality of the sentimental as a cultural mode in postwar America. The power of sympathy, as June Howard has defined it, lies in its "capacity for engendering solidarities." Middlebrow sentimentalism flourished during the Cold War because it allowed Americans to imagine themselves moving out into the world in non-imperial ways. It provided a language for telling stories about Americans who were making homes in Asia, developing friendships with Asian people, and integrating themselves into local Asian communities. It provided a vocabulary for articulating the idea of America-in-Asia—America as a familiar, legitimate, non-threatening, and beneficial presence in the decolonizing world. The literary characters crafted by Dooley, Lederer, Burdick, and the other authors of people-to-people narratives can be seen as inheritors, not of the parlor-bound sentimentalism of Susan Warner's 1850 bestseller *The Wide, Wide World,* but of the expansive sentimentalism of Herman Melville's *Moby Dick.* Like Ishmael befriending the pagan Pacific Islander Queequeg, Dooley and the assorted non-ugly Americans learn to embrace all kinds of cultural difference and, through that, to signal their apartness from an imperial project even as they participate in American expansion.[65]

CHAPTER 3

How to Be an
American Abroad

James Michener's The Voice of Asia
and Postwar Mass Tourism

Neither imperial Rome nor Britain in all their glory ever
dreamed of any such many-sided penetration of the world
as ours.

> William Harlan Hale, *Saturday Review,* 1959

On July 20, 1955, a riot erupted in the South Vietnamese capital of
Saigon when a protest marking the first anniversary of the Geneva Accord turned violent. The angry mob was not protesting the increased
number of Americans who arrived in their country after the end of the
French-Indochina war the previous year; as members of the Cao Dai religious sect, the rioters allied themselves with the South Vietnamese government and its U.S. supporters. Rather, they were protesting the Geneva Accord's creation of communist North Vietnam, and they sacked
two hotels housing members of the International Truce Commission as
a way of expressing what the *New York Times* described as "their dis-
taste for the international commission and communism." The rioters
rammed the door of the Hotel Gallieni with a jeep and set the lobby
ablaze; they tore out the elevators at the Hotel Majestic, broke down
doors with axes, and threw furniture out the windows. Fifty-seven
Americans were living in the Majestic at the time of the attack. Among
them were U.S. foreign aid officials—the kind of people that Lederer
and Burdick would critique three years later in *The Ugly American*—
and Angier Biddle Duke, head of the International Rescue Committee,
which in the following year would begin financing Dr. Tom Dooley's
activities in Laos and managing the creation of his public persona. Two

of the hotel's inhabitants fended off the "anti-red" rioters by identifying themselves as Americans and thus "friends." One of them was author James A. Michener.[1]

Michener managed to pen a letter to a friend in the midst of the chaos, in which he described his near escape from physical harm.

> I stayed here in the Majestic and listened to them coming down my hall. They completely annihilated the room next door and then started in on mine. I thought the lock would hold, but it didn't, so when the door crashed in I stood with my typewriter and said, "I'm an American writer. Behave or I'll write bad things about you." They stood there for a second and then we all laughed.

Michener protected himself not only by asserting his friendship with the Vietnamese rioters, but also by wielding his typewriter and his power to portray them to the American public. This episode offers a startlingly literal example of the influence Michener possessed during the 1950s as a representer of Asia to postwar America: his decision whether or not to "write bad things" about Asia carried great weight at home and abroad.[2]

Michener's anecdote about the riot in Saigon captures something of the double-edged quality that travel to Asia carried in the 1950s. Travel to this part of the world could be risky and dangerous, as the smashed-in door of Michener's hotel room suggests. The new nations of the decolonizing world were volatile places, in the midst of tremendous social and political upheavals, and unsuspecting tourists could easily get caught up in events beyond their control. Tourists also ran the risk of falling prey to the rising anti-American sentiment. At the same time, however, travel to Asia offered the possibility of dissolving barriers of ignorance and mistrust, and held out the promise that Asians and Americans might come to understand each other better. Michener, after all, survived the encounter unharmed, and the conflict dissolved into shared laughter and affirmations of friendship.

The postwar period saw a boom in travel writing. Newspapers hired full-time travel writers, magazines designed special sections and even whole issues around travel, and new magazines devoted exclusively to travel, such as *Holiday,* sprang up. The publishing industry put out a steady stream of travel accounts and guidebooks about Asia and the Pacific. Supreme Court Justice William O. Douglas wrote four accounts of his travels in Asia and the Middle East: *Strange Lands and Friendly People* (1951), *Beyond the High Himalayas* (1952), *North from Malaya* (1953), and *West of the Indus* (1959). In 1950 Lowell Thomas Jr. pub-

lished *Out of This World: Across the Himalayas to Forbidden Tibet,* an
account of the trip he and his father, CBS radio broadcaster Lowell
Thomas, took to Lhasa at the invitation of the Tibetan government,
which feared a Chinese invasion and wanted to call the world's attention
to its vulnerable situation. The Indian-born and Wellesley-educated Santha Rama Rau wrote about her Asian travels in *Home to India* (1945),
East of Home (1950), *This Is India* (1954), and *View to the Southeast*
(1957). In 1957 Philip Wylie, author of the 1942 bestseller *A Generation of Vipers,* published *The Innocent Ambassadors,* an account of his
around-the-world tour that focused almost exclusively on Asia. European travel writers, such as Henri Michaux, author of *A Barbarian in
Asia* (1949), and Thor Heyerdhal, author of *Kon Tiki* (1950) and *Aku
Aku* (1960), also found large American audiences. *Reader's Digest* carried articles by many of these writers, and the *Saturday Review* often reviewed their books. At the same time, travel emerged as a theme in other
popular media. Frank Sinatra released an album of travel-related songs
in 1958, *Come Fly with Me;* Broadway lampooned the explosion of tourism in Noel Coward's *Sail Away* (1961), which had as its hit song "Why
Do the Wrong People Travel?" and the 1956 film version of Jules Verne's
Around the World in Eighty Days offered widescreen vistas of scenic
sights in Taiwan, Burma, Thailand, and fifty other countries.

James Michener was among the most prolific and popular of these
postwar travel writers about Asia. Although he worked across a range
of literary genres—he wrote short stories, novels, war reportage, political analyses—he became identified as a travel writer, in the broadest
sense of the term: he traveled widely throughout Asia and the Pacific and
reported back on the people and events he had seen. Through scores of
articles and nearly a dozen fiction and nonfiction books, he helped create the postwar Asia-Pacific region as a knowable part of the world for
American readers. His articles appeared on the front pages of newspapers
and in the highest-circulation magazines, and by 1958 his books had
sold six million copies and been translated into twenty-four languages.
From the late 1940s through the 1950s, Michener served as one of the
most influential producers of Asia and the Pacific in the postwar American imagination.[3]

This explosion of travel writing about Asia, by Michener and others,
must be read in relation to the postwar emergence of mass global tourism. As a social practice, tourism entailed the temporary migration of
millions of Americans out to the far reaches of the world. As a cultural
practice, the representation of travel became a preferred way to imagine

and assign meanings to the diffusion of all kinds of Americans, not just leisure travelers, around the globe. Tourism functioned as a discourse through which Americans could enact and imagine the transition from what William Harlan Hale of the *Saturday Review* saw as their prewar "total isolation" to their postwar "total immersion" in world affairs. Like the jungle doctor, the tourist became a favorite figure of American internationalism.[4]

Many middlebrow writers of the 1950s eschewed the nostalgic search for the premodern and the authentic that has characterized so much Western travel writing about the non-West. Instead, they favored a head-on encounter with the modern. They used the travel genre to explore the issues that shaped America's postwar relations with the nations of Asia: the collapse of the European empires, the rise of Asian nationalism, the increasing presence of Americans in Asia, the consequences of white racism, the appeal of communism, the threat of Soviet or Chinese domination. Postwar travel writing, and Michener's in particular, regularly narrated the American encounter with Asia not through scenes of heroic discovery, but through moments of personal exchange in which traveler and host engage in some kind of verbal, intellectual, emotional, or financial give-and-take. In a move typical of narratives of anticonquest, these accounts revolved around what Mary Louise Pratt has called "dramas of reciprocity." For Pratt, this textual emphasis on exchange is bound up with the economic impulses of Western expansion. "Reciprocity," she suggests, "has always been capitalism's ideology of itself."[5]

Postwar travel and travel writing thus need to be read in relation to America's fear of "losing" Asia, especially of losing economic access to its markets and resources. The discourse and practice of travel served as a cultural space in which the anxiety over losing Asia could be—at different moments—expressed, managed, and imaginatively resolved. It provided a venue in which the threat of loss and the hostility toward the U.S. that lay behind it could be acknowledged; it also provided an arena in which balms for that hostility and strategies for preventing that loss could be proposed. Above all it functioned as a cultural space in which Americans could be trained to imagine and practice the kinds of exchanges that would strengthen the nation's global ties.

TOURISM AS SOCIAL PRACTICE AND POLITICAL DISCOURSE

Although mass international tourism emerged in the U.S. in the 1920s, it was not until the 1950s that it took off and became a prominent feature of the social and cultural landscape. Many factors contributed to its rapid postwar growth. On the economic front, the U.S. economy was booming, Americans had more money to devote to leisure activities, and countries around the world hungered for U.S. dollars to help rebuild economies shattered by the war. On the technological front, during World War II engineers had built airstrips around the world in locations that had previously been inaccessible, and the new postwar aerospace industry made air travel more commonplace. The introduction of commercial jet travel in 1958 made international travel cheaper, faster, and more comfortable than ever before. Suddenly the trip to Europe came within the range of the "average" American and members of the expanding middle class were able to afford vacations well beyond the borders of the nation. On the psychological front, Americans had a renewed desire to see the world: those who had fought overseas in World War II were often anxious to return to former battlefields in peacetime, while civilians confined by the Depression during the 1930s and war during the 1940s were eager to leave the country after nearly twenty years of restrictions. The militarization of America's relations with the rest of the world during World War II and the Cold War also promoted much overseas travel: one 1958 survey by the University of Michigan found that of the 20 percent of adults who had been overseas at some time in their lives, two thirds of them had traveled in the armed services.[6]

After World War II, the number of Americans who traveled abroad increased each year. In 1947, only 200,000 Americans had valid passports; in 1953 more than a million Americans traveled overseas, surpassing the number of Americans who crossed the Atlantic during the peak year of 1920s prosperity. By 1959, 7 million Americans were going abroad, 1.5 million of them to places other than Canada and Mexico. For these overseas travelers, Europe held the greatest attraction: it hosted 204,000 Americans in 1948, 400,00 in 1953, and more than 800,000 in 1961. Fewer Americans went to Asia: only 2 percent of all tourists in 1959 and about 500,000 total in 1961. In spite of these relatively small numbers, Asia figured prominently in postwar travel discourse as an exciting new destination, a formerly remote area that had suddenly become accessible. Horace Sutton, the *Saturday Review*'s travel editor, captured the euphoric sense of Asia's new availability to Americans after 1958:

> Flying the jets into New Delhi, the new traveler could buzz off to the Taj Mahal or to Jaipur, or explore South India before flying off again to explore Singapore, go south to Jakarta and thence to Bali. Bangkok was

a wild dream of gilded temples and mosaic figures of delicate people pad-
dling canoes along the murky klongs. And then there was Hong Kong, suddenly revealed as a capsule of China, immensely colorful, brim-full of bar-
gains, and critically short of hotels. Tokyo had shaken off the war and the
occupation and was a bustling city with new restaurants, a new outlook
and a dozen plans for new hotels. The jet age unleashed a tremendous
burst of energy, particularly in the Orient. It started a new vogue in travel
for round-the-world trips.

With his breathless tone, Sutton creates an impression of Asia as suddenly wide open to Americans and available for their visual and economic consumption. Such accounts of "round-the-world trips," many
of which focused on Asia, developed a special cachet in the 1950s. Not
only did they contribute to a new jet setting aesthetic, but they also
served, with their detailed itineraries and catalogues of miles traveled, as
a convenient way to represent the world—most often the "free" world
—as a coherent, integrated whole.[7]

As part of the "massification" of travel, the category of tourist broad-
ened in the postwar years to include all those who participated in the
global growth of American power. The U.S. government in 1955 defined
a tourist not simply as a "sightseeing traveler," but used "the term in its
broadest sense" to include "the bona fide non-immigrant who desires to
make a temporary visit to a foreign country for any legitimate purpose."
Diplomatic historian Foster Rhea Dulles—cousin to Secretary of State
John Foster Dulles and CIA head Allen Dulles—noted in 1964 how in
addition to the familiar "hordes of vacationing sightseers . . . trying to
see the entire continent in a few hurried weeks," the transatlantic traveler in the mid-twentieth century "ranged from a president flying abroad
for a Summit Conference to a party of five hundred TV dealers taking
a twelve-day tour sponsored by the General Electric Company; from a
young draftee reporting for military duty in Germany to a wealthy so-
cialite spending a weekend in Paris." The category of tourist now included all the agents of America's political, economic, and military expansion. Government employees delivering aid and advice to foreign
governments constituted a whole new subset of travelers, as did educators and students: between 1949 and 1957, 2,000 professors funded
by the GI Bill and the Fulbright Act went to Europe, as did 10,000 students funded by government and foundation grants, and 1,500 more on
junior year abroad programs. The number of American missionaries
abroad also grew in the postwar period, with more than 30,000 working in 117 countries in 1959. By the close of the decade, the 1.5 million

Americans temporarily living and working around the world included 800,000 GIs and their families, 50,000 civilian government workers, and 100,00 members of what the *Saturday Review* called a "voluntary Third Force" of missionaries, students, businessmen, and teachers. In the late 1940s and 1950s, "tourism" became a framework within which to think about what William Harlan Hale called America's "many-sided penetration of the world." [8]

Tourism and U.S. global expansion not only occurred simultaneously, but also shared a common material infrastructure. The commercial airline industry, so vital to the growth of overseas travel, played a key role in fostering international military integration. In the late 1920s and early 1930s, the U.S. government subsidized the expansion of Pan American Airways into Latin America by giving it an exclusive contract to carry U.S. airmail, which enabled the company to establish a virtual monopoly on air travel in the region. During World War II, Pan Am contracted with Washington to build and improve airports around the world in order to facilitate the waging of the war. In the postwar period, private airline companies proved crucial to the development of overseas military bases and the securing of foreign air-transit rights, and U.S. officials encouraged airlines to locate their operations in areas they considered vital to ensuring U.S. security. Developing the means to move Americans around the world easily was both a commercial endeavor and a military necessity. [9]

Tourism and global expansion also developed close discursive links, as middlebrow intellectuals and political elites converged in their depiction of travel as a form of geopolitical engagement. Tourism opened up a space for the participation, both real and imagined, of millions of ordinary Americans in the drama of U.S. expansion. Horace Sutton, like many other travel writers, promoted tourism as a way to put the middlebrow aesthetic of political commitment into practice. At a time when the U.S. had assumed "a position of immense global responsibility," he wrote in 1960, all travelers needed to "accept a personal part of the responsibility that leadership entails." Americans could no longer afford to think about travel "as the purest of larks." Rather, American tourists were "millions of ambassadors" who needed to treat their international movements as a consciously chosen political activity. Echoing the Eisenhower administration's language, Sutton promoted travel as part of the "overseasmanship" that postwar Americans needed to learn. The Eisenhower administration modeled this ideal of the politically engaged traveler by taking personal diplomacy to a new level. While previous high administration officials had traveled abroad on diplomatic missions, none traveled as often or as extensively as did members of the Eisenhower White House. *Travel* magazine recognized Secretary of State Dulles and Vice President Nixon as exemplars of the new tourism and bestowed its annual Mr. Travel award on Dulles in 1955 and Nixon in 1958. Eisenhower himself visited eleven nations in Europe, North Africa, South Asia, and the Middle East in 1959, and toured Latin America, Paris, and East Asia in 1960. The president treated these trips less as opportunities for substantive diplomacy and more as symbolic gestures of international interdependence; he saw them as a means to "reaffirm and strengthen the common purposes of the non-Communist world." [10]

The ordinary American tourist also came to be seen as an active figure in the economic integration of the capitalist world. Political elites and observers saw the exchange of bodies across national borders as a form of economic exchange, an integral component of the expanded trade in goods and raw materials that they sought to encourage between the U.S. and its allies. In the *Saturday Review*'s discussions of foreign economic policy, the American traveler loomed large as a "major economic fact" capable of pumping billions of U.S. dollars into foreign economies eager for exchangeable currency. The Truman administration recognized the value of this flow of dollars, and the Economic Cooperation Administration—the bureaucratic arm of the Marshall Plan—actively encouraged travel to Europe as a means of further infusing U.S. dollars into war-shattered economies. In a 1949 *Reader's Digest* article Juan Trippe, president of Pan American Airways, articulated the economics of global tourism and explained how tourist dollars ultimately found their way back into the U.S. economy:

> We Americans have a tremendous stake in foreign travel. Millions of people abroad are ordering our machine tools, trucks, food, medicine and thousands of other articles—30 billion dollars worth since 1945. But unless foreigners somehow obtain dollars, they cannot pay their bills to Americans. The pleasantest means of getting dollars abroad is for American visitors to take them over. The dollars they leave behind will ultimately be spent in the United States.

In 1954, the State Department estimated that tourists provided enough dollars to pay for 10 percent of all purchases that foreign countries made from the United States. By 1959 Americans spent $2.3 billion abroad. Tourists were seen as objects of trade in and of themselves, economic units that could be measured annually. But they were also seen as facilitating much larger flows of trade. Eisenhower thought that by forging "friendships" that cultivated the "knowledge and mutual understanding" on which international trade depended, the tourist would smooth the channels through which the world's chromite, tin, cobalt, hemp, and manganese flowed into the United States.[11]

Eisenhower vigorously promoted tourism as part of his foreign economic policy. He endorsed the findings of his Commission on Foreign Economic Policy, which recommended that the government "encourage the promotion of tourism," and in his messages to Congress in 1954, 1955, and 1960, as well as in the 1954 Mutual Security Act, he emphasized that he saw increased travel as a vital component of U.S. foreign policy. The Eisenhower administration also promoted tourism in international venues, such as the Rio economic conference of 1954 and the U.N. Economic and Social Council in 1955. In 1955 Commerce Secretary Sinclair Weeks designated Eisenhower as one of the world's most "enthusiastic boosters for international travel." [12]

A number of observers saw tourism as a way to resolve one of the key foreign policy difficulties of the Eisenhower administration: the opposition to foreign aid. Tourism was often invoked in an effort to resolve the conflict in foreign economic policy between advocates of private investment and trade on the one hand and advocates of government-funded foreign aid programs on the other. Like foreign aid programs, tourism produced a direct transfer of U.S. dollars to foreign nations desperate for hard currency. Yet, like private investment and trade, tourism entailed exchange rather than a handout: it allowed private American citizens to get something valuable in return for their dollars. For the Eisenhower administration, tourism proved an easier political sell than foreign aid: it was much easier to persuade Americans to travel overseas than it was to persuade Congress to approve foreign aid bills. The *Saturday Review* supported those in Washington who advocated "increasing the outward flow of American tourists" as a solution—"not only effective but relatively painless politically"—to the problem of "implementing our foreign economic policy." "Another million Americans traveling abroad by land, sea, and air," the editorial pronounced, "would markedly reinforce the world's precarious dollar balances." And tourism would satisfy the American need to feel it was getting an even exchange: "Instead of paying taxes to underwrite international trade deficits, the Americans would be watching the changing of the guard in front of Buckingham Palace, strolling down the Champs Elysées, gazing at St. Peter's, watching the sun rise over Fujiyama." In 1959, the *Saturday Review* applauded the more than $2 billion that American tourists spent overseas

in the previous year as "a massive private Foreign Aid program in addition to the official one." [13]

These political and economic meanings came together in a vision of
the tourist as an emblem of America's benign, non-imperial internationalism. The *Saturday Review* contrasted touristic internationalism with
what it presented as the imperialist aggressions of Europe and the Soviet
Union. In early 1957, only a few months after the Suez Crisis (in which
British, French, and Israeli troops attacked Nasser's Egypt and seized
the newly nationalized Suez Canal) and the Soviet invasion of Hungary
(which initiated a flood of refugees into neighboring Austria), the magazine praised tourism as a peaceful way to "cross a frontier." Unlike the
"invader, bringing death and terror," and the "refugee, fleeing death
and terror," the tourist aspired only to the "peaceful sharing of the
world's wide treasure of history, culture, and beauty." The *Saturday Review*, in keeping with the global imaginary of integration and its structure of feeling, hailed travel for its unique ability to "move peoples back
and forth across all boundaries" in ways that eroded "old prejudices"
and yielded "new tolerances." [14]

TRAVEL AS POLITICAL EDUCATION

U.S. officials and middlebrow intellectuals joined one another in promoting tourism as an instrument of popular education. They saw tourism as a means for producing subjectivities appropriate to citizens of a
global power. Unlike *The Ugly American* and Dooley's narratives, which
offered models of how to be a good American in Asia, travel was a concrete social practice: it was something that millions of Americans actually
did with their bodies, their time, and their money. Travel was a widespread activity, rather than just a story, that could be politicized. Like
the People-to-People program, the official discourses and regulation of
travel were attempts to orchestrate the flow of millions of Americans out
into the world. Washington wanted to guide the exchanges that Americans entered into abroad and shape the meanings that they generated.
Policymakers and middlebrow intellectuals aspired to produce a tourist
who possessed a global consciousness, yet was free from attitudes and
patterns of behavior that would be read by others abroad as imperialist.
They aimed to produce a specifically sentimental tourist who would forge
bonds with people around the world by engaging in meaningful exchanges, while at the same time avoiding displays of wealth, power, or
racism that could render America's power visible in unattractive ways.

Fearing the rise of anti-American sentiment, Washington and middle-brow intellectuals alike tried to guide Americans' encounters with people abroad, so that these encounters would not become opportunities for local populations to express their resistance to the political, military, and economic policies of U.S.-led integration.

In 1954 the State Department began putting into every passport it issued a pamphlet that advised travelers on how to behave as political actors. Seeking to impress travelers with the seriousness of their position and an awareness of their nation's new global stature, the State Department "fervently . . . hoped" that they would act "in a manner befitting their station." The pamphlet ascribed to tourists a power that they could use either for or against the nation's interests, and it warned that those who interacted inappropriately with people abroad—who "assume[d] an air of arrogance" or violated "the common bonds of decency"—could "do more in the course of an hour to break down elements of friendly approach between peoples than the Government [could] do in the course of a year in trying to stimulate friendly relations." The State Department strengthened this message in 1957 by including a letter from Eisenhower himself in each passport. In it, the president informed Americans who traveled, especially to those parts of the world where America was "less well understood," that they "represent[ed]" the nation and that their behavior and attitudes would "help to mold the reputation of our country." The Eisenhower administration, deeming the tourist to be of significant potential value to the achievement of its objectives abroad, set out to teach its citizens how to become politically useful travelers.[15]

The State Department actively sought to enlist travel writers in this project of public education and subject formation. In 1954 the *Department of State Bulletin* published an article entitled "Americans Abroad," written by Francis J. Colligan of the International Educational Exchange Service, one of the State Department's cultural diplomacy offices. Colligan praised those travel writers and cultural institutions, such as the Book-of-the-Month Club and *Reader's Digest,* that were already stimulating the desire to travel, and he offered suggestions for directing that desire into politically useful channels. The primary goal of travel writers, he suggested, should be to increase the presence of Americans around the world: they should promote "trips to areas of the world which few Americans visit" and encourage tourists "to travel for longer periods of time." Since most Americans traveled within North America and to Europe, this effectively meant encouraging tourism to the less developed parts of the world, such as Asia, Africa, and Latin America. Travel writers should also train Americans to understand their "responsibilities" in this "age of crisis." They should take a pedagogical, rather than a merely entertaining, approach and help travelers gain "a knowledge of a country, its language, and its peoples," which would include developing "some idea of its relations with the United States." At a more personal level, travel writers should promote an attitude of tolerance among travelers, specifically "a desire to share common interests" with the people they encountered and an ability "to understand significant differences." [16]

The *Saturday Review* and *Reader's Digest* needed no prompting from the State Department on this subject, having committed themselves to educational and political travel writing at the dawn of the Cold War. Both magazines launched regular travel series—Horace Sutton's "Booked for Travel" column in the *Saturday Review* and *Reader's Digest*'s Armchair Travelogue series—in 1947, the year of the Truman Doctrine and George Kennan's articulation of the containment policy, and they expanded their travel coverage over the course of the following decade. The travel articles they published tended to satisfy the criteria that the State Department laid out in 1954. Many of them gave readers a mini-education in Cold War geopolitics. *Reader's Digest* specialized in articles that combined the familiar generic elements of the travel essay—brief histories, sights to see, picturesque natural scenes—with political analysis, most often an evaluation of the degree of communist threat. The *Saturday Review* tended toward more comprehensive overviews: its 1961 World Travel issue included a lengthy "Political Guide for Tourists" that gave capsule evaluations, written by experts in the field, of the political relations between the U.S. and dozens of countries around the world. The articles about Asia usually created a global political map that located individual nations within a network of ties to the U.S. and a web of dangers from the Soviet Union and China. Both magazines used travel writing as a device to educate all their readers, travelers and nontravelers alike, about the nation's relationships with other countries. In their view all Americans, as citizens of a global power, needed to become at least armchair if not actual travelers.

Reader's Digest, in keeping with its preference for "how-to" articles, published didactic articles that gave tourists specific lessons in how to carry the burden of economic and political meaning that had been loaded onto them. Often these articles exhorted readers to develop feelings of sympathy and cultural tolerance. One 1949 article, entitled "How to Be an American Abroad," urged Americans to embrace the differences they encountered: "Instead of looking down your nose at those who are different, enjoy them and their ways." Leland Stowe, in a 1952 article that the State Department's Francis Colligan singled out for praise, urged his readers to develop a universalistic perspective. Stowe, like Cousins, rejected American parochialism as a form of "miseducation," and he praised travel for revealing the bonds that linked American and foreign cultures. Intelligent travel, he suggested, teaches us that "we owe a huge debt to foreign cultures and peoples" and that "we Americans are directly related to almost every people on earth." The greatest benefit of travel comes when "you gradually realize that, underneath, we are all quite alike" and "you discover, with an elation born of sharing, that there are no geographical boundaries to the human heart." For Stowe this knowledge of global connection enables a quasi-imperial sense of ownership: to be a "citizen of the world," for Stowe, means that "the world and its people belong to you, just as you belong to the world." Stowe, like other *Reader's Digest* and *Saturday Review* travel writers, sought to inculcate in his readers a cosmopolitan sensibility that would allow them to move confidently through the world without generating what *Newsweek* in 1957 would call "frictions." [17]

International travel often did cause friction, however, along what the *Saturday Review* called the "potentially combustible lines of race." The crossing of national boundaries between the U.S. and Asia often exposed to the world at large the legal boundaries that divided blacks and whites within the U.S. In one well-publicized episode, the dining room staff at the Houston airport separated out the Indian ambassador from other guests, an embarrassing incident that called forth apologies from Secretary of State Dulles. Vice President Nixon, in a 1954 televised speech reporting on a recent trip through Asia, described a similar incident in which an Asian legislator derived "an unfavorable impression of America because he visited a city in which he got on a bus and the bus driver made him move to the back of the bus because his skin was not white." Nixon categorized such acts of legalized racism, which were "blown up by the Communists abroad," as a threat to national security on a par with atomic espionage, and he invited his viewers to help prevent Asia from "falling into Communist hands" by "practicing and thinking tolerance and respect for human rights every day of the year." [18]

Racial tolerance became an integral component of the global subjectivity that travel writers sought to cultivate in Americans. The millions of tourists fanning out from the United States, each one carrying their racial views with them, became points of potential vulnerability for the nation, and travel writers tried to ease the frictions that such tourists risked generating. To a surprising degree, the educational travel essays in *Reader's Digest* and the *Saturday Review* foregrounded the global implications of American race relations. They presented racism as a glaring departure from the desired state of sympathy and as a mark of illegitimate forms of internationalism, such as imperialism and fascism, that they associated with Europe. Magazine writers like Leland Stowe urged travelers to "treat people as your equals" and avoid adopting the "attitude of superiority" displayed by "colonizers" like the British and the Nazis, who behaved as if they belonged to a "master race." In doing so, Stowe and others encouraged a certain disaffiliation with Europe in order to encourage a sense of affiliation with Asia. In the political education that travel writers supplied, the ability to respond to angry questions about America's race relations figured as among the most important things the tourist had to learn. For Norman Cousins, American race relations constituted the "number one question" tourists would face in Asia: "Why do Americans practice race prejudice and discrimination?" *Reader's Digest* prepared its readers for interrogations about the burgeoning civil rights movement: "If you are a democracy, why can't Negroes go to school, ride the buses and eat at lunch counters with whites?" Questions about international expressions of racial prejudice were also to be expected: "Isn't it true that the United States dropped the atomic bomb on Japan because it was a colored race and that the bomb would never have been dropped on a white people?" Promoters of tourism believed that if Americans could refute these accusations persuasively, rather than simply denying them, they could provide invaluable protection from the more damaging charge of imperialism, with which American racism was so intimately linked. To that end, travel writers often encouraged tourists to admit that racial inequality still existed within the United States, but to emphasize that great progress had been made toward remedying it and was continuing. The tourist thus became an integral part of the state apparatus for managing the overseas perception of domestic American race relations: encouraging Americans to be racially tolerant while abroad was far easier, and more politically palatable, than enacting substantive civil rights legislation at home.[19]

Middlebrow intellectuals also lauded tourism for its power to incorporate average Americans into the vast educational machinery that was producing knowledge about the contested portions of the world. As part of their effort to shape tourists into cosmopolitan subjects, middlebrow brokers sought to turn them into educators of others. In a 1956 editorial entitled "Everyman as Reporter," Cousins articulated his vision of the ideal tourist as one who traveled to the politically contested nations in the decolonizing and communist world. He or she visited the front lines of the Cold War, places that most tourists avoided like "the Soviet Union, Egypt, Turkey, Israel, India, Pakistan, Afghanistan, and Indonesia." (It is worth noting that within nine days of this editorial Israel attacked Egypt in the Suez Crisis; one month later, the Soviet Union rolled tanks into Eastern Europe; and relations between India and Pakistan were so tense throughout the 1950s that their border was considered one of the flash-points of the Cold War.) Cousins praised tourists who did not spend all their energy visiting sights and shopping, but managed to "meet people and spend some time with them"—who engaged in substantive exchange with people abroad. Above all, he singled out tourists who acted as "reporters" and not just "eyewitnesses": those who came back "with something to say and to show—either films or slides or snapshots." He wanted tourists to document the insights they gained from their encounters. He held up his neighbors as examples to be emulated: after visiting "the trouble zones," they reported the average Soviet to be "intensely human and likable," they gave an "intimate" picture of the problems of Egypt "from the point of view of the Near Eastern peoples," and they explained the "greater respect" they had gained for the problems in the newly independent nations of the Indian subcontinent. Cousins's neighbors produced a sentimental knowledge about the world: travel transformed their "feeling" for others, it led them to discover that others were more similar than different from themselves, and it enabled them to see things from a foreign point of view.[20]

This push to turn tourists into producers of knowledge must be understood within the context of America's relative lack of information about the decolonizing world. Because the U.S. never acquired as extensive a formal empire in Asia as the British or the French, and because those European empires restricted American access to large portions of the globe, the U.S. in the early years of the Cold War did not possess a large, professional, institutionalized machinery for producing knowledge about Asia. On top of this, domestic containment policies silenced many of the scholars, diplomats, and journalists who did possess sophisticated knowledge about Asia, especially China. In order to fill this gap, political elites and middlebrow intellectuals put pressure on travelers themselves, as well as on professional travel writers, to produce useful knowledge about Asia. The representation of travel thus served as a sort of emergency, stop-gap measure, a means to get at least some basic

information about this crucial part of the world into circulation among
ordinary Americans. The knowledge about Asia had to be of a certain
kind, however—it had to be untainted by 1930s radicalism, or by sympathy with Chinese communists, or by too rigorous support for Asian
nationalists.

In 1954 the *Saturday Review* further encouraged tourists to act as
producers of knowledge about the contested parts of the globe when it
began sponsoring an annual World Travel Photographic Awards contest. One unspoken goal of the competition seems to have been to encourage the representation of and travel to the developing world, especially Asia: although a minority of travelers went to Asia in the 1950s,
many of the prize-winning photographs were taken there. The full-page
advertisement for the contest declared "East is East and West is West
and the twain shall meet in a camera." It situated the tourist photograph
within the cultural machinery that was producing the global imaginary
of integration: the tourist's camera, it implied, was where the joining of
America and Asia would actually take place. The advertisement affirmed
the idea of American exceptionalism by implicitly contrasting America
with Europe and identifying it with Asia instead. By reworking Kipling's
dictum, the *Saturday Review* politely repudiated its imperialist ideology
of the absolute difference between East and West. In doing so, it implied
that Americans did not share the political and racial ideologies that had
underwritten European imperialism. Where European culture, exemplified here by Kipling, worked to police and reinforce the boundaries of difference, the *Saturday Review* suggests that the quintessentially middlebrow art of amateur photography could break down those barriers. The
ordinary tourist, the contest implied, could serve as the agent of this
historic "meeting"—or integration—of East and West. This revision of
Kipling's famous lines, which expressed the core principle of the culture
of integration, became a familiar motif running through middlebrow
representations of "free" Asia. It surfaced in discussions of Broadway
musicals, Hawaii's claim to statehood, and academic institutions.

The actual photographs that *Saturday Review* readers produced, however, show the limits of middlebrow culture's ability to shape the popular
perception and representation of Asia. The prize-winning photographs
taken in India, Thailand, Hong Kong, and Ceylon that the magazine
published in its pages do not show the "twain" of East and West meeting,
so much as they reproduce the Othering tropes of traditional Orientalist discourse. To be sure, the photographs studiously avoid the negative
terms of containment, and never represent Asia as deviant, threatening,

Figure 7. "Two Korean Elders," third-prize winner of the *Saturday Review*'s World Travel Photographic Awards. (photo: Donald D. Julin, *Saturday Review*, January 2, 1954)

or ugly. Yet, though they convey a sympathetic approach to their subject matter—a quality that the judges looked for in choosing winners—they nonetheless construct Asia in terms of difference: it is, variously, old, traditional, feminine, poor, crippled, and exotic. None of the photographs shows Asians and Americans together, nor do they capture evidence of East-West exchange. The photograph that took the third prize in 1954, for example, depicts "Two Korean Elders" (Figure 7). Taken by one Captain Donald D. Julin of Washington, D.C. only a year after the end of the Korean War, it stands as evidence of the blurred boundary between tourism and military expansion. Despite the photographer's military status, his picture betrays no evidence of the destruction of the country, the massive influx of American military personnel, or the extensive interactions between Americans and Koreans that took place as a result of the war. Rather, it presents Korea as premodern, authentic, and untainted by the West—the way a tourist who had traveled half-way around the world in search of something he or she could not find at home might most desire to see it.

JAMES MICHENER: THE MAN WHO "MAKES ASIA REAL TO US"

James Michener was in many respects the ideal 1950s tourist. Widely acclaimed as a citizen of the world, he spent the decade traveling through Asia and the Pacific, interacting with the people he met there, and writing about his encounters. Michener embraced the middlebrow role of the travel writer as educator: he used his writing to direct Americans' attention toward Asia and to introduce them to the foreign policy issues of the Cold War. In the process, he became America's foremost popular expert on Asia. *Newsweek* praised Michener for introducing "the world of the trans-Pacific into almost every American home" and singled him out as the man who "makes Asia real to us" (Figure 8).[21]

Michener was well qualified to take on the role of public educator. Born and raised in poverty in Doylestown, Pennsylvania, Michener received a scholarship to Swarthmore College, where he found a mentor in the literary scholar Robert Spiller, who would go on to have a long and distinguished career as an institutionalizer of American Studies as an academic discipline. After graduating in 1929 and teaching at a private high school for several years, Michener in 1936 enrolled at the Colorado State College of Education, where he earned a Master's degree in education and became an associate professor and a teacher of social

Figure 8. James Michener (left), the model 1950s tourist: "He makes Asia real to us." (*Newsweek*, January 25, 1954)

studies in its laboratory school. Michener seems to have absorbed some of Spiller's ideas, perhaps only latent in the 1920s, about an American Studies approach to the study of culture, and he put them into practice in Colorado. He developed an innovative interdisciplinary method and regularly incorporated music and literature into his social studies lessons. As a professor of education, he published widely on pedagogical issues, editing *The Future of Social Studies: Proposals for an Experimental Social Studies Curriculum* (1939), co-authoring *The Unit in Social Studies* (1940), and writing fifteen articles for academic journals, many of which, like "Bach and Sugar Beets," advocated an interdisciplinary approach. His first successful piece of fiction, "Who Is Virgil T. Fry?" was published in an academic journal and reprinted a half-dozen times; it told the story of a popular high school teacher who challenges his students to think for themselves and is dismissed by the school board for his unconventional pedagogy. On the strength of this publication record, Harvard's Graduate School of Education offered Michener a year-long visiting lectureship in 1939 and he began there, but never completed, a Ph.D. Two years later he left Colorado when the Macmillan publishing house in New York offered him a job editing textbooks.[22]

World War II derailed Michener from this quietly academic track and propelled him into the Pacific, introducing him to a world that he would imaginatively inhabit for the next fifteen years. He enlisted in the Navy in 1943 and served as a lieutenant in the Pacific theater, where he became a self-described "superclerk" inspecting installations, delivering messages, and replenishing supplies on forty-nine islands. Reenlisting for a second tour of duty that continued after war's end, he became an official naval historian of Pacific battles and served as a naval secretary to several Congressional committees. Whereas Tom Dooley's internationalism arose primarily out of the missionary tradition, Michener's grew directly out of World War II: military service provided Michener with the means to see vast areas of the Pacific firsthand (he traveled more than 150,000 miles with the Navy), gave him the time he needed to write his first book (he drafted *Tales of the South Pacific* while stationed on French New Caledonia), and aligned him politically and intellectually with the official forces of U.S. expansion.[23]

Michener first came to public prominence when *Tales of the South Pacific,* a collection of stories set in the Pacific theater during World War II, won the Pulitzer Prize for fiction in 1947. He became famous—and was embraced as an expert on Asia—after Rodgers and Hammerstein turned some of these stories into their hit 1949 musical *South Pacific.* The success of *South Pacific* gave Michener the financial freedom to write full-time, and he spent the 1950s traveling through Asia and the Pacific and producing a mountain of magazine articles, essays, short stories, and novels about contemporary events taking place there. Much of his prose first saw print in newspapers and magazines, including the *Saturday Review,* and he developed an especially close relationship with *Reader's Digest.* He worked as a roving editor for *Reader's Digest* for eighteen years, publishing more than sixty articles in its pages. In 1951 he published two books: *The Voice of Asia,* a collection of essays based on interviews he conducted in Asia, and *Return to Paradise,* a follow-up to *Tales of the South Pacific* that combined short stories with travel essays and became a Book-of-the-Month Club selection and one of the top ten bestsellers of the year. Two years later he published *The Bridges at Toko-Ri,* a novel which translated Washington's rationale for the Korean War into a story about an aircraft carrier fighter pilot facing his fears and ambivalence about the war (and which the *New Republic* criticized as sounding too much like a Voice of America broadcast). In 1954 he published *Sayonara,* a cross-racial romance about an American fighter pilot in Tokyo who falls in love with a Japanese woman. Michener took a break from Asian themes to write *The Bridge at Andau* (1957) a nonfiction work about Hungarian refugees fleeing a failed uprising against their Soviet-backed government; the State Department so valued it as an exposé of communism that it aided in the publication of fifty-three foreign editions. He concluded his fiction writing on Asia and the Pacific with the publication of *Hawaii* in 1959. Several of his books, including *Sayonara* and *The Bridges at Toko-Ri,* were made into movies. Michener also published four books about Japanese *ukiyo-e,* or woodblock prints, which he began collecting in the early 1950s. Like Norman Cousins, Michener facilitated the flow of Asian art into the United States and helped make the work of Japanese artists like Hokusai—creator of the "Thirty-Six Views of Mount Fuji" series of prints—familiar to Americans.[24]

Michener became famous not for writing about Asia and the Pacific per se, but for narrating America's encounter with Asia and the Pacific: his fiction and journalistic books feature Americans who live, work, or travel in the non-communist East. (China was absent from Michener's oeuvre because the Chinese government expelled all the Americans from the country in 1949.) Michener credited his success to a fortuitous accident of timing, noting that he started to write at the moment when "World War II and the airplane opened the horizons and Americans suddenly wanted to read about the rest of the world." He saw himself as a by-product of America's turn toward international engagement. "I published my books," he explained, "at the precise time when Americans were beginning to look outward at the entire world rather than inward at themselves. . . . Had I come along fifty years earlier, when America was isolationist, I doubt if anyone would have bothered much with my writing." The United States, however, was hardly "isolationist" fifty years before he began writing: the turn of the twentieth century marked the peak of U.S. territorial imperialism in the Pacific and the Caribbean. Michener, like so many other cultural and political figures, here constructs America's postwar expansion as wholly new, and in doing so, he both elides the history of U.S. territorial imperialism and carves out a unique role for himself. His writing performed the cultural work of managing America's "outward" turn: it tried to shape what Americans saw when they turned their gaze toward Asia and to teach them how to think about themselves in relation to what they saw.[25]

By 1953 Michener had become so closely identified with Asia and the Pacific that the *New York Times* announced that to "think of the Pacific is to think of Michener." Contemporary observers explained Michener's popularity by pointing to Cold War geopolitics. *Newsweek,* for instance, published a lengthy article in 1954 that situated Michener in relation to the political turmoil in Asia: after noting that there had never "been such need as now for Americans to know their Asiatic enemies and respect their Asiatic friends," it went on to assert that "no popular writer has done more than James A. Michener to interpret, in friendship and understanding, Asia to the Americans." A. Grove Day, his first biographer, explained Michener's popularity in 1964 by pointing to the need for Americans to understand their place in the postwar world: "He is probably the person who has done most to make his fellow Americans aware of the dangers and challenges that the United States must face as the course of empire, taking its westward way, has come full circle and is now eyeball to eyeball with the East." Day also read Michener as offering instruction in postwar national identity. "So long as modern Americans need to know who they are, in a world of wars hot and cold," he wrote, "so long will Michener's books be read." Such comments suggest the extent to which Michener's work, like so much middlebrow culture, was read by contemporaries as a guide to a new and confusing world.[26]

These contemporary readings of his work meshed with Michener's own sense of himself as a politically engaged writer. Michener's writing emerged out of the same middlebrow poetics of education and commitment that editor Norman Cousins articulated in the pages of the *Saturday Review*. In interviews, book reviews, and manifestoes, Michener dismissed what he called "pure art" as too arid and called for a literature of "utility" and "purpose" that expressed writers' willingness "to commit themselves" to exploring "the problems of current society." Viewing writers as the "conscience of the world," he identified himself with socially engaged writers like Steinbeck, Faulkner, and Hersey, who he felt made it impossible for Americans to "kick around the dispossessed," "go on lynching Negroes," and "drop as many atom bombs as [they] like" with a sense of impunity. Although Michener echoed the aesthetic values of the Popular Front, he positioned his calls for a "committed" and "didactic" authorship securely within a Cold War framework. In his advice to other writers, Michener described his own work: he urged writers to take up the issues raised by America's new "world responsibilities," embrace the "world novel," and recognize that "in the last few years it is the entire world that has become our battleground of ideas."[27]

In keeping with his embrace of the middlebrow aesthetic, Michener retained his professorial air long after he left academia. Balding, mild-mannered, and bespectacled, he often struck interviewers as having "the sincere, convincing air of an inspired college professor." To his biographer and friend A. Grove Day, Michener was a "professor *malgré lui*" whose writing functioned as an "extension of his teaching activities." Michener put this professorial reputation into the service of higher education in 1953, when he became president of the Asia Institute, which at the time was the only graduate school in the U.S. devoted exclusively to Asian affairs. Michener's third biographer, John Hayes, captured his appeal to the education-minded middlebrow audience when he described Michener's readers: "Trying to improve themselves, if even painlessly, Middle Americans have likened Michener's books to a seminar, and read them as a way of continuing their education." When President Ford awarded Michener the Medal of Freedom in 1977, he commended him not only as an author, but also as a "teacher and popular historian" who had "expanded the knowledge . . . of millions." [28]

In assuming this role as popular educator about Asia, Michener largely displaced the popular China experts from the 1930s and 1940s, such as Edgar Snow and Agnes Smedley. Snow and Smedley, the most famous fellow-travelers of Asian communism, wrote books that combined the conventions of travel literature and political reportage. Snow began his career as a foreign correspondent with a series of articles that he wrote while touring the Chinese railway system. In 1938 he published *Red Star over China,* a best-seller based on five months spent with the Red Army during their famous Long March, which presented a favorable picture of Mao. Agnes Smedley also traveled widely through China as a journalist sympathetic to the communist cause. Her best-known work, *Battle Hymn of China* (1943), described her travels with the Red Army from 1938 to 1941. Established houses published Snow's and Smedley's accounts, which received good reviews from critics across the political spectrum and found enthusiastic readers among the general public. During World War II, when the U.S. valued China as an ally, the mainstream press turned to Snow and Smedley as experts on China: Snow became an editor at the *Saturday Evening Post* and *Reader's Digest* solicited articles from Smedley (although none were ever published). Smedley and Snow fared badly in the postwar climate of anticommunism, however. Both were blacklisted, eased out of jobs, and generally muzzled by government officials and private employers. Agnes Smedley found speaking and publishing venues closed to her after MacArthur's headquarters in Japan falsely accused her of spying for the communists in 1949; Edgar Snow experienced a similar fate after he resigned from the *Saturday Evening Post* in 1951.[29]

Pearl S. Buck was of course the best-known of the Chinese experts from the 1930s and 1940s. A child of missionaries, Buck spent most of her first forty years in China. The success of *The Good Earth* (1931), a classic middlebrow novel, brought Buck into the public sphere, and she went on to write and speak widely about Asia. Buck shaped Americans' perception of China for many years and did much to create the sense of friendship, identification, and solidarity that many Americans felt toward China in the 1930s and 1940s. She published scores of books and articles, and, with her husband, John Day publisher Richard Walsh, a magazine about Asia. In 1938 she became the first American woman to receive the Nobel Prize in literature. Buck straddled the middlebrow political divide represented by *Reader's Digest* and the *Saturday Review.* Like *Reader's Digest,* in whose pages she often appeared, she supported Chiang Kai-shek and worked tirelessly to raise funds for his government during World War II and the civil war, although she also criticized Chiang's corruption and elitism. At the same time, she shared many of the liberal beliefs of the *Saturday Review,* where she also appeared regularly. Upon her return to the United States in the mid-1930s Buck became active in the early civil rights movement. She worked on anti-lynching campaigns, spoke out against European imperialism, and urged black Americans to link their civil rights struggles with national liberation movements around the world. She condemned the internment of Japanese Americans during World War II—one of the few prominent Americans to do so—and led campaigns against the Chinese exclusion laws. She also became an outspoken critic of missionaries, among whom she had lived in China, for their bigotry and cultural imperialism.[30]

Buck began to fall out of public favor with the onset of the Cold War, partly because the "loss" of China deprived her of her primary subject matter, but more directly because of her political views. Unlike Cold War liberals, Buck refused to accept anticommunism as the primary principle that should determine America's foreign and domestic policy agendas. She criticized Washington's foreign policy, especially its military emphasis, and accused the U.S. of pursuing an imperialistic path in Asia, views which earned her public accusations of anti-Americanism and brought her to the attention of the FBI and HUAC, who investigated her affiliations with allegedly communist front organizations. As a consequence, Buck found many publishing and public speaking venues closed to her. Although she continued to publish books with her husband's company and they continued to sell well, she lost much of her visibility and legitimacy as a public expert on Asia.

Michener, unlike Buck, Smedley, and Snow, embraced the political and economic premises of Cold War foreign policy and saw his role as public educator in terms of cultivating an understanding of and support for those policies. A classic Cold War liberal, he exemplified the postwar synthesis of left and right internationalist visions of America's proper role in the world. In keeping with the traditions of right internationalism, he argued that Asia was more important to the United States than Europe and that U.S. bungling had enabled the communists to seize power in China; he fetishized U.S. military power and especially air power; and he saw the U.S. nuclear arsenal as the key to national security. In keeping with the traditions of left internationalism, he dismissed territorial imperialism as a dead system, advocated free trade and private investment as its successor, and promoted human rights and democratization under U.S. tutelage. He accepted anticommunism as the necessary foundation of America's internationalism and supported military interventions in the developing world, including Vietnam, in order to contain communism's spread. At the same time, he deplored the hysterical anticommunism of McCarthyism at home and its attacks on civil rights: in 1954 he mounted the first successful campaign to legally overturn the firing of a federal employee accused of being a communist. A life-long Democrat, he supported Adlai Stevenson in 1956 and campaigned for Kennedy in 1960, convinced that the Republicans were blind to the revolutionary changes ushered in by decolonization. He blamed Eisenhower for allowing the U.S. reputation to slip abroad and for his timidity in the face of the civil rights revolution at home. Michener even ran for Congress himself in 1962, but lost.[31]

In keeping with his ideal of the politically engaged writer, Michener put his literary skills and celebrity directly into the service of the U.S. government. Unlike Dooley, who served the CIA unwittingly, Michener actively and consciously worked for the government in ways that fostered the integration of Asia into the U.S.-backed international system. In 1953 Michener assumed, at Washington's behest, the presidency of the Asia Foundation, a CIA-funded organization that sponsored People-to-People-type development projects and cultural exchanges with Asia. Washington, concerned that the foundation was supporting communist projects, asked Michener to take charge as the organization weeded out suspected communists and radicals in its midst, which he willingly did. (In 1954 Michener helped establish a similar People-to-People-type organization, the Fund for Asia, which sponsored development aid projects through private American organizations; Michener supported the organization with the royalties from his writing until 1956, when it folded.) At some point in the 1950s, according to Hawaii Congressman Daniel K. Inouye, he helped the government of Malaya suppress a communist insurgency that threatened to destabilize the government. Michener nearly entered the diplomatic corps himself: in 1960 President Kennedy offered Michener the ambassadorship to Korea, but Michener declined out of fear that his Japanese American wife would encounter hostility. He also worked with cultural diplomacy programs. Beginning in the 1960s and continuing for the next twenty-five years, Michener served on various government supervisory boards, including a five-member commission that oversaw the news, public relations, and propaganda efforts of the USIA in the early 1970s. In 1972 he traveled as a reporter with President Nixon on his historic visit to China that ended the estrangement that had begun with the "loss" of China in 1949. (The seventy-nine-year-old Buck desperately wanted to return to China with the Nixon entourage, but the Chinese government rejected her appeals.) Michener continued to work with the government until 1989, when he "retired" at the age of eighty-two.[32]

Michener put his writing into the service of the government as well. Even when not working directly for the government, he helped to disseminate its views, not because he belonged to some illicit propaganda machine, but because he shared Washington's perspective on events unfolding in Asia and America's relation to them. In 1953, *Reader's Digest* sent an article Michener wrote about the Korean War to the Department of Defense for vetting prior to publication; when they requested some changes to the final paragraph in order to promote the cause of the war more firmly, Michener willingly complied. He later wrote a magazine article on the B-52 bomber as a way to alert U.S. allies that Washington had a new weapon for their defense. Throughout the decade he accepted invitations from State Department officials, ambassadors, and members of foreign governments to visit and write about their concerns in Korea, Japan, Thailand, and other Southeast Asian nations, to the point that, according to one biographer, "it was difficult at times to separate Washington's interests from Michener's work." He even proposed a People-to-People-type TV series called "War for the World," which would cover the "exploits and adventures of Americans working overseas and engaged in the endless struggle for our people to help new nations find security." Congressman Inouye recognized the political value of Michener's work on Asia, and in 1962 he saluted Michener from the floor of the House as "one of our most effective anti-communist weapons in the world-wide struggle." As a well-known private citizen who explained the government's positions on events in Asia, Michener served as the quintessential "paraphraser" that the National Security Council was looking for: he translated Cold War ideology into popular narrative and explained it in terms that the man on the street could understand and accept.[33]

THE VOICE OF ASIA

Michener does quite a bit of such "paraphrasing" in *The Voice of Asia*, his first book devoted exclusively to Asia rather than the Pacific. Published in 1951, it gives an account of Michener's experiences during a tour through Asia in 1950. The book consists of sixty-eight short essays, some of which had previously appeared in the *New York Herald Tribune, Life,* and *Reader's Digest.* Part political reportage and part travelogue, it captures the revolutionary changes sweeping the region in the aftermath of World War II: it brings the reader into the cities and villages of former U.S. enemies (Japan), former Japanese colonies (Korea), former European colonies (Indonesia, Burma, India, and Pakistan), and colonies currently struggling for their independence (Singapore, Indochina). The essays do not cover China, because Michener could not travel there, or the former U.S. colony of the Philippines, for reasons which Michener does not explain. The Literary Guild chose it as a main selection, and it was translated into fifty-three languages.

The Voice of Asia effectively paraphrases NSC 48, a series of National Security Council documents that laid out American "objectives, policies, and courses of action in Asia." Michener toured Asia and wrote his essays at the same moment that political elites were becoming seriously concerned with the possibility of "losing" Asia. The NSC began drafting the series of documents in late 1949 as part of its reevaluation of U.S. policy in light of Mao's success in China and the Soviet explosion of an atomic device. Considered by historians to be the blueprint for postwar foreign policy in Asia, NSC 48 extended the Europe-based policies of containment and integration into Asia. The fifth paper in the series, NSC 48/5, was written in 1951—the same year that *The Voice of Asia* was published—and reviewed U.S. policy after the outbreak of the Korean War.[34]

The Voice of Asia and NSC 48 both present Asia as a region in danger of being politically and economically "lost" to the U.S. Like the members of the National Security Council, Michener presents the Kremlin and Peking as bent on bringing East Asia, Japan, and the major islands of the Western Pacific under Soviet control. Michener uses everyday language to explain the principles and assumptions that structure the National Security Council reports: that the global balance of power hangs in the balance in Asia, that the most serious threats to U.S. national security are coming from Asia, that the spread of communism there must be contained, that nationalist movements are vulnerable to communist influence and subversion, and that the loss of any one of several key Asian nations would cause the United States and the rest of the "free world" to become unacceptably vulnerable. Both *The Voice of Asia* and NSC 48/5 map Asia in a systematic, thorough, and country-by-country fashion. Both evaluate each country's strategic value to the U.S. by enumerating its material resources, the military significance of its geography and population, and its industrial capacity. Both make note of America's reservoir of good will in Asia and point out that rising anti-American sentiment is rapidly depleting that reservoir.

NSC 48/5 makes abundantly clear that the U.S. goal in Asia is economic integration. At nine different points in the thirty-page document, the drafters spell out that one of America's primary objectives is to "maximize the availability, through mutually advantageous arrangements, of the material resources of the Asia area to the United States and the free world generally, and thereby correspondingly deny those resources to the communist world." This statement articulates two key concepts that undergirded policymakers' thinking about Asia. The first concept is "availability": the U.S. must act in such a way as to ensure exclusive and uninterrupted access, for itself and its major allies, to the rice, rubber, oil, tin, manganese, jute, and atomic materials of Asia. The second concept is "mutually advantageous arrangements": the U.S. seeks access to these resources not through force or coercion, but through a system of trade that ostensibly benefits all parties. Exchange, rather than seizure and exploitation, is America's goal. This insistence that U.S. relations with Asia were based on the principles of availability and reciprocity, rather than on domination or exploitation, marks the ideological ground on which the U.S. denial of empire rested. NSC 48/1 expresses quite explicitly the need to distance the U.S. from the appearance of imperialism. Washington must not take actions that will "expose the U.S. to charges of 'imperialism'" and must work instead to preserve "the U.S. traditional reputation as a non-imperialistic champion of freedom and independence for all nations."[35]

The Voice of Asia, like NSC 48/5, also articulates the fear of "losing"

Asia, the goals of access and exchange, and the need to deny imperialism; these concerns embody the cultural logic which unites these two contemporaneous texts. As a popular writer rather than a policymaker, however, Michener handles these ideas in a fundamentally different manner from the National Security Council: it is here that one must pay attention to questions of genre and form. Michener has written a piece of popular travel writing, not a statement of policy, and he is bound by the literary conventions of his chosen vehicle. As a result, he translates the threat of loss and the goals of availability and exchange into scenes, characters, and modes of expression that the genre makes available to him. Whether Michener knew about NSC 48, or wrote his essays in coordination with policymakers as a means of publicly disseminating Washington's views, is a moot point. The general principles expressed by NSC 48 circulated widely in newspapers, magazines, and political speeches as part of the government's efforts to educate the public about its foreign policy agenda, and Michener did not need any special access to Washington in order to publicize them. The more important point is that, whatever Michener's formal relationship to Washington in 1951, his essays disseminated the core principles of U.S. foreign policy in Asia.

Michener begins his book by introducing his readers to a volatile and contested Asia, one that bears alarming animosity toward the United States. Writing only a year after the triumph of communism in China, Michener fears the further estrangement of the people of Asia from America. He raises the specter of an alternative form of integration, warning that Asia might ally itself with Russia and create a monolithic "Asia-Europe-Africa" coalition that could surround the U.S. in a stranglehold. Michener highlights the dire economic consequences of such an alliance: it would leave the U.S. "cut off from many critical raw materials" with the result that "American life as we know it would vanish." He also implies that, far from being at home in Asia, as Cousins, Dooley, and Burdick and Lederer would suggest toward the end of the decade, Americans were in danger of being driven out of Asia:

> An American today in Asia had better not go out at night. He is likely to get shot. He cannot get into China at all. Siberia is closed to him. If he is caught in the jungles of Malaya or the back roads of Indonesia or the suburbs of Manila he is likely to be murdered. In India, Pakistan, and Thailand he is welcomed, but he had better duck for cover in Indo-China.

Michener's overheated prose presents the Cold War in Asia as a sentimental crisis: he imagines that America will be destroyed through separation from the people of Asia and the loss of their affection. Michener's goal in writing the book is to prevent this economic, political, and emotional loss and to preserve Asia as a field for American action.[36]

The most important step for Americans, Michener writes, is to develop a new conceptual framework for thinking about Asia. The first lesson they need to learn is that "colonialism is dead"—as are the ideologies that accompanied it. Americans have "got to give up the old ideas" that undergirded imperialism and abandon the racist clichés— that Asians are "yellow hordes," "backward," "inscrutable," "mysterious," or that they simply "aren't like us"—that reproduce a consciousness of separateness and difference. If Americans want to "get back into Asia," they will have to cultivate "a new orientation of mind and heart" and make an "honest-to-God acknowledgment of the fact that all men are brothers." Only if Americans embrace a humanistic universalism, grounded in the values of "tolerance" and "humility," can the U.S. avoid the disaster that Michener sees looming in the near future.[37]

Throughout his book, Michener models the new mental attitude that he thinks Americans should adopt. Largely eschewing a gaze-based narrative of grand vistas and picturesque sights, which Mary Louise Pratt identifies as characteristic of imperial travel narratives, Michener instead constructs his text around a series of personal encounters that entail some sort of exchange. These moments of reciprocity serve as cultural cousin to NSC 48/5's insistence on "mutually advantageous" trade, and through them Michener enacts a suitably non-imperial identity of an American in Asia.

In a few of his essays Michener represents himself as participating in explicitly economic relations of exchange, so common in the literature of postwar tourism, in which sights and experiences are bartered for cash. In "Three Rupees, Sahib," for instance, he tells the story of his encounter with Sikantor, a boatman on the Irrawaddy River in Rangoon, Burma. Michener hires Sikantor for three rupees to ferry him across the river, but the entrepreneurial Sikantor has other ideas and persuades Michener, almost against his will, to see sights further along the river for a gradually increasing price. Sikantor ferries him up the river for five rupees, then into a side-canal for eight rupees, and finally to a group of rice mills for fifteen rupees before turning back. When they reemerge onto the river after nightfall, Michener beholds a spectacular view of the Irrawaddy aglow with stars and city lights and blazing Buddhist temples; at this moment he realizes that Sikantor has planned the whole expedition to culminate in this vista. Having initially feared being taken advantage of, Michener realizes the exchange has been a fair one all along and he gladly pays his fifteen rupees.

Pratt has identified the "seeing man," the Western traveler who achieves a masterful gaze over a non-Western landscape, as a recurring figure of colonial power. Although Michener does become the viewer of a beautiful sight at this moment, he refuses to become a "seeing man." Declining any dominance over the vista, he insists on his own passivity and gives all credit for arranging the view to Sikantor, who is not the shadowy native enabler of Western mastery found in narratives of discovery, but a fully developed character in his own right. Michener fashions himself as a guest in Burma, rather than a claimant of any sort of ownership over what he sees. In fact, the point of the essay is not the sights at all, but rather the series of exchanges with Sikantor that lead Michener to discover the basic decency and financial acuity of the Burmese.

The essay ends with Michener's return to his hotel, "where a hot-shot commission of big-time American businessmen had arrived to advise the Burmese Government on ways by which Burma could make more money," at which point he experiences "the curious feeling that the wrong men had been sent to the wrong country." Michener thus presents the American presence in Burma—his own and by implication that of the businessmen—in terms of a mutually advantageous economic exchange in which the Burmese are quite capable of looking out for their own interests. Michener implicitly denies any possibility of economic exploitation of the Burmese by the Americans. If exploitation is going to take place, he suggests, it will most likely be perpetrated by the Burmese.[38]

Michener embeds the principle of reciprocity into his text's structuring logic. In keeping with his title, he organizes *The Voice of Asia* around extended interviews he conducted with over one hundred "ordinary citizens" from across the social and political spectrum, including peasants, nationalists, European colonists, American businessmen, former members of the Japanese imperial army, refugees living in Nationalist China, and even a few communists. He describes how he immersed himself in the milieu of his interviewees, leaving his hotel to meet people in their own environments, sharing their meals, and making every effort to understand them from their own perspective. These meetings, which lasted between two and ten hours each, began as interviews in which Michener would ask questions, but at a certain point he would turn the format around and invite the interviewee to ask questions of him. It was at this point,

Michener explains, that his companion would often reveal his "soul" as the one-sided interviews turned into "tremendous conversations."[39]

Michener presents these conversations as reciprocal exchanges among social equals. With a few exceptions, his interviewees are adults who come across as well-spoken and politically conscious, and he respects the differences of opinion that arise. These are intellectual rather than emotional exchanges: his interviewees, none of whom resemble Dooley's sick peasants, offer Michener and the reader insights into social and political issues rather than alliances based on the shared experience of suffering. In these conversations, Michener mingles the sentimental ideal of forging personal bonds with the middlebrow ideal of self-education: as a participant in these exchanges, Michener presents them not as displays of his superior American knowledge but as opportunities to correct what he describes as his own intellectual deficiencies.

Michener uses these conversations as the book's central structuring device, thereby locating the logic of reciprocity within his text's very form. Michener builds each essay around a condensed version of a single interview, which he presents as a lengthy quotation in the interviewee's own words, bracketed by a few paragraphs of Michener's own commentary. Although Michener guides the conversations by the questions he asks and necessarily shapes them in the condensing process, he insists that he has not edited his interviewees' thoughts. Seeking to avoid some of the pitfalls of Western representations of non-Western peoples, Michener emphasizes that the interviewees are representing themselves. The result is a three-hundred-page book in which scores of Asians apparently tell their own stories in their own words.

Many of these essays operate according to a logic of availability rather than exchange. Michener often fades into the background of his conversations, serving more as a shadowy amanuensis than an active participant, and the dialogue often reads like monologues by his interviewees. By absenting himself and reproducing the words of his interviewees, Michener creates the impression that the reader is being spoken to directly in an unmediated fashion. This in turn creates a sense of immediacy that allows the reader to temporarily see the world from the interviewee's perspective and to develop a sympathetic appreciation for his or her situation. In a narrative move typical of the sentimental, Michener serves in these essays as a conduit for the flow of empathy from his readers to his characters; he becomes an intermediary, or medium, who can make available to the reader the thoughts, emotions, and life experiences of a young Japanese woman, an Indonesian magazine editor, an

Indian feminist, a Malayan schoolteacher, and a Pakistani sheik. Michener refuses to recognize any barriers to communication and accessibility, and he gets a story from everyone he talks to. Even an aged Korean peasant, who speaks only in grunts and untranslatable verbal torrents, is made to reveal his story of poverty and hard work during the Japanese occupation and the Korean War.

Through his essays, Michener delivers access to the thoughts, emotions, and personalities of Japanese, Chinese, Korean, Indonesian, Burmese, and Indochinese people. Michener wants to supplant the old knowledge about Asia—that presented it as "mute," "mysterious," and "remote"—with a new knowledge that renders it familiar, articulate, and approachable. Far from being inscrutable, Michener wants to prove to Americans that Asians are "easy to know and to love." His openness to the people he encounters allows him to enter into an ideal state of multiracial, multinational collectivity, and he reports being permanently changed by the "overwhelming experience of friendship, understanding and brotherhood" that he feels. Like the People-to-People program, which the book anticipates by several years, Michener presents himself and his interviewees as leaping governments and engaging in direct communication with each other. In doing so, he reassures the reader that Asia is still accessible to an American, that exchange is still possible, and that the alienation of Asia from America is not inevitable.[40]

Michener's insistence on reciprocity leads him to avoid producing himself as a heroic protagonist in possession of Western privilege and power. Far from being a "seeing man," Michener produces himself as what might be called a "listening man." Passive and blandly self-effacing (the source, no doubt, of his much-commented-upon "professorial" air), he refuses to assert a strong subjectivity over and against that of the people he interacts with. More often than not, he lets them act upon him, as in his description of how he found people to interview: "I went into a nation, sat quiet, and in time found that all sorts of people wanted to talk with me." Fashioning himself as a passive receptor rather than an active agent, he reports that in Singapore he "listened for fifteen or sixteen hours a day." Rather than presenting himself as a figure who dominates the world that he travels through, Michener depicts himself as submitting to that world as part of his quest for understanding. Utilizing another favorite trope of the sentimental, and playing it for humor at the same time, he presents his body in pain as evidence of his heightened state of receptivity. In an essay about his visit to a Thai doctor, he describes a massage he receives:

So he moved me to a spot near a window, whose sill he grabbed with both hands while he walked up and down my body. When he found a good place to stop he started to apply subtle and overpowering pressures with his toes. At one point he placed his big toes on the inside blood vessels of my leg and pressed down until I thought I must break in half. . . . It felt wonderful.

In scenes like this, Michener models the middlebrow ideal of a curious and open-minded American presence in Asia. In contrast to Dooley, Michener doesn't construct a sentimental "fellowship of pain." The only person suffering is Michener, and he's not suffering very much. Rather, his quasi-comic experience of pain demonstrates the depth of his commitment to bridging the gap between himself and the people in Asia. It also serves as an implicit disavowal of imperial power relations, in that he presents himself as physically vulnerable—and trusting—as he puts his body in the hands of an Asian man. Michener offers himself up—as listening man, as receptive man—as the model for how the U.S. should represent itself in Asia: "America should have some of its ablest young men doing for months and years what I did for some days."[41]

Michener perceives a danger that Americans will adopt the wrong model of how to be a Westerner in Asia—the colonial one. In "The New Mem-Sahibs," Michener brings together the issues of economic expansion, imperialism, and racism in an essay that imagines the U.S.-Soviet struggle for Asia as a competition among women who hold different attitudes about race. Michener claims, rather implausibly, that in colonial India it was British women rather than men who were "largely responsible for the hateful policy of arrogant supremacy." He thus expresses dismay at his discovery that many American women, "in the first flush of America's world responsibilities," have "picked up the mem-sahib racket right where the Englishwomen left off." He describes growing angry when he hears women spout the racist views of a bygone era —"If we Americans pulled out of here tomorrow, within six months these characters would be back in trees"—and he presents these women as a threat to America's foreign policy agenda. If Americans persist in "playing" that colonial "role," Michener warns, then "our efforts to win Asia to our side are absolutely doomed," because communist China and Russia are sending to Asia "extremely powerful and impressive women" who are "undoing the damages done by the mem-sahib."[42]

Michener suggests a bit of remedial education to prevent these women from permanently estranging Asia from the United States: "All American firms sending employees to Asia, all governmental agencies having business there, and all friends seeing vacationists off should see to it that the women who go along are given a pamphlet explaining what happened to the English and the Dutch and French and Australian societies that were built upon the tacit assumption that all people who are not white are feeble-minded." The racist American "mem-sahib" poses a threat to the nation, Michener suggests, because she creates the impression that Americans are imperialists. But even as she invites the specter of imperialism, as a literary device she allows Michener to deflect it. Through her, Michener genders racism as feminine and thus suggests that it is malleable and ultimately ephemeral, rather than embedded in material relations and institutions. By defining imperialism as racism and locating racism exclusively within the white American woman, Michener detaches the question of imperialism from the expansion of America's economic, political, and military power, processes that were controlled by white American men. American women's racial attitudes, Michener suggests, and not "American firms" or "governmental agencies" are the instruments of imperialism; prejudice, not economic exploitation or political domination, generates anti-American attitudes in Asia. Michener suggests that if American businesses and government agencies can change the attitudes of their employees, especially those of their employees' wives, they will be able to operate in Asia without opposition. He implies that the U.S. need not alter its economic or military policies in Asia, but only encourage its citizens to modify their attitudes. Michener thus imagines the cultivation of racial tolerance as a relatively painless solution to the crippling charges of imperialism, one that would not endanger America's economic and strategic interests in Asia.[43]

Michener's essay helps us to understand one of the reasons why the liberal critique of racism as individual prejudice proliferated in the late 1940s and 1950s. Within popular political discourse, imperialism was almost always defined as a function of white racism, rather than as the direct or indirect domination of one country by another through economic, political, and military means. The keenly felt need to deny American imperialism thus required only the condemnation of personal racial prejudice, which many Americans were quite willing to do. They were not so willing—or able—to critique the expansion of U.S. economic, political, and military power around the world. None of the middlebrow intellectuals or political elites who expressed concern over accusations of U.S. imperialism urged Washington to scale back its overseas military bases, remove itself from political alliances with colonial regimes and repressive postcolonial governments, or restrict the flow of foreign trade. Those critics who did characterize U.S. foreign policy as imperialistic— such as Paul Robeson, W. E. B. Du Bois, and Pearl Buck—soon found themselves the objects of domestic containment policies that restricted their access to the public sphere. In the place of substantive critiques of U.S. capitalism and militarism, liberal Americans condemned individual racial prejudices as the only acceptable—and ultimately, least challenging—way to discuss U.S. imperialism. At least some agents of U.S. economic expansion found this critique of personal prejudice eminently acceptable: in 1957, Michener reported that "The New Mem-Sahibs" had become his single most widely read piece of writing, in large part because many U.S. corporations included it in the instruction booklets they gave to new employees heading off to the Third World.[44]

Michener's effort to cultivate a sentimental, racially tolerant subjectivity in his readers should not be read as an act of altruism, but as part of his effort—openly announced in the book's introduction—to keep Asia within the U.S. sphere of influence. Michener's antiracism constituted an integral component of the legitimating ideology of U.S. global expansion. At the same time, it would be a mistake to dismiss Michener's liberalism as only a mystification of neocolonial expansion. Michener did impress upon his millions of readers that racism was a pressing social problem that they could do something about. He popularized the link between domestic racial practices and foreign policy and insisted that questions of race belonged at the center of foreign policy discussions. Ultimately, he publicized the disastrous geopolitical consequences of racism, which in turn kept some pressure on American political leaders to do something about it.

CONTESTED TERRAINS AND COUNTERNARRATIVES

Travel and travel writing became a contested political terrain in the late 1940s and 1950s, more so than the above discussion would perhaps suggest. As part of their effort to manage the flow of Americans abroad, the Truman and Eisenhower administrations promoted only certain kinds of travel by certain kinds of people and prevented other kinds of travelers from leaving or entering the country. Beginning in 1947, the Truman administration regularly denied passports to American communists, communist sympathizers, unrepentant former communists, and strong critics of U.S. foreign policy. In 1952, Secretary of State Acheson explained that the Department of State would withhold a passport from anyone who it had "reason to believe" was a Communist Party member, whose "conduct abroad is likely to be contrary to the best interest of the United States," or who might be "going abroad to engage in activities which will advance the Communist movement."[45]

The State Department's Passport Office withheld passports from many Americans, barring some three hundred citizens from traveling abroad in 1951–52 alone. It refused passport requests from politicians friendly to the Communist Party (Congressman Leo Isaacson), blacklisted film and theater actors (Edward G. Robinson), authors (Howard Fast, Arthur Miller), civil liberties lawyers (Leonard Boudin), intellectuals (W. E. B. Du Bois), and academic Asia specialists (Owen Lattimore). Many people who eventually did get their passports experienced delays lasting from several months to more than a year. The Truman and Eisenhower administrations also restricted visas allowing foreign nationals to enter the United States. Communist Party members, labor leaders, scholars, artists, and journalists were among the categories of individuals whose presence within the United States, even for brief visits, the State Department deemed a threat to national security. For all their discussion of "flow" and free exchange of goods and ideas, the Truman and Eisenhower administrations treated the national border as impermeable when it suited their interests to do so.[46]

In seeming contradiction of its promotion of travel and travel writing as engines of racial tolerance, the State Department restricted the travel of black Americans, such as Paul Robeson, who criticized U.S. racial practices too sharply. In the 1930s, Robeson had been a classic fellow-traveler, both literally and figuratively: he adhered to the Communist Party line without ever becoming a member, and he traveled around the world speaking out on racial and political issues. When he protested Truman's decision in 1950 to send U.S. troops into Korea, the State Department seized his passport. State Department officials declared that they considered domestic race relations to be a "family affair" inappropriate for discussion in foreign countries; U.S. attorney Leo Rover called Robeson "one of the most dangerous men in the world" because "during the concert tours of foreign countries he repeatedly criticized the conditions of Negroes in the United States."[47]

This characterization of Robeson's racial views as "dangerous" points up some of the differences between the liberal critiques of racism so pervasive in postwar middlebrow culture and the more radical critiques that the U.S. government felt it needed to suppress. In contrast to Michener or Norman Cousins, who saw racism in terms of individual prejudice,

Robeson critiqued racism as a systematic problem rooted in economic structures and in exploitation. He rejected the idea of racism as a regional problem unique to the South or even a national problem, and instead saw American race relations as continuous with the systems of racial exploitation that Europe exercised in its Asian and African colonies. The fight against racism within the United States, in Robeson's view, had to be connected to the struggle for independence by the colored peoples in Asia and Africa. It was this affiliation of domestic American race relations with European colonialism that the State Department found so politically damaging that it had to suppress it. Robeson talked about the wrong kind of international interdependencies when he linked the U.S. and European nations together as imperialist and racist powers, and in doing so he encouraged Asian nationalists to distance themselves from the U.S.

These postwar contestations around travel—the official promotion of one kind of travel, side by side with official restrictions on other kinds —must be read within the larger context of the Cold War delegitimation of Popular Front internationalism, as discussed in Chapter 1. In the 1930s travel served as a major avenue for far-left internationalism, with travel abroad, especially to the Soviet Union, Spain, and China, serving as a route to political awakening and as an expression of international solidarities. This literal traveling by leftist artists and intellectuals in the 1930s, and the accounts they wrote about it, helped establish travel as a politically infused activity. The State Department appropriated and transformed this Popular Front idea of travel as a form of political engagement: just as the People-to-People program displaced the banned Popular Front organizations on the attorney general's list of subversive organizations, so the State Department's promotion of the Cold War tourist displaced the politically engaged "fellow traveler" of the 1930s. The State Department sought to restrict the flow of those Americans, like Robeson, who it feared would engage in the wrong kind of people-to-people contact, just as it sought to restrict the expression of alternative forms of internationalism more generally.

Although many American accounts of travel in Asia published during the 1950s adhered to the sentimental model of interpersonal encounter and exchange, not all of them represented these encounters as successes. J. Saunders Redding's *An American in India* (1954) offers a powerful counternarrative to that of Michener. Although he follows the sentimental template, he emphasizes his failures to achieve the desired relationship of reciprocity, understanding, and sympathy. In doing so, he highlights the different meanings that could be attached to the principle of international integration and the difficulties of representing America as a nation committed to racial equality.

At the same time that the State Department prevented Paul Robeson from leaving the U.S., it promoted the travel of many other black artists, writers, and cultural figures through its various cultural diplomacy programs. In 1952 the State Department sent Redding, a black scholar of African American literature, to India under the auspices of the International Educational Exchange Service. His goal in touring India, like Michener's in writing *The Voice of Asia,* was to "win friends for America." Unlike Michener, however, he went not as a listening man but as a speaking man, delivering a series of lectures designed to "interpret American life to the people of India." As "a teacher" and "a bringer of truth," Redding tried to explain to Indians, who were the sharpest critics of American racial practices, that the U.S. was not an irredeemably racist country.[48]

Redding narrates his encounters with the Indians as spectacular failures. Despite hours of briefings with State Department officials, he is overwhelmed when the Indians accost him with statistics of lynchings, riots, and segregation, and he is unnerved by the constant specter of Robeson, whom the Indians see as a more legitimate representative of black America. When he tries to explain the recent improvements in black life, his listeners tell him flat out, "We do not believe you." When he speaks of democracy, they drown him out with accusations of "imperialism." His first speech begins "badly" and turns into a "fiasco"; in discussions with other writers he feels "like a stupid pupil in a class of bright ones." In the question-and-answer periods after his lectures, he is often overwhelmed and silenced by the audience's unremitting critiques, so that instead of communicating with them he stands "dumb" and tries to imagine ways of "escape." In contrast to Michener, Redding cannot enter into a sympathetic relationship with his auditors; he cannot adopt their perspective nor persuade them to understand his. In fact, he barely communicates with them at all. During one particularly unpleasant encounter, he comes to see his audience not as potential friends and allies but as a hostile enemy:

> My eyes searched for the man in the audience, the tormentor, the enemy, but I could not distinguish him. It was very strange. I looked to the place where I had seen him rise. In my mind was an image of him—brown skin taut-stretched to gray over the fine bone of his cheeks, eyes aglint, mouth tightened like a miser's purse—but I could not see him. He had lost definition as an individual. They had all lost definition. The enemy had no face.

Instead of transcending the barriers of Otherness, Redding lapses into an older, less liberal tradition of representation: he can only see his audience as the faceless, inscrutable Asian enemy of World War II and Korean War movies.[49]

The Indians reject Redding's appeals for political alliance with him as a representative of a fellow democratic nation, and offer instead an alternative solidarity based on race and the shared experience of exploitation. This vision disturbs Redding deeply. For thirty years, Redding writes, he had struggled against the primacy of race as the determinant of his selfhood, and he felt that he had recently succeeded in ridding himself of this "emotional baggage." But his first experience in India forces him to accept it once again. Riding through Bombay in a horse-cab with a white American woman he met at the airport, Redding is confronted by a dark-skinned beggar who, upon discovering that Redding is an American, touches Redding's dark-skinned arm, smiles with "recognition and wonder," and says to him, "Same like me . . . Like by you." Redding bristles at this assertion of racial solidarity:

> All at once I knew I was closer to this nameless man than I could ever be to Rena Mark, who pressed against my side in fear. The feeling and the knowledge came spontaneously, unbidden, without the intercession of my will, and I tried to deny it, ignore it, stamp it out. . . . The barriers of language, culture and national birth dissolved before it, and I stood face to face with an indestructible truth: the color of my skin was still the touchstone. I did not like it.

This dissolution of "barriers" based on racial solidarity contradicts the ideal of a multiracial, multinational community that Redding (and Eisenhower) seek. While the process of identification is similar, the basis of that identification is all wrong—shared humanity and a commitment to democracy, not the simple fact of race, should be the uniting factors. The Indians' "color-consciousness" appalls Redding, and he is shocked by what he sees as their inability "to conceive of a dark-skinned American as being other than the enemy of white, or of having a loyalty that goes beyond color."[50]

An American in India writes back to the optimistic vision of tourism offered by Michener, the State Department, *Reader's Digest*, and the *Saturday Review*. Like Michener undergoing his Thai massage, Redding suffers in Asia. Yet where Michener's physical suffering marks his commitment to understanding things from his hosts' point of view, Redding's emotional suffering marks the chasm that separates him from his Asian hosts and his American home. Redding never experiences the soothing sense of universal brotherhood that Michener does. Instead, his exchanges with Indians lead to heightened feelings of isolation and to a more deeply felt awareness of racism in America. In the end, and perhaps inadvertently, Redding narrates the failures of integration: both of black and white Americans at home and of Asians and Americans abroad. His story testifies to the firmness of the boundaries of race and nation that still separate peoples. By foregrounding this failure, Redding undermines the sentimental narratives which cast tourism as a series of reciprocal exchanges leading inexorably to mutual understanding. And by dramatizing the Indian resistance to his efforts at exchange, Redding illustrates Washington's limited ability to shape how its global expansion was perceived abroad. He documents the force with which Asians can resist exchange and tell their own stories about America.

In India Redding confronts an alternative vision of internationalism based on racial consciousness and resistance to oppression. Although he ultimately rejects this view, he does narrate the extent to which it shakes his faith in the liberal assertions of improved race relations. This alternative exists within his narrative as an emergent internationalism, one that can only be glimpsed in 1954 but that would appear full-blown in the 1960s, when the Third World, anti–Vietnam War, and Black Panther movements asserted their own visions of U.S.-Asian solidarity.

· · · · ·

As Redding's narrative suggests, the politicization of the tourist as an agent and emblem of American expansion carried a certain risk. Far from deflecting the charge of imperialism, the American traveler abroad sometimes made U.S. power visible in a human form and thus more easily contestable. Anti-American sentiment mushroomed worldwide during the late 1950s: more than fifty USIA centers in twenty-one countries were attacked between 1948 and 1958, and anti-American riots erupted in Taiwan, South Korea, Algeria, Lebanon, and Turkey. Newspapers and magazines, in stories such as "The U.S. Tourist: Good or Ill-Will Envoys?" connected anti-American sentiment to the increased flow of tourists abroad and turned the "ugly American" into an epithet for the vulgar tourist who generated hostility around the world by advertising the nation's unparalleled power and wealth. Tourism emerged as an arena in which Americans expressed their own anxieties about their role as a global power: in 1961 the *Saturday Review* ran a baleful cartoon of a woman asking a beleaguered travel agent, surrounded by posters of

"Where aren't we hated, as of this moment?"

Figure 9. Tourism served as a space in which anxiety about U.S. global expansion could be expressed. (*Saturday Review,* January 28, 1961)

Cuba, the Orient, and France, "Where aren't we hated, as of this moment?" (Figure 9).[51]

The nation's highest-level tourists sometimes found themselves at the center of these anti-American demonstrations. In 1958 protesters in Caracas attacked Vice President Nixon—recent winner of *Travel* magazine's Mr. Travel award—during a good-will tour through Latin America. In 1960 rioters took to the streets in Tokyo for two weeks in protest over the revised U.S.-Japan security pact. Angry mobs trapped Ambassador Douglas MacArthur II in his limousine for more than an hour, and some thirty thousand demonstrators paraded in front of the U.S. Embassy (Figure 10). Dancing in the street and shouting "Eisenhower don't come" and "Ike, stay home," the rioters forced the president—whom the U.S. commerce secretary had recently dubbed one of the

Figure 10. Some of the thirty thousand demonstrators in front of the U.S. Embassy in Tokyo, 1960; the partially obscured horizontal banner at left demands that Eisenhower cancel his trip to Japan. (© Bettman/Corbis)

world's most "enthusiastic boosters for international travel"—to cancel a much-anticipated goodwill visit to Japan. These riots differed markedly from those in which Michener found himself caught up in Saigon in 1955. Far from culminating in an expression of friendship with the U.S., they marked a rupture in the sentimental discourse of tourism. The Japanese rioters rejected rather than embraced a U.S.-Asian encounter: they produced a hostile confrontation rather than mutual understanding, and they affirmed rather than bridged the boundary separating the U.S. and Japan. Like the U.S. State Department when it denied passports to Paul Robeson and others, the Japanese protesters claimed the right to render their national boundaries impermeable. The riots, which were widely reported in the U.S. press as a product of communist agitation, raised the specter of the separation of the U.S. from its most important ally in Asia. Like Redding's tour through India, these anti-American riots produced humiliation for the U.S.: they provided a worldwide audience for the public denunciations of the United States as an "imperialist" power.[52]

CHAPTER 4

Family Ties as
Political Obligation

*Oscar Hammerstein II, South Pacific,
and the Discourse of Adoption*

[Oscar Hammerstein II] brought superduper, musical extrav-
aganzas to Broadway and Hollywood featuring live, sprightly
music, and sparkling lyrics, sometimes with an ideological
touch.

U.S. Representative Philip J. Philbin, 1960

In the early 1950s Broadway lyricist Oscar Hammerstein II wrote a musical with his son-in-law called *With the Happy Children*. The show
played before local audiences in Bucks County, Pennsylvania, a rural
area not far from New York City where a number of middlebrow artists who wrote about Asia made their homes. Hammerstein wrote the
show to publicize Welcome House, an adoption agency that Pearl Buck
had launched in 1949 specifically to find families for Asian and part-
Asian children born in the United States whom other agencies refused
to handle. The agency revolutionized American adoption practices by
placing children with parents of different racial backgrounds. It also
caught the attention of a number of middlebrow cultural figures: Hammerstein and James Michener worked with Buck at Welcome House, and
Reader's Digest and the *Saturday Review* published enthusiastic stories
about it (Figure 11).[1]

The idea for Welcome House emerged out of Buck's long-standing
ties to China. The rise to power of the Chinese communists in 1949
deeply distressed Buck, as did the intervention of Chinese forces against
U.S. troops during the Korean War and Washington's inability, or unwillingness, to work with many of the nationalist independence move-

Figure 11. Oscar Hammerstein II with Pearl S. Buck and child at Welcome House, Buck's adoption agency that worked with Asian and mixed-race children born in the United States. (Archives, Pearl S. Buck International)

ments throughout Asia. Like many Americans, she saw U.S. influence in the region declining after 1949. In a 1952 *Saturday Review* article, Buck suggested that hybrid Asian and American families created through adoption could eventually facilitate better political relations between the United States and Asia. U.S. policy had failed in China, she believed, because too few Americans could understand both China and America and mediate between them. She proposed Welcome House as part of a solution to America's foreign policy problems: in her view, the mixed-race children available for adoption were "key children" who could facilitate relations between the U.S. and Asia and perhaps prevent further losses of Asian nations to communism.[2]

A number of Buck's contemporaries shared this view of the family as a lens through which to understand America's foreign policy difficulties in Asia. Over the course of the 1950s, several political observers located one source of Washington's problems in Asia in Americans' weak sense of political obligation toward Asia. If more Americans saw themselves as affected by the political upheavals in Asia, they reasoned, then Washington could implement its policies of containment and integration more effectively. Several Asia experts traced this weak sense of political obligation back to the history of Asian immigration to the United States. Loy Henderson, the U.S. ambassador to India, addressed this question of obligation in a 1950 speech before the Indian Council of World Affairs. Henderson explained to his audience that he sincerely regretted Americans' looser sense of commitment to Asia than to Europe, but he nonetheless deemed it "only natural." Because "most people of the United States or their ancestors migrated from Europe," he explained, Americans "have had comparatively close relations with the countries of Europe" in contrast to "those of Asia." James Michener echoed this view in 1956. Americans have rarely thought of themselves as bound to Asia, he wrote, because "the average American is at heart a European. . . . Few Americans are descended from Asian ancestors, few bear Asian names, even fewer speak an Asian tongue." Harold Isaacs voiced a similar opinion. In his 1958 study of popular American perceptions of Asia, he sought to explain why "vagueness about Asia had been until now the natural condition even of the educated American." He, too, began by noting the absence between Americans and Asians of that "intricate web of bonds" rooted in immigration.[3]

Henderson, Michener, and Isaacs each cast the problem of political obligation to Asia as a problem of family: Americans did not feel bound to Asians because they had rarely belonged to the same families and thus shared few of the ties of culture, religion, and language that families knit across oceans and generations. All three men saw immigrant families as incubators of knowledge about the world, and saw the small number of these families as part of America's problem in Asia. For Michener, given the paucity of immigrant ties, "our difficulty in knowing Asia is understandable." Henderson saw the absence of substantial family-generated knowledge as a "handicap" in the achievement of U.S. policy goals. In making these connections between families and foreign policy, each of these observers inadvertently pointed to the legal history of American racism. Family ties to Asia were limited in the 1950s because race-based immigration and citizenship laws had hindered the formation of Asian American families since the late nineteenth century.

What does Hammerstein's and Buck's work for Welcome House have to do with Henderson's, Michener's, and Isaac's comments on absent immigrant ties to Asia? Each of these episodes highlights how, in the late

1940s and 1950s, the issues of Cold War geopolitics and American racism intersected with the burgeoning discourse of family formation. Western culture has a long tradition of imagining East-West relations in familial terms. *Madame Butterfly,* which originated as an American short story in 1887 before becoming famous as Puccini's opera in 1904, has long been a preferred Western vehicle for imagining America's encounter with Asia. It structures its narrative around the twin poles of a failed marriage and a successful adoption: Benjamin Franklin Pinkerton is an American Navy officer in Nagasaki who pretends to marry and then impregnates and abandons a Japanese woman, who patiently awaits his promised return; when Pinkerton finally returns after several years, he comes with his white American wife, and together they adopt his mixed-race child, as Butterfly, in a gesture of self-sacrifice, commits suicide. Gina Marchetti has explored how a number of post–World War II movies—including *Love Is a Many-Splendored Thing* (1955), *Sayonara* (1957), *China Gate* (1957), *The Crimson Kimono* (1959), and *The World of Suzie Wong* (1960)—took up *Madame Butterfly*'s theme of romance between a white man and an Asian woman and used it to figure Americans' liberalizing views on race. Less noticed, however, has been the proliferation of postwar stories, both fictional and nonfictional, focusing on the other strand of the *Madame Butterfly* narrative: the adoption of Asian and part-Asian children by white American parents.[4]

During the postwar period the hybrid, multiracial, multinational family created through adoption became a familiar feature of middlebrow culture. These families offered a way to imagine U.S.-Asian integration in terms of voluntary affiliation: they presented international bonds formed by choice (at least on the part of the American parents), rather than by biology. In doing so they foregrounded the idea of alliance among independent parties—the model of postwar integration—rather than the idea of an empire unified by blood and force. These mixed-race families also offered a way to imagine Americans overcoming the ingrained racism that so threatened U.S. foreign policy goals in Asia. In part because the family balanced emotional unity with internally structured hierarchies of difference based on age, it served as a model for a "free world" community that included Western and non-Western, developed and underdeveloped, established and newly created nations. The family became a framework within which these differences could be both maintained and transcended, and offered an imaginative justification for the permanent extension of U.S. power, figured as responsibility and leadership, beyond the nation's borders.

THE HIROSHIMA MAIDENS

The family has long been used to represent the nation in microcosm. As a metaphor, the family reworks the abstract bonds that unite a community too large ever to be experienced directly into the intimate biological and emotional bonds that unite parents, children, and extended relatives. During the late 1940s and 1950s, the U.S. became "family centered" in new ways. In the aftermath of war, the rush to earlier marriages and more pregnancies produced a baby boom among all classes and ethnic groups. The combined effects of increased savings, a growing economy, and government subsidies led to an exodus out of cities and into suburbs, where parents and children lived apart from other relatives in single-family homes. Experts hailed this new nuclear family as the building block of a strong society and as the best means to fulfill all of the individual's personal, emotional, and recreational needs. As the institution of the family changed, so did gender roles. Men experienced new pressures to marry, have children, assume the role of breadwinner, and become more actively involved in the rearing of children. Women, who had enjoyed increased financial and personal freedom during the war years, were pushed out of high-paying jobs and encouraged to redomesticate themselves as wives, mothers, and homemakers. Individuals who departed or were excluded from these conventions were often seen as deviant.[5]

Popular media presented the white, middle-class, suburban family as one of the foundations of postwar national identity, an emblem of a prosperous and secure America. It often reinforced this identification through a contrast with communist nations, which it represented as bent on destroying the family and replacing it with the state. One 1958 *Newsweek* article about China quoted a girl of seventeen who described commune life by saying, "The family does not count anymore. . . . We provide all needs." Three photos accompanied the article: men raising guns in the air, women carrying hoes in a field, and children lined up in formation, with captions declaring "Men Without Women," "Women Without Men," and "Children Without Parents" (Figure 12). This sundering of family ties under communism became a familiar theme in the cultural containment of China that took place after 1949.

The family could be invoked in other ways, however. In its discussion of international affairs, the *Saturday Review* regularly imagined extending the family, and especially its love, beyond the borders of the nation. Norman Cousins gave the political discourse of familial love its clearest

Figure 12. Communist China, as
depicted in the pages of *Newsweek*
in 1958: "The family does not count
anymore." (Eastfoto)

expression when he wrote about the Hiroshima Maidens, a group of
twenty-five young Japanese women who had, as schoolchildren, been
scarred and disfigured by the dropping of the atomic bomb. In 1953
Cousins launched a four-year project of bringing these women to the
United States for reconstructive plastic surgery. Cousins raised funds for
the project from *Saturday Review* readers and promoted it as a voluntary, people-to-people-type effort that would allow readers to participate
in world events. He coordinated the voluntary efforts of scores of people
and institutions who represented the forces of global military and economic integration as well as of humanitarian internationalism. Dr. Ar-

thur J. Barsky, a prominent plastic surgeon, took charge of the operations and persuaded Mt. Sinai hospital to donate surgical facilities; a number of Quaker families, under the auspices of the American Friends Services Committee, provided homes for the women; the U.S. Air Force flew the Maidens to the U.S. from Japan; and Pan American Airways flew them back to Japan after their operations had been completed.[6]

During World War II, U.S. propaganda had represented the Japanese in racialized and dehumanizing terms—as apes, vermin, supermen, inferior men, primitives, savages, madmen—which fostered an exterminationist attitude. At war's end, however, Japan's global role shifted from reviled enemy to Washington's most valued Asian ally. Japan was the first Asian nation to receive substantial U.S. aid, and Washington promoted the occupation and reconstruction of its former enemy as a model of American selflessness and proof of America's benign global aspirations. The need to secure Japan's integration into the capitalist "free world" shaped U.S. foreign policy for the rest of Asia: the U.S. increased its involvement in Southeast Asia in order to guarantee Japanese access to that region's economy, and thereby prevent Japan from becoming dependent on trade with communist China and thus vulnerable to political pressure from Beijing.[7]

Cousins charted the Hiroshima Maidens' progress in a series of editorials which expressed this shift in American attitudes toward Japan. In one of them Cousins offered a vision of America bound to Asia through ties of familial love. He quoted, and endorsed, the response that the American-born Japanese chaperone gave when one of the Maidens asked her why Americans were so generous to a former enemy:

> Suppose . . . that some people have a philosophy of life which enables them to regard all human beings as belonging to a single family. Even though they might not actually know each other, even though they might live thousands of miles apart, they might still believe in their closeness to one another and in their duty to one another. The same love that members of a family feel for one another can be felt by these people for all others, especially for those who are terribly in need of help.

In these editorials, the plastic surgery that the girls receive becomes a metaphor for the "reconstruction" of postwar Japan. Cousins casts the relationship between the United States and Japan in the intimate terms of one family member feeling "love" and a sense of "duty" to another. This familial rhetoric figures the political and economic forces of reconstruction in personal, private terms, while also constructing a seemingly natural hierarchy. Cousins presents the U.S. as the healthy and strong family member that can aid weaker members who are "terribly in need of help." Cousins launched the Hiroshima Maidens project a year after the U.S. occupation ended, and the family that he invokes echoes the dual logic of independence and interdependence that structured the 1951 peace and security treaties. These treaties restored Japan's sovereignty, yet also bound Japan and the U.S. tightly together through a series of political, military, and economic agreements that not only granted Washington extensive military base rights, but also forced Japan to conform to U.S. policies designed to contain communist China. Cousins's "single family" philosophy, which he ascribes to all Americans, subsumes the complex economic and security bases of the U.S.-Japan relationship to a purely personal, affective bond that deflects all charges of American self-interest.[8]

The Hiroshima Maidens, who appeared frequently in American media, marked the shift away from the terms of wartime propaganda and toward new terms that fit with Japan's postwar status as ally and subordinate partner. No longer vermin, these Japanese were innocent virgins, victims, and patients. Their wounds marked them as human beings with whom Americans could identify and feel sympathy, and their femininity distanced them from the masculinity of the Japanese military. These characteristics also clearly cast the Maidens as subordinate figures dependent on American generosity.

Cousins locates the Maidens within a sentimental, rather than eroticized, vision of the family. He distances this global "single family" from any biological or sexual ties and makes it a function of common humanity and individual sympathy instead. Within the tradition of American sentimentalism, the family has long represented the most prized form of community. It embodies and institutionalizes the primary values of compassion and sympathy. In contrast to romantic or sexual love, which are tainted by self-interest, familial love is seen as a generous love which motivates a selfless concern for others. It gives form to the ideals of responsibility and commitment to others, and implies a permanence not susceptible to the vicissitudes of romantic love. With its hierarchies of age and sex, the family also serves as a sentimental model for managing unequal social relations. Nineteenth-century sentimental narratives used the figure of the family to integrate symbolically into the social order those socially marginal figures whose humanity had been questioned on grounds of race, criminality, or mental capacity. This extension of the family reached its cultural apex in Harriet Beecher Stowe's *Uncle Tom's Cabin,* when Little Eva extended her proto-maternal love out to the naughty slave-child Topsy and thus brought her within the nurturing and disciplining domestic sphere.[9]

Cousins's vision of the family worked as a similarly inclusive device to encourage a sense of identification with the Japanese, whose humanity had so recently been denied. In contrast to the *Newsweek* article, which used the family as a wedge to distinguish the U.S. from communist China, Cousins's formulation welcomed the Japanese into the American family—and, by extension, into the family of democratic nations—rather than figuring them as threats to it. The Hiroshima Maidens project shows how the postwar global imaginary did not depend exclusively on a logic of exclusion, of keeping communists out of the U.S. and out of the "free world." Rather, it also depended on a logic of inclusion, of strengthening the "free world" by inviting many nations and peoples into its protective embrace. Cousins imagined a hybrid, all-encompassing family that could tame previously threatening differences by incorporating them rather than by containing them. The family emerges here as an answer to the "What are we for?" question: it offered a way to claim some of the communitarian energy associated with communism, while avoiding the conflation of the community with the state. As one *Reader's Digest* article put it, the family as a model of collectivity offered a way to bridge the ideological gap between the "ruthless collectivism" of communism and the "selfish individualism" with which the U.S. was so often identified.[10]

Cousins's assertion of a single global "family" did not produce a single, coherent meaning, however. As much as the Hiroshima Maidens project echoed certain aspects of Washington's foreign policies for Asia, it threatened to publicly undermine others. The State Department expressed strong reservations about the project from the outset and at one point tried to stop it altogether. U.S. officials knew Cousins as an outspoken critic of U.S. atomic policy who advocated disarmament and a halt to nuclear testing, and they worried that the Maidens would fuel the budding antinuclear peace movement. They feared that leftist critics in Japan and throughout the world would use the project to reiterate their attacks on the U.S. for dropping the atomic bomb and for testing nuclear weapons in the Pacific, and that the Maidens would end up provoking rather than soothing anti-American sentiment. At a moment when the Eisenhower administration was promoting its "Atoms for Peace" campaign, the disfigured bodies of the Maidens threatened to make atomic energy's destructive capacities all too visible. The State Department also did not want the project to be read as an admission of American responsibility or expiation for the bombing of Hiroshima. Although Cousins, careful not to exploit the suffering of the Maidens, kept the public focus on the humanitarian angle, the project's meanings were not so easy to control. Many Americans, especially among the liberal readership of the *Saturday Review,* did feel tremendous guilt over the dropping of the atomic bombs, and they eagerly donated funds to the Maidens project as a way to expiate that guilt.[11]

THE CHRISTIAN CHILDREN'S FUND

The Hiroshima Maidens was not the first international project that the *Saturday Review* coordinated: already in 1949 Cousins had organized the moral adoptions program, through which readers of the magazine "adopted" four hundred Japanese children orphaned at Hiroshima. Because U.S. law blocked the immigration of actual Japanese persons, these adoptions were virtual and consisted primarily of the donation of funds and the exchange of letters. *Saturday Review* readers responded eagerly to the program, which they saw as a moral act through which they could express what one reader described as their "responsibility for others in the world." Cousins did not invent this idea of Americans "adopting" Japanese children, however; in all likelihood, he got it from the Christian Children's Fund.[12]

The Christian Children's Fund fine-tuned the equation of political obligation as familial obligation by establishing adoption as a trope through which one could imagine one's relationship with the developing world. Presbyterian minister Dr. J. Calvitt Clarke founded the Christian Children's Fund (originally the China's Children Fund) in 1938 to raise money for Chinese children orphaned and rendered homeless by the Sino-Japanese war. As a fundraising innovation, Clarke appealed to prospective American donors by representing their relationship with the children they sponsored as one of "adoption." The adoption campaign proved so successful that not only did other aid organizations begin using it, but it enabled the CCF to expand its operations throughout Asia in step with the Cold War. By 1955 the CCF was supporting children in fifteen Asian countries, many of them refugees from communist China and North Korea.[13]

This rhetoric of adoption symbolically "solved" the problem of America's racially exclusive immigration laws. It freed the idea of family from its biological roots and dependence on physical proximity and made it a function of sentiment instead. Asians did not actually have to enter the United States in order to become tied to Americans through family bonds; instead, the American family, and the love and aid that went with it, could extend out beyond the borders of the nation. This idea of a multiracial, multinational family repudiated the history of American racism without the difficulties of putting that position into practice at the level of social and political policy.

In the late 1950s, the CCF and its "adoption" program garnered public prominence as a success story in the fight against Asian communism. In 1957 and 1958 Clarke received awards and commendations from the anticommunist governments of Japan, Taiwan, and South Korea. In 1957, Universal Pictures released *Battle Hymn,* a Korean War film based on the true story of Air Force Colonel Dean Hess who, as the communists moved in on Seoul in 1950, evacuated nearly one thousand CCF orphans to an offshore island, whereupon CCF staff arranged their "adoption." That same year saw the publication of *Children of Calamity,* an organizational history of the CCF written by sometime *Reader's Digest* contributor John C. Caldwell that included a foreword by Pearl Buck and described Clarke on its opening page as an "un-ugly American"; a second history, Edmund Janss's *Yankee Sí!,* was published in 1961 and sent out to each sponsor. Janss framed these "adoptions" within the political discourse of familial love: he dedicated his book "To those who have helped make America loved" and emphasized the CCF's role in stemming the spread of Asian communism. Describing "adoptees" as "tiny ambassadors" for America, Janss compared CCF sponsor dollars to the billions of dollars in military aid pouring into Southeast Asia, remarking that "the best investment dollar-for-dollar, however, will be the tangible love sent by Americans who 'adopt' Asia's babies." This public promotion of CCF efforts helped make Clarke's strategy of "adoption" a familiar way for millions of Americans to imagine their relations with Asia.[14]

The CCF's print advertisements appealed to Americans to take a specific action that would commit them personally to Asia. Published in the pages of middlebrow magazines such as the *Saturday Review,* they seared the idea of "adoption" into millions of Americans' minds as an effective means to fight the Cold War. Written by Clarke, the advertisements kept pace with the changing focus of the Cold War, offering children from

Taiwan, Korea, and India to American readers. Instead of merely feeling a familial tie to the people of Asia, the advertisements urged readers to act on their feelings and become "parents" to an Asian child, through the simple act of writing a check.

A typical advertisement from 1952, published in the midst of the Korean War, works by first provoking the reader's anxiety about communism and then offering parenthood as a means to defuse it (Figure 13). A photograph of a middle-aged white man and woman holding a "hunger-limp" Indian baby dominates the advertisement; beneath the caption "Am I My Brother's Keeper?" Dr. Clarke takes the reader on a three-hundred-word tour through the trouble spots of the Cold War—India, Korea, Japan, Germany. Clarke describes the children of these countries as starving victims of poverty and war, vulnerable to communism because "Communists care enough to make very successful capital of democracy's failures." Clarke figures both the "failures" of democracy and the menace of communism in terms of decimated families: in Japan, orphanages are full of GI babies "deserted by their American fathers"; among Korean refugees fleeing communist forces, "there is hardly a family not broken, fathers taken prisoner or shot, mothers abused and carried off or left dead behind a broken wall"; in West Germany, escapees from communist East Germany "won their freedom at great cost. Few families escaped intact. Children, parents, wives and husbands shot down or dragged off to labor camps." The logic undergirding this advertisement, and much of the CCF's promotional material, is that family breakdown, whether caused by communists, war, or poverty, leads to hungry children; hungry children are susceptible to communist promises of a better future; thus hungry children threaten the security of Americans. As Clarke phrases it in the concluding line of his tour, "The hungry children of the world are more dangerous to us than the atom bomb."

The advertisement invokes the twin paralyzing anxieties of the Cold War—communism and the atomic bomb—only to offer an easy solution. It concludes by inviting the reader to "adopt a child . . . for ten dollars a month" in any of the fourteen countries in which the CCF runs orphanages. The advertisement thus resolves imaginatively what cannot be so easily resolved politically: while the average individual can't protect America from the atom bomb, the advertisement suggests that, for a modest sum, she can save Asia and thus indirectly herself. The advertisement invites the reader to save herself from atomic war, and the child from communism, by extending the American family out into the world. The photograph of the white couple holding the starving child makes

Handwritten margin notes: "- About Schmidt", "- missionary impulse", "- problems of adopters"

this solution easy by offering a model of behavior with which the reader can identify visually.

An advertisement from 1954 (Figure 14), the year Ho Chi Minh's communist forces defeated the French at Dien Bien Phu, suggests that Americans must step in as parents to Asian children in order to prevent the communists from doing so first. Under a menacing headline—"This Picture is as DANGEROUS as it is PITIFUL!"—it presents a picture of a stern, well-fed Asian man holding an emaciated, naked Asian boy on his knee. The text warns that the photograph "threatens to take from us all that we hold most dear—life, liberty and the pursuit of happiness." The text under the photograph interprets the image for the reader by identifying "the misery of human beings" as "the most powerful weapon in the hands of the Communists." The image and text together invoke the threat that an Asian man—a communist—will assume the paternal obligation of feeding this starving child and thus manipulate him into accepting communism. Like the earlier ad, this one also appeals to the reader to step into the world of the photograph, only this time to displace the Asian man as parent to the Asian child. In that same year the Save the Children Federation made the equation between adoption and the U.S. political and military expansion into Southeast Asia more explicit in an advertisement that suggested that Americans needed to step in and save the French after their inglorious defeat in Vietnam. Using a melodramatic headline that recalled a telegram—"Dateline: Dien Bien Phu. The Republic of France regrets to inform you . . ."—the advertisement implied that the French had given up fighting communism in Vietnam and were appealing to Americans to take over that job.

One can imagine a multitude of meanings that "adoption" carried for the people who participated in the Christian Children's Fund program; like Cousins's assertion of a single global family in relation to the Hiroshima Maidens project, the parent-child relationship is inevitably polysemous. One way to read the CCF's "adoption" program is as an invitation to participate in the Cold War struggle for Asia. The advertisements conclude on a note of vigorous affirmation and a pledge to take action: at the bottom of the page, the 1954 advertisement offers a box for the reader to check off that says, "YES! I want to do what I can to help the starving, homeless children of the world," with a blank space to fill in for the amount of money that the reader will include. CCF newsletters and books carried numerous stories of ordinary individuals making quiet, yet heroic, efforts to save children from poverty, starvation, and the consequences of communism. Adopting a child made the reader a

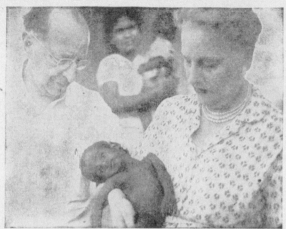

Am I My Brother's Keeper?

IN INDIA I asked myself this question when I saw thousands of homeless sleeping in the streets of Calcutta and Bombay. When I saw half starved children and "hunger limp" babies like the one above.

IN KOREA (My schedule did not permit me to examine the 28 orphanages in which CCF assists Korean children). There is only ugliness and misery in Korea. Wandering refugees, little ragged children, destroyed homes. There is hardly a family not broken, fathers taken prisoners or shot, mothers abused and carried off or left dead behind a broken wall. A destroyed country of rubble, rags, disease, hunger and human misery.

IN JAPAN in the Elizabeth Saunders Home for GI babies, deserted by their American fathers, and 18 other CCF orphanages, all over-crowded.

IN GERMANY where I saw some of the several million people who are refugees in their own country. Those who escaped from East Germany won their freedom at great cost. Few families escaped intact. Children, parents, wives and husbands shot down or dragged off to labor camps. Those who escaped are destitute. They can't find work and have inadequate food and shelter.

The sick little children of India, the wandering orphans of Korea, that flaxen haired German miss, who saw her father killed, does God charge me with their plight? I have returned from overseas with the realization that the Communists care enough to make very successful capital of democracy's failures and with the strong conviction that we Americans can not close our eyes or stop our ears to the cry of a hungry child anywhere in the world — black, brown, yellow or white. The hungry children of the world are more dangerous to us than the atom bomb.

CCF assists children in 97 orphanages in the following countries: Borneo, Brazil, Burma, Finland, Formosa, Indonesia, India, Italy, Japan, Jordan, Korea, Lapland, Lebanon, Malaya, Okinawa, Pakistan, Philippines, Puerto Rico, United States and Western Germany. You can adopt a child in any of these countries for ten dollars a month and the child's name, address, picture and information about the child will be furnished. Correspondence with the child is invited. Smaller gifts are equally welcome. God sees not the coin but the heart that gives it.

For information write to:

Dr. J. Calvitt Clarke
CHRISTIAN CHILDREN'S FUND, INC.
RICHMOND 4, VIRGINIA

Figure 13. Christian Children's Fund advertisements appealed to Americans to "adopt" Asian children. (Courtesy Christian Children's Fund)

Figure 14. "This Picture is as DANGEROUS as it is PITIFUL!": advertisement for Christian Children's Fund. (Courtesy Christian Children's Fund)

participant in this large, dramatic historical struggle, and because the CCF asked the sponsors to support the child for at least a year, adoption entailed a commitment rather than just a gesture.

In one sense, the advertisements figure participation in terms of consumption: for $10 a month, the reader can purchase a child, protection from communism, and relief from a sense of political powerlessness. John C. Caldwell captured this sense of adoption as commodity consumption in his 1957 book on the CCF, *Children of Calamity,* when he described the cables CCF headquarters in Virginia regularly sent to the Hong Kong office. They sound like nothing so much as department store back orders: "Need 4,000 more children!" "Rush me 500 orphans," "Need 200 Koreans, 10 Japanese mixed-blood, 50 Chinese, 10 Arabs." The advertisements make purchasing a political act, and purchasing the idea of the family becomes a mechanism for creating ties between the U.S. and Asia.[15]

The "adoption" process also opened a route to participation in terms of education, in ways that echoed the contemporary discourse of travel. In checking the box marked "YES! I want to do what I can," the reader expressed a willingness to learn more about the countries in which the children resided. The exchange of information played an important role in the "adoptive" relation. American "parents" and their "adoptees" exchanged personal narratives, letters, and photographs, thereby fostering a personal bond of intimacy that incorporated the Asian child, emotionally and textually, into the American family. This new family thus became a two-way site of education: the parents learned about the misery that communism bred, and the child learned about the material abundance and personal generosity that the capitalist "free world" offered. Like so many other forms of middlebrow culture, these "adoptive" families generated an interest in and knowledge about Asia that Washington deemed necessary for the success of its foreign policy. The CCF also linked its program to tourism more directly. CCF newsletters printed many reports of "parents" who had traveled to the far reaches of Asia and elsewhere to visit their "children," and had seen firsthand how the people they were helping lived. CCF adoptions provided an impetus for Americans to go beyond an imaginary tour of Asia and, like Cousins's ideal tourist, embark on their own fact-finding expeditions.

Finally, "adopting" a child enabled a sense of participation in U.S. foreign policy. At the most abstract level, one can see the donation of funds as a confirmation of support for the enormous financial costs of the containment/integration foreign policy agenda. The CCF's appeal to feed starving children meshed with the logic of American food aid to Asia. When India faced widespread famine in 1950, advocates of aid urged Washington to send shipments of wheat, arguing that it offered not only a way to communicate America's concern for the people of Asia (particularly important at a time when the U.S. was being criticized for killing Asians in Korea), but also an opportunity to depict the United States as motivated by positive ideals other than anticommunism. CCF advertisements reinforced the logic of this aid effort and provided an opportunity for Americans to participate in it at the individual level. Both the CCF and Washington understood "adoption" as a form of foreign aid. The CCF worked to make the connection between its program and government policies clear to potential parents by promoting its efforts as part of Eisenhower's People-to-People program. At the same time, the State Department recognized "adoption" programs as part of its own Cold War efforts and oversaw them through its Advisory Committee on Voluntary Foreign Aid. In all these ways, "adoption" linked political participation and political obligation to feelings of pleasure, love, and domestic fulfillment.[16]

This representation of the Cold War as a sentimental project of family formation served a doubly hegemonic function. These families created an avenue through which Americans excluded from other discourses of nationhood could find ways to identify with the nation as it undertook its world-ordering projects of containing communism and expanding American influence. Like Dooley's medical mission in Laos, the CCF adoptive families helped to integrate socially marginal people within the United States, as well as Asians outside the nation. At a time when American social and cultural institutions privileged the nuclear family as the ideal form of personal relations and stigmatized those who did not marry and have children as selfish or perverted, the opportunity to "adopt" a child opened up the institution of the family in inclusive ways. The expansion of the American family out into Asia enabled those excluded from the national-domestic ideal—the elderly, single, divorced, homosexual—to feel that they were integral parts of American society. CCF literature published regular testimonials on the pleasures of "parenthood" by childless and unmarried individuals. The discourse of adoptive family formation thus performed a dual function: it helped construct a broadly inclusive historical bloc within the U.S. at the same time that it cultivated support for the integration of noncommunist nations around the world.

SOUTH PACIFIC

Richard Rodgers and Oscar Hammerstein brought the topic of trans-racial adoption to the attention of millions of Americans in their 1949 musical *South Pacific*. Rodgers and Hammerstein occupied a privileged position in postwar American culture. From their first musical collaboration in 1943 through Hammerstein's death in 1960, they were the most successful songwriting team in American history. During their peak years of 1943–1952 their musicals dominated Broadway, and their songs suffused popular musical culture. Together they wrote eleven shows—including *Oklahoma!, State Fair, Carousel, South Pacific, The King and I, Flower Drum Song*, and *The Sound of Music*—that circulated throughout American culture in a variety of formats: as Broadway shows, national touring companies, Hollywood movies, radio broadcasts, TV shows, magazine stories, sheet music, LP (long-playing) recordings, and local theater productions. Critics showered the shows with awards, and civic organizations honored the authors with citations. Millions of ordinary people sang their songs. By the mid-1950s Rodgers and Hammerstein were earning $15 million a year, an amount that even in the age of General Motors made them "decidedly Big Business."[17]

Many contemporaries saw Rodgers and Hammerstein's musicals as expressions of an authentically American national identity, a form of modern folk culture that formed an integral part of the nation's "cultural heritage." As articulators of "America" at a time when the United States was assuming an ever-greater role in global affairs, Rodgers and Hammerstein also represented the nation around the world. One and a half million servicemen saw a special USO production of *Oklahoma!* that toured U.S. military bases in the Pacific in 1945; in 1951 the State Department sent the show to Berlin; and by 1955, commercial companies had staged it in London, South Africa, Sweden, Denmark, Australia, Paris, Rome, Naples, Milan, and Venice. In 1958, as part of the cultural exchange efforts that emerged out of the thaw in Cold War tensions, Moscow accepted the film version of *Oklahoma!* as one of ten American films that it agreed to distribute throughout the Soviet Union. From 1947 through 1956 the Drury Lane Theatre in London staged Rodgers and Hammerstein's shows exclusively. When General George C. Marshall returned from his failed mission to resolve the Chinese civil war in 1947, he announced that Rodgers and Hammerstein's movie musical *State Fair*, which was playing in China at the time, "did more to tell [the Chinese] about America, about its heart and soul and about its people than I could possibly have told them in hours of talking." [18]

South Pacific opened on Broadway in April 1949. Based on James Michener's *Tales of the South Pacific* and starring Mary Martin and Ezio Pinza, it became a phenomenal success. It had a record-breaking five-year run on Broadway, where it won the Pulitzer for drama (as well as the New York Drama Critics Circle Award, eight Tonys, and nine Donaldsons) and then toured nationally and internationally for several years more; for decades it formed a staple of regional, community, and high school theater productions. The show's original cast album, one of the first popular LP records, sold one million copies and held the Number 1 position on the charts for sixty-nine weeks, while the sheet music sold over a million copies in the first four months. The show proliferated throughout print media as well, as magazines and newspapers published interviews with the stars, and *Life* gave it a big photo spread. Even before the movie rights were sold, *South Pacific* earned profits exceeding five million dollars. In 1958, Twentieth Century Fox released *South Pacific* as a film musical starring Mitzi Gaynor and Rossano Brazzi. It garnered three Academy Award nominations, winning for best sound. The soundtrack album, displacing the original cast album, stayed in the U.S. top ten for two years, including fifty-four weeks in the Number 1 spot, and became the biggest-selling soundtrack of the decade with sales of five million.[19]

Much postwar middlebrow culture, including Dooley's jungle doctor narratives and Michener's travel essays, condemned racial prejudice and urged Americans to become more tolerant; *South Pacific* suggested how they might in fact be able to overcome their racism. The show and the movie (the latter a faithful adaptation of the former) focus on two love stories culled from Michener's collection of nineteen sketches. The narrative revolves primarily around Ensign Nellie Forbush, an enthusiastic young nurse from Little Rock, Arkansas, stationed in the South Pacific during World War II. When the story opens Nellie is a self-described "fugitive," having fled the confines of her Southern home and joined the Army in order "to see what the world was like" and "meet different kinds of people." On the island Nellie falls in love with Emile De Becque, a wealthy, sophisticated, and considerably older French plantation owner. After accepting his proposal of marriage, she discovers to her horror that he has fathered two children with a now-deceased Polynesian woman, thereby confronting Nellie with a racial dilemma. In Michener's more explicit *Tales,* the children pose a "nigger" problem: "Emile De Becque had lived with the nigger. He had nigger children. If she married him, they would be her step-daughters." Overwhelmed by the very prejudices she had tried to flee, she calls the marriage off. When Emile embarks on a life-threatening mission for the American military, she realizes her love for him is more powerful than her prejudice, and when he returns alive she welcomes him back and accepts his children as her own. The show ends with Nellie deciding to marry Emile and live on his Pacific plantation with her new, mixed-race family. The subplot follows a similar racial line. It tells the story of Joe Cable, a Marine lieutenant who falls in love with Liat, the beautiful daughter of an entrepreneurial local woman named Bloody Mary who has her eye out for an American son-in-law. Sharing Nellie's racial antipathies, the Princeton-educated Cable initially refuses to marry Liat because he can't imagine bringing her home to his family. Love eventually conquers his racism as well, and he decides to marry Liat and remain in the Pacific with her; before he can carry out his plan, however, he dies on the mission with Emile.[20]

South Pacific uses much of its dramatic energy to repudiate American racism and to establish love as the only force capable of eradicating it. The song "You've Got to Be Carefully Taught" voices the show's explicitly antiracist message. In singing it, Joe Cable rejects Nellie's claim that her revulsion at the thought of Emile's Polynesian lover is natural and "something that is born in me." Instead, as he explains to a confused Emile, both he and Nellie have been indoctrinated with racial prejudices. Raised since childhood "to hate all the people your relatives hate," they are victims of a perverted pedagogy of "hate and fear": as Southerners, and as Americans, they have been "taught to be afraid" of "people whose eyes are oddly made" and "people whose skin is a different shade." The drama of the show revolves not only around the process of romantic couple-formation—which forms the central narrative trajectory of most musicals—but also around Nellie's and Cable's gradual overcoming of their racism.[21]

South Pacific pairs this antiracist theme with one focusing on America's expansion into the Pacific. The show presents Nellie as a quintessentially American heroine who leaves home and never returns, opting instead to create a new life in the Pacific. Years later Michener explained that even as he wrote *Tales of the South Pacific* during World War II, he could see that the United States would dramatically expand its presence in the Pacific in the postwar years. He claims that he wrote his stories in part to ease the way for that expansion: he wanted to correct any negative impressions about the Pacific that the war, with its horror stories about Bataan and Guadalcanal, produced. "If America was committed to the retention of bases in the Pacific," he wrote, "then many Americans would have to live in that region, and living there would not be as bad if silly preconceptions were not allowed to prejudice first judgments." Describing his tales as a kind of promotional literature for postwar expansion, he pointed out that "the standards of living and enjoyment were greater than comparable standards in many parts of the States." [22]

Although *South Pacific* appealed to still-fresh memories of the war, the show's focus on the American military presence in the Pacific also resonated with postwar expansion. In the years after 1945, the U.S. assumed control over virtually the entire Pacific. The U.S. already controlled Hawaii, Wake, Midway, Guam, and Samoa as a result of its first wave of Pacific expansion in the nineteenth century, and over the course of World War II it established military bases on numerous other Pacific islands as it advanced upon Japan. As part of its occupation of Japan, the U.S. assumed control over the Japanese main islands, as well as the outlying island chains of the Ryukyus, the Bonins, and the Volcanos; it claimed near-total authority over Okinawa for an indefinite period of time and turned the island into a major military base. In 1946, the U.S. obtained 99-year leases on more than twenty bases in the Philippines. In 1947, it formalized its control over key islands within the Micronesian archipelagos of the Caroline, Marshall, and Mariana Islands (including the Bikini atoll on which it tested atomic bombs in 1946) when they became U.S. trust territories. These island bases complemented those that the U.S. maintained on the Asian mainland: in China, until Chiang Kai-shek's defeat in 1949, and in Korea, where U.S. forces occupied the southern half of the peninsula. As this expansion unfolded, U.S. policymakers and journalists resurrected the nineteenth-century imperial idea of the Pacific as an "American lake." Michener participated in the planning for this expansion: before returning to civilian life and publishing *Tales of the South Pacific,* he served as a naval secretary to several Congressional committees that were deliberating the future of American military bases in the South Pacific. The producers of the movie version of *South Pacific,* in turn, benefited from this military presence: they filmed the musical in cooperation with the U.S. Navy, a relationship which received prominent acknowledgment in the opening credits.[23]

South Pacific brings these themes of antiracism and global expansion together via the tropes of family formation and adoption. Set at Emile's plantation, the final scene presents Nellie and the children, Ngana and Jerome, awaiting the Frenchman's return from his secret mission. The scene triumphantly resolves Nellie's moral crisis: she has overcome her racism and decided to marry Emile and accept his mixed-race children as her own. No longer a parochial Southern racist, Nellie is on her way to becoming a tolerant citizen of the world. This final scene serves as the musical's ideological center, because it shows that Americans can overcome their racism and that this will enable them to move into the Pacific with a clean conscience. Overcoming racism becomes here a precondition for successful expansion, and expansion the reward for overcoming racism. At the heart of this process lies Nellie's embrace of motherhood.

The final scene illustrates how representing U.S.-Asian relations in familial terms could carry a powerfully idealistic, even utopian, charge. It shows the creation of an international community that transcends the potentially divisive boundaries of race, nation, sex, and generation. Nellie's new family brings together whites and Asians; an American, a European, and two Pacific Islanders; male and female; young and old. Music provides the glue that binds Nellie, as a mother, to this community. The musical number begins when the children demand that Nellie sing a song for them. In asking her to sing "Dites Moi" the children invite Nellie into their motherless family, since the song is one that they have previously sung with their father. In the middle of the song Emile returns and joins in, and the lovers realize they have surmounted all the obstacles to their love. The number shows the work of community formation in progress: Nellie, unsure of the words, struggles to remember them as Emile and the children help her. Nellie's learning process here invokes and repudiates her previous education in racism that "Carefully Taught" exposed: by singing with the children, Nellie expresses her willingness to abandon her prejudices. Nellie is Hammerstein's answer to Schlesinger's call for Americans to abandon their "sin of racial pride." Making her Broadway debut in the same year that *The Vital Center* was published, she shows that Americans can change, they can overcome their racism, and they can create a community that includes people of other nations and races.[24]

Nellie's embrace of motherhood and her entrance into an international community also works, however, as a claim to power. The scene opens with Nellie looking out over the ocean with the children and naming the different kinds of ships as they steam off to attack the Japanese. Previous scenes have made clear that this attack will be the turning point of the Pacific War, the moment when the U.S. launches the offensive that will lead to Japanese defeat. The scene thus presents us with the origins of America's postwar dominance of the Pacific. Yet it represses this military power as soon as it invokes it: even as Nellie identifies the ships, she turns away from them and tells the children that the soldiers will now be largely absent from the island. As part of this deflection away from militarism, Nellie exercises greater authority in this scene as a mother than she has in the rest of the show as a military officer and nurse. No longer the "knucklehead" that her friends call her, Nellie acts for the first time with an air of responsibility and efficiency. She commands the children to do her bidding, even in her absence: "Now you have to learn to mind me when I talk to you, and be nice to me, too. Because I love you very much." Repudiating her racism, Nellie declares maternal love in its place.[25]

Nellie reinforces her maternal claim of authority with a physical gesture: she puts a hand on each child's head and forces them into their seats at the table. Director Joshua Logan deemed this gesture so central to the scene's meaning that in rehearsals for the Broadway show he demonstrated how it should be played ("more forcefully"), made actress Mary Martin practice it, and then reproduced it in the movie version, which he also directed (Figures 15 and 16). While playful, the gesture —and the physical response it produces in the children—suggests the authority that maternal love bestows on those who wield it. It makes visible the subtextual claim to power that animates the entire sentimental discourse of love, family, and adoption. As a form of what Richard Brodhead has called "disciplinary intimacy," maternal love becomes here an instrument for exercising authority over others. By repudiating her racism, Nellie does not so much sacrifice her authority as gain added influence over her new Asian children.[26]

The difference between the beginning of this scene, when Nellie looks out at the warships, and the end, when the family has been united, suggests a historical development in the nature of American power in the Pacific. Formerly based on military strength, it will now be exercised through maternal values of nurture and protection. Pushing military force into the background, the scene visualizes the idea that familial love, not global military power, explains America's presence in Asia: America's job is to love, feed, and support others, not dominate them. This scene suggests that while the United States may have won World War II on the basis of military strength, the Cold War, as a struggle for allegiances, demands the skills of a parent, not a soldier.

Even as Nellie's new-found maternity enables her to disavow overt racial prejudice, it also maintains the white-Asian racial hierarchy by mapping racial differences onto differences of age. The musical distin-

Figure 15. Maternal love as a claim to power: director Joshua Logan demonstrates how actress Mary Martin can "play it more forcefully" for *South Pacific* on stage, 1949. (Photofest)

guishes between two kinds of love: romantic love, which Nellie feels for Emile and Joe Cable feels for Liat, and maternal love, which Nellie feels for the children. These different kinds of love work differently within the narrative. While the romantic love that Nellie and Cable feel for another adult enables them to lay down their burden of racial prejudice, only Nellie's maternal love for the children offers a sustainable model of in-

Figure 16. "Now you have to learn to mind me. . . . Because I love you very much": Nellie Forbush (Mitzi Gaynor) displays her maternal love in the film *South Pacific,* 1958. (Museum of Modern Art/Film Stills Archive)

terracial relations. *South Pacific* endorses a feminine, maternal love over a masculine, erotic love as the basis of relations between Asians and Americans: it kills off Cable before he can marry Liat, while clearing the way for Nellie's love for her step-children. Nellie's maternal love foregrounds the politically resonant ideals of responsibility and obligation for others in ways that Cable's erotic love does not. It also echoes the structure of *Madame Butterfly,* which likewise forecloses on the erotic cross-racial love between adults by killing off Butterfly, while sustaining the parental love that Pinkerton and his white American wife feel for Butterfly and Pinkerton's mixed-race child. In preventing a cross-racial marriage, the musical further suggests the limits of the liberal imagination on race. Cable and Liat's marriage would not only break the lingering taboo against miscegenation, it would also undermine the racial hierarchy that Nellie's parental relationship maintains in disguise.

　　South Pacific's multiracial, multinational family embodies a variation on the U.S.-French-Vietnamese relationship that was being forged at the same time. In 1950—the year after the show opened on Broadway—

Washington began openly financing its French ally's colonial war in Vietnam and delivering aid to its puppet government in Saigon. After the
French defeat at Dien Bien Phu in 1954—the year *South Pacific* closed
on Broadway—the U.S. took over their war against the communists in
the North. *South Pacific* evokes the French colonial situation in Southeast Asia directly when it identifies Bloody Mary and Liat as Tonkinese
—that is, as natives of colonial Vietnam whom French planters have
brought to the Pacific islands as indentured laborers. When *South Pacific*
opened on Broadway, audiences might not have been fully conscious of
their nation's emerging relationship with the French in Indochina. But
over the course of its five-year run and the years that it toured nationally, public awareness of America's involvement in Southeast Asia grew.
In 1955, a year after Dien Bien Phu fell to the North Vietnamese and
South Pacific closed in New York, Norman Cousins published an editorial in the *Saturday Review* describing Americans as "up to our hips" in
the war in Vietnam and urging his readers to educate themselves about
that part of the world.[27]

The final scene figures this alliance as a product of American abundance and protection. At the end of "Dites Moi," Nellie gathers the
French and Asian characters around her at the table. Generous and benevolent, she bestows her healthy sexuality upon the graying Emile and
doles out soup to her Asian dependents. Like Washington's aid programs
in Indochina, this family invigorates an aging and weary France, gives
provincial America access to the colonial sources of French wealth and
prestige, and maintains the childlike Asians in a condition of security
and dependence. *South Pacific* anticipates the postwar alliance of Americans and French designed to manage, as it were, Indochina's transition
from colonial status to independence. It visualizes and narrativizes America's emerging role in Southeast Asia. (The musical does not display mi-
raculous powers of foresight, however: already in 1943, when Michener
wrote *Tales of the South Pacific,* political observers could see that the
postwar Pacific would see both the retreat of the European colonial powers and an increased American presence.) The Broadway show and the
Hollywood film end with an identical arrangement of characters. In a familial gesture suggestive of both containment and integration, the American Nellie and the French Emile join hands with each other and encir-
cle their small Asian children in the arc of their arms (Figure 17).

Forty-seven years after writing *Tales of the South Pacific,* Michener
suggested that the war in Vietnam always existed as a latent subtext in
the musical. When Asian American author Gish Jen wrote an article in

Figure 17. A familial gesture suggesting both containment and integration concludes the film *South Pacific,* 1958. (Museum of Modern Art/Film Stills Archive)

the *New York Times* accusing *South Pacific* of perpetuating stereotypes of Asian women as delicate, docile, and willing to sacrifice themselves for their men, Michener responded with a letter to the editor in which he begged to differ. He described Bloody Mary as "a 1944 prevision of those stubborn little Vietnamese women of 1965 who played a major role in defeating the entire American Army." In his autobiography Michener described the real Bloody Mary, a Tonkinese worker he encountered on a French plantation in the New Hebrides. Her name derived not from her penchant for chewing betel nuts, as in his stories, but from her politics: she was committed to the "advocacy of Tonkinese rights" and possessed of a "strong resistance to exploitation." This Bloody Mary was a "potential revolutionary" who planned to return to Vietnam at World War II's end in order "to oppose French colonialism." As America's involvement in Vietnam escalated into war during the 1960s, Michener wondered if American leaders realized that "the enemy they were fighting consisted of millions of determined people like Bloody Mary." Michener and Hammerstein together repressed this historical Bloody

Mary and transformed her revolutionary anticolonial politics into a sentimental story of family formation.[28]

If *South Pacific* imagined the integration of the U.S., France, and Vietnam into an international political alliance, it likewise imagined the domestic integration of middle-class white women. *South Pacific* gave American women, and mothers in particular, a prominent role in the postwar national project of expansion. Nellie serves to assuage the wartime fears, sparked by Philip Wylie's charge of "Momism" in his 1943 bestseller *Generation of Vipers,* that the American wife and mother posed a threat to national security. Wylie accused mothers of emotionally smothering their sons and thus producing dependent, psychologically weak men who were unfit for military service. Michael Rogin has suggested that the wartime anxiety over Momism carried over into the Cold War, where it fused with anxiety over communism to become a central feature of containment-culture texts such as *The Manchurian Candidate.* But the integrationist side of the Cold War exacted different demands that gave a positive value to Mom's "natural" qualities. Her ability to nurture, feel empathy, and exercise moral authority through love and persuasion became a political asset. By 1957 Wylie shifted his critique away from "Momism" and toward "whitemanism"—that is, racism—as the source of the nation's vulnerability. Like so many other contemporary political observers, Wylie condemned racism for alienating the colored people of the world whose alliance the U.S. needed. *South Pacific*'s Nellie shows that rather than hindering the power of the state, Mom can help it expand, precisely because her maternal qualities allow her to free herself from the constraints of "whitemanism." [29]

South Pacific also spoke to the changing social roles of women in the postwar period. In her transition from nurse to mother, Nellie enacts in miniature the postwar move of millions of women out of military and defense jobs and back into the home. Nellie joined the Navy to escape the confinements of Little Rock, and her desires to have new experiences are potentially rebellious; she raises the possibility of a female flight from commitment akin to the male version that Dooley undertakes. Nellie expresses her independence when she sings "I'm Gonna Wash That Man Right Outta My Hair," a rousing, proto-feminist song in praise of female autonomy and choice. Nellie does indeed escape Little Rock—but not domesticity. The show redirects her energies into the service of the nation by channeling them into a domestic sphere that now encompasses the world. By giving Nellie—as wife and mother, not as military officer—a role in the expansion of America's global power, the show helps defuse the discontent of real women who resented their ouster from well-paid jobs and their confinement within the home. *South Pacific* symbolically maintains the social order within the United States by projecting potentially disruptive elements out into the Pacific. Just as the CIA and the International Rescue Committee found a way to put Dooley into the nation's service despite his homosexuality by sending him to Laos, *South Pacific* likewise puts Nellie's anarchic energies into the service of the nation. The musical illustrates how postwar domestic ideology could serve as an expansionist ideology. Like the gesture of familial embrace that closes the show, domestic ideology intertwined containment and integration: it contained women's desires for independence by enlisting them in the project of international integration.

Contemporary viewers did read *South Pacific* as a commentary on domestic integration—but of black Americans, not white women. Despite its wartime setting and the absence of any major black characters, *South Pacific* was seen as speaking to the nascent civil rights movement. In some sense the show made the question of black-white relations easier to address by deflecting it out into the Pacific and recasting it into Asian-white terms. Liberal white reviewers in the mainstream press often embraced "You've Got to Be Carefully Taught" as "a kind of international anthem for racial tolerance," and although some described its philosophy as "elementary," they also saw it as a "bold" and "remarkable" statement for a Broadway lyricist to make in 1949. For years the song served as an inspiration to civil rights activists who struggled to put their racial politics into practice: Frank Power, the headmaster of Charlestown High School in Boston, kept Hammerstein's lyrics under the glass top of his desk, where he could read them every day as he oversaw the busing of black students into his overwhelmingly white school during the late 1960s and early 1970s. As an educator, Power no doubt appreciated the song's take on racism as a lesson that could be unlearned.[30]

After the Little Rock school crisis of 1957, viewers around the world read *South Pacific* as a commentary on Jim Crow segregation. When Governor Orval Faubus defied the Supreme Court's 1954 *Brown vs. Board of Education* ruling and called out the National Guard to halt the integration of Little Rock's Central High School, he created a global public relations disaster: newspapers around the world published photographs and articles about the confrontation, which did enormous damage to U.S. prestige, especially in the decolonizing world. *South Pacific* helped make Little Rock an icon of American racism. As President Eisenhower later wrote in his memoirs, Faubus's "outrageous action called to my mind the first act of the Rodgers and Hammerstein musical *South Pacific* in which the hero, a Frenchman, mistakenly calls the heroine's American hometown 'Small Rock.' Before September 1957, that line was meaningless for foreign audiences. Thereafter, no one anywhere would miss the point: the name of Little Rock, Arkansas, would become known around the world." The State Department, in an effort to turn this knowledge of Little Rock to its advantage, enlisted *South Pacific* in its campaign to improve the nation's reputation. At the 1958 Brussels World's Fair, the State Department tried to address head-on the controversy over American race relations with a social scientific exhibit based on the theme of "Unfinished Work." Through the display of photographs, newspaper headlines, statistical charts, and explanatory text, the exhibit acknowledged racism and segregation as problems that the nation was working to remedy. The State Department closed the show down, however, after it generated too much controversy at home, especially among Southern politicians. In its place the State Department arranged for screenings of *South Pacific,* through which it presented an antiracist message in a more muted form.[31]

Mainstream black publications also used the show to publicize the issue of racism. The casting of the African American actress Juanita Hall as the Tonkinese Bloody Mary facilitated the show's conflation of Asian-white relations abroad and black-white relations at home (Figure 18). *South Pacific* made Hall a star—she played a major character, sang two prominent songs, and was the only actor to appear in the Broadway version, the national touring company, and the movie version. In interviews with the black press, Hall praised the show for saying "a great deal" about racial prejudice and for being so "effective" in delivering its message of tolerance. *Ebony* profiled Hall in a lengthy story in 1950, and in 1958 it published a photo essay about the movie that emphasized the racial story lines, the advocacy of interracial marriage, and the multiracial cast. The article concluded by quoting a prediction by the actor who played Joe Cable that "*South Pacific* should make more people understand the need for free, unrestricted association between races and religions." Headlined "South Pacific: Lavish Film Scores Racial Hate among U.S. Troops," the story resonated with African American experiences of racism in the armed forces during World War II and the Korean War, the violence that had been visited upon returning black World War II veterans, and the recent desegregation of the U.S. military.[32]

White viewers with more conservative racial politics, in contrast, found *South Pacific* offensive. One audience member at the New Ha-

Figure 18. African American actress Juanita Hall as the Tonkinese Bloody Mary in the film *South Pacific*, 1958. (Photofest)

ven tryouts, calling "Carefully Taught" an "ugly" and "untimely" song, urged Rodgers and Hammerstein to cut it. Two segregationist Georgia state legislators, after seeing a performance in 1953, condemned the song as a "justification of interracial marriage" and introduced legislation to outlaw such works of entertainment that had "an underlying philosophy inspired by Moscow." The South African government shared this view, and in 1964 it banned *South Pacific* as a "plea for racial mix-

ing." The variety of critical and institutional responses to the show, from
support in Washington to condemnation in Georgia, point to the complex position that questions of race occupied in the Cold War's ideological landscape.[33]

THE SOCIAL PRACTICE AND MEANINGS OF ADOPTION

Trans-racial adoption was not just a story that Americans in the 1950s
liked to tell themselves, but also a social practice that many of them
lived. This was especially true for the middlebrow intellectuals of Buck's
County, Pennsylvania. When Pearl Buck launched the Welcome House
adoption agency in 1949—the year *South Pacific* opened on Broadway
—she was already the mother of two adopted bi-racial children. Oscar
Hammerstein and James Michener shared Buck's commitment to cross-
racial adoption as a social practice. Hammerstein, of course, knew Michener as the author of *Tales of the South Pacific;* he also knew Buck
through her writing, having read *The Good Earth* aloud to his wife Dorothy in 1931 when she was in the hospital giving birth to their first son.
In 1949, Michener approached Hammerstein for his help in supporting
Welcome House. Hammerstein agreed, and, when his daughter Alice
adopted one of the agency's first children, he became one of the first
Welcome House grandfathers. Hammerstein went on to serve as president of the Board of Directors from 1953 until his death in 1960. Richard Rodgers, as a birthday present for Hammerstein in 1955, paid off the
mortgage on Welcome House, and Hammerstein's wife Dorothy worked
with Welcome House as a tireless fund-raiser. Michener also served with
Hammerstein on the Board of Directors and, with his second wife, Vange
Nord, adopted two boys from Welcome House. Michener and Nord divorced before the second adoption became final, however, and they returned the child to Welcome House. Other middlebrow cultural figures
also adopted Asian children: Norman Cousins took one of the Hiroshima Maidens into his family, and Yul Brynner, star of Rodgers and
Hammerstein's *The King and I,* adopted two girls from Vietnam in the
mid-1970s.[34]

Middlebrow intellectuals were not the only Americans who adopted
Asian children. International adoptions arose after World War II as a direct consequence of the global expansion of U.S. military power. Stationed in countries around the world, U.S. soldiers fathered and then
abandoned children that host countries neither wanted nor had the resources to care for. A series of legislative acts, including the War Brides

Act (1945) and the Displaced Persons Act (1948), allowed Americans to adopt European children outside of normal immigration quotas. The Korean War, in combination with the passage of the Immigration and Nationality Act of 1952, which lifted the racial bar on Asian immigration, cleared the way for the adoption of Asian children. Two legislative acts of 1953 authorized a number of nonquota visas for orphans, and in 1957 amendments were made to the Immigration and Nationality Act that authorized unlimited orphan visas. The passage of the 1953 and 1957 acts permanently shifted the primary countries of origin from Europe to Asia. Between 1953 and 1963, Americans adopted 8,812 children from Asia. South Korea, whose families and social welfare system had been decimated by war, provided the majority of these children. Harry Holt, a prosperous Oregon farmer, gained publicity in December 1956 when he arranged what he called a "babylift" mission that flew ninety-one Korean children to the U.S. for adoption before emergency measures allowing special entry for Amerasian children expired. He and his wife then created Holt International Children's Services, the first U.S. agency to handle international adoptions. In the late 1950s Buck's Welcome House also began coordinating international adoptions and began finding families for children from Japan, Korea, Hong Kong, and Taiwan. Over the course of the 1950s, Americans created thousands of multiracial, multinational families in which white parents raised their Asian children.[35]

The white mother that figured so prominently in postwar middlebrow culture, and in the lived experiences of middlebrow intellectuals and other Americans, possessed a complex genealogy and carried a contradictory set of meanings. The figure of the white parent to the nonwhite child has long worked as a trope for representing the ostensibly "natural" relations of hierarchy and domination. The infantilization of racialized Others and marginalized social groups has been a standard rhetorical means of legitimating unequal power relations. Images of trans-racial parenthood figured prominently in American imperialist discourse: as the U.S. acquired colonies in the Pacific and the Caribbean at the turn of the century, political cartoonists regularly represented Puerto Rico, Cuba, and the Philippines as children subject to the discipline of an American parent. As a practice, trans-racial or trans-ethnic adoptions have also served as a means of social control. In the early twentieth century, Progressive reformers promoted the adoption of urban, ethnic, immigrant children by middle-class white women as a way to prevent these children from becoming threats to the social order.[36]

The parent-child model undergirded the idea of the "special relation-ship" between the U.S. and China. In 1958 Harold Isaacs observed that "peculiarly parental emotions . . . are threaded through the whole mesh of American-Chinese relations." In the early nineteenth century Ameri-cans began to see the Chinese as wards who needed to be protected and guided toward maturity, modernity, and Christianity by benevolent American guardians. Missionaries played a key role in developing these parental emotions and adoption, in turn, played an instrumental role in their activities. In the form of sponsorship, adoption served as a popular fund-raising device and encouraged long-term financial commitments between American congregations and potential Chinese converts. Adop-tion also served as a tool for evangelization and education. Female mis-sionaries often "adopted" destitute Chinese children themselves, which usually meant that they provided funds for the children's support and education while the children continued to live at home, with a Christian Chinese family, or in a missionary-run school. These children not only served as conduits for the missionary into the local community, but also became bearers of missionary values from within Chinese society. Adop-tion thus worked to further the cultural transformation of China along American lines.[37]

This parental logic became a preferred way to solicit support for China during the Sino-Japanese war and World War II. In 1937 *Life* published a photograph of a Chinese baby—its body blackened, its clothes torn, its mouth open in a wail—sitting alone amidst the rubble of Shanghai after a Japanese attack (Figure 19). A classic sentimental image, it captured a profound sense of loss: it represented China as a weak and vulnerable infant, and appealed to an implicitly adult American viewer to extend some kind of parental aid. The photograph, which was widely repro-duced to solicit funds for China relief, points to Henry Luce's power as a shaper of American views of China in the 1930s and 1940s. Born and raised in China as the child of missionaries, Luce used his role as publisher of *Life, Time,* and *Fortune* to further the idea of the "special relationship." For two decades he presented the relationship between the U.S. and China as a parental one: under America's tutelage and Chi-ang Kai-shek's leadership, China would be raised up to become a Chris-tian, democratic, industrial nation that mirrored its American "parent." Millions of Americans, prompted by stories and images like that of the baby in Shanghai, embraced this view of China and developed an in-tense emotional bond with the Chinese people. This long-standing sense of a parent-child relationship helps explain the depth of the emotional

Figure 19. A Chinese baby in the streets of Shanghai after the Japanese bombing, 1937. This image was widely reproduced to raise funds for China relief. (© Corbis)

trauma caused by the "loss" of China in 1949, in which the popular triumph of communism was experienced as a profound rejection of more than a century of parental love.[38]

During the Cold War *Reader's Digest* used adoption to imagine the U.S. relationship with all the people in the capitalist "free world." It published numerous stories about Americans adopting children from China, Japan, Korea, France, Germany, Italy, and Greece, as well as displaced persons from communist Poland and Latvia. Some of these articles were expanded and published as books, such as Helen Doss's *The Family Nobody Wanted* (1954), which charted her and her husband's adoption of twelve children from white, Chinese, Japanese, Filipino, Korean, Mexican, and Native American backgrounds. In these stories the adoptive relationship became a way to figure Americans' acceptance of the worldwide responsibilities, commitments, and obligations which *Reader's Digest* saw as the essence of postwar national identity. The adoptive relationship also served as a way to figure those international obligations as beneficial to the United States: several stories featured children who repaid their parents' love by joining the U.S. military when they grew up and helping the nation defend itself against foreign enemies.[39]

These were not the only meanings that adoption carried in the 1950s, however. Pearl Buck and her supporters saw the adoption of Asian children by white Americans as a socially progressive and antiracist act. A fierce critic of American racism, she saw such adoptions as a practical means of challenging white Americans' assumptions about racial difference and white supremacy. In June 1958, the *Saturday Review* awarded its Anisfield-Wolf Award in Race Relations to Jessie Bennett Sams for her memoir, *White Mother,* in which she told the story of how she and her sister, two black girls living in the South, were adopted and raised by a white woman. Buck, who announced the award, read the memoir as offering a solution to the nation's, and the world's, problem of racial conflict. She advocated trans-racial adoption as a course of action that all concerned Americans could take:

> When any American asks the question of what he—or she—can do to bring an end to prejudice in our country and in the world, that one has only to read 'White Mother.' The answer is there. You do what the white mother did. There are children everywhere in deep need of love and faith and opportunity. The dearth is in white mothers and fathers. I am not saying too much when I declare that were we all to follow in the footsteps of this one white mother, we would need not ask how to achieve peace on earth. Peace would be here.

For Buck, the white mother to the nonwhite child became the emblem of antiracist commitment and the vehicle for achieving racial harmony on a global scale. She advocated motherhood across the racial barrier as an actual step that ordinary Americans could take to reduce global tensions and help solve the anxiety-provoking problems of the postwar world.[40]

As much as Buck's promotion of trans-racial adoption grew out of her long-standing commitment to racial justice, it also grew out of the domestic containment policies that silenced her on more explicitly political issues. As McCarthyist pressures pushed Buck out of the public sphere of foreign policy debates, she retreated into the private, traditionally female sphere of the family. Through her adoption work, she was still able to speak out on the issues of racism and U.S.-Asian relations, although in a less direct way. Other strong critics of American racism also retreated to the domestic sphere in the face of political harassment. During the early 1950s, African American singer Josephine Baker came to the attention of the U.S. State Department when she spoke out against racism during her overseas concerts. Alarmed that she was damaging the nation's reputation, the State Department pressured foreign governments to restrict her speeches, urged the military police in Cuba to interrogate her, and blocked her reentry into the U.S. (she had given up her U.S. citizenship in 1937). Baker succumbed to the pressure, and when she returned to France, where she had lived since the 1920s, she stopped speaking publicly about U.S. race relations. Instead, she decided to create a family that could serve as a model for racial harmony. In 1954, she and her French husband began adopting children of various races and religions, creating what she called a "Rainbow Tribe" family that eventually included twelve children. One can see Buck and Baker as being contained against their will within the familial sphere, where their critical views could be tamed, neutered, and rendered innocuous—that is, domesticated. At the same time, one can also see their adoptive families as safe havens for their political values and actions. In some sense, the practice and advocacy of trans-racial adoption offered a cultural space in which Baker and Buck could sustain and even promote their racial politics in the midst of a political climate that was overtly hostile to them.[41]

OSCAR HAMMERSTEIN II

Hammerstein's involvement with Welcome House, like Buck's creation of the agency, arose from his long-standing social and political convictions. Although not often remembered today as such, Hammerstein was an active participant in the Popular Front and was seen by his contemporaries as a politically and socially engaged artist. With Richard Rodgers, he extended the social consciousness of Popular Front musicals such as Marc Blitzstein's *The Cradle Will Rock* (1937) and Harold Rome's *Pins and Needles* (1937) into the postwar period and transformed the light-hearted musical comedy of the 1920s and 1930s into the "serious musical" of the 1940s and 1950s. Audiences and critics embraced Hammerstein's work precisely because he contravened Moss Hart's famous advice to "Let Western Union carry the messages" and reinvented the musical theater as "a place of ideas and even ideals." Throughout the 1940s and 1950s audiences identified Hammerstein with the struggle against racial prejudice.[42]

Hammerstein merged his aesthetic of social significance with one that privileged emotion and feeling. However much they praised his political views, his critics never let them overshadow what they saw as his greatest skill: his ability to write "desperately sincere and right-minded" songs that were bathed in "sweetness" and that spoke directly to the "hearts of millions" of listeners. Eschewing both the "cleverness" of his predecessors in musical comedy and what he called the "'waste-land' philosophy" of his highbrow literary contemporaries, Hammerstein embraced the label of "sentimentalist." His sentimentality was inseparable from his social consciousness: Hammerstein didn't simply "preach" against racism, he wrote stories and songs that turned the principle of antiracism into a sentimental structure of feeling that audiences could embrace.[43]

By the time he wrote *South Pacific,* Hammerstein had been working to expose and eradicate American racism for over twenty years. Oscar Clendenning Greeley Hammerstein II was born in New York City in 1895, the son of theater manager William Hammerstein and the grandson and namesake of opera impresario Oscar Hammerstein I. After a brief stint at Columbia studying law, Hammerstein began writing songs for the stage: in 1920 he contributed a song to *Tickle Me,* a comedy about a film crew in Tibet, and wrote the book and lyrics for *Always You,* a World War I romance with overtones of *Madame Butterfly.* Hammerstein began using the stage to express his liberal racial politics in 1927, when he created *Show Boat* with Jerome Kern. Although this was the thirteenth musical for which he had written the libretto and lyrics, it was the first since 1920 that he had written without a collaborator and that expressed his own philosophy. Set on the Mississippi River in the 1880s, *Show Boat* foregrounded the tragedies of Jim Crow segregation while treating its black characters with a degree of humanity and sympathy unusual for the time.[44]

During the 1930s and 1940s Hammerstein's commitment to the cause of racial justice drew him into the cultural milieu of the Popular Front, and he took up projects that explored some of the Front's favorite themes. Hammerstein first worked with Paul Robeson, who would become one of the Popular Front's iconic figures, on the 1928 London production of *Show Boat,* a show which provided Robeson with one of his first major stage successes. Robeson subsequently appeared in the 1932 New York revival of the show and in the 1935 film version, and in the process he turned "Ol' Man River," which Hammerstein called "a song of resignation with a protest implied," into one of his trademark songs. As a result of this film collaboration, Hammerstein, Jerome Kern, and director James Whale became interested in making another film as a vehicle for Robeson, and in 1935 they bought the film rights to *Black Maj-*

esty, the radical Trinidadian C. L. R. James's play about Toussaint L'Ouverture. Toussaint, the black revolutionary leader of the 1791 uprising against the French colonial regime in Haiti, was a favorite figure in Popular Front culture, and his story became an allegory for contemporary anticolonial struggles. Initially enthusiastic about the project, Hammerstein's interest faded, and the project died. In 1938 he produced *Glorious Morning,* an antifascist play about a woman modeled on Joan of Arc, another Popular Front hero, and her followers who live in a totalitarian society and die before a firing squad rather than recant their belief in religious freedom. In 1939, Robeson consulted with Hammerstein on the possibility of working together on *John Henry,* a play about the working-class, black folk hero who was yet another typical Popular Front figure; Robeson did appear in this play in 1940, but apparently without Hammerstein's involvement.[45]

Hammerstein became an institutional player in the Popular Front as well, and while working in Hollywood during the 1930s he participated in numerous Popular Front organizations. In 1936 he helped found the pro-Soviet Hollywood Anti-Nazi League, which Larry Ceplund and Steven Englund describe as "the most important Popular Front organization in Hollywood," and worked as chairman of its cultural commission, which organized radio broadcasts, articles, and short films "to combat racial intolerance and thus combat Nazism, which uses intolerance as a weapon to attain power." He served as a founding member of the Hollywood League for Democratic Action, a successor to the Hollywood Anti-Nazi League, and in 1945 he helped create the Independent Citizens' Committee of the Arts, Sciences, and Professions, which promoted "day to day participation" in democratic politics; it was branded by the California Tenney Committee as a "Communist front" organization and singled out by Arthur Schlesinger as the quintessential emblem of liberal fellow-traveling. In 1946 he joined Paul Robeson, Marc Blitzstein, Lena Horne, E. Y. (Yip) Harburg, Alain Locke, Pete Seeger, Woody Guthrie and others as a founding member of People's Songs, which the California legislature's Committee on Un-American Activities described as vital "to Communist proselytizing and propaganda work because of its emphasis on appeal to youth and because of its organization and technique to provide entertainment for organizations and groups as a smooth opening wedge for Marxist-Leninist-Stalinist propaganda." In 1948, he joined the Freedom from Fear Committee to raise money for the legal defense of the Hollywood Ten.[46]

Hammerstein also worked with other liberal organizations that were not specifically connected with the Popular Front but shared its goals of racial justice. In 1942 he helped found the Writers' War Board, which devoted itself to combating racism and anti-Semitism within the United States and pressuring government and private organizations to stop racist practices; its efforts were instrumental in getting the Army to hire black medical personnel and the Red Cross to stop typing blood by racial group. In the 1940s left-liberal intellectuals took on racial blood typing as one of their political issues; by the early 1950s, federal loyalty board members saw it as evidence of communist sympathies.[47]

In 1945 Hammerstein took charge of writing and presenting to the communications industry an essay entitled "The Myth That Threatens America," which urged writers, radio producers, and advertising people to avoid inadvertently perpetuating racism through the use of racial and ethnic stereotypes. In the late 1940s he joined the Authors Guild, which took as one of its aims the abolition of such stereotypes. Hammerstein also joined the NAACP and served as a vice-president of its national board of directors until his death. Hammerstein's antiracist views were perhaps shaped by his own Jewish background and by the experiences of his brother-in-law (his wife's sister's husband), Jerry Watanabe, a Japanese citizen living and working in New York whom the government interned for several months on Ellis Island when the war broke out; Watanabe's daughter lived with the Hammersteins during her father's internment.[48]

Hammerstein's dedication to Popular Front cultural and racial politics culminated in his creation of *Carmen Jones,* an adaptation of Bizet's opera *Carmen* with an all-black cast. The idea first came to him in Hollywood in the mid-1930s when he saw a concert version of *Carmen,* and he began collaborating with Duke Ellington to write a movie with an original score. The choice of Ellington made sense—Ellington himself began planning his own all-black "social significance show" in 1936 and throughout the 1930s there were reports that Ellington's "dream" was to do "a musical with an entire Negro cast." The collaboration didn't work out, however, and Hammerstein shelved the project, returning to it in 1941 when he was at a low point in his career. Hammerstein retained Bizet's score while translating the lyrics into colloquial English and updating the setting to a contemporary World War II parachute factory in the South. Hammerstein "loved" working on the project, the first he had ever written without a commission and a guaranteed producer, and reported that it gave him "more pleasure than anything [he] had written heretofore." *Carmen Jones* opened on Broadway in 1943 to tremendous acclaim and quickly became a runaway success, playing in New York for over a year before embarking on a sixty-city national tour.[49]

Carmen Jones was a triumphant showcase of Popular Front theatrical aesthetics that achieved critical, popular, and commercial success. The show's producers shared a set of social-aesthetic ideals with Orson Welles and John Houseman's Mercury Theater: they democratized elite culture by reworking a classic so as to emphasize its contemporary significance, and they made it available to a broad public through low ticket prices. The show also merged the traditions and aesthetics of African American popular musical culture with those of European high culture, specifically opera, a goal that numerous Popular Front figures —including Duke Ellington, Langston Hughes, Kurt Weill, and Marc Blitzstein—had set out to reach, with mixed results.[50]

Carmen Jones was also an exemplary instance of Popular Front social practice. At first no producer would take the show, claiming it would be too difficult to stage, but in 1942 Billy Rose agreed to take it on and hired John Hammond, the jazz producer and promoter who was active in the Popular Front, to do the casting. This task proved a heroic one: because of the operatic score, none of the established black stars, such as Lena Horne, could sing the parts, and because of the color line, none of the established opera singers were black. Hammond criss-crossed the country in search of African Americans who could sing opera and gradually put together a cast of talented amateurs, many of whom had never appeared on stage before. When the show opened in 1943, the show's program foregrounded the working-class identity of the cast (it referred to the show as "The Triumph of the Obscure") and identified the performers in terms of their jobs: "employed in a Philadelphia camera shop at $15 a week, . . . a checker in the Philadelphia Navy Yard, . . . a New York City policeman, . . . a social worker, . . . a housewife, . . . a chauffeur, . . . a bellhop, . . . a receptionist, . . . a prize fighter."[51]

Critics at left-leaning publications in particular praised the show as a "deeply significant" social act as well as a satisfying aesthetic experience. The *New Masses* declared it "a people's triumph; above all, *the* people's triumph" and praised it for exposing the consequences of segregation by showcasing talent that segregation normally kept out of view. The *Daily Worker* announced it as "a great Negro triumph" that "proves once and for all that the Negro people are prepared to give fresh, rich quality to our operatic and musical comedy stage." *The Worker* saw it as a radical break from traditional Negro musicals that were "replete

with minstrel jokes, Step-n-Fetchits and all the other stock characters."
Hammerstein himself emphasized the social significance of the show in
an advertisement he took out in the *New York Times* in 1946 when the
show returned to New York: he announced his pride in the show because it served as "an illustration of the great musical and dramatic talent to be found among the colored people of the United States. And the
more cities we demonstrate this fact to, the greater will be the achievement of the play." *PM* praised the show for democratizing the high art
of opera, a view shared by many reviewers who commented favorably
on the inexpensive ticket prices that made the show available to a broad
audience.[52]

Highbrow critics, both black and white, more often criticized the
show, less for its racial politics than for its aesthetic politics. Miles Jefferson, writing in the African American journal *Phylon* in 1945, found
the show passable as "entertainment," but disapproved of the "popu-
larization" of Bizet and pointedly compared it unfavorably to the *Carmen* he had seen at the Metropolitan Opera House, thereby affirming his
own credentials as highbrow intellectual. James Baldwin, writing about
the movie version of *Carmen Jones* in *Notes of a Native Son* (1955), also
disapproved of the merging of popular culture with "classic . . . art,"
which he felt to be an effort to present the black American as respectable
by in effect "repudiating any suggestion that Negroes are not white."
Both of these critics pursued the same line of criticism as the New York
intellectuals did in their attack on middlebrow culture in general. James
Agee, writing in the *Partisan Review,* railed against *Carmen Jones* (as
well as Robeson's *Othello* and Rodgers and Hammerstein's *Oklahoma!*)
as "vicious pseudo-folk" culture that in seeking to dissolve the line between "folk" and "classical" art only succeeded in producing "deceit,"
"decay," and "corruption."[53]

Carmen Jones marked the end of one stage in Hammerstein's career
and the beginning of another. Immediately after completing the book
and lyrics for the show in 1942, he got a call from Rodgers inviting him
to work on what would become *Oklahoma!*—a show that brought his
ten-year commercially unsuccessful period to an abrupt end and established him as the most influential lyricist on the Broadway stage. While
it is tempting to see the transition from *Carmen Jones* to *Oklahoma!* as
a sharp break in Hammerstein's career, a moment in which he left his
socially engaged work behind in favor of a safer, tamer form of theater, it
would be a mistake to do so. Hammerstein used his success and celebrity
to support his commitments to Popular Front ideals even as he estab-

lished himself within the cultural politics of the Cold War. From the position of relative safety that his financial and commercial success earned him, Hammerstein hired and gave moral support to actors, such as Howard Da Silva and Hy Kraft, who had been accused and blacklisted by the House Un-American Activities Committee (HUAC), and defended Paul Robeson in a television interview.[54]

Hammerstein also publicly announced his agreement with the racial politics of the Communist Party. In 1948 he defended himself from charges of inadvertent racism in an unusual place—the *Daily Worker*. A columnist for the Communist Party newspaper, while praising a revival of *Show Boat* overall, suggested that Rodgers and Hammerstein delete some of the "Uncle Tom business" that presented "the Negro as the object of patronizing ridicule" so that the show would not inadvertently "help the Rankins and the other monstrosities on our national scene." (Rep. John Rankin of Mississippi was a key member of HUAC who established it as a permanent investigative committee in 1945; he expressed sympathy for the Ku Klux Klan and proposed the 1947 investigation of Hollywood.) Rodgers and Hammerstein responded with a lengthy reply that the *Daily Worker* published the next month. In a letter "not written to complain" but with "the attitude of welcoming a chance to say these things on the general topic of the stereotype evil," they offered their letter as a "clarification of [their] own ideas about 'Jimcrowism' and 'Uncle Tomism' on the stage." Insisting that "these ideas, we are certain, coincide with yours," they proceeded to explain in some detail why the show "could never be considered as anything but pro-Negro and anti-Jimcrow." This public pledge of agreement with the Communist Party newspaper is significant because it took place in 1948—after the Truman Doctrine had established anticommunism as an ideological foundation of U.S. foreign policy, after Truman had instituted loyalty tests in the State Department, after the attorney general's list had been drawn up, after HUAC had begun its investigations of communism in Hollywood, and after the Hollywood Ten had been tried and convicted.[55]

Throughout the 1940s and 1950s Hammerstein continued to put his racial politics into practice by writing librettos and songs that not only created a space for black actors on Broadway but also propelled them into stardom. *Show Boat* gave Paul Robeson an early starring role and provided him with one of his favorite protest songs. Juanita Hall achieved fame as Bloody Mary in *South Pacific* and Madame Liang in *Flower Drum Song*. *Carmen Jones* launched Muriel Smith on a successful acting and singing career, and she went on to achieve stardom in Europe by playing Bloody Mary in *South Pacific* and Lady Thiang in *The King and I* in London. The movie version of *Carmen Jones* made Dorothy Dandridge the first black actor to earn an Academy Award nomination as a star. Some of these actors, including Hall, Smith, and Dandridge, never again found roles as complex and satisfying as those that Hammerstein wrote for them—in large part because of Broadway and Hollywood's adherence to the color line—and eventually faded from the acting scene. That they could not sustain the stardom that they first achieved performing Hammerstein's work indicates how far ahead of his contemporaries Hammerstein was in his commitment to African American advancement on the stage.

Although McCarthyism affected Broadway less than it did Hollywood, Hammerstein's racial and cultural politics did draw the attention of the official communist-hunters. In 1953 Hammerstein ran afoul of the State Department Passport Division. The State Department had received information that raised doubts about Hammerstein's loyalty, and when he applied for a passport, they demanded that he first submit a statement of his political beliefs. Hammerstein complied and wrote a twenty-nine-page affidavit in which he detailed his Popular Front political activities, including his support for the Hollywood Anti-Nazi League and his annual $2 contribution to the Abraham Lincoln Brigade. He defended himself by noting that his songs praised ideals that "Communists call *bourgeois*," while also declaring that he had a healthy "but not a hysterical fear" of international communism. He also defended Robeson's right to speak and made clear that he opposed blacklisting and travel restrictions as violations of the Constitution.[56]

When Hammerstein died in 1960, Congressman Philip J. Philbin praised Hammerstein's work for having an "ideological touch." That assertion of ideology had an ambiguous meaning in 1960. Although *South Pacific*'s "You've Got to Be Carefully Taught" was indeed "mild" and "gentle" in its social criticism, as even Hammerstein's admirers acknowledged, it trailed roots back into the more radical cultural politics of the Popular Front. Hammerstein was not, however, a radical who "sold out" his politics in order to protect his career: the liberal political views that he expressed from the 1920s to the 1950s show greater continuity than disruption. Rather, his significance lies in his ability to illuminate the perimeters of and overlaps in the violently shifting coalitions of the postwar era: his participation as an intellectual in both the Popular Front and the Cold War historical bloc marks the area of continuity and contact between these two formations. Hammerstein straddled the boundaries between them. He belonged to that liberal sliver of the Popular Front coalition that found its way into the Cold War coalition and that marked its leftmost limit. He worked in the border where the distinction between dominant and residual formations, legitimate and illegitimate ideologies, became blurred. Hammerstein's criticism of racial relations was as strong as it could be without costing him his access to the major outlets of Broadway, Hollywood, radio, and print media. The more radical critics of American race relations—Robeson, Du Bois, even Buck— had their access to that public sphere severely restricted. With *South Pacific* Hammerstein preserved his liberal racial politics by linking them up with the new ideological issues of global expansion. This was the way that he found to keep the issue alive in a changing political climate. In his musicals, he merged into a single "bath of sweetness" elements of the racial and geopolitical ideology of both the Popular Front and the Cold War. He created a structure of feeling that joined these two seemingly opposite ideological systems, and in doing so eased the way for middlebrow Americans to transfer their own affiliations from the cultural politics of antifascism to those of anticommunism.

· · · · ·

The familial language of political obligation that middlebrow culture produced throughout the late 1940s and 1950s proved to be a valuable reservoir from which political leaders could draw. The Eisenhower administration mobilized the idea of the multiracial, multinational family as a metaphor for the international interdependence that it was promoting so heavily during the 1950s. It did so most explicitly when it sent "The Family of Man" on a worldwide tour. "The Family of Man" was an exhibition of 503 photographs taken in sixty-eight countries that Edward Steichen curated for the Museum of Modern Art in 1955. A classic example of middlebrow culture, it attracted huge audiences in New York and other American cities, graced the cover of the *Saturday Review,* and earned the contempt of the New York intellectuals. The show offered perhaps the fullest expression of the ideals of humanistic universalism that so many middlebrow intellectuals embraced in the postwar years. Steichen captured the essence of this universalism when he described the goals of the show. "From day to day we are brought face to face with the differences in life," he explained in an interview. "They are differences of race; they are differences of creed; they are differences of nation." In his show he sought to emphasize as his "prevailing theme" not these differences, but rather "the things that we are alike in." "We can't overlook the differences," he said, "but unless we arrange these pictures so that they stress the alikeness—the similarity—we have lost out." For Steichen, it was the emotional, affective bonds of love that united the "Family of Man": "Unless we have the element of love dominating this entire exhibition—and our lives—we better take it down before we put it up." [57]

Between 1955 and 1962, over nine million people saw "The Family of Man" as the USIA arranged its tour through thirty-eight countries. As a work of cultural diplomacy, the show aimed to reinforce Washington's policies of international integration: it toured countries that were secure U.S. allies, such as Japan; countries that the U.S. hoped to win over as allies, such as Laos; and countries that had recently been contested terrain, such as Iran. Its itinerary often coincided with Washington's political and military agenda: the USIA sent it to Lebanon shortly after Eisenhower sent in the U.S. Marines; to Tito's Yugoslavia, the sole communist country that refused to join the Soviet bloc; and to the U.S. Trade Fair in Moscow, where it formed part of the backdrop for the Nixon-Khrushchev "kitchen debate," which was itself a prime example of Cold War domestic-ideology theater. The exhibition drew enthusiastic crowds around the world and cultivated tremendous good will toward the United States. In publicizing the idea that all humanity belonged to the same family, the show reinforced the terms through which the U.S. explained and justified its reshaping of the international order. America's claims of global "responsibilities," "obligations," and "commitments" became more acceptable when they were embedded in a logic of family. Imagined as an extension of family love, the extension of American power became somewhat less objectionable. The bonds of family rendered the inequalities of political and economic power less visible and partially defused the charges of racism and imperialism. [58]

Like so many of the postwar assertions of a global family, however, this one was polysemous. The most outstanding photograph in the exhibition—the only one in color, the only one that had a whole room to itself—showed the 1954 explosion of a hydrogen bomb on the Bikini Atoll. As many viewers of the image would have known, the explosion not only decimated the small Pacific island, it also horribly sickened the crew of a Japanese fishing vessel, the *Fortunate Dragon*, that happened to be downwind of the blast. The exhibition thus not only celebrated the idea of a global family, it also opened up a space for a critical awareness of the military threats to that family that the Cold War posed. [59]

After 1954, South Vietnam was the part of Asia that the U.S. worked hardest to integrate into its political, military, and economic system. Senator John F. Kennedy relied on the middlebrow logic of political-obligation-as-parenthood in a 1956 speech to the American Friends of Vietnam. In articulating Washington's deep commitment to President Diem's two-year-old government, he used language that would have been comfortingly familiar to the millions of *South Pacific* viewers and the readers of Christian Children's Fund advertisements. "If we are not the parents of little Vietnam," explained Kennedy, "then surely we are the godparents. We presided at its birth, we gave assistance to its life, we have helped to shape its future. As French influence in the political, economic and military spheres has declined in Vietnam, the American influence has steadily grown. This is our offspring—we cannot abandon it, we cannot ignore its needs." Kennedy exhorted Americans to commit themselves to South Vietnam—and to an expansionist foreign policy throughout Asia—by recasting a fundamentally political relationship into the personal terms of adoptive parenthood.[60]

Diplomatic historians who have thought about the Cold War in terms of gender have often focused on the process of masculinization. They have explored how political elites and cultural producers ascribed to the nation and its representatives qualities traditionally associated with men: toughness, hardness, virility, heroism, strenuousness, aggressiveness, physical competence, courage. At the same time, social and cultural historians of the postwar period have often argued that domestic ideology functioned as a force of constraint, turning women's attention inward and restricting their symbolic and actual spheres of action to the home and family. Both of these positions have merit: masculinization and domestic ideology were indeed crucial components of the cultural logic of containment both at home and abroad. But the push toward global integration demanded a national identity formulated in less confrontational and more affiliative terms than discourses of masculinization could provide. The result was that America's global power was often figured in maternal, adoptive, and familial terms. The expansionist discourse of the Cold War was heterogeneous rather than uniform: in the 1950s the white mother stood alongside the tough man as an iconic figure of the nation. Domestic ideology in some instances facilitated the outward turn toward global engagement that the Cold War demanded. Maternal love was imagined as a force capable of overcoming racism and a source of benign global power. The adoptive U.S.-Asian families, both imaginary and real, created through this love met many of the ideological demands of the Cold War. They encouraged a sense of political obligation to a part of the world with which most Americans had limited ties; they assigned re-domesticated women a role in the national project of global expansion; they gave millions of Americans a sense of personal participation in the Cold War. Perhaps most important, they affirmed that Americans, despite their nation's history and their own prejudices, were not irredeemably racist or imperialist.[61]

CHAPTER 5

Musicals and Modernization

The King and I

The musical is—and always has been—America's most political theater.

John Lahr, 1996

In the late 1950s and early 1960s Yul Brynner starred in two films that
imagined the relationship between the United States and the developing
world. In 1956 he played the King in *The King and I*, Rodgers and Hammerstein's musical about an English schoolteacher in the royal court of
Siam. Four years later he appeared in *The Magnificent Seven*, John Stur-
ges's Western about a group of American gunfighters hired by beleaguered Mexican villagers to protect them from a local bandit. Both of
these films, although set in the nineteenth century, are imbued with what
Michael Latham has called the postwar ideology of modernization. Together they suggest the extent to which the conceptual framework of
modernization theory, so beloved by postwar social scientists and foreign policymakers, extended beyond the realms of the political elite and
suffused contemporary popular culture as well.[1]

Richard Slotkin, in his monumental, three-volume study of the myth
of the frontier in American culture, has shown how the Western has long
served as a bearer of ideology about U.S. expansion, national identity,
and the idea of progress. *The Magnificent Seven*, he has argued, offers a
fantasy of counterinsurgency modernization. Working within the well-
established conventions of the Western genre, it anticipates and models
the logic of Kennedy's foreign policies in Vietnam: Brynner heads up
a group of professional, Green Beret–like killers who cross the border
into Mexico, defend a peasant village from the political tyranny of a lo-

cal warlord, and in a spectacular act of violence—what Slotkin has described as a commando-style "surgical strike" on the village itself—kill
the warlord and eliminate the threat to the peasants. Having restored
peace, the gunfighters return back across the border, leaving behind a
newly Americanized native leadership that will guide the village into the
future.[2]

The King and I also engages directly with the issue of modernization.
Brynner's character here is based on Siam's legendary King Mongkut
who opened up his country to Western influence in the 1860s, and the
film imagines with some nuance the advantages, as well as the costs, of
Westernization. The King and I shares with The Magnificent Seven certain narrative similarities: although it replaces the band of male gunfighters with Anna Leonowens, a female schoolteacher, The King and I
tells the story of an Americanized figure, hired because of her specialized
skills, who defends a non-Western community from political tyranny
and sets it on the road to progress and democracy under a newly Americanized leadership. But where The Magnificent Seven employs the language of the Western, The King and I views modernization through the
sentimental lens of the musical. Here, "backward" Siam is transformed
through love and friendship, and the premodern is swept away in a spectacular episode of song and dance.

A reading of The King and I in relation to postwar modernization
theory allows us to see the musical as an ideological genre on a par with,
but radically different from, the more familiarly ideological genre of the
Western. Film scholar Thomas Schatz has distinguished between Westerns and musicals by classifying them, respectively, as genres of order and
genres of integration. Westerns tend to feature individual male heroes
who embrace a masculine code of self-reliance; their dramatic conflicts
are externalized as violence and resolved through the elimination of the
threat to the social order. Musicals, in turn, tend to feature a collective
hero, usually a couple or a community, in which feminine and familial
values dominate. They express their dramatic conflicts as emotion and
resolve them by integrating antagonistic characters into a harmonious
community, usually through the mechanism of romance. Social readings
of these genres proceed from their respective emphases on the elimination or incorporation of antagonistic forces. The Western's ideological
power derives largely from the way it imagines violence: who can legiti-
mately use it, against whom, and in the defense of what. The musical's
ideological power, in turn, resides in the way it imagines community: the
differences among people that can be transcended, the kinds of bonds

that can be forged, and the nature of communities that can be created. If the Western translates ideology into ritualized forms of action, the musical translates it into structures of feeling. What the Western imagines as a gunfight, the musical imagines as a dance.[3]

As a genre, the musical opens up its ideological workings to include the viewer in ways that the Western never does. Broadway lyricist E. Y. (Yip) Harburg, who had been a Popular Fronter in the 1930s and 1940s before being blacklisted in the 1950s, understood better than most of his peers "the essentially political nature of song." In his view, the musical's ideological force arises from two sources: its ability to translate controversial ideas into easily absorbed emotions and the inescapability of song in the age of mass culture. According to Harburg, the "power" of a song "is its invisibility." Where a book or a painting must be sought out by the reader or the viewer, the "song seeks you." A popular song "is ubiquitous and sinewy. It pursues you every minute. It's your shadow. You're sitting in a dentist's chair. There it is. Or in the elevator. Or the supermarket. Or a car. You may catch the song from somebody else. Its ideas may infect you." A listener, surrounded by a musical's songs as they circulate throughout the culture, can easily become caught up in its vision of the world. Donal Henahan recalled that Rodgers and Hammerstein's songs achieved a level of ubiquity in the late 1940s and early 1950s that few contemporary songwriters could match: "Few inhabitants of America in 1949 could have failed to know every dramatic nuance and singable note of *South Pacific*. . . . the Rodgers score penetrated every layer of American culture. . . . For years, no American ear could escape. . . . The songs oozed out of every radio and television set, assailed one in elevators, restaurants and washrooms. A generation of susceptible youth could hardly avoid them, and did not try." The infectious quality of the Rodgers and Hammerstein songs also opened them up to popular participation. Designed to be sung by as many people as possible, they invited listeners to sing along with their catchy tunes and rhyming lyrics. This singability allowed audience members to step out of their role as passive observers and temporarily join in the process of community formation that was taking place on stage or on screen.[4]

Given these generic differences, the Western and the musical were ideally suited to express the two strains of Cold War ideology. Westerns, with their emphasis on the frontier as a border between civilization and savagery and their resolution of conflict through violence, fit comfortably within the category of containment culture. *The King and I*, in turn, offers an exemplary instance of the culture of integration: it imagines that

Others, rather than being exterminated, could be modernized through an intimate embrace.

A NARRATIVE OF MODERNIZATION

The King and I was, along with *The Ugly American,* one of the most popular representations of Southeast Asia produced in the 1950s. The second in Rodgers and Hammerstein's trilogy of Asia-Pacific musicals (along with *South Pacific* and *Flower Drum Song*), it opened on Broadway in 1951 with Gertrude Lawrence starring as Anna and Yul Brynner playing the King. The show ran in New York for three years, toured nationally for a year and a half, and played in London for two and a half years. In 1956, Twentieth Century Fox faithfully translated the show into a film version, this time pairing Yul Brynner with Deborah Kerr; the film won six Academy Awards, and its soundtrack remained on the charts for 274 weeks.[5]

The King and I had its roots in European imperial and American missionary history. The real Anna Leonowens was an Englishwoman born and raised in colonial India. She worked as a teacher in the royal court of Siam from 1862 to 1867 and wrote two fictionalized accounts of her experiences, *The English Governess at the Siamese Court* (1870) and *The Romance of the Harem* (1873). Margaret Landon, an American, rediscovered Leonowens during a decade spent in Siam with her husband, an educational missionary who later went on to work on the Far Eastern staff of the State Department. Landon combined Leonowens's accounts with her own archival research to produce *Anna and the King of Siam,* a fictionalized biography that became a bestseller in 1944 and that *Reader's Digest* condensed. In 1946 Twentieth Century Fox turned Landon's novel into a nonmusical film of the same name. Rodgers and Hammerstein's version of Anna's story must thus be understood not as an exclusively postwar text, but as part of a narrative tradition that stretches back to the mid-nineteenth century.[6]

The story of Anna Leonowens and the King of Siam has served since the nineteenth century as America's favorite narrative about Thailand. In writing his libretto, Oscar Hammerstein retained many of the fundamental pieces of the story that Leonowens, Landon, and the Hollywood screenwriters in 1946 developed. In all the versions, King Mongkut of Siam, seeking a Western education for the royal family, hires the young English widow as a teacher for his large brood of children. Although an Englishwoman, Anna is an Americanized figure who uses the politics and culture of the Civil War—Lincoln's struggle to free the slaves, Harriet Beecher Stowe's *Uncle Tom's Cabin*—as her frame of reference. The King stands on the cusp of a new era: a traditional ruler, he realizes that he must bring Siam into closer conformity with modern Western intellectual and social currents in order to protect his country from Western domination. Anna becomes the King's partner in his project, and during her tenure in Siam she educates the King's wives and children in Western habits of behavior and thought. She teaches them Western science and geography, Western social rituals and table manners, Western forms of dress, and Western political ideals. The King's awkward position between tradition and modernity often leads to tensions with Anna, and their relationship is marked by conflicts. Eventually, however, the King comes to trust her judgment, and he promotes her from tutor to secretary to political advisor. When the King dies, his son and Anna's most avid student, Prince Chulalongkorn, takes over the throne and expresses his commitment to further his father's program of bringing Siam into closer harmony with the West.

Hammerstein's libretto, which he based on Landon's novel and the 1946 screenplay, modified the narrative in several ways. In keeping with his own liberal racial politics, Hammerstein excised much of Leonowens's and Landon's ethnocentric and racist language and bypassed the "yellow-peril" characterizations of the 1946 film. He downplayed the notion of unbreachable cultural differences and heightened the message of tolerance and mutual understanding. He also turned Leonowens's proto-feminist tale of female bonding across the racial divide into a heterosexual romance of unconsummated trans-racial love. Only in Hammerstein's version does the friendship and mere hint of attraction between Anna and the King—presented for the first time as an attractive, eroticized man—turn into love. Hammerstein also heightened Anna's Americanness by giving *Uncle Tom's Cabin* a more central role in the narrative. In all its versions, however, the story of Anna and the King is a story of how a Western woman promotes the modernization and democratization of a small Southeast Asian nation: Anna Leonowens is an agent of the West who remakes Siam along Western lines. The repetition of this narrative, from Leonowens's nineteenth-century accounts to Hammerstein's postwar version and on into the 1999 film *Anna and the King*, starring Jodie Foster and Chow Yun-fat, attests to the appeal, for Americans at least, of this model of U.S.-Asian relations.

Rodgers and Hammerstein made their reputation writing musicals that captured iconic scenes of Americana, from the Western frontier in

Oklahoma! to a Maine seacoast village in *Carousel.* What led them to create a musical about nineteenth-century Thailand? One answer is that *The King and I,* like *South Pacific,* grew partly out of Hammerstein's political values. As much as Hammerstein worked to improve domestic race relations, he was also a committed internationalist who thought deeply about how nations around the world should work together. Hammerstein's internationalism, like that of Norman Cousins, took the form of world federalism. Hammerstein joined the world government movement in 1947, the year that the Truman Doctrine established containment as one of the twin poles of postwar foreign policy, and he actively promoted its goals until his death in 1960. He used his celebrity to educate the public about international issues and to advocate a global political system that would bind Americans more tightly to other nations around the world. He served as vice president of the United World Federalists (Cousins was president), delivered numerous public speeches, and wrote articles for the *Saturday Review* and the *Congressional Digest.* Cousins, who praised Hammerstein as "one of the first starry-eyed and divinely discontented astronomers to bring the Federalist concept to our attention," saw his gift as the ability to bring out the "human" dimensions of internationalism.[7]

The King and I explored some basic world federalist issues, such as the unwillingness of national leaders to sacrifice a degree of their sovereignty in order to achieve a greater, collective good. In the song "A Puzzlement" the King debates with himself the need to forge international alliances and his unwillingness to trust allies too much:

> Shall I join with other nations in alliance?
> If allies are weak, am I not best alone?
> If allies are strong with power to protect me,
> Might they not protect me out of all I own?
> Is a danger to be trusting one another,
> One will seldom want to do what other wishes . . .
> But unless someday somebody trust somebody,
> There'll be nothing left on earth excepting fishes!

The song also suggests the prospect of nuclear annihilation, the specter of which drove the world federalism movement. The King, who does eventually learn to trust Anna, serves as Hammerstein's model of a wise national leader who learns to give up some of his power in order to achieve a greater security. Yet part of what makes *The King and I* interesting is that these ideals of world federalism, which occupied a distinctly marginal position within the Cold War consensus, coexist with the much more dominant discourse of modernization theory.[8]

The twentieth-century popularity of Anna Leonowens's story coincided with the increased geopolitical importance of Thailand to the United States. Although Japanese-occupied Thailand was officially part of the Axis during World War II when Landon published her novel, the Thai people remained strongly pro-Western, and their underground resistance movement welcomed American OSS agents. In the decade between 1946 (when the first film version of *Anna and the King of Siam* was released) and 1956 (when the film version of *The King and I* was released), Thailand became one of America's strongest allies on the Asian mainland. After the "loss" of China to communism in 1949, U.S. policymakers increasingly saw the countries of Southeast Asia, in the words of Secretary of State John Foster Dulles, as "the forward positions against which the waves of Communism are beating and where the issues of war and peace, of freedom and captivity, hang in precarious balance." Within this increasingly volatile region, Americans saw Thailand as a unique island of stability. Alone among its neighbors, Thailand had remained free from European colonial domination, which meant the Thai people did not harbor the anti-Western sentiments that hampered U.S. dealings with other nations in the region. It was also the only Southeast Asian nation not wracked by nationalist and communist-supported revolutions, and was thus seen by Washington as a dike against the surrounding "waves" of destabilization. When Thailand's rulers made clear their pro-Western and anticommunist orientation, the U.S. responded with generous financial support. In 1950 the Truman administration pledged $10 million in military, economic, and technical aid to Thailand, and over the course of the 1950s the Eisenhower administration poured in hundreds of millions of dollars more.[9]

Although most of this money went to the Thai police and military forces, which turned Thailand into a repressive police state, the official goal of this aid was to help Thailand modernize and Westernize. The U.S. began funding cultural and scientific programs in Thailand with its first infusion of aid in 1950. Washington brought in technical experts to improve Thailand's agriculture, irrigation, transportation, communications, harbor facilities, commerce, and public health. It also funded educational advisors and established an American-supervised language center for teaching English. These programs established a tutelary relationship between the two nations, with the U.S. assuming the position of teacher and guide to modernization, and Thailand the position of eager student.[10]

U.S. officials in these years grounded their policies toward Thailand in the principles of modernization theory, which, beginning in the late 1940s and 1950s, became a primary conceptual framework for thinking about U.S. relations with the developing world. The U.S.-assisted modernization of Asia did not begin in the postwar period, of course: Japanese modernizers had sought U.S. assistance after the Meiji restoration of 1868, as had Thai reformers after 1900, and Chinese reformers following the collapse of the Qing dynasty in 1911. But it was not until the Cold War that modernization theory fully developed in the U.S. as both an academic field and a political project. Universities and think tanks gave it an institutional foundation, government officials translated it into foreign policy, and W. W. Rostow popularized it in his "non-communist manifesto," *The Stages of Economic Growth* (1960). Rostow and his colleagues at the Center for International Studies at M.I.T. were universalists: they posited that all societies existed on a singular continuum between "tradition" and "modernity" and that each one must inevitably progress from one condition to the other through a clearly marked set of stages. As policy advisors, they aimed to intervene in the process in order to accelerate it and direct it in ways compatible with U.S. interests. Modernization theory thus intersected neatly with the larger Cold War goals of integration and containment: by helping "backward" nations become "modern," the U.S. hoped to alleviate the conditions that made communism an attractive option and thus secure these nations' participation in the "free world" alliance. For these theorists, modernization looked very much like Americanization: taking the U.S. as the epitome of the modern state, they held it up as a model for developing nations to emulate, and they formulated policies designed to reproduce American social, political, and economic structures in developing nations. According to Rostow, U.S. history offered a "blueprint" that the developing world must inevitably follow.[11]

Modernization theory, far from being a postwar invention, belonged rather to a long tradition within U.S. foreign policy discourse. As part of a continuing effort to deny its own imperialism, the U.S. has regularly explained its overseas expansion in terms of progress and modernization. In contrast to European imperialism, which many Americans saw as based on naked exploitation and self-interest, U.S. expansion was seen as fostering economic development, infrastructure modernization, political liberalization, and the promotion of free trade. In reality, however, modernization theory continued many of the precepts of the "civilizing mission" which had underwritten Western colonialism. It assumed that the nonwhite portions of the world were backward, that they needed to be educated and uplifted by the West, and that they would need long periods of supervision before they would be ready for complete self-government. Modernization theory thus recycled many of colonialism's legitimating ideas: it saw the developing world as trapped in a timeless past, unable to help itself, and bound to follow Western models. In contrast to nineteenth-century imperial ideology, however, modernization theory eschewed an explicit ideology of racial hierarchy in favor of a more social scientific ideology of Western developmental superiority. Not coincidentally, modernization theory emerged simultaneously with decolonization. It offered a means to continue Western access and authority, and Third World dependency, in the absence of formal colonial ties.[12]

Culture played an important role in postwar modernization projects. Academic and policy experts sought to create new attitudes in the developing world as well as new social, political, and economic systems. As part of their effort to achieve this goal, U.S. officials launched a broad range of cultural diplomacy initiatives. The Fulbright exchange program, the State Department's International Information and Education Exchange program, the USIA, and the CIA all aided in the global dissemination of American culture that took place during the Cold War. The Fulbright program aimed to stimulate an in-depth understanding of America in Asia, and around the world, through the exchange of students and teachers. It arranged exchanges with China and Burma in 1947, the Philippines in 1948, India and Pakistan in 1950, Japan in 1951, and Ceylon in 1952. While the content of these exchange programs was important, the form of them was as well: many Fulbright participants emphasized that the substance of the academic exchange often proved less valuable than the more basic experience of working with and getting to know people from other cultures.[13]

These programs served a number of functions. One of their primary goals was to eliminate doubts about America's global intentions by educating other nations' elite classes about American history, culture, and values. Through such educational and cultural exchanges, the U.S. tried to demonstrate that it shared a fundamental body of beliefs and aspirations with other countries, and that as a result these nations should not fear the U.S. as a coercive outside power, but rather accept it as the strongest member of an organic community. These initiatives aimed to create a sense of common ground between the U.S. and developing nations, which would in turn provide a foundation on which modernization programs could take root and grow. According to USIA director Theodore Streibert, the agency aimed to "emphasize the community of interest that exists among freedom-loving peoples and show how American objectives and policies advance the legitimate interests of such people." In addition, cultural diplomacy programs reinforced the universalizing assumptions of modernization theory by offering proof that, in spite of their differences, Americans and people in developing nations could learn to understand each other. These cultural programs also served a vital economic function: they opened up markets and created audiences for U.S. culture industries in countries that were too poor to have fully developed mass-media industries of their own, or whose entertainment industries had been weakened by the war. Like modernization theory itself, these cultural programs trailed long roots into the history of U.S. global expansion. Since the turn of the century, U.S. officials had funded cultural and educational programs as part of their efforts to "modernize" Asia. After the Boxer Rebellion of 1900, Washington used the Chinese government's forced indemnity payments to set up scholarships for Chinese students studying in the U.S. And as part of its colonial policy in the Philippines, the U.S. established a comprehensive educational system based on the American public school system. By instructing Filipinos and Chinese in the English language and American culture, these programs sought to facilitate the achievement of U.S. interests in Asia through nonmilitary, nonpolitical means. While both the Philippine education system and the Boxer scholarships were held up as proof of American benevolence and commitment to modernization, they also served as cultural instruments for pursuing U.S. economic and political interests abroad.[14]

The King and I tells a story of sentimental modernization. According to Vicente Rafael, the political discourse of sentimental modernization stretches at least as far back as the conquest of the Philippines. It represents colonialism as a feminized project of modernizing backward peoples by inculcating in them a set of habits and a consciousness associated with middle-class domesticity. Instead of exterminating backward peoples through savage war, as imagined by the frontier discourse of continental expansion, sentimental modernization called for their incorporation through a process of nurture and education. As a sentimental modernizer, Anna Leonowens exercises her influence in Siam not through violence or force or political coercion, but through the power of love and the tools of culture.[15]

Anna wields the ideology of middle-class domesticity as a progressive force, a body of values whose acceptance will facilitate Siam's transition into modernity. Much of Anna and the King's relationship revolves around a quarrel over whether she will live in a separate house, as originally promised, or within the palace, that is, the harem. This argument serves as a device through which the multiple differences between Anna and the King can be animated—differences of sex, gender, culture, religion, and status. This debate over competing models of sexuality and domestic life serves primarily, however, as a vehicle for their larger argument over traditional vs. modern political authority. The King desires to modernize his country, but at the same time he expects to continue exercising power as an authoritarian ruler. The harem serves as the concrete manifestation of his traditional authority: he rules absolutely over a household of hundreds of women and children who must do his bidding unquestioned, who can never oppose him, and who show their submission by prostrating themselves in his presence. Anna, in turn, champions Western liberal political ideology, whose abstractions she communicates via the terms of middle-class domesticity and sexuality: she uses romantic love, monogamy, the nuclear family, and the private home as her examples for explaining the rights of the individual and the rule of law. Anna's critique of the harem, therefore, becomes the core of her challenge to the King's premodern political authority. This conflict over Anna's living quarters also resonates with the concerns of world federalism. Anna claims that the King's promise of a house has the status of a legal contract; the King claims that as the absolute sovereign of Siam he can make and break promises as he pleases. When Anna insists that the King respect his promise, she makes the world federalist argument that a system of international law should override prerogatives of national sovereignty.

With *The King and I*, the American narrative of anticonquest reached its apex. Far from being an imperialist, Anna helps preserve Siam's independence by deflecting the unwanted attentions of a colonial power. Like the modernization theorists themselves, Rodgers and Hammerstein found a receptive audience because they told a familiar story that tapped into a long-standing American and Western tradition of imagining overseas expansion as the liberalization of oppressive societies. Rodgers and Hammerstein's Anna, like M.I.T.'s Walt Rostow, was only the latest in a long line of Europeans and Americans who claimed to be modernizing the East by educating it in the ways of the West.

MUSICAL NUMBERS AS SPECTACLES OF MODERNIZATION

Anna Leonowens is an explicitly feminized modernizer whose power derives from her access to the sphere of culture. She is a teacher, and she transforms Siam by bringing in new ideas. Margaret Landon, in her novelized biography of Leonowens, gave Anna an internal monologue in which she voiced her goal of transforming the East through Western education. In it, Anna imagined herself teaching not just a few children but the whole nation: she dreamed of "shaping" the "child mind" of a "future king" and thus enabling him to lead "a new and better world." Burning with a secular sense of "mission," she imagines herself a "liberator" who will "fight with knowledge" rather than guns to instill a respect for "human freedom" and "human dignity" in her charges. Rodgers and Hammerstein's Anna extends this characterization. In her hands, modernization becomes a maternal task of shaping the consciousness of children and students by introducing them to Western, and specifically American, culture.[16]

As a musical, *The King and I* communicates much of its meaning through its deployment of song and dance. Its musical numbers serve as spectacles of education and cultural transformation, reworking the ideology of modernization into utopian moments of community formation. I want to consider three numbers and read them as successive steps in the process of modernization: the first, an appeal to the West for education by the Siamese; the second, the process of education itself; and the third, the results of that education displayed.

"The March of the Royal Siamese Children" takes place early in the narrative. Soon after arriving in Siam Anna threatens to leave because the King has broken his promise of a separate house; in this number the King entices Anna to stay by showing off his large and charming brood of children. The number shows that Anna does not impose modernization on the Siamese against their will, but rather that they request it. An orchestral number with no singing or dialogue, it opens with Anna and the King alone together and progresses as the King directs a small throng of his children, her future pupils, to greet Anna. The children enter the room one by one, quiet, stately, and lavishly dressed; they salute Anna with a bow, touch their heads to her hands in a sign of respect, then back away from her and sit down a few feet away, at no time turning their backs to her. As the number proceeds ritualistically, Anna's changing expression reveals her emotional response: the children's quiet charm and beauty win her heart, she falls in love with them, and she agrees to remain. Even as it bathes the scene in a warm glow of feeling, the number establishes a hierarchical relation of teacher and student between Anna and the Siamese. The Siamese children, although charming and appealing, are mute; they seek enlightenment and guidance from the representative of the West, who alone possesses knowledge. Employing a standard trope of colonial discourse, the number displays the Siamese invitation to the West to intervene.

"Getting to Know You," which follows soon after, takes place in the palace schoolroom as Anna teaches a group of children and wives a geography lesson. This number displays the process of education that the children have requested and figures it in terms of cultural exchange and transformation. With this song Anna inculcates a liberal internationalist perspective in her students as she introduces them to Western knowledge: while she sings of her pleasure in "getting to know" and "like" the people of Thailand, she teaches the children Western social rituals so that they may behave as Westerners. The number, and the educational process itself, work through mimicry: first Anna sings and shows them how to shake hands and curtsey, then the children reproduce her words and her movements. After Anna teaches them her dance, the children, with the aid of a dancer, teach her a fan dance, thereby enacting a process of cultural exchange in which the West and the East learn to understand each other's culture. The equality of the exchange, however, is deceptive: although Anna learns a new dance, the goal of the scene is to change the Siamese, not her. The use of sound effects in the original stage version marks the profound nature of their transformation: up to this point, the women and children's voices have been represented by orchestral sounds, and it is only as they learn English in this scene that they begin to speak lines of intelligible dialogue. On the one hand this can be seen as an attempt at cultural verisimilitude, an effort to avoid misrepresenting the Siamese as already speaking English. On the other hand, however, it suggests that only through Westernization do the Siamese acquire the markers of full humanity, the ability to speak and to represent themselves.[17]

"Getting to Know You" presents education as a process of East-West community formation. Anna uses song and dance to transform the children into an intellectual community, a Westernized native elite that can articulate Western ideas in a Western language. Emotional as well as intellectual ties forge the bonds of this community, and sentiment and pleasure work as the mechanisms of the children's transformation. The number presents teaching as an act and expression of love and as a pro-

cess of creating emotional bonds. Anna does not drill the children mer-
cilessly; rather, she plays with them, expresses her fondness for them,
and at the end of the number, sweeps several of them up in her arms to
hug them. The children are willing to change because Anna makes their
transformation a pleasurably emotional experience.

The King and I has as its showpiece number "The Small House of
Uncle Thomas," in which the Siamese display the effects of their Western education. Two main themes converge in this number: the idea of
modernization as cultural transformation and the idea of domesticity as
democratic political ideology. The King has approached Anna for advice
about a developing crisis: British imperialists are threatening to make
Siam a "protectorate" of the crown, using its supposed lack of civilization as a pretext. Anna, outraged, advises the King to outwit the British
by inviting them to see a display of how civilized Siam has already become. This display takes the form of a twenty-minute musical number,
a show-within-a-show Siamese version of Harriet Beecher Stowe's Uncle
Tom's Cabin. Performed before an audience that includes Anna, the King,
and the British officials, the number condenses Stowe's novel to focus on
the episode in which the slave Eliza and her baby escape from Simon Legree by running across the frozen Ohio River to join her husband George.

This number marks one of Hammerstein's greatest departures from
the previous versions of Anna Leonowens's story. Leonowens had used
Stowe's sentimental abolitionism as the intellectual foundation for her
condemnation of Thai slavery and the harem, and she modeled some of
her characters and episodes on those in Stowe's novel; Landon, in her
1944 novelized biography, played up the references to Stowe. The 1946
film version introduced the idea of Anna as an anti-imperialist figure
who helps the King ward off European imperialism by staging a show,
but in that version the show is a display of Siamese history and is only
referred to rather than presented visually. Hammerstein expanded on
these references to Stowe's novel and turned the staged performance of
Uncle Tom's Cabin into the heart of the show.

Within the plot of the musical, this number exerts incredible political
power. At one level, it preserves Siam's independence. The British, convinced that Siam is indeed on the road to Westernization, withdraw their
threat of colonization and depart, leaving Siam the independent country
that U.S. and Thai Cold Warriors would later hail as a fellow "land of
the free." At another level, it creates a public forum for the only direct
opposition to the King's authoritarian rule. The performance is written
and narrated by the Burmese concubine Tuptim, an early convert to

Anna's domestic ideology; she is in love with a young countryman and wants to escape the King's sexual slavery to form a monogamous relationship. Anna had earlier given Tuptim a copy of Stowe's novel as a way to comfort her and reinforce her aversion to slavery, and from it Tuptim selected the scene of escape and marital reunification that forms the basis of the show. Tuptim uses the stage performance as an opportunity to denounce the King and make a public appeal for her freedom: after joyfully announcing the death of "King" Simon Legree in the icy waters of the Ohio River, Tuptim breaks out of character as the narrator and declaims to the King and assembled guests that she is happy to see the death of any king who would prevent a slave from being with her lover. At the end of the number, Tuptim puts her beliefs into action and runs away with her lover. This act of political protest, like the defeat of the British imperialists, results from Anna's education. In giving Tuptim a copy of Stowe's novel, Anna has given her a model for political rebellion, a manual for opposing her own slavery and claiming her individual right to marriage. Anna's teaching results in the discourse of romantic love functioning as the only effective way to articulate opposition to the King's authoritarian rule. Tuptim, by insisting on her right to monogamous sexuality, becomes the first member of the royal family to fully embrace modernity.

What is it about this number that makes it such a powerful political —specifically anti-imperialist and anti-authoritarian—weapon? First, the number proves that Siam is becoming like the West by offering a spectacle of the integration of Western and "Siamese" cultural forms. While the narrative of escaping from slavery and all the characters are recognizably American, the music, costumes, and style of dance and acting are all "traditional" Siamese (by way of Broadway): the characters wear saffron-colored costumes, golden headdresses, and carved masks, while Uncle Tom's cabin sports the turned-up wings of traditional Siamese architecture. A group of the King's wives perform the number's music on Thai instruments, and Tuptim narrates in a charmingly stilted English that rephrases "Uncle Tom's Cabin" as "The Small House of Uncle Thomas." The number brings to fruition the lessons in Westernization that began in the classroom scene of "Getting to Know You": putting their education on display, the characters emphasize the role of snow and ice—part of Anna's geography lesson—in helping Eliza escape across the Ohio River. The number is a spectacular melding of American and Siamese cultural forms, both for the internal audience of British colonialists and for the viewer. It develops the idea of a U.S.-Asian

intellectual community from "Getting to Know You" and presents Siam
as sharing a cultural common ground with the United States.

In doing so, the number translates some of the assumptions of modernization theory into a spectacle of song and dance. As the culmination
of the show's process of national transformation via education and cultural exchange, the number shares a certain logic with Cold War cultural diplomacy programs. Both embrace the idea of culture as a medium of political communication and revolve around the idea that the
U.S. does not force its influence on other nations, but engages in a mutual exchange of ideas. More pointedly, Anna offers American history
and culture as a universal blueprint which the more backward Siamese
can follow in order to progress up the ladder of modernity. By giving the
Siamese American culture, Anna gives them a vehicle with which to express their political desire for independence from colonial domination.
She gives them a fictional incarnation of American political history—
the abolitionist movement—onto which they can graft their own political dilemmas. She seems to suggest that only by using the language and
forms of American culture can the Siamese effectively speak their anticolonial and democratic desires. That Siam retains its political independence as a result of this indigenous retelling of an American story suggests that the U.S offers a model of progress that the decolonizing world
can and should follow.

What is one to make of Hammerstein's decision to give the show's
most prominent number over to an abolitionist drama and to link it to
the cause of anti-imperialism? What might it have meant to invoke the
history of American slavery, set within a Southeast Asian context, in
1951? Actually, this invocation of abolitionism in the 1950s is not quite
so odd as it first appears: by the late 1940s the whole idea of slavery had
already been resurrected and put into the service of the Cold War as a
familiar framework through which to comprehend the unfamiliar situ-
ations that the Cold War gave rise to. From the earliest days of the Cold
War, Truman had made "slavery" one of his preferred synonyms for Soviet communism, and since then it had become entrenched within the
American political vocabulary. One of the basic statements of Cold War
foreign policy, NSC 68, invoked slavery to mark the distinction between
communist and noncommunist nations—"There is a basic conflict between the idea of freedom under a government of laws, and the idea of
slavery under the grim oligarchy of the Kremlin"—and presidential candidate John F. Kennedy, like Anna Leonowens, compared himself to Lincoln as he conflated nineteenth-century slavery with twentieth-century

communism: "In the election of 1860 Abraham Lincoln said the question was whether this nation could exist half-slave or half-free. In the election of 1960, and with the world around us, the question is whether the world will exist half-slave or half-free." [18]

As a metaphor for communism, "slavery" became linked in Cold War rhetoric with both "imperialism" and the "Oriental." In an attempt to discredit communism and link it with the collapsing European empires, American political leaders regularly described Soviet domination in Eastern Europe and Soviet aspirations in the developing world as "imperialistic" and affiliated communism with the "Oriental" qualities of Soviet secretiveness and conspiracy. At the same time, these invocations of slavery served as an inspiring history lesson. Like the many cultural diplomacy efforts that addressed the question of American racism, they were part of an effort to acknowledge and lay to rest a dark period in the American past by suggesting that the worst wrongs of racial oppression had been resolved a hundred years ago. These references to slavery suggested that America was best represented by its traditions of antiracist activism rather than by its racist, slave-holding history and its lingering consequences. This rhetorical strategy of defining the United States in opposition to slavery was part of the larger effort to identify it as a revolutionary force in the world, rather than ceding that status to the Soviet Union.[19]

By directly incorporating *Uncle Tom's Cabin* into this musical, Hammerstein makes explicit what was implicit in so much Cold War culture, namely, that the sentimental was alive and well as a mode of political discourse. "The Small House of Uncle Thomas" displays the debt that postwar discourses of modernization and expansion owed to nineteenth-century sentimentalism. It allows us to see the ways in which the representations of Cold War internationalism carried the residual traces of older discourses that imagined transcending boundaries of difference at home. By foregrounding Stowe's sentimental abolitionism, Hammerstein implies that the American-led modernization of Asia is a continuation of progressive reform movements—such as temperance, child protection, and urban reform—that had existed within the U.S. for over a century.

The theme of Western education unfolds through these three numbers, from an appeal for education by the Siamese in "The March of the Royal Siamese Children," through its enactment in "Getting to Know You," to its fruition on stage before British imperialists in "The Small House of Uncle Thomas." Throughout, this process of education has been figured in cultural—as opposed to military or conventionally political—terms: the embrace of Western, specifically American, cultural forms marks the successful modernization of the country. Because Anna works in the realm of culture, she remains untainted by charges of "imperialism"; in fact, the cultural transformations she initiates protect Siam from imperialism. Feelings are what her cultural education produces: feelings of friendship for her as a figure of the West, feelings of romantic love that undercut the King's authority. This collaboration of culture and sentiment, linked as it is with the overall feminization of the idea of progress, serves to legitimate the principles of modernization by stripping them of any imperialist overtones of force, coercion, and exploitation. Anna's explicit anti-imperialism—an invention of the postwar versions of the story—and its expression through the deployment of American culture, serves to establish American-oriented modernization as a clear alternative to imperialism and as an agent of political independence. But while *The King and I* rejects imperialism's methods of outright domination and rule, it does not reject the principle of wholesale transformation under and according to Western standards. Rather, the entire narrative revolves around achieving some of the ends of imperialism through non-imperial means.

Anna's effort to bring Siam into harmony with the West culminates in the number "Shall We Dance?" in which she teaches the King to polka in celebration of their success at fending off the British. The scene serves as the culmination of the sexual tension that has been building up between them, and, like that sexual tension, it is another of Hammerstein's inventions. The scene opens by reiterating the equation between Western gender roles and Western respect for individual rights that Anna has been insisting on all along. Anna and the King, seated in an empty ballroom, debate the relations between men and women: the King argues for the harem, a hierarchical relation of male dominance, while Anna argues for monogamous marriage, a more egalitarian relation between the sexes.

As part of her argument in favor of marriage, Anna introduces the polka as a ritual of Western courtship, an initiation into the Western sexual and, by implication, political order. Anna begins to dance by herself and the King, transfixed, looks at her with desire and joins in as she sings about dancing with a lover. The King demands to learn this dance and Anna complies, teaching him the polka's "1-2-3-and" rhythm; after some humorous interplay, he catches on and they dance together, only to stop abruptly when the King declares that they are not dancing the way he saw the "Europeans" dance that evening. In the film, a long pause fol-

Figure 20. The spectacle of Siam's Westernization: Anna (Deborah Kerr) and the King (Yul Brynner) dance a polka in the film *The King and I,* 1956. (Museum of Modern Art/Film Stills Archive)

lows as the music stops and the camera frames the two in a close shot: Anna slowly admits the King's point, and the King, looking her straight in the eye and with his hand rigidly outstretched in an unmistakably phallic gesture, takes her in a firm, close embrace around the waist; they look at each other intently, their breasts heave, and when the music erupts they begin to dance and whirl around the room (Figure 20). The number is intensely erotic: Anna wears a low-cut gown that, for the first time, displays her in a sexual manner, while the King wears a loose costume that exposes his hairless chest and bare feet; their dancing brings their bodies into close and active contact. The dance enacts the key moment of couple formation: in their first and only musical number together—and the last number of the show—Anna and the King finally surmount the barriers of race, sex, and culture that have kept them at odds for so long.

This number works as a spectacular moment of East-West integration, as the Western woman and the Asian King coordinate themselves with each other through the shared effort of the dance. Their voices and their movements bind them together into a harmonious unit, their synchronized bodies offering a physical manifestation of a joint effort undertaken to express a common sentiment. Their exaggerated costumes express their absolute difference from each other as Victorian lady and Oriental despot, yet at the same time each one's opulence complements the other visually. The scene evokes visually the pluralistic universalism of so much middlebrow culture, in which difference is first constructed and then ostentatiously bridged. It is a moment of perfect understanding between East and West, as Anna teaches, the King learns, and they communicate their feelings for each other through words and music, looks and touches.

This number brings to a climax the processes of cultural transformation initiated in "Getting to Know You." It is structured as an educational moment: Anna teaches the King how to polka, showing him the steps, the beat, and teaching him the words to the song. Like the children earlier on, the King mimics Anna's words and movements, only this time he repeats romantic words about individuals falling in love. Anna sings the first chorus of the song alone; the second time around, the King, having learned the words, joins in, finishing in harmony with Anna the lines that she had begun alone. As in "Getting to Know You," sentiment works here as the medium of education: the King wants to learn the polka because the respect and friendship he feels for Anna is turning into love. However, the veneer of cultural exchange has dropped away, and the King demands to dance just like the Europeans do.

Extending the dynamic of "The Small House of Uncle Thomas," "Shall We Dance?" offers a final spectacle of Siam's Westernization. As Anna converts the King to her domestic ideology of romantic love, she converts him also to her political ideology of respect for individual rights. When he demands that Anna teach him how to dance, the King demands that she teach him how to express with his body the very ideology that he rejects with his mind, and as he learns the form of this Western ritual, he imbibes its underlying content as well. The King performs his love for Anna in Western liberal and romantic rather than Oriental despotic form. The dance expresses Anna's liberal belief in individual rights and equality: unlike the relations between men and women of the harem, in which the women must prostrate themselves before the King, here the man and the woman stand and face each other as partners. The very song they sing—"Shall We Dance?"—takes the form of a request that may be accepted or rejected in contrast to the King's usual commands to "Eat. Eat. Eat" or "Sit. Sit. Sit" that can only be obeyed. The scene represents a moment of delicate balance between Anna and the King—he still has the power to command her, but he commands her to teach him the objective correlative of Western liberal ideology, the same ideology that enabled Tuptim to defy his authority publicly.

The ideological power of this number, and of the musical as a genre, derives from its ability to invite the viewers to participate in the events taking place on screen. Just as the King is drawn in to Anna's liberal political ideology by joining in her song and dance, so we are led to embrace the ideals of international integration and Third World modernization by our own sense of participation. We are first drawn in by the physicality of the number. As the dancers whirl around the room, the camera moves with them and seems to move us, too, so that we share in their sense of motion and exhilaration. Their obvious pleasure in dancing together is infectious—it spills out into the audience and makes us want to dance, too. The billowing fabric of Anna's dress has an almost tactile quality that, when combined with the dancers' exposed bodies, offers an unexpected sense of physical intimacy. The educational quality of the number also invites us in. As the King learns the words to the song and the steps to the dance, so do we, and we cannot help but at least mentally sing along. The number gives us the sense that we are participating—joyfully—in the King's political transformation and that we, too, can join the mixed-race, multinational community that is being forged on screen.

The heightened sense of participation that the viewer feels in this number brings to light how this sense of inclusion has been operating over the course of the whole show. Since so many of the numbers have revolved around the process of education, they have drawn us in as participants throughout. As Anna has been teaching the children and the King about how to become more like the West, she has been drawing the viewer into the process of national transformation that she undertakes.

By the end of the show many of the songs have become deeply, if not permanently, embedded in the brains of audience members, who can now sing them on their own. As a moment of community formation, "Shall We Dance?" echoes the final musical number in *South Pacific,* in which Nellie, De Becque, and the children join together to sing "Dites Moi." Both numbers invite the viewer to join a mixed-race, multinational community that is being forged through song and dance. In each case the song invites us, through simple words and repeating lines, to learn the song that a character is learning and to mentally sing along.

Singing along with a musical number can express any number of meanings, from identification with a particular character's state of mind to the pleasure that comes from lifting one's voice in song. One can read the musical numbers of *The King and I* as bringing millions of people together into an imagined community of Asians and Americans, and in the process fostering a sense of participation in Asia's transformation. This inclusive potential expanded as the musical numbers circulated through the cultural landscape, on Broadway, in movies, in touring companies, in amateur productions, on sheet music, on the radio, and on record albums. In singing along with Rodgers and Hammerstein's catchy tunes, Americans joined each other, if only momentarily, in affirming the project of modernizing Southeast Asia. As millions of Americans purchased the songs of *The King and I* in any of their multiple forms, they purchased a vision of themselves in relation to Southeast Asia that shared a fundamental logic with U.S. policies for the region.

"Shall We Dance?" marks the turning point in Siam's modernization. The number comes to a crashing halt when the King's aides drag in Tuptim, whom they caught trying to run away with her lover, and hold her spread-eagled and face down on the floor. The King pushes Anna away and, furious at Tuptim's challenge to his sexual and political authority, seizes a whip. As he raises it to strike Tuptim, Anna cries angrily, "You've never loved anyone. . . . You *are* a barbarian." Anna accuses the King of acting not out of love but out of brute power; he wants to whip Tuptim not because she has made him jealous, but because she has defied his absolute authority. Anna condemns him for his failure—inseparable in her mind—to love in the Western fashion and to recognize Tuptim's rights as an individual.[20]

Anna's accusation traps the King by demanding that he finally choose between modernization and tradition. Desirous of Westernization, yet hesitant to renounce the sexual and authoritarian underpinnings of his rule, the King snaps: he throws the whip to the ground and runs from the room, clutching his heart. He cannot bring himself to trample on Tuptim's right as an individual to love whomever she chooses. He realizes that the modernization he has set in motion has destroyed his ability to rule in his traditional manner, that the force of Westernization has proved more powerful than himself. Recognizing Anna's responsibility for the King's collapse, the Prime Minister shouts at her, "You have destroyed King. . . . He cannot be anything that he was before. You have taken all this away from him." In Anna's hands the romantic musical number becomes a political tool, a weapon capable of toppling a head of state—her polka kills the King.[21]

The musical concludes a few minutes later, as the King lies on his deathbed and his more democratically inclined son—and Anna's protégé—takes over the throne. In his first proclamation as ruler of Siam, Prince Chulalongkorn declares that henceforth Siam will be governed with greater respect for the individual and that no longer will the Siamese have to prostrate themselves before the king. He proscribes the physical manifestation of his father's authoritarian rule—"No bowing like toad. No crouching. No crawling"—and replaces it with the physical expression of respect between individuals that "Shall We Dance?" introduced: "You will stand with shoulders square back, and chin high . . . face king with proud expression . . . looking in each other's faces with kindness of spirit, with eyes meeting eyes in equal gaze, with bodies upright." In calling for individuals to stand upright and face each other with mutual respect, he repudiates his father's authoritarian rule, embodied in the image of Tuptim held prostrate on the floor awaiting her whipping, and institutionalizes the politically liberal image of Anna and the King dancing together. By making his first political act in effect an emancipation proclamation, Chulalongkorn suggests that Siam has learned the lessons of *Uncle Tom's Cabin* and will henceforth follow the blueprint of American history.[22]

Chulalongkorn stands as a model of the enlightened, democratically inclined leadership that Washington hoped would be produced by its modernizing mission in Southeast Asia. Biologically the King's child and politically Anna's, the Prince stands as the offspring of their joint effort to modernize Siam. While Anna did not physically give birth to him, both she and the King recognize that she is his intellectual parent, the source of the revolutionary content of his speech. The Prince, as the dying King acknowledges with ambivalent pride, has been "trained for Royal government" by a Westerner. Chulalongkorn meets the requirements that U.S. policymakers developed for the nationalist leaders they cultivated in Southeast Asia throughout the 1950s: like Phibun in Thailand, Magsaysay in the Philippines, and Diem in Vietnam, Chulalongkorn is an indigenous leader sympathetic to the West, imbued with the ideals of individualism and individual rights, yet thoroughly native even down to his dress, and youthful enough to lead his nation into the future. These pro-U.S. leaders were crucial not only for supporting U.S. policies in the region but also for shielding the U.S. from accusations of imperialism: as one policy memo explained in 1949, "The long colonial tradition in Asia has left the peoples of that area suspicious of Western influence. We must approach the problem [of communism in Asia] from the Asiatic point of view insofar as possible and refrain from taking the lead in movements which must of necessity be of Asian origin. It will therefore be to our interest wherever possible to encourage the peoples of India, Pakistan, the Philippines and other Asian states to take the leadership in meeting the common problems of the area."[23]

With the leadership of the fictional Siam now in the hands of a mere boy, Anna survives at the end of the musical as the last adult authority figure. This ending echoes the genres of order, like the Western: the King, as a relic of the old system and a potential threat to the Westernized new social order, must be killed off. At the same time, the ending reaffirms the community initially forged in "Getting to Know You." Acceding to a young princess's plea that she not let them "fall down in darkness," Anna decides to stay on as caretaker to oversee Siam's transition to modernity. In having her do so, the ending redraws the boundaries and structure of the royal family community, so that it will be led by a white, Western woman rather than by an adult Asian male. Anna's parental love for the King's children reveals itself here as the force that will guide Siam into the future and thus locates *The King and I* within the insistent postwar discourse of trans-racial adoption. *The King and I* is a variation on the *Madame Butterfly* narrative: a representative of America comes to Asia, falls in love with an Asian, the romance doesn't work out, the Asian dies, and the American takes over the upbringing of their shared child. *The King and I* inverts the sexes, but in many ways the gender remains constant: Anna is partially masculinized as the bearer of Western knowledge and authority, while the King is partially feminized by his ignorance and his intense eroticization. And like the *Madame Butterfly* narrative and *South Pacific* as well, *The King and I* pairs and contrasts two kinds of love that cross the racial divide: the romantic love between Anna and the King, which remains unconsummated, and the parental love she feels for her students, which finds full expression throughout.

The King and I picks up where *South Pacific* ends, in that it shows how a white mother actually raises up the Asian children with whom she has chosen to affiliate herself.[24]

As a teacher and a mother, Anna becomes an ideal representative of the United States as a modernizing force in Asia. Anna's goal has been to reproduce herself in the children, to mold them in her own image, so that their ideas and values echo hers: her job has been to produce a new nation by producing children who possess a new consciousness. Anna's loving instruction establishes an exemplary hegemonic relationship: it achieves its goals through sentiment rather than through physical force and by inculcating a desire on the part of its objects to behave in a certain way. It suggests power exercised not through direct political or military control, but through relations of exchange and influence. Anna's influence, like American-guided modernization, results in local leaders governing themselves but always according to Anna's precepts.

DANCING WITH THE CHINESE COMMUNIST PARTY

Hammerstein was not the first to use the dance between Eastern and Western partners as a symbol for peaceful international integration. Others committed to a vision of left internationalism had done the same in the late 1930s and early 1940s. "Shall We Dance?" recalls a similar scene from Wendell Wilkie's *One World*, the 1943 best-seller that, with its sympathetic treatment of the Soviets and the Chinese, captured the spirit of wartime internationalism and provided the rallying cry for the post-war world federalism movement. In describing a night he spent in the Middle East, Wilkie offered an image of East and West integrating themselves with each other via a romantic spectacle of song and dance:

> After a few formal speeches, the dinner became a concert, and the concert became an exhibition of Arab dancing girls, and this in turn became a Western ball with English nurses and American soldiers up from Basra on the Persian gulf and Iraqi officers dancing under an Arabian sky. No man could have sat through that evening and preserved any notion that the East and West will never meet, or that Allah is determined to keep the Arabs a desert folk, ruled by foreigners from across the sea.

With this scene, Wilkie creates an internationalist vision of a multinational, multiracial community bound together by a commitment to fight fascism and moving inexorably toward freedom from imperialism. "Shall We Dance?" visually and politically echoes Wilkie's image of East and West, bound together through music and dance, moving together into an increasingly close, and specifically non-imperial, relation.[25]

In the writing of left-leaning journalists Agnes Smedley and Edgar Snow, this vision of an East-West dance communicated a more radical vision of internationalism. Smedley lived and worked as a reporter in China from the late 1920s through the early 1940s, and was unwavering in her support for the communist cause. During the winter of 1937 she taught the leaders of China's Communist Party how to dance. Recovering in the mountains of Yan'an with the Red Army after its grueling Long March, Smedley was convinced that the survivors and the newly arrived young revolutionaries needed to relax; she also wanted to break down the rigid social codes imposed by the wives of the leading cadres that kept men and women apart. Encouraged by Mao and Zhou Enlai, she tracked down a phonograph and records of "On Top of Old Smokey," "Red River Valley," and "She'll Be Comin' Round the Mountain When She Comes," and arranged regular dance parties. In a letter to Edgar Snow, Smedley reported, "I have not yet corrupted Mao with dancing but I'll probably succeed soon. He wants to learn dancing and singing in case he has the chance to go abroad. Thus it was imperative he learn the latest fox trot."[26]

Drawing on her letters, Snow described Smedley's interactions with Mao:

> He and Agnes were the same age, and he questioned her in detail concerning her life, including her love life. Mao had read some Western poems in translation, and he asked Agnes whether she had ever experienced romantic love of the type poets such as Byron, Keats, and Shelley praised. . . . Mao wanted to know exactly what "love" meant to Agnes. . . . Agnes later said to me, "I was surprised at his childish curiosity." And again, "He said that he wondered whether the type of love that he had read about in Western novels could really exist and he wondered what on earth it was. . . . He seemed to feel that somehow he had missed out on something."

Like Anna Leonowens, Smedley teaches the revolutionary Asian leader about Western notions of love as she introduces him to Western social rituals. But unlike Anna, she teaches the common folk dances so beloved by Popular Fronters, as well as the classic dances of Western courtship. For Smedley, these dances with the Chinese communists in the mountains of Yan'an, tinged as they were with romantic overtones, expressed her internationalist aspirations for a deeper bond between America and China. They also, however, expressed her desire to modernize the outdated social customs that held sway among the revolutionaries. It was this social modernizing impulse that provoked dissen-

sion in the camp and ultimately forced Smedley to leave Yan'an. According to Snow, "The dancing, however, continued. Smedly considered
this a significant victory—a step toward removing the vestiges of feudal
thinking from Chinese society. Square dancing became popular beyond
Yan'an."[27]

RECEPTION

The King and I, according to this reading, was imbued with the geopolitical ideals of modernization and integration. But did contemporary
viewers actually read the show and the film in relation to foreign affairs?
To a surprising degree, they did.

Musicals in general were often seen in political and economic terms
in the late 1940s and 1950s. They figured prominently in the massive
global dissemination of American culture that took place after the war,
under both commercial and government auspices. Critics treated musicals as a particularly potent export, in part because they communicated
a sense of America's postwar power without carrying a negative national
image the way that many thought Hollywood movies did. *Newsweek*
announced the "New Empire of the American Musical" in 1956 and
lauded the Rodgers and Hammerstein–influenced Broadway show as
not only America's premier postwar cultural form, but also "one of the
great and indisputably successful U.S. exports of the mid-twentieth century." Under the headline "The American Musical Conquers Europe,"
the *Saturday Review* wrote approvingly about a U.S. occupation official in Austria who staged a Hammerstein-heavy review called "From
Show Boat to South Pacific" that garnered State Department support
and played in over five hundred venues in Germany and Austria. The article cheered that this official's production of *Kiss Me, Kate* had "done
more to promote the United States in Central Europe than half-a-dozen
ambassadors and/or cultural exchange programs." The State Department also used Broadway musicals as a high-visibility component of its
racial and cultural diplomacy efforts, as when it sent Gershwin's *Porgy
and Bess* on a European tour.[28]

Reviewers of *The King and I* often connected the show, despite its
nineteenth-century setting, to the contemporary political world. Some
praised it for its "social commentary" and its willingness to engage with
"serious" issues, while others condemned it as a "sermon" and com-
plained that its songs tended to dissolve in a "paroxysm of social commentary." A number of reviewers saw *The King and I* as grappling with

the same issues that policymakers did when they looked out at Asia: the
"conflict between East and West," the need to protect "individual . . .
rights," and the need for "social reforms" in non-Western countries.
Some saw the King as a "dictator" and Anna as an instructor in the ways
of "democracy." Others read it as a parable of modernization, and either
approved of Anna as a bearer of "progress" to a "backward country" or
questioned the validity of her nineteenth-century vision of the West as
"the giver of light and knowledge" to the East. At least one reviewer connected the show to decolonization, by noting the show's relevance at a
time when "Eastern lands have impinged themselves" on the American
consciousness through the "widening independence movement" and the
"fight against what they regard as Western imperialism and domination." Even Richard Rodgers turned to politics to explain his and Hammerstein's decision to do the show: they were drawn, he said, by "the
theme of democratic teachings triumphing over autocratic rule."[29]

News magazines used the familiar story of Anna and the King to introduce their readers to Thailand as an important U.S. ally. They frequently identified the current king of Thailand as the great-grandson
of Anna's employer, King Mongkut, and the grandson of her protégé,
Prince Chulalongkorn. In 1954, *Newsweek* invoked the show to teach
its readers about the long history of friendship between the U.S. and
Thailand and to justify the latest increases in economic and military aid.
Foreign affairs journalists looked to *The King and I* as a conceptual
bridge between Americans and their increasingly valuable ally in Southeast Asia; they used it to teach readers about complex issues in international relations and to remind them of what they already knew about
Thai history.[30]

Even before Rodgers and Hammerstein produced their musical version, popular nonfiction writers used Anna Leonowens's story as a template for narrating America's democratizing influence in Asia. In January 1948 *Reader's Digest* published "Elizabeth and the Crown Prince of
Japan," an article about Elizabeth Gray Vining, an American Quaker
who was hired by the Emperor of Japan to tutor the Crown Prince. The
article, which echoed the themes as well as the title of Margaret Landon's *Anna and the King of Siam,* detailed how an American woman
integrated herself into the Japanese imperial family in the years after
World War II and helped transform a former enemy into an ally. Continuing the discursive tradition of sentimental modernization, the article
presented Vining as a feminized emblem for the entire U.S. occupation
and reformation of Japan: "The work of one American woman," it sug-

gested, "may have untold influence on the future of 78,000,000 Japanese." Several years later *Reader's Digest* published another article that drew on Anna Leonowens's story, this time filtered through the musical version, to explain the modernization of Nepal. In February 1957, it published "Erika and the King of Nepal," a first-person account about a German masseuse who became incorporated into Nepal's royal family as a bearer of Western knowledge and who taught the King how to dance the foxtrot. When the King confided to her that he was trapped between an impending attack by communist China and an authoritarian prime minister who had seized control of the government, Erika served as a go-between to sympathetic forces in India. Her efforts succeeded, and the King, now safe from both communism and authoritarianism, set Nepal on the road to modernization.[31]

A number of political actors and observers saw the liberal internationalist sentiments of "Getting to Know You" as capturing Eisenhower's ideal of personal diplomacy. Organizers of the People-to-People program selected "Getting to Know You" as the program's theme for 1958. The song also served as the motto for Project Hope, the People-to-People hospital ship that traveled throughout Southeast Asia in the late 1950s dispensing medical services. For some of Eisenhower's critics, "Getting to Know You" came to summarize all that they disliked in his foreign policies. The writer Christopher Isherwood lambasted the musical for its implicit geopolitics—"I *hate* Anna, that sweetly smiling, gently snooty apostle of democracy and 'our' way of doing things"—and described "Getting to Know You" as containing some of the "vilest" lyrics that Hammerstein had ever written. George Kennan, head of the State Department's policy-planning section under Truman and originator of the containment doctrine, expressed his skepticism toward what he saw as Eisenhower's amateurization of diplomacy by pointedly noting that U.S. relations with Asia could not be effectively handled, "as many Americans like to believe, merely by thrusting ordinary people together and 'letting them get to know each other.'"[32]

The King and I was connected to Thailand's economic development in material as well as symbolic ways. When costume designer Irene Sharaff dressed the cast of the show in a distinctive silk fabric made in Thailand, she launched a major fashion trend. Before long, stylish American women and Hollywood actors were wearing clothes made from opulent and richly colored Thai silk. Jim Thompson, the American owner of a Thai silk company in Bangkok, had supplied Sharaff with the fabric and helped her with the costume designs, and when she credited his U.S. distributor in the theater program, orders began flowing in. Thompson had been in Thailand immediately after the war with the OSS (precursor to the CIA), and when he returned to Bangkok in 1947 he single-handedly reinvigorated the foundering silk industry. Within a few years dozens of companies were employing thousands of workers, and Thai silk had become the nation's fastest-growing export. Thompson was thrilled with the competition: his goal, as he explained it, had never been to exploit Thailand's underdevelopment for his own profit, but to use capitalism to better the lives of the Thai people. He looked askance at the huge American development projects that were appearing in Thailand in the 1950s and adamantly opposed those foreign companies who came in with the sole intent of extracting huge profits. Thompson favored forms of economic development that were grounded in the local social structure and respected local traditions. He put these views into practice in his own company, which maintained traditional weaving practices and was owned primarily by Thai stockholders. Thompson saw himself as a new breed of Western modernizer: with tongue only partially in cheek, he described his job as being "like a missionary but with better visual results." [33]

Thompson's success made him the best-known American in Thailand, and when dozens of American publications told his story, he became something of a legend at home as well. As the U.S. became increasingly involved politically and militarily in Southeast Asia, he stood out as an unambiguous success story—so much so that William Lederer and Eugene Burdick used him as a model for one of their "non-ugly" characters in *The Ugly American.* The increasing number of American tourists traveling in Southeast Asia made a beeline for his store, while his Bangkok home—built in traditional Thai style and filled with Thai art—became a regular destination for many of the political and cultural figures who were shaping American perceptions of Asia. His guests included Senator William J. Fulbright, who was an enthusiastic supporter of foreign aid and a loud critic of *The Ugly American,* travel writers Philip Wylie and Santha Rama Rau, and *South Pacific* director Joshua Logan. His home also became a gathering place for gay men in Southeast Asia, including Dr. Tom Dooley.[34]

Thompson's success took on a larger significance in the postwar discussions of modernization and development. The fiscally conservative *Reader's Digest,* which regularly promoted private capitalist investment in the developing world as an alternative to taxpayer-funded foreign aid, trumpeted the story of Thai silk as a model of how U.S.-Asian economic

relations should be structured. In 1959 it published an article that hailed
the convergence of Thompson's Thai Silk Company and *The King and I*
as "an example of 'foreign aid' at its best." It reported that Thompson
paid his workers well, gave them a share of the profits and a bonus of
three-months' wages every year, and that soon they were able to buy
American-produced household goods, luxuries, even automobiles. When
the principles of the free market were adhered to, it suggested, both
nations' economies would benefit. The liberal *Saturday Review* also
publicized Thompson's private model of economic development. Travel
editor Horace Sutton, who visited Bangkok during a 1959 around-the-
world trip, reported that in the aftermath of *The King and I* Thompson's
company was earning almost $1 million a year and his weavers were
"buying television sets and sending their sons off to U.S. colleges." Both
Reader's Digest and the *Saturday Review* suggested that private capital
investment, aided by American popular culture and the fashion sensibilities of American women, could help modernize Thailand by elevat-
ing the levels of living standards, consumption patterns, and even education to approach those in the United States.[35]

As much as the Thai people liked Jim Thompson, they detested Anna
Leonowens. In the 1870s Leonowens's books greatly offended those
Thai, relatively few in number, who read them, and the government apparently tried to buy up the whole edition of *The English Governess at
the Siamese Court* to prevent its distribution. When Margaret Landon
resurrected her story for a much larger audience in 1944, their offense
turned to outrage. With its global dissemination, Rodgers and Hammerstein's version only made matters worse, and the government banned the
musical as an insult to the monarchy. Visitors to Bangkok in the 1950s
were warned not to mention Anna and the King because "it makes the
Thais furious." The Thai people, recognizing the power of Western popular culture to shape the world's understanding of their country, resented the way that the story distorted history by giving credit for Thailand's modernization to a relatively minor—and Western—employee of
the court, rather than to their own forward-looking King Mongkut. The
Thai aversion to *The King and I* was so strong that when the King and
Queen visited Australia in 1962, the government radio network banned
the music from its airwaves for the eighteen days of their visit. When
Queen Sirikit eventually saw a New York performance of the show in
1985—at Yul Brynner's personal invitation—her spokeswoman reported the Queen thought it "fun" and added, "We all know that the
court would never act like that."[36]

•   •   •   •   •

Rodgers and Hammerstein's King of Siam held a powerful appeal for postwar Americans: Yul Brynner spent the rest of his life playing the leader of a developing nation who welcomes the West into his country and willingly dies rather than impede the process of modernization. *The King and I* made the transition to modernity seem painless, as long as native elites followed the West's instructions and knew when to step aside. But nine years after first playing the King, he starred in *The Magnificent Seven*, in which he played an American who must force modernization and freedom on a developing people almost against their will. These two roles suggest a fundamental ambivalence that always existed at the heart of modernization theory: while the peaceful transformation of the developing world was most desirable, it would be achieved through violence if necessary. Walt Rostow, like Yul Brynner, expresses this ambivalence in his own career: the academic planner of Third World development was also a hawk on Vietnam. This ambivalence allows us to see how the ideals of integration and containment, community formation and violence, polkas and gunfights always existed side by side in both the politics and the culture of the Cold War. By thinking about *The King and I* and *The Magnificent Seven* together, we can see how both sides of this ambivalence circulated throughout postwar culture in two of the most popular and distinctively American genres, the musical and the Western.

CHAPTER 6

Asians in America

Flower Drum Song *and* Hawaii

Hawaii will be the first state with roots not in Europe but in
Asia. This is bound to have a profound effect on America's
future in the entire Far East. . . . In Asian eyes, the U.S. is
the land of the white man, and all too frequently it is tarred
with the brush of "colonialism." Hawaii the 50th state could
change all this.

"Enchanting 'State,'" *Newsweek*, 1959

James Michener, after publishing *Tales of the South Pacific* with Macmillan in 1947, decided he wanted a different publisher to bring out his
second book. Years later he described his decision to move to Random
House as an expression of social conscience. "I had visited the Random
House offices," he explained,

> and had noted that their receptionist was a charming young Negro girl (she
> later appeared in the musical *Carmen Jones*). Most publishing houses at
> that time did not even employ Negroes in their shipping rooms. I imagined
> that Random's choice of a receptionist might cost some patronage, and I
> felt that an outfit willing to risk prejudice by such an act of faith would be
> a good one to associate with. So I got on the Fifth Avenue bus at Washing-
> ton Square, rode up to 50th Street, and handed that Negro girl the manu-
> script of *The Fires of Spring*.

Michener criticized the export of American racism in much of his writing
about Asia and the Pacific during the 1940s and 1950s. In his anecdote
about Random House, he shows that he was also concerned with racial
inequality within the United States and eager to put his social criticism
into practice by working with a publisher that shared his convictions.[1]

In exploring the role of race in the Cold War, it is useful to think in
terms of racial formations—the historically specific and socially con-

structed racial categories within which people live their lives. Racial formations are a product of both social structures and ideas: they result from the process of defining how race is organized socially and legally and what race means. In the century prior to World War II, racial formation in the U.S. largely revolved around the process of racialization, which separated peoples into distinct and incompatible biological categories called races. The racialization of African Americans was achieved, in part, through the system of segregation, which separated black people from whites legally, physically, socially, and politically. The racialization of Asian Americans, in contrast, was achieved through a series of laws regulating immigration and naturalization. Congress passed the first Chinese Exclusion Act in 1882, restricted Japanese immigration in 1907 with the so-called Gentlemen's Agreement, and created the Asiatic Barred Zone, which prohibited immigration from South Asia and the Pacific Islands, in 1917. The 1924 National Origins act sealed off virtually all immigration from Asia, while the Tydings-McDuffie Act of 1934 closed the last loophole that had allowed immigration from the Philippines, which was still a U.S. colony. Restrictions on the naturalization of Asians already in the U.S. followed a similar trajectory, beginning in 1870 with the Chinese and culminating in the Supreme Court's 1923 ruling that the "free white persons" criterion for naturalization categorically excluded all Asians. Collectively, these laws established the meaning of Asianness as foreign, as unassimilable, as "alien."[2]

In the 1930s and 1940s the racial formation of people of color within the U.S. began to change, as racialization gave way to ethnicization. With ethnicization, the socially and culturally defined category of ethnicity replaced the biological category of race as the preferred way to explain differences among populations. During World War II, official and unofficial propagandists celebrated America as a racially, religiously, and culturally diverse nation, and in the process they transformed the ethnic immigrant from a marginal figure into the prototypical American. This vision of America, as Nikhil Singh has suggested, served as one of the ideological foundations upon which the U.S. claim to world leadership rested, both during and after war. As a democratic nation of immigrants, this reasoning went, America alone possessed the ideals and the experiences to lead a multiracial world of independent nations in which imperialism had lost all legitimacy. Only America contained the principle of internationalism within its own borders: it alone could claim to be what Gunnar Myrdal described as "humanity in miniature" and what Carey McWilliams called "a nation of nations."[3]

The pervasive racial discrimination against African Americans and Asian Americans undermined this claim of world leadership, however, creating what Myrdal in 1944 called the "American dilemma." In order to justify the claim, the social organization of race within the U.S. had to be brought into alignment with professions of equality for all. Recognizing this imperative, the federal government instituted a series of legal and legislative reforms that, over the course of the 1940s and early 1950s, partially transformed the economic, political, legal, and social structures that regulated race in the United States. In a series of reforms aimed at African Americans, the federal government forbade racial discrimination in defense industries, prohibited the white primary, ordered the desegregation of the military, invalidated restrictive housing covenants, desegregated interstate travel, and ordered the desegregation of public schools. During this same period, a separate series of legislative reforms reopened the door to Asian immigration and allowed Asians within the U.S. to become naturalized citizens. Congress repealed the Chinese Exclusion Acts in 1943, passed laws allowing the immigration and naturalization of Filipinos and Indians in 1946, and in a 1947 amendment to the War Brides Act it allowed Asian Americans serving in the military to bring home Asian-born wives. In 1952 the McCarran-Walter Act abolished the principle of Asian exclusion by invalidating the racial bar to naturalization; it also created annual quotas for immigrants from the Asia-Pacific area, and added a family reunification provision. Several pieces of special legislation allowed the entry of Chinese refugees from communism after 1949 and allowed Asian children to come in as adoptees. By 1952, and for the first time in U.S. history, all Asians were allowed to become immigrants, and all Asian immigrants inside the U.S. were allowed to become naturalized citizens. Together, these reforms had as their ultimate goal the integration of Asian and African Americans into the political and social mainstream of American life.[4]

These changes in the social regulation of race were both real and limited: their significance often derived more from the legal precedents they overturned or established than from any dramatic social changes they ushered in. School desegregation did not follow automatically from the 1954 Supreme Court's *Brown vs. Board of Education* decision, nor did the 1952 Immigration and Nationality Act entirely eradicate the principle of Asian racial difference. Although the act did officially remove the racial bar to naturalized citizenship, it also perpetuated the racially discriminatory aspects of the 1924 law in a disguised form: Asians would be allowed into the country under what Neil Gotanda has called "quasi-racial, ancestry based quotas" rather than the strictly national quotas that applied to Europeans. This meant that the tiny Chinese quota would apply to all persons of at least 50 percent Chinese background, regardless of their national origin. Nevertheless, the 1952 law had a significant effect on immigration from Asia. Even though the quota for Japan was set at only 185 immigrants per year and China's was set at 205, the combined legal changes enabled about 45,000 Japanese and 32,000 Chinese immigrants to enter the U.S. over the course of the 1950s. These legal reforms and increased immigration began to change the meaning of Asianness within the United States: no longer legally aliens, Asians could begin to claim the status of "immigrant" at the very moment that it was being held up as a privileged category of American national identity.[5]

These legal reforms allow us to see the double meaning of integration in the postwar period: the domestic project of integrating Asian and African Americans within the United States was intimately bound up with the international project of integrating the decolonizing nations into the capitalist "free world" order. Many of the proponents of these reforms recognized this connection, as did middlebrow cultural producers. Michener's anecdote about choosing Random House because it employed a black receptionist and his reference to Oscar Hammerstein's all-black musical, *Carmen Jones,* allow us to see how the same cultural producers who narrated the international integration of the United States and Asia also grappled with the question of the integration of minorities within the United States. As the social structures organizing Asian people within the United States changed, the meaning of Asianness did as well. Hammerstein and Michener, through the musical *Flower Drum Song* and the novel *Hawaii,* participated in the changing racial formation of Asian Americans by articulating some of the new meanings that Asianness carried.

FLOWER DRUM SONG

In 1942 C. Y. Lee, the son of an impoverished gentleman landlord, left war-torn China to attend graduate school in the United States. Lee started at Columbia and then transferred to the creative writing program at Yale, where he received an MFA in 1947. After graduating, Lee left New Haven and headed west: he planned to return to China and write for the film industry there, but news of Mao's successes in the Chinese civil war interrupted his journey. Getting as far as California, he settled in San Francisco's Chinatown, where he took a job as a journal-

ist with a Chinese-English newspaper. Lee spent his spare hours writing
fiction, and in 1949—the year Mao's forces took control of China—
one of his short stories won first prize in a writing contest. That same
year Lee became a naturalized American citizen and started work on his
first novel, a lighthearted story about a wealthy family of refugees from
communist China living in San Francisco's Chinatown. In 1957 Farrar,
Straus and Cudahy published *Flower Drum Song,* and to Lee's surprise
the novel quickly climbed the bestseller lists.[6]

The popular success of Lee's novel should be seen within a broader
context of Asian American writing. The growing acceptance of the ethnicity paradigm opened up a new cultural space for minority writers.
Although the 1930s saw a flowering of writing by Asian American authors, some of whom, such as Toshio Mori and H. T. Tsiang, were affiliated with the Popular Front, World War II proved to be the real water-
shed. Just as the war prompted changes in the legal structures affecting
Asians in the U.S., it likewise dramatically increased their access to a national literary and cultural apparatus, although it did so unevenly. The
emotional bond that Americans felt with the people of China and the
Philippines as allies in the Pacific war created a greater awareness of and
sympathy toward Chinese and Filipinos living in the U.S., which translated into a national audience for the stories they had to tell. Established
publishing houses became increasingly interested in bringing out the
work of writers of Chinese and Filipino descent, and non–Asian Americans were increasingly interested in reading them. Carlos Bulosan's
America Is in the Heart (1946), for example, an autobiographical novel
about a migrant Filipino worker on the West Coast during the Depression, won critical and popular acclaim and was selected by *Look* magazine as one of the fifty most important works of American literature.
Published in the year the United States granted independence to the Philippines, Bulosan's book benefited from a concentrated, if brief, interest
in America's Asian colony. Americans had far less interest in reading the
works of Japanese American writers, who were identified with the wartime enemy and whose traumatic experiences in the internment camps
challenged the idea of America as a racially tolerant and inclusive society. John Okada's 1957 novel *No-No Boy,* for instance, which explored
the bitter aftereffects of war and internment on a Japanese American family, generated little enthusiasm among white or Asian American readers.[7]

Among the most popular Asian American literary works of the 1940s
and 1950s were those written by Chinese Americans: Pardee Lowe's *Father and Glorious Descendant* (1943); Jade Snow Wong's *Fifth Chinese*

Daughter (1950); and C. Y. Lee's *Flower Drum Song*. Each of these works was published by an established East Coast publishing house, garnered glowing reviews in the national press, and found a large readership across the country. Pardee Lowe's novel and Jade Snow Wong's autobiography, as the first book-length works published in English by American-born Chinese writers, were groundbreaking achievements; Wong's book enjoyed enormous longevity, and was the most financially successful book by a Chinese American author until at least 1982. All three works share certain similarities of theme and character, including a focus on the family. Each narrative revolves around generational conflicts between immigrant parents, who uphold many "traditional" aspects of Chinese culture and life, and their American-born children, who struggle to integrate themselves into white American society. Each of these authors also embraced the role of cross-cultural mediator: they used their writing to introduce non-Chinese readers to the people and customs of San Francisco's Chinatown.[8]

Lowe's, Wong's, and Lee's narratives each have a touristic quality. Motivated by an educational and sociological impulse, they guide their readers like privileged tourists through the inner workings of Chinese families, businesses, social relations, and customs. Chinatowns, of course, had been tourist destinations for white Americans since the 1880s and had appeared as such in musicals, magazine fiction, travel narratives, tourist guides, and journalistic exposés. These early works usually represented Chinatown in terms of absolute foreignness, constructing a trip there as either a visit to an exotic land or as a dip into a world of social pathology and vice. The narratives of the 1940s and 1950s, written when racial restrictions on Asian immigration and citizenship were being eased, offered a fundamentally different vision of Chinatown. They need to be seen, in part, as domestic counterparts to the postwar literature of international tourism in Asia: like Michener's *The Voice of Asia*, they introduce Americans to a people whose integration has become a geopolitical imperative. These three narratives ethnicize Chinese Americans by representing their difference in cultural rather than racial terms. It is in the display of ethnic culture—conceived in Boasian terms as a whole way of life—that the touristic nature of these narratives is most visible. Jade Snow Wong, for instance, brings the reader into a garment factory and an herbalist's shop, elucidates New Year's rituals and marriage customs, provides recipes for steamed rice and tomato with beef, and explains Chinese family structure and attitudes toward education. Pardee Lowe explains the importance of gift exchange and how Chinese language schools operate, while C. Y. Lee enumerates the distinctions between Chinatown restaurants aimed at tourists and those that cater to local tastes. These displays of Chinese ethnicity are balanced by displays of Americanization, as characters' consciousness and behavior are gradually transformed along American lines. Noteworthy scenes include those in which characters attend American schools and universities, enter into a Western hospital, become engrossed in a baseball game, use a commercial bank, and graduate from citizenship school. Chineseness in these texts thus becomes a matter of culture rather than race, and ceases to be a rationale for exclusion from an American society that increasingly defines itself in terms of cultural pluralism.[9]

The process of ethnicization can also be seen in these books' reliance upon the literary conventions of the family centered, ethnic-immigrant narrative that had been established by Euro-American authors in the late nineteenth and early twentieth centuries. Families, both nuclear and extended, figured centrally in the experience and literature of white ethnic immigrants. In contrast, the Chinatowns of the 1930s and 1940s— the period that Lowe's and Wong's texts cover—were bachelor societies composed largely of a single and male population. U.S. laws prevented Asian immigrants from forming families by restricting the immigration of Asian women, stripping the citizenship of American-born women who married noncitizens, and criminalizing miscegenation. By presenting Chinatown families as somehow representative, when in fact they were a rarity, Lowe, Wong, and Lee construct a similarity between Chinese and European immigrants around one of the issues that most clearly marked the racialization of Asians. This cultural work of ethnicization that these texts performed was a product not only of the authors, but of the entire literary apparatus of editors, publishers, and reviewers who selected which narratives would be published and shaped how they were promoted and received. The equation of Chinese Americans with white European immigrants became one of the lessons that these works taught. As one reviewer of *Father and Glorious Descendant* noted, "If the story it unfolds is at all typical, the development of Chinese Americans is much the same as that of many other immigrants." [10]

The commercial success of Lee's *Flower Drum Song* in 1957 attracted the attention of numerous film and theater producers, including Joseph Fields, Richard Rodgers, and Oscar Hammerstein. Their enthusiasm about the novel derived in part from their familiarity with the conventions of white ethnic theater. Producer Joseph Fields, who read Lee's novel first and approached Rodgers and Hammerstein about it, was the son of Lew Fields, a former member of a German-dialect vaudeville team that had been very successful in the turn-of-the-century ethnic theater. Rodgers and Hammerstein, in turn, had in 1944 produced *I Remember Mama,* John Van Druten's heartwarming play about a Norwegian immigrant family growing up in San Francisco, and their 1943 musical *Oklahoma!* featured an ethnic character who assimilates into a quintessential American frontier community. Together Rodgers, Hammerstein, and Fields won out over the competition, and in 1958 their musical version of *Flower Drum Song* opened on Broadway. The show was a respectable success, although not as overwhelming a hit as its predecessors *South Pacific* and *The King and I.* It played on Broadway for a year and a half, toured nationally for another year and a half, and played in London for a year. In 1961 Hollywood producer Ross Hunter released a film version of the show that was nominated for five Academy Awards.[11]

Flower Drum Song should be read as both a cultural narrative and a social practice—as a popular story and as an investment of capital, a body of hiring practices, and a series of marketing decisions. As it circulated around the country on stages and movie screens, *Flower Drum Song* created a focal point around which the integration of Asian Americans was enacted, performed, promoted, and publicized. It became a forum for the articulation of liberal views on race and for the repudiation of the older racial formation of racialization, and it created a cultural space in which Asian Americans could be publicly embraced as "real" Americans.

Rodgers and Hammerstein's version expanded the novel's work of ethnicization in a number of ways. In reworking Lee's story into a libretto, Hammerstein emphasized the ethnic elements in the story while cutting out Lee's limited, but significant, exploration of the racial discrimination experienced by Chinatown's residents. Amid an otherwise comic framework, Lee had included a number of episodes that revealed the intersecting exploitations based on race and class that Chinese Americans experienced. Lee's novel forced the reader to confront racism in the labor market, when college-educated Wang Ta could find no job other than as a dishwasher; it illustrated the proletarianization of educated workers, when a character with a Ph.D. in political science could only find work in a grocery store; and it depicted the sexual and emotional frustrations of life in a bachelor society, in which immigration restrictions had made marriage and family formation extremely difficult. Hammerstein omitted these discomforting scenes and instead crafted a narrative about the relative ease with which Chinese Americans were integrating into America. He pushed the character of the father into the background and, in keeping with the conventions of the musical genre, focused the story on the formation of two heterosexual couples: the elder son, Wang Ta, and Mei Li, a picture bride from China; and night-club owner Sammy Fong and Linda Low, a singer and stripper in his club. When Hammerstein wrote the lyrics for "Chop Suey," which the characters sing at a party celebrating Madame Liang's graduation from citizenship class, he produced a paean to a pluralistic American society. Hammerstein takes "chop suey" as his metaphor for an ethnically and culturally diverse America, and gives it form in a musical number that the Chinatown residents perform in a shifting variety of Western dance styles, from the square dance to the waltz. As a spectacle of assimilation, the number celebrates the permeable boundaries of cultural difference and the pleasingly "mixed-up" quality of contemporary American life.

Rodgers and Hammerstein understood this narrative of ethnicization as a liberal message about American race relations. Rodgers, when asked in an interview to explain the show, replied: "What's the show about? Well, it's the story of the confrontation of the Far Eastern and American civilizations, told in terms of the conflicts between first- and second-generation Chinese Americans in San Francisco. The usual thing you hear, you know, is East is East, and West is West, and all that nonsense. We show that East and West can get together with a little adjustment." In rejecting Kipling's dictum, Rodgers repudiates the prewar racial formation of Asians as absolute Other. Like the advertisement for the *Saturday Review* travel photo contest, Rodgers rejects the colonial mindset that insists on the absolute difference between East and West. Now that Americans have taken over from Europeans the mantle of the "West," he implies, such differences can be bridged. Rodgers's belief that East and West can "get together with a little adjustment" positions the show firmly within the postwar politics of cultural pluralism and liberal universalism and within the global imaginary of U.S.-Asian integration.[12]

Rodgers and Hammerstein's commitment to Asian American ethnicization evoked a variety of responses from reviewers. A number of them recognized and drew attention to the show's recycling of the conventions of earlier white ethnic narratives: the *New York Times* critic, for instance, saw the film as reproducing "the characters and comedy that used to bloom in any number of plays about German or Swedish or Jewish immigrants coming from the old to the new country . . . in years gone by," while the *New Yorker*'s reviewer noted that "back of the dragonish false front . . . we catch the oddest glimpse of 'The Jazz Singer' and 'Abie's Irish Rose.'" Other reviewers emphasized the show's racially liberal message, praising it as a "tuneful lecture on tolerance and good manners" and singling out the number "Chop Suey" as "a witty ode to U.S. pluralism." A number of reviewers, however, condemned the musical as "patronizing" and took it to task for inauthenticity. The *New Yorker* chastised the show as a "stale Broadway confection wrapped up in spurious Chinese trimmings" and dismissed the film as a "preposterous" and "pseudo-Oriental" "fraud," in which the "phony Chinese apothegms flow like tiger-bone wine, and the settings are every bit as authentic as Fu Manchu." *Variety* rejected the film as "distasteful" and unlikely to amuse Chinese American audiences: "It is as if we are being asked to note 'how darling' or 'how precocious' it is of them to undertake the execution of American dances, . . . to comprehend the science of baseball, or to grapple with U.S. idioms." Even *Time,* which had publicized the Broadway show assiduously, took a swipe at the movie version. Criticizing its use of Asian actors of various ethnicities to play Chinese characters, it protested, "Honestly, fellows, they really don't all look alike." These comments indicate the extent to which, by 1958 and even more so by 1961, Rodgers and Hammerstein's mild brand of liberal antiracism was coming to be seen as inadequate and outdated.[13]

Flower Drum Song must be seen, however, not just as a narrative of integration but as a material and social practice that enabled the integration of real people. The late 1950s saw a proliferation of Asian-themed plays and movies: *Rashomon, Kataki, Cry for Happy, The Cool Mikado,* and *The World of Suzie Wong* were all playing on New York stages when *Flower Drum Song* opened in 1958, and Hollywood had recently released *Love Is a Many-Splendored Thing* (1955), *Tea House of the August Moon* (1956), and *Sayonara* (1957). But Rodgers and Hammerstein did what no other Broadway producers had done before: they told an Asian American story and they told it using Asian American actors. Of the original cast of fifty-nine, only two were non-Asian; one was white and the other black. *Flower Drum Song* remained until *The Joy Luck Club* (1993) the only major Hollywood film—and until David Henry Hwang's new version of the show in 2002, the only mainstream Broadway musical—to feature an almost exclusively Asian American cast. Because of these casting decisions, the musical was also a source of pleasure for many Asian Americans. Young people especially enjoyed the rare opportunity of seeing versions of themselves represented positively as Americans who could speak without accents and who participated in contemporary social and cultural life.[14]

In a manner similar to Hammerstein's all-black *Carmen Jones,* the stage and film versions of *Flower Drum Song* gave work to hundreds of Asian Americans at a time when these actors had limited professional opportunities. Over the course of its New York run and national tour, the producers scoured cities, towns, and Chinatowns across the country for fresh Asian American talent, checking out small nightclubs, local theaters, YWCAs, and beauty pageants. As had been the case with *Carmen Jones* fifteen years earlier, the producers tapped into a pool of talent whose access to the Broadway stage had been restricted because of race. The show provided exposure to amateurs who were appearing on a commercial stage for the first time, and it boosted more established performers to stardom. The burst of Asia-themed narratives on Broadway and in Hollywood in the late 1940s and 1950s had created a small pool of experienced performers. The Broadway cast included Pat Suzuki (the first U.S.-born Japanese American to achieve popular music success), Miyoshi Umeki (the first Asian American woman to win an Academy Award), Jack Soo (later of TV's *Barney Miller*), and Keye Luke (who played the number one son in the long-running Charlie Chan film series); the film version added Nancy Kwan (who had recently starred in *The World of Suzy Wong*) and James Shigeta (the first Japanese American man to attain star status in theater, television, and music and the first to be groomed by Hollywood since Sessue Hayakawa in the early 1900s). Like *Carmen Jones,* the musical expanded the cultural space allotted to actors of color in mainstream theater and movies, allowing them to play a wide range of roles, including those, such as romantic male lead, usually reserved for whites. The movie version of *Flower Drum Song* also called attention to Chinese American painter Dong Kingman, a well-known watercolorist whose work had appeared on the cover of the *Saturday Review,* by using a series of his paintings in its opening credit sequence. In cover stories in *Time* and *Newsweek,* in a photography spread in *Life,* on the stages and screens of countless American cities and towns, *Flower Drum Song* made Chinese Americans visible as ethnic Americans, and not as an alien "yellow-peril" threat, at the very moment when immigration from Asia was starting up again after a quarter-century hiatus (Figure 21).[15]

The *Flower Drum Song* programs that theater audiences received furthered the show's narrative construction of Asian Americans as immigrants and as "real" Americans; like the program for *Carmen Jones* in 1943, they played an important role in the circulation of meaning around the show. Where the biographical sketches in the program for *Carmen Jones* had, in keeping with its Popular Front cultural politics, emphasized

TIME

THE WEEKLY NEWSMAGAZINE

Miyoshi Umeki & Pat Suzuki
in
"FLOWER DRUM SONG"

Philippe Halsman

Figure 21. *Flower Drum Song* made Asian Americans visible as ethnic Americans. Miyoshi Umeki and Pat Suzuki appeared on the cover of *Time*, December 22, 1958. (TimePix)

the working-class identity of the show's performers, the programs for *Flower Drum Song* identified the actors in terms of their ethnic mix, their immigrant origins, and their place of birth. Instead of simply noting each actor's previous stage work, the biographies identified the actors as "native Japanese, . . . Californian, . . . part Chinese and part Hawaiian, . . . from Shansi Province in North China, . . . native of Seattle, . . . born in Manila, . . . American of Korean extraction," and so on. Some programs even called attention to the citizenship status of the actors' parents: Pat Suzuki's parents were identified as "Californians of Japanese birth and American citizenship," Keye Luke's were simply "American citizens," and the father of Cely Carrillo from Manila was identified as "a retired Lt. Colonel in the U.S. Armed Forces, who fought in Bataan." Others acknowledged the internment of Japanese American actors during the 1940s and explained how some actors had changed their names —from the Japanese Goro Suzuki to the Chinese-sounding Jack Soo, for instance—as a way of avoiding the anti-Japanese racism.

In some sense, the need to identify these actors as American exposes the depth of the assumption that Asian Americans are inherently foreign. Such a national identification of the black actors in *Carmen Jones* would have been unthinkable, since the racialization of black Americans did not involve a denial of their Americanness. One can also read these programs, however, as extending the mediatory social function of Lowe's, Wong's, and Lee's Chinatown narratives. They introduced audiences not just to a fictional narrative about Chinese Americans, but to a large and ethnically diverse group of Americans with roots in countries throughout Asia. By naming national origins, the programs identified some actors as belonging to the emblematic American category of immigrants; by describing others as "natives" of the states in which they were born, they asserted an Americanness not identified in racial terms; and by defining some as Americans of a particular national "extraction," they emphasized how American nationality supersedes but does not eliminate ethnic identity. By including the citizenship status of foreign-born parents, the program called attention to the newly established race-neutral criteria for U.S. citizenship, and when it identified one father's service in the U.S. military, it hinted at the links between the growing presence of Asian Americans and the history of U.S. expansion in the Pacific. Perhaps most important, these mini-biographies created a continuity between the fictional characters on stage and the real actors who performed them, thereby expanding the show's narrative of inclusion to encompass the real actors. If audiences could accept a story about Chinese becoming Americans, the program suggested, they should also be able to accept these flesh-and-blood Korean, Japanese, Filipino, and Hawaiian Americans as real Americans, also.

One could read this process of ethnicization that occurs within and around *Flower Drum Song* as a process of "whitening": by depicting Chinese Americans in the same terms used to represent European immigrants, and by ignoring the history of race-based exclusion, proletarianization, and ghettoization, the musical and the surrounding publicity imply that there were no racially specific differences in the experiences of European and Chinese immigrants. One could argue that the show and the film construct Asians, like Europeans, as racially unmarked —"white"—as they assimilate into a national American identity that ostensibly renders racial identities obsolete. The power of the show to elevate a national over a racial identity and to extend its narrative of integration into the lives of its actors affected even Juanita Hall, the show's black actress, who played Madame Liang. A story about Hall in *Ebony* recounted how C. Y. Lee had once asked Hall, who had also played the Tonkinese Bloody Mary in *South Pacific,* if she had much "Chinese blood," because she seemed so Chinese on stage. "There was a time," the reporter wrote, "when she quickly corrected such a mistaken impression by explaining proudly, 'I am a Negro.' Now, a little older, wiser, more tolerant, she smiles, says, 'I'm an American.'" Hall, in keeping with the show's vision of tolerance and integration, rejects the racial label and defines herself in the ostensibly racially unmarked—and increasingly inclusive—terms of nationality instead. Like her character Madame Liang, who graduates from citizenship class during the show, and like the thousands of black civil rights activists, Asian immigrants, and newly naturalized Asian American citizens, Hall stakes a claim to an Americanness that is becoming less restricted on racial grounds.[16]

The film version of *Flower Drum Song* makes this whiteness reading an easy one to make. The story focuses on eldest son Wang Ta's romantic choice between two women: the American-born and wholly assimilated Linda Low, played by actress Nancy Kwan (who has a Chinese-Scottish background), and the recent immigrant Mei Li, played by actress Miyoshi Umeki (who was born in Japan). The terms of his choice are laid out in two musical numbers that develop the character of each woman.

Linda Low's character-defining number, "I Enjoy Being a Girl," makes a visual spectacle out of the equation of assimilation with whiteness. The number takes shapes as Linda, dressed only in a skimpy wrap-around, sings about the social and sexual pleasures of being a "girl," such as her "curvy" silhouette, the "whistle" she attracts from men, and her future life with a "brave and free male." Set in her boudoir before a multi-paneled mirror, the number is overwhelmingly white: the furniture, the carpeting, the walls, her costume, the phone are all blazing white. In a quasi-surreal moment, three separate Lindas appear in the mirror, each one wearing a different stylish outfit. The number presents Linda Low as the epitome of the assimilated, Americanized, Asian woman. There is nothing particularly "Chinese" about this number: her clothes, or lack thereof, are standard issue for a white star in a Hollywood film, and her body conforms to mainstream standards of beauty—she's tall, leggy, has fine features—and no modesty prevents her from displaying it (Figure 22). Her song defines her in gendered rather than racial or ethnic terms. She sings about being a "girl" rather than being "Chinese," and she cares about what all "girls" in the 1950s are supposed to care about: clothes, hairdos, and dates with a boy named "Joe or John or Billy." The number does not present her as fundamentally different from any other Hollywood bombshell—Marilyn Monroe or Doris Day could perform this number without any real changes. It is hard not to read this scene as a visual representation of Chinese American whiteness—the overwhelming paleness of the costume and decor seems to literalize her assimilation.[17]

Linda Low's character and visual presentation stand in marked contrast to the film's other instance of Chinese femininity, the immigrant Mei Li. Mei Li's signature number is "A Hundred Million Miracles," which she sings in a street-corner park. She has just arrived in San Francisco with her father, fresh off the boat from Hong Kong, and is trying to track down the man to whom she has been betrothed as a picture bride. This number presents Mei Li as typically "Chinese": her costume is Hollywood's version of traditional dress— black satin pants, a smock with a mandarin collar, a cap, and black slippers. She even wears her hair in a long queue, the stereotypical emblem of Chineseness in the late nineteenth and early twentieth centuries. She sings with a noticeable accent, her demeanor is modest, she doesn't expose much of her body, and she bows often. The song she sings, like the flower drum she performs with, is a putatively traditional Chinese one, and in introducing it to the audience, her father invokes the traditional ideal of "filial piety" and the foreign images of "ghosts" and "loyal officials." The staging of the number also emphasizes her separateness from the Chinese Americans who surround her as an audience and who wear Western clothes and hair-

Figure 22. Assimilation as a spectacle of whiteness: Linda Low (Nancy Kwan) enjoys "being a girl" in the film *Flower Drum Song,* 1961. (Photofest)

styles. In contrast to Linda Low, Mei Li's musical number marks her heavily as Chinese, as ethnic, as foreign (Figure 23).[18]

Wang Ta, the young male protagonist, starts out in love with Linda Low but ends up marrying Mei Li. The comparison of these two scenes raises the question—why choose the one over the other? In a show that celebrates the process of becoming American, why privilege a character

Figure 23. The "foreign" Mei Li (Miyoshi Umeki) sings about Chinese traditions in the film *Flower Drum Song*, 1961. (Photofest)

that highlights foreignness over one that emphasizes assimilation? One
possible answer comes from reading these two characters as the two poles
of the stereotypical Asian American woman. Linda Low is the hyper-
eroticized sexual expert, the kind of woman Nancy Kwan had portrayed
the previous year in *The World of Suzy Wong*. Mei Li, on the other
hand, is the docile, subservient Asian woman, similar to the character

Miyoshi Umeki portrayed, and won an Oscar for, in *Sayonara* four
years earlier. According to the logic of Hollywood, a decent leading man
might fool around with Linda Low, but he has to marry the more do-
mestically inclined Mei Li.

A different, and more historically grounded, reading would be that
what the film values in Mei Li is precisely her Chineseness, her strong
marks of ethnicity. The problem with Linda Low is that she is too assimilated, she is too "white," she has lost any significant ties to China.
Her romance with Wang Ta collapses because she does not adhere to
what the show has defined as traditional Chinese values: she offends his
family with her materialism, her explicit sexuality, and her lack of family ties, all of which come together in her job as a nightclub stripper.
Although Mei Li adopts numerous Americanisms—she picks up some
slang and learns how to kiss from watching TV—she never loses all her
conventional markers of Chineseness: her halting speech, her quiet modesty, her way of dressing and bowing. She is the heroine because she
holds assimilation in balance with ethnicity. Mei Li offers an example
of what literary critic Frank Chin has described as "dual identity": her
consciousness contains both Chinese and American elements. Chin, as
well as many other Asian Americanist scholars, condemns dual identity
for perpetuating the idea that Asian Americans are permanent foreigners, racialized aliens forever identified with countries they may never
have seen. The literary work that Pardee Lowe, Jade Snow Wong, and
C. Y. Lee produced during the 1940s and 1950s abounds with dual-
identity characters like Mei Li who bridge the gap between Chineseness
and Americanness. Their privileged position in these popular narratives
suggests, however, that they represent something more complex than
simple alienness.[19]

I want to suggest that in the 1940s and 1950s it was precisely the dual
identity—the foreignness—of Chinese Americans that gave them value
as Americans. *Flower Drum Song* hardly advocates the "melting" of
Asian difference into a homogenous sameness of postwar American
whiteness. The idea of dual identity—as opposed to wholesale assimilation—was crucial to the changing racial formation of Asian Americans and other ethno-racial minorities during the 1940s and 1950s and
had everything to do with the global imperatives driving the reformula-
tion of American national identity as a pluralistic nation of immigrants.
Dual-identity characters like Mei Li possess cultural and political value
precisely because their non-American parts connect America to the rest
of the world. Although they are not exclusively foreign, their partial for-

eignness makes them worth assimilating into American society, because it legitimates the nation's claim to be "a nation of nations." Mei Li's obvious and persistent Chineseness contributes far more to the argument for America as "humanity in miniature" than does Linda Low's spectacular whiteness. In an era of global expansion, these residual ties to other nations and other peoples carry significant ideological benefits.

The creators of *Flower Drum Song* were not the only people who valued Asian Americans' continued ties to their ancestral homelands: Washington did as well. Over the course of the 1940s and 1950s the U.S. government regularly employed ethno-racial minorities as agents and legitimators of U.S. expansion. During World War II, for example, the U.S. Marines recruited hundreds of Navajo Indians as radiomen in the Pacific theater because their language provided a code that the Japanese were unable to break. During these same years the OSS drew upon the local knowledge and community ties of Sicilian immigrants living in Middletown, Connecticut, to plan the invasion of Italy. This enlistment of "ethnic" Americans of all colors expanded during the Cold War. In 1948, when the U.S. feared that Italy was on the verge of voting the Communist Party into power, U.S. officials encouraged a letter-writing campaign in which Italian Americans urged their relatives back home to preserve democracy and vote against communism. In these cases, Washington employed ethnic Americans as agents of expansion: they took actions that helped the U.S. spread and preserve its influence around the world.[20]

The U.S. government also employed ethno-racial minorities as legitimators of expansion during the Cold War, in an effort to deflect the criticism of Asian and African leaders. The State Department and the USIA employed numerous African Americans as cultural ambassadors, sending them abroad to spread the word that while discrimination still existed in parts of America, it was on the way out. Washington also enlisted the services of Asian American cultural producers, including two of the artists associated with *Flower Drum Song*. In the early 1950s the U.S. Army hired C. Y. Lee, who had not yet written *Flower Drum Song*, to teach Chinese languages at its California Language School, and between 1955 and 1957, when he had finished his novel but not yet published it, Lee worked as a feature writer for USIA's Radio Free Asia. In 1954 the State Department sent Dong Kingman, the artist who had painted the movie's opening credit sequence, on a Goodwill Ambassador tour of Asia as part of its cultural exchange program. Kingman spent five months lecturing and exhibiting his work in India, Korea, Japan,

Taiwan, Hong Kong, the Philippines, Singapore, Thailand, and Malaysia. When he returned, he submitted his report to the State Department in the form of a forty-foot-long painted Chinese-style scroll, which *Life* magazine reproduced.[21]

In 1952 Washington sent Jade Snow Wong, author of *Fifth Chinese Daughter*, on a forty-five-stop speaking tour through Asia. Wong was the first Chinese American sent overseas by the State Department, and she received a hearty welcome, in part because the department had previously arranged for her book to be translated into a number of Asian languages, including Chinese, Burmese, and Thai. The State Department had originally booked Wong for a two-month tour, but American embassies were so eager to have her visit their posts that they extended her visit to four months. Wong stopped in Japan, the Philippines, Hong Kong, Malaya, Thailand, Burma, India, and Pakistan, where she spoke about the United States and the life it offered for Chinese Americans. As she later explained, Wong understood her "dual heritage" as a political asset for the nation, one that allowed her to internationalize the role of cultural mediator that she had constructed in her autobiography. She embraced the role that Washington offered her because she felt "a moral obligation to interpret what she knew of the United States to fellow Asians." She also felt her tour "would be good for the image of the United States" and "inspiring" to Asians who were "searching for identities" in the midst of decolonization: it might encourage wavering and nonaligned peoples to decide to look more favorably at the United States. Wong used her speeches, as did many of the cultural ambassadors of color, to defend America from the ubiquitous charges of racism. When asked about prejudice, she acknowledged that she had experienced it, but emphasized that "racial prejudice had never stopped her from getting where or what she wanted." She defended America as a racially inclusive country and shifted the blame for the effects of discrimination onto Asian Americans themselves: the "fear of prejudice," in her view, ultimately proved more "damaging" than any white bigotry because it offered an "excuse" for "personal failure." Wong put the ideals of cultural pluralism and assimilation on display for audiences throughout Asia and, as a representative of the nation, performed her integration into American society.[22]

In *Fifth Chinese Daughter*, Wong had constructed herself as a discursive tour guide to Chinatown for American readers; in 1956 she turned this literary fiction into a social practice when she and her husband guided a group of American tourists on a trip to Hong Kong and Japan.

Two years later the flow of American tourists to Asia had increased to the point that Wong and her husband started a travel agency and began organizing regular tours to Asia, where they introduced Americans to Madame Chiang Kai-shek in Taiwan, Buddhist monks in South Vietnam, and indigenous art in Cambodia. As a tour guide and travel agent, as well as a cultural diplomat and Chinese American, Wong facilitated the flow of persons and information between the U.S. and Asia that many Americans believed would help foster closer ties between these parts of the world. In becoming a travel agent, she transformed her status as an ethnic mediator within the U.S. into a new role as an international mediator between the U.S. and Asia.

Washington valued these "ethnic" Americans as protectors, representors, and explicators of the nation precisely because it saw them as being, in some way, still Navajo, Sicilian, African, and Chinese, as well as American. It sought to tap into and mobilize their ethnicity and cultural difference in support of internationalism and expansion. This is not to suggest that all expressions of ethnic identity found favor in the government's eyes. To the contrary, only those that could be safely subsumed to a larger national identity and that did not question the fundamental principles of foreign policy were encouraged. This is also not to suggest that all people who participated in these efforts served as simple propagandizers for U.S. globalization; while some of them certainly did, others forged alternative understandings of internationalism or found their awareness of American racism heightened by encountering Third World criticisms of it firsthand. What we do see in these examples is the U.S. government drawing upon and encouraging a sense of ethnic identity as a means of advancing the material and ideological projects of international integration.[23]

STATEHOOD FOR HAWAII

Like Oscar Hammerstein, James Michener in the late 1950s turned from writing narratives about the international integration of America and Asia to write a narrative about the domestic integration of Asians within American society. While Hammerstein focused on San Francisco's Chinatown, Michener wrote about the territory of Hawaii. For Michener, as for many observers, Hawaii more than any other place in the country affirmed America's status as a "nation of nations" and as "humanity in miniature."

The Hawaiian Islands had played a material role in America's expansion into the Pacific since the early nineteenth century. American sailors involved in the China trade began stopping at the islands in the late nineteenth century, and Nantucket whaling ships followed soon thereafter. New England missionaries arrived in the 1820s, riding the first wave of evangelical zeal that carried Americans into China, India, and Southeast Asia. Together with merchants, they began transforming the social, political, and economic structure of the islands along American lines. By the 1880s American sugar planters had led the islands securely into the U.S. economic orbit, and in 1893, acting with the support of the U.S. minister to the islands, they overthrew the native government of Queen Liliuokalani. Washington annexed Hawaii five years later during the Spanish-American war, incorporating the islands into a territorial empire that encompassed the Philippines, Puerto Rico, and Cuba. In the twentieth century the U.S. developed Hawaii as the anchor of its string of Pacific military bases, and during World War II Hawaii became a major jumping-off point for operations in the Pacific.[24]

Hawaii's role as a staging area for U.S. expansion into Asia and the Pacific increased dramatically with the Cold War. The islands became ever more militarized as the U.S. occupied Japan and waged war in Korea and Vietnam; with sixteen major military installations on Oahu alone, it became the central supply node in America's network of military bases spanning the Pacific. Defense dollars poured into the islands and became a pillar of the post-plantation economy, providing a livelihood for fully one-fourth of the islands' population; more than any other state, Hawaii depended financially upon the continuation of the Cold War. The U.S. government also treated Hawaii as an important location from which to wage the struggle for the hearts and minds of Asia. In 1959 Washington launched the East-West Center in Honolulu, which the *Saturday Review* hailed, in yet another reworking of Kipling, as the place "Where the Twain *Will* Meet." (In 1964 it offered the job of director to Norman Cousins, who turned it down for personal reasons.) The East-West Center promoted both cultural policies of integration and military policies of containment. Designed as a counterpart to Moscow's Friendship University, it brought Asian, Pacific, and American students together in one setting; at the same time, it coordinated grants for Indonesian military officers who were undergoing small-arms training before the 1965 military coup that, with the goal of eradicating communism, left a half-million Indonesians dead. Hawaii also facilitated the postwar flow of American civilians into the East, serving as a jumping-off point for tourists traveling to Asia and the Pacific.[25]

The growing material significance of Hawaii after 1941 was matched by its increasing visibility in American culture. The islands had been familiar to the mainland since the 1920s as an elite vacation destination and source of popular music, but the Japanese attack on Pearl Harbor fixed the territory in the public mind as an integral part of the nation. Both the militarization of the islands and the advent of commercial jet service in 1959 made Hawaii increasingly available to middle- and working-class mainlanders. Tourism to the islands grew exponentially during the 1950s, making it one of the foundations of the islands' economy: tourist spending jumped 350 percent between 1950 to 1959, from $24 million to $109 million, while the number of tourists increased from 34,000 in 1945 to 243,000 in 1959. Hawaii proliferated throughout popular culture in travel essays, advertisements, and movies such as *From Here to Eternity* (1953) and Elvis Presley's *Blue Hawaii* (1961), and contributed to the postwar fascination with all things Polynesian that found expression in Pacific-themed restaurants and hotels. It also provided a material basis for much of the cultural representation of Asia and the Pacific in general during the postwar period: William Lederer, *Reader's Digest*'s roving editor in Asia and coauthor of *The Ugly American,* lived in Hawaii and used the islands as a base for much of his writing about Asia; Dr. Tom Dooley polished his draft of *Deliver Us from Evil* there; *South Pacific* was filmed in the islands; numerous around-the-world travel narratives, such as Philip Wylie's *The Innocent Ambassadors* and Horace Sutton's 1959 series in the *Saturday Review,* used the islands as their gateway between America and Asia; and a number of *Flower Drum Song*'s cast members, including James Shigeta, the film version's leading man, came from Hawaii.[26]

Hawaii's campaign for statehood, which ran more or less continuously from 1945 to 1959, kept the territory alive in the nation's political culture. It also served as one of the primary sites in which the changing racial formation of Asian Americans became visible. As a U.S. territory, Hawaii enjoyed a liminal status. An integral part of the nation legally, its residents paid federal taxes, were subject to the laws of the United States, and, if they met national eligibility requirements, were U.S. citizens. At the same time, however, residents of Hawaii could not vote in presidential elections, the president appointed their governor, and their elected representative to Congress had no voting power. Although the statehood debate involved a number of questions, such as whether the nation could include a noncontiguous state, race was the big issue: people of Asian and Pacific background outnumbered whites

three to one. Plantation owners had begun importing Asian laborers in
the mid-nineteenth century, and by 1959, 54 percent of the population
was Asian. The Japanese formed the largest group at 35 percent, followed by Filipinos at 12 percent, Chinese at 6 percent, and Koreans at
1 percent. Full or part native Hawaiians accounted for 18 percent of the
population, while 2 percent was Puerto Rican. Only 25 percent of the
population was white. There was no legal segregation on the islands and
intermarriage was common, with about 10 percent of marriages before
World War I and more than 30 percent in the 1950s taking place between people of different races. The territory of Hawaii was thus simultaneously Asian, in terms of its population, and American, in terms of its
political relationship with the U.S. The debate over Hawaii's statehood,
which raged in the national press and in the halls of Congress for fourteen years, was largely a debate over the relationship between these two
categories, Asian and American: Were they mutually exclusive? Could a
people be both Asian and American? Could America in some way be an
Asian nation? The struggle over Hawaiian statehood became a struggle
to define both the meaning and the social organization of Asianness in
America.[27]

As a pivotal moment of Asian American racial formation, the postwar statehood movement should be seen in relation to the black civil
rights movement that was taking shape in the American South during
the same years. Both movements raised similar issues about the legal
rights of racial minorities, and both were fueled by the demands of veterans—blacks in the South and Japanese Americans in Hawaii—for full
access to the benefits of citizenship that they had defended with their
lives during the war. At the same time, significant differences distinguished them. The civil rights movement was a grassroots mass movement that challenged the legal organization of race as it structured daily
life in the South, and this challenge provoked confrontations, such as the
Montgomery bus boycott, the march on Selma, the freedom rides, and
the conflict over school desegregation in Little Rock, that captured the
nation's attention. The Hawaiian statehood movement, in contrast, was
neither a mass nor a specifically race-based movement: spearheaded by
the elected officials of Hawaii and waged peacefully in the halls of Congress, it did not seek to restructure the everyday organization of race in
the islands per se, but to secure for all the territory's residents the full
rights of U.S. citizenship.

Supporters and opponents of statehood often made their arguments
by discursively mapping Hawaii onto a national and global geography.

Physically, the Hawaiian islands are isolated in the midst of the Pacific Ocean: they are located 2,000 miles west of the continental U.S. and 4,000 miles east of Japan; Alaska looms 3,000 miles to the north, while the nearest major Pacific islands are 2,000 miles to the south. Part of the statehood debate involved determining where Hawaii "belonged" politically, culturally, and racially. All sides agreed with Joseph R. Farrington, Hawaii's Congressional delegate in 1949, that Hawaii stood as the "gateway to the South Pacific and the Far East" and the point "where east meets west." They parted company, however, in the meanings that they assigned to this position of U.S.-Asian convergence.[28]

Opposition to statehood, as to the civil rights movement, came primarily from Southern Democrats such as Senators James Eastland of Mississippi, Strom Thurmond of South Carolina, and Herman Talmadge of Georgia. Struggling to maintain the legal separation of races in their own states, they were threatened by the prospect of a multiracial state that eschewed legal segregation and would likely elect nonwhite and pro–civil rights senators. Strom Thurmond argued against statehood by mapping Hawaii in relation to Asia and denying its ties to the United States:

> There are many shades and mixtures of heritages in the world, but there are only two extremes. Our society may well be said to be, for the present, at least, the exemplification of the maximum development of the Western civilization, culture, and heritage. At the opposite extreme exists the Eastern heritage, different in every essential—not necessarily inferior, but different as regards the very thought processes within the individuals who comprise the resultant society. As one of the most competent, and certainly the most eloquent, interpreters of the East to the West, Rudyard Kipling felt the bond of love of one for the other; but at the same time he had the insight to express the impassable difference with the immortal words, "East is East, and West is West, and never the twain shall meet."

Thurmond emphatically embraces, rather than reworks, Kipling's emblematic phrase. He constructs Asia and America as mutually exclusive categories which represent the "extreme," and by implication pure, categories of East and West. Because Hawaii is Asian, Thurmond suggests, it cannot possibly also be American. Thurmond uses the phrases of culture rather than race—he speaks of "civilization" and "heritage," and disavows the idea that the East is inherently "inferior"—but he makes a racialist and segregationist point, namely, that the difference between Asians and whites is absolute and "impassable." In arguing that the Chinese, Japanese, Filipinos, and Koreans of Hawaii are fundamentally unassimilable, Thurmond resurrects the racializing logic of the exclusionary immigration laws which deemed Asians to be aliens ineligible for citizenship. The specter of miscegenation haunts Thurmond's view, so that in spite of the "bonds of love," the racial separation must be maintained. With his positive invocation of Kipling, Thurmond also maps America in relation to Britain: America has Northern European roots that must be maintained.[29]

Other opponents of statehood mapped Hawaii in relation to the Soviet Union. In the late 1940s, labor leader Jack Hall organized Hawaii's mostly Asian plantation and dock workers into the radical International Longshoremen and Warehousemen's Union. Hall's success drew the attention of Washington's communist hunters to the islands, and in 1953 he and six other union leaders were convicted under the Smith Act of conspiring to overthrow the government. (The decision was overturned on appeal in 1958.) Opponents of statehood latched onto these accusations and, linking the union's nonwhite membership with its political radicalism, charged Hawaii with being irredeemably "tinctured with Communism." The American Communist Party's well-known commitment to racial equality made this equation of integration and communism as easy to make in Hawaii as it was in the rest of the country, where HUAC investigators, Southern segregationists, and FBI members regularly accused civil rights activists of being party members and fellow-travelers. Senator Hugh Butler launched this anticommunist argument in 1949—the year Mao took power in China—when he announced that the American Communist Party supported Hawaiian statehood and was working for a state constitution that would be "dictated by the tools of Moscow in Hawaii." Imagining Honolulu as bound to Moscow, Butler saw Hawaii's position as gateway to the East as a point of national vulnerability: he accused the islands of being "one of the central operations bases and a strategic clearinghouse" for the worldwide communist campaign against America. Four years later, as the Korean War wound down to its unsatisfying conclusion, Senator John Pillion likewise represented Hawaii as a doorway through which communists could enter the nation at will. He warned against statehood as a Russian plot and declared that admitting Hawaii into the Union would be to "actually invite two Soviet agents to take seats in our U.S. Senate."[30]

Statehood advocates, in turn, turned Hawaii's racially diverse people —and the relative harmony in which they lived— into a benefit that the islands would bestow upon the rest of the nation. Where statehood opponents argued in the decreasingly legitimate terms of racialization, supporters mobilized the increasingly dominant terms of ethnicization. Already in the 1920s social scientists began applying the principles of the ethnicity paradigm to the islands and pointing to their polyglot population as proof that multiple races could live together in harmony. By the 1930s Hawaii had earned a reputation as a racial paradise and the "melting pot of the Pacific." After World War II the mainstream media seized upon Hawaii as the place where the American promise of equality for all was being worked out in practice. In 1945, for example, *Life* published an effusive article, entitled "Hawaii, a Melting Pot, a Score of Races Live Together in Amity," that rejected the principle of biological racial difference and praised the islands as "the world's most successful experiment in mixed breeding, a sociologist's dream of interracial cultures." With so many races and mixtures, the article insisted, prejudice had become "simply impractical." The article rejected the racializing notion that intermarriage produced inferior hybrids and applauded that "a new race"—"tolerant, healthy and American"—is "emerging and stabilizing" in the islands, a claim that it illustrated with numerous photographs of attractive women accompanied by captions identifying their ethno-racial backgrounds. While articles such as these acknowledged the racial conflict that did exist in the islands—*Life* noted that only a week before a race riot had broken out between white sailors and people they attacked as "gooks," and other magazines mentioned the racially charged Thalia Massie rape and lynching case of 1931—they tended to downplay such incidents as deviations from a normal state of racial harmony. *Life* also deemphasized racial difference by constructing gender difference: by depicting Hawaii in the form of attractive women, it imagined statehood as a kind of sexual union between a feminized Hawaii and an implicitly masculine mainland.[31]

James Michener became an outspoken advocate of statehood. In 1953 he published his first essay on Hawaii in *Holiday* magazine, which *Reader's Digest* condensed, and he went on to write additional pieces for the *New York Times Magazine, Reader's Digest, Look,* and the Honolulu *Star-Bulletin,* many of which combined the conventions of travel writing with pro-statehood arguments. Michener's arguments did not differ significantly from those of others who advocated statehood. Rather, he used his literary skills, celebrity, and status as an expert on Asia and the Pacific to bring the pro-statehood arguments into greater prominence.

In much of his writing Michener promoted statehood as a strategic move in the Cold War. International politics had always impinged upon the race-and-statehood debate: in the 1930s and early 1940s, when an expansionist Japan threatened U.S. interests in the Pacific, many Americans saw the Japanese American population of Hawaii as an undesirable element, a potential fifth column. In the postwar period, however, the need to secure the allegiance of the decolonizing nations changed the political currency of Hawaii's people. Michener saw Hawaii's Asian-Pacific population as having an enormous geopolitical value: by granting them the full rights of citizenship, the U.S. would do much to invalidate the charges of racism and imperialism that so damaged its reputation abroad. Michener advocated statehood as a way for Washington to prove the racially inclusive nature of American democracy. "In Asia, Hawaii has become a symbol of the fair and just manner in which we treat Orientals," he wrote in a 1958 *Reader's Digest* article. "Quietly, the word has circulated that in Hawaii Chinese do well, that Japanese get elected to office, that Filipinos get a fair shake. If now we slap Hawaii in the face and say, 'You cannot have statehood,' the slap will reverberate." Statehood would also ease the memory of U.S. imperialism in the Pacific and establish a clear distinction between the United States and the European colonial powers, by making Hawaii's territorial status seem a temporary stage in the development toward full inclusion in the nation, rather than a permanent colonial condition suitable for a nonwhite population.[32]

In contrast to statehood opponents, Michener mapped Hawaii in relation to the mainland. He specifically constructed Hawaii as an alternative to Little Rock, as a positive instance of a multiracial society. In a 1959 article in the *New York Times Magazine,* Michener noted that the "bad publicity stemming from Little Rock" had been "a serious bar" to American efforts to win the support of "uncommitted or wavering nations." Statehood for Hawaii would offer concrete proof to these nations that Americans do not "hate Orientals" and could "accept men of varying colors." It would facilitate the integration of the decolonizing world by making "the job of every State Department official in Asia and Africa ... a little easier" and "the words of every U.S. Information Service man ... a lot more persuasive." Michener also imagined the Asians of Hawaii as healers of the South's bitter racial conflicts. He cast Hawaii's future congressmen as rescuers of America from the "grave internal problems arising from race relations." Michener constructs the Asian Americans of Hawaii as reasonable figures who will mediate the highly charged and long-simmering racial conflicts between blacks and whites. Part of the value of Hawaii's statehood, then, becomes its ability to smooth over the racial divisions within the nation by interjecting Asian Americans as a third term between the poles of black and white.[33]

Michener also mapped the islands in relation to Asia. To Michener, Hawaii's familial and cultural ties to Asia made it worth incorporating into the union. He saw the people of Hawaii as an exploitable natural resource who could facilitate U.S. global expansion by serving as native informants and guides: they were a "splendid resource from which our government can draw in these difficult days of trying to work with many foreign governments." Other statehood advocates shared this view. *Businessweek* in 1950 explained that "the islands have brought to the U.S. a new national resource—a population that is the logical stepping stone between the U.S. and the Orient" and went on to praise these people as the "logical intermediaries to carry an understanding of U.S. democracy to the Orient." One of the Congressional committees investigating statehood came to a similar conclusion: "Many of her people have their racial background in that Asian area, giving the nation a unique medium of communication and understanding with Asiatic peoples"; as a result, Hawaii could become a "natural training ground for leaders to administer American interests in this area." In the nineteenth and early twentieth centuries, Americans looking for a stepping stone to China valued Hawaii for its geographical location. In the second half of the twentieth century, it was Hawaii's Asian population that held out the promise of securing access to the markets and resources of Asia.[34]

If Hawaiian statehood rendered America a little less white and Western in its national identity, that was apparently fine with many statehood advocates. *Businessweek,* noting that "America has always had cultural ties to Europe," appreciated that the "thousands of citizens of Chinese, Japanese, Korean, and Filipino ancestry, who understand the customs, and, in some cases, speak the language of the country of their fathers and grandfathers," could now bestow upon the nation those same ties with Asia. *Newsweek* in 1959 similarly noted that "Hawaii will be the first state with roots not in Europe but in Asia" and looked forward to the "profound effect" that this would have on America's future in the Far East: no longer would America be known as a "land of the white man" and "tarred with the brush of 'colonialism.'" *Time* in turn celebrated statehood as an act through which America "leaped over its old, European-rooted consciousness of Caucasian identity." The incorporation of Hawaii into the union, in the eyes of these advocates, would benefit America's role as world leader by making the nation at least partially Asian.[35]

While opponents of statehood succeeded in blocking legislation for many years, their views were not widely held. By 1954, 78 percent of

Americans approved of Hawaii's efforts to join the union, as did the Departments of State, Defense, and Justice, the Democratic and Republican parties, and the eleven Congressional committees that had investigated statehood. In 1959 the racial arguments of statehood opponents finally lost their persuasive power, and Congress approved legislation making Hawaii the nation's fiftieth state.[36]

MICHENER'S *HAWAII*

Michener's interest in Hawaii culminated in 1959 with the publication of *Hawaii,* his first epic historical novel, his first book to approach one thousand pages in length, and his last major work on the Asia-Pacific region. *Hawaii* took shape at the intersection of the discourses of statehood, racial integration, and tourism. Excerpted in *Reader's Digest* and *Life,* chosen as a main selection by the Book-of-the-Month Club, and republished as a Reader's Digest condensed book, *Hawaii* quickly became a bestseller, selling five million copies by 1978. The novel capped Michener's decade-long promotion of Asia and the Pacific as tourist destinations and as a primary arena in the Cold War. Written as a manifesto for statehood and published a few months after that goal was achieved, *Hawaii* served as an expanded tourist guidebook to the new state and became the definitive representation of the island for millions of people around the world for years to come. In 1962 Hawaii's Congressman Daniel K. Inouye praised the novel from the floor of Congress as "the semiofficial guide to our lovely shores." "Today," he said, "when a ship or airplane deposits visitors on our shores, sometimes as many as half of them arrive with copies of his book under their arms. And the important thing about this is that they all have derived from Michener's writing an appreciation of the wonderful strains of the human family that have blended together to build our paradise." *Hawaii* was not simply a representation of the islands, but part of a cultural-educational apparatus that deployed the islands as a means through which Americans could learn the value of racial tolerance. It was both a representation of racial integration and a device for achieving that integration in practice. With this novel, Michener took on the task of teaching his readers the political and racial lessons of Hawaii.[37]

In keeping with his didactic view of literature and his guidebook inclinations, Michener constructs his novel as a history of Hawaii. After announcing in a brief prologue that his work of fiction is "true to the spirit and history of Hawaii," he builds the novel's skeleton around the major events that have shaped the islands' history. The novel begins with the islands' birth in a series of volcanic eruptions and goes on to narrate all the high points of the islands' social, political, and economic history, from the migration of the native Hawaiians from Polynesia in the ninth century, through the annexation by the U.S. in 1898, to the aftereffects of World War II. He fictionalizes key figures in Hawaii's history, from the missionary Hiram Bingham to the insurgent Democratic party leader John Burns, and he incorporates major episodes from the islands' social history, including the spread of leprosy in the 1870s, the plague-induced burning of Chinatown in 1900, the creation of the Japanese American 442nd Regimental Combat Team during World War II, and the big labor strikes of the 1940s. He explains the climate and the plant and animal life of the islands, and provides the kind of local information, on things like the origins of the ukulele and the multiple uses of the coconut palm, that tourists like to know. Reviewers described the novel as a "comprehensive social history of our 50th state," praised its "wealth of scholarship," and located it in literary-historical terms as an heir to the "documentary novel of the Nineteen Thirties." [38]

Around this framework, the novel traces the history of the islands' four major racial and ethnic groups—native Hawaiian, white American, Chinese, and Japanese—via the formula of the multigenerational, multifamily saga. The novel consists of six chapters: the first focuses on the island's geological history, the next four on each major ethno-racial group, and the last brings together the main characters from the previous chapters. The novel covers, with some large gaps, fifty-six generations of the native Hawaiian Kanakoa family, six generations of the white Whipple and Hale families, fifty generations of the Chinese Kee family, and three generations of the Japanese Sakagawa family. Eight pages of genealogical charts help the reader keep track of the relationships among dozens of characters.

Through this multifamily formula, *Hawaii* translates the ethnicity paradigm into a compelling narrative, as each group lives out sociologist Robert Park's four-stage race relations cycle of contact, conflict, accommodation, and assimilation. Michener does not shy away from the islands' history of racial conflict and exploitation: he documents the brutal conditions on the ships that transported Chinese laborers, the systematic exclusion of Japanese children from public schools in order to keep them on the plantations, and the limited education received by native Hawaiians in white-sponsored schools that trained them for work in menial jobs. (The implicit comparison, of course, is with the experiences of black Americans on slave ships, in segregated schools, and in vocational education programs such as those offered by the Tuskegee Institute.) But the novel universalizes this history by locating it within a global context. During World War II various characters encounter British imperialism in Fiji, segregation in Mississippi, and Nazism in Europe, after which they appreciate anew Hawaii's high degree of racial harmony. The novel also charts a progression away from this structurally embedded racism and toward the institutionalization of racial egalitarianism. Michener ends the novel in November 1954, at the very moment when the white minority is losing its historic control over the islands' political and economic life. Newly naturalized Asian-born residents have turned out to vote in record numbers, the multiracial Democratic party has won control of the legislature from the white Republican elite, and Japanese Americans have been elected to a majority of seats in the territorial legislature. Michener suggests that Hawaii, while clearly not a racial paradise, is closer than any other multiracial society to putting the ideal of racial integration into practice.

The novel also narrativizes the ethnicity paradigm by unfavorably contrasting characters who think in narrowly racial terms with those who have embraced the more flexible terms of culture. The novel's heroes are those who can select the best elements of each group's culture and combine them to create something new. The home of the Chinese matriarch Nyuk Tsin embodies this Hawaiian ideal of cultural hybridity: "In food, language and laughter the establishment was Hawaiian. In school-book learning, business and religion it was American. But in filial obedience and reverence for education it was Chinese." The narrative structure itself communicates the ideal of liberal universalism by drawing parallels between each of the different ethno-racial groups, in everything from their shared experience of a nightmarish ship journey to the islands, to their tendencies toward ancestor worship and quasi-incestuous marriage. Michener, like Hammerstein, articulates his message that "all men are brothers" in a manner difficult to miss. Many readers of the novel understood this message and liked it: the *Chicago Sunday Tribune* reviewer, for instance, praised *Hawaii* as "one of the most enlightening books ever written, either fact or fiction, about the integration of divergent peoples into a composite society." [39]

Michener makes sense of this vast narrative and this proliferation of characters by organizing the book spatially: he uses his generation- and continent-spanning families as the skeins that knit America together with the rest of the world. Michener's families are in motion, traversing

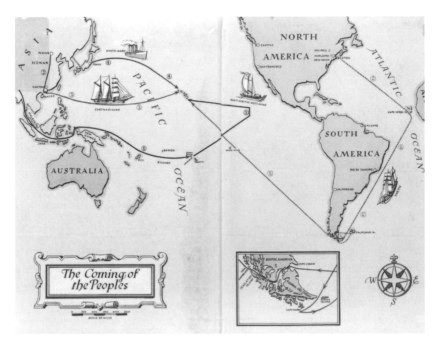

Figure 24. In his book *Hawaii* (1959), James Michener maps the immigrant flows out of Polynesia, New England, China, and Japan and into Hawaii. (courtesy Random House)

the vast expanses between the American mainland, Hawaii, the islands of the Pacific, and Asia. Immigrants and travelers, their routes map Hawaii as the center of a complex web of flows that bind Asia, the Pacific, and America together.

Michener organizes the novel according to three sets of flows, each of which has Hawaii at its center. The first set consists of the flows of migration that span a thousand years and that carry the characters away from their original homes in Bora Bora, New England, central China, and Japan. Michener emphasizes this first set of flows in his chapter titles— "From the Sun-Swept Lagoon" (Polynesians), "From the Farm of Bitterness" (Americans), "From the Starving Village" (Chinese), "From the Inland Sea" (Japanese)—and in the full-color map that forms the book's frontispiece (Figure 24). Rendering his project of transnational mapping literal and visual, this map, titled "The Coming of the Peoples," charts the flows of each of his four ethnic groups out from their places of origins in North America and Asia and into Hawaii. Together with the genealogical trees at the back of the book, this illustration maps the family structure of the narrative onto the space of the Pacific basin. Michener's families are international entities.

As the map makes clear, all of the novel's groups are immigrants, but Michener inflects each group's travel with different meaning. He frames the Polynesian characters' travel as an adventure narrative: setting sail in big canoes, they travel for thousands of miles using only the stars to navigate and establish a new society on uninhabited islands. The white New Englanders' travel is cast as a narrative of national expansion: fired by missionary zeal, they leave the United States in order to spread American culture, values, and institutions beyond the nation's borders. The Chinese and Japanese characters follow the literary path of the classic ethnic immigrant narrative. Driven from their homes by economic hardship and limited opportunity, they travel to Hawaii in search of expanded opportunities. Once arrived, they begin the slow but steady process of integrating themselves into and rising up through Hawaii's Americanized society: while the first generation begins as servants and plantation laborers who maintain their original languages and traditions, their Hawaiian-born offspring imbibe American culture, attend public school, become successful businessmen, and eventually enter into political life.

Casting the Chinese and Japanese stories as familiar ethnic narratives was key to the novel's political argument: Michener wanted to show that the islands' majority Asian population was composed not of unassimilable racial Others but of familiar immigrant types who, like previous generations of European immigrants, embraced the traditional virtues of hard work, loyalty to family, and love of education. By making them familiar immigrants, Michener's work does culturally what the 1952 McCarran-Walter Act did legally: it shows that Chinese- and Japanese-born people can be Asian and American at the same time. The family bonds established by this first set of flows enable Michener to trace the roots of Hawaii, and by extension America, back to multiple origins in the Pacific islands, New England, China, and Japan. Michener directs his educational impulse to these places as well as to Hawaii itself, and he teaches his readers about religious tensions in Bora Bora, ethnic differences among the Chinese, and courtship traditions in rural Japan. The effect of this is to render New England, traditionally the birthplace of the nation, as only one among many originary sources of the nation's identity. He makes the South Pacific, China, and Japan into equivalent "old countries" to the more familiar white ethnic homelands of Ireland, Italy, and Eastern Europe. In doing so, he introduces his mainland readers not only to their new fellow citizens, but to their Asian-Pacific cultural roots as well.

The novel's second set of flows reinforces and sustains these ties to Asia and the Pacific by sending characters back, either literally or figuratively, to their ancestors' homelands. Unlike many immigrant narratives, Michener's does not sever the characters' ties with their points of origin: their Americanization does not require the loss of all contact with their ancestral homes. Rather, after mapping their flow into Hawaii, Michener posits a partial flow back out of Hawaii as his fully assimilated characters recognize, maintain, or reestablish the unbreakable bonds of family and culture that tie them to Asia and the Pacific.

In keeping with Michener's views of the people of Hawaii as a national "resource" upon which Washington could draw, his Japanese and mixed-race characters return to their Asian and Pacific origins as agents of U.S. expansion. Hoxworth Hale, a part-Hawaiian member of the white elite, travels to the South Pacific as a military officer during World War II. Claiming Tahiti as the "islands from which his people had come," he describes Bora Bora as "like a sacred home." When he fathers a child with a native woman—at her invitation—he asserts that he will be "forever a part of Bora Bora." This episode recapitulates a typical imperial fantasy of sexual conquest and colonization. Yet Michener complicates this fantasy by making his white man part-Polynesian, which frames his sexual encounter not as an imperial gesture of control and domination, but as a migrant's return to his roots. Hale's racial hybridity thus works to obscure the imperial nature of the military expansion that he enacts. Establishing the bonds to Japan requires a more careful negotiation. Michener does sever ties based on national loyalty: Kamejiro Sakagawa's devotion to the Emperor leads to penury, unhappiness, and "schizophrenia" and must eventually be renounced during World War II in favor of loyalty to the United States. But his sons' cultural tie to Japan, specifically their ability to speak Japanese, enables them to return to their parents' homeland as part of the U.S. occupation forces and work as translators for General MacArthur's land reform expert. The biological and cultural ties to Asia and the Pacific that these characters possess make their presence there, and by extension that of the U.S. government, which they represent, that much more natural and thus legitimate. With this return set of flows out of Hawaii and back into Asia and the Pacific, Michener constructs the immigrant bonds of his characters as two-way roads, routes through which Americans can flow out into Asia and the Pacific as easily as Asians and Pacific Islanders can flow into

America. These immigrants bestow upon the nation at large the very thing that political observers feared was lacking in America and undermining U.S. foreign policy in Asia: a familiarity with Asia rooted in the intimate bonds of family and common culture.[40]

Michener's third set of flows consists of populations migrating around the world over the course of millennia. This flow is at once more abstract and more all-encompassing, and more than any other it establishes America, through Hawaii, as a "nation of nations" located within a truly global matrix of family ties. The novel culminates in a chapter that celebrates Hawaii as the incubator of a glorious new type of person, whom Michener dubs the Golden Man. Although Michener invented this term for the novel, the narrator ascribes it to a group of sociologists who in 1946 perfected a concept whose outline had preoccupied them for years. The sociologists' Golden Man, as a figure who first appears earlier in the century but does not fully mature until after the war, is thus the apotheosis and embodiment of the ethnicity paradigm, the incarnation of changing ideas about race and culture. The Golden Man is primarily an intellectual, rather than a racial, hybrid who combines the best of both Eastern and Western cultures: "He was a man influenced by both the west and the east, a man at home in either the business councils of New York or the philosophical retreats of Kyoto, a man wholly modern and American yet in tune with the ancient and the Oriental."[41] Michener focuses on four such Golden Men, one from each of his ethnoracial groups, and they bring to fruition the themes of cultural relativism, pluralism, and syncretism that have been developing over the course of the novel: like the heroic figures in earlier chapters, they are characters who can understand, embrace, and learn from other cultures.

Michener uses the Golden Men to discredit biological theories of racial purity and hierarchy. Although each of his four characters thinks of himself as racially pure, Michener invalidates their narrowly racial thinking by tracing their genealogies back centuries and connecting them to all the races of the world. Hoxworth Hale, his ostensibly white Golden Man, for instance,

> was one-sixteenth Hawaiian, inherited through the Alii Nui Noelani, who was his great-great-grandmother. He was also part-Arabian, for one of his European ancestors had married during the Crusades, part-African through an earlier Roman ancestor, part–Central Asian from an Austrian woman who had married a Hungarian in 1603, and part-American Indian through a cute trick that an early Hale's wife had pulled on him in remote Massachusetts.

Hong Kong Kee, his Chinese Golden Man, has a similar background. His "ancestors had picked up a good deal of Mongolian blood, and Manchurian, and Tartar, plus a little Japanese during the wars of the early 1600's, plus some Korean via an ancestor who had traveled in that peninsula in 814, augmented by a good deal of nondescript inheritance from tribes who had wandered about southern China from the year 4000 B.C. on." Ultimately, Michener connects all his Golden Men, and the separate groups they represent, back to a single mythic family, which he imagines alternately as "two ancient Malayan brothers" or "three ancient Siberian brothers," whose descendants form the populations of Polynesia, New England, China, and Japan—that is, the original homes of Hawaii's four major population groups. These Golden Men embody the ideal of the "brotherhood of man" so popular among middlebrow intellectuals, from Edward Steichen to Pearl Buck: when Hammerstein, in an insensitive moment, referred to the children of Welcome House as "half-castes," Buck snapped, "We don't use that ugly term around here: we're all half-castes if you trace it back far enough."[42]

The Golden Men are the means through which Michener achieves the novel's central ideological project of redeeming the United States from the accusations of racism and imperialism. Michener presents these Golden Men as the ultimate benefit that Hawaiian statehood can bestow upon America. Spanning the globe through their multiple bloodlines, these new Americans represent a globalism that is natural and inescapable, not imperial or coercive. They allow the reader to see America and the world not only as fundamentally interconnected, but as always having been so. They take the ideal of U.S.-Asian integration out of the realm of contemporary foreign affairs and project it back into the mists of prehistory and biology. It becomes a result of sex and marriage, of migrations and flows, rather than politics. The hybrid Golden Men, as emblems of Hawaii, deflate the accusation of imperialism by showing that America already and harmoniously contains all the world's people within itself.

With Nyuk Tsin, the Chinese matriarch, Michener creates the novel's quintessential immigrant and most memorable character. In doing so, he establishes the Asian immigrant woman as an emblematic figure of the domestic integration of Asian Americans—a cultural counterpart to the jungle doctor, white mother, and tourist who serve as the era's figures of international U.S.-Asian integration. Michener makes hers a classic immigrant story: a poor village girl who is kidnapped and sold into prostitution, Nyuk Tsin arrives in Hawaii as the second wife of a Chinese gambler; she works hard, educates her sons, and gradually builds up and

oversees a huge financial empire run by her children and grandchildren.
Her values, while presented as traditionally Chinese, are also comfortingly familiar: she values thrift, education, private property, and the
basic principles of capitalism. Her immigration to Hawaii, rather than
threatening the U.S. by injecting into it alien customs, strengthens the
nation's social and moral foundations. The progenitor of ninety-five descendants (according to her genealogical tree) who travel the world and
intermarry across many racial and ethnic lines, Nyuk Tsin becomes, in
effect, the mother of a new multiracial and global America.

The novel's three sets of flows come together in Nyuk Tsin. As an immigrant, she participates in the initial flow out of China and into Hawaii. She participates in the second flow back to China when she sends
money to her husband's first wife, who remained behind in the ancestral
village, and when she sends her children's and grandchildren's names
back to be registered in the village's records. In these ways family ties are
maintained across the Pacific, so that even though none of the family has
ever physically returned to China, when the eldest Kee child goes to college on the mainland, "he was not only head of a burgeoning family left
behind in Honolulu, but also the member of a powerful clan whose
existence had continued in the Low Village for thousands of years."
Nyuk Tsin embodies the third, more global, flow when she names
her five sons after the continents of Asia, Africa, Europe, America, and
Australia. In this way, she extends her family like a web around the
globe, making it coterminous with all the other peoples of the world. In
the final pages of the novel, her immigrant trajectory comes to its ultimate conclusion as she takes advantage of the naturalization provision
in the 1952 McCarran-Walter Act and, eighty-eight years after immi-
grating, becomes a U.S. citizen. With this episode Michener injects the
novel's only direct reference to the Cold War in Asia: as Nyuk Tsin takes
her citizenship test, a bevy of newsreel cameras, brought in by the immigration officials, film the interview as a "dramatic" event that they
can "use for publicity in Asia." Having completed the cycle from immigrant to citizen, and having facilitated the integration of Asia and
America in many small ways, Nyuk Tsin dies at the age of one hundred
and six.[43]

· · · · ·

Hawaii in the 1950s had an ideological value unmatched by any other
part of the United States. For one reason, it was a multiracial society that

contained a negligible number of African Americans. It thus allowed Michener and other commentators to recast American race relations in Asian-white terms rather than in the more fraught black-white terms. Writing about Hawaii enabled Michener to champion the ideal of racial equality and the practice of racial integration without having to grapple with the entrenched and often violent racism, rooted in the history of slavery, that the black civil rights movement was revealing in the American South and bringing to the forefront of national consciousness. By using Hawaii as "proof" that racism was not permanently entrenched in the American psyche and society, Michener effectively "solved" the nation's race problem by excising blacks from America.

Hawaii's other main ideological advantage was that it allowed Michener to sidestep the single greatest act of anti-Asian racism: the internment of Japanese Americans during World War II. As Caroline Chung Simpson has argued, the fact of internment and its public remembering during the postwar years threatened, as did other well-known instances of racial injustice, to destabilize the nation's claims to being a democratic, tolerant, and pluralist nation. To remember internment was to risk remembering that Americans had until very recently been committed to the idea of Asians as unassimilable foreign Others. Hawaii offered Michener the possibility of acknowledging the history of internment while limiting its ideological damage: while California, Washington, and Oregon forcibly interned 120,000 of their residents of Japanese background, most of whom were U.S. citizens, Hawaii interned only 1,444. The difference resulted from widespread opposition to internment among Hawaii's elite, from logistical considerations and, most important, from self-interest: to lock up or evacuate one third of the islands' population and a high proportion of its agricultural and skilled work force would have devastated the economy and endangered the security of the islands. Because internment did not dominate the history of Asians in Hawaii, Michener was able to contain its ideological threat by embedding its remembering within a larger narrative of Asian integration.[44]

Flower Drum Song offered a similar opportunity to publicly raise and contain the memory of internment by locating it within a larger narrative of Americanization. In its 1958 cover story on the show, *Time* presented the life stories of stars Miyoshi Umeki and Pat Suzuki as two models of how Asians could also be Americans. Umeki, whom the article described as "American by solemn determination," offered a model of Asians becoming American though the process of U.S. global expansion. Born and raised in Japan, Umeki's Americanization was set in motion by the postwar occupation of her country. Encouraged to sing by American GIs who befriended her family, she began performing with GI bands in their service clubs; later she learned to copy the style of singers such as Doris Day whom she heard on the U.S. Army radio and became a hit on Japanese radio and TV. Her success prompted her to move to the U.S., where she found work in nightclubs, on TV, and in Hollywood. She married an American and settled in the U.S. permanently. *Time* presented the California-born Pat Suzuki, on the other hand, as "American by instinct": temperamentally as well as legally American, she was filled with wanderlust as a child and "chafed by restrictions, careless of customs, and in a hurry" as an adult. The article presented her childhood as a typical one, noting that she sang songs like "I Am an American" at county fairs. The bombing of Pearl Harbor derailed this uneventful life: she and her family were "shipped to the Amache relocation camp at Lamar, Colo.," and after the war they spent a year working on a Colorado sugar-beet farm before finally returning home. *Time* acknowledged but downplayed the significance of Suzuki's incarceration, presenting it as an interruption of an otherwise average American life story. The article did not mention racism, the violation of civil rights, or the economic exploitation of people forced to abandon their homes and property. Instead it described Suzuki's life in the camps as "a matter of school as usual," and implied that the experience made little impression on her, claiming that her only memories were of the weather and of the Nisei Boy Scouts who raised the American flag each morning. The article presented Suzuki as completely American even as she was ethnically Japanese, and it never suggested that internment entailed any denial of her Americanness. The article cast her experiences as a rough spot in an American childhood, but refused to read it as evidence of a widely held view that people of Japanese background were fundamentally foreign. In doing so it contained, as did Michener's novel, the destabilizing potential that public rememberings of internment threatened to raise.[45]

Hawaii and *Flower Drum Song* make clear that the racial formation of Americans has never been a simple domestic process. The meanings and the regulation of ethno-racial difference within the nation have always taken shape in relation to events and processes occurring beyond the nation's borders. The foreign and the domestic spheres, far from being neatly separated as they have been in most accounts of American political and cultural history, impinge on each other in unexpected ways. The racial formation of Asian Americans shifted between the early 1940s, when Japanese Americans were interned, and the 1950s, when Asian Americans were legally and symbolically integrated into the nation as immigrants and citizens, and one cannot fully understand that change outside of a transnational framework that takes into account the political and ideological demands of World War II, the Cold War, and the ongoing process of U.S. global expansion.[46]

Conclusion

A new Anna Leonowens appeared in American movie theaters in the fall of 1999. Played by Jodie Foster in the $70 million Hollywood production *Anna and the King*, she was once again the teacher, governess, and advisor to the royal court of Siam. The producers promoted the film as a new version of Leonowens's story, based on her original nineteenth-century accounts, but the Rodgers and Hammerstein classic inevitably echoed throughout, despite the absence of musical numbers. The unconsummated romance between Anna and the King still smoldered, and their feelings for each other still culminated in an erotically charged dance, now performed as an extended, swaying embrace rather than a rousing polka. This Anna, however, fits more comfortably with late-twentieth-century political sensibilities: her transition from British arrogance to American-style tolerance is more marked, as is her condemnation of imperialism. The filmmakers also modeled this King more closely on the Mongkut that exists in Thai history books. A dignified and mature ruler, he lacks the hysterical, imperious quality that characterized Yul Brynner's King. A wholehearted rather than ambivalent modernizer, he no longer needs to die at the end but remains vitally alive to guide his country along the road to Westernization.

Rodgers and Hammerstein's *The King and I* had never wholly disappeared from the American cultural scene. It was revived on Broadway and in regional theaters across the country throughout the 1970s and 1980s, including a much-acclaimed version in 1996, and it came to life as a short-lived television series in 1972 and as an animated children's film in 1999. The continued popularity of this story points to the almost arbitrary nature of historical periodization. I have chosen to end this study in 1961, but the processes that the preceding chapters have explored continued long after this endpoint. The investments that Americans made in Asia during the 1940s and 1950s—economic, political, military, and cultural—played themselves out over the course of the succeeding decades in both predictable and unpredictable ways. The foreign policies of containment and integration led the U.S., seemingly inexorably, into the debacle of the Vietnam War. The Third World and antiwar movements of the 1960s gave a radical twist to the idea of forging political bonds between a multiracial America and the colored peoples of the world. The immigration act of 1965 expanded the reforms begun with the McCarran-Walter Act of 1952, permanently abolishing the national origin system and opening the doors to a great flow of immigrants from Asia, many of whom came from communist China, either directly or via Taiwan, as refugees and from countries where the U.S. during the 1940s and 1950s had waged war or maintained a strong military presence, such as South Korea, Vietnam, and the Philippines. This demographic growth, combined with the rise of ethnic studies and multiculturalism, returned Asian Americans to mainstream cultural visibility in the 1970s and 1980s. Meanwhile, the popular interest in Asian culture that figures like Norman Cousins, James Michener, and the Beats had stimulated in the 1950s and 1960s took off in the 1980s and 1990s, as millions of Americans began practicing Buddhism, martial arts, yoga, and traditional forms of Chinese medicine such as acupuncture.

The return of Anna and the King in 1999 belongs to this ongoing American engagement with things Asian, but it also points to the opening of yet another distinct chapter in that history. When the Soviet Union collapsed in 1991 and the Cold War came to its sudden end, capitalism, sometimes accompanied by democratic political reforms, began spreading into countries and regions that had previously marked the limits of the "free world": the former Soviet Union, Eastern Europe, Vietnam, China. A host of developments, lumped together under the rubric of globalization—free trade agreements, regional integration, the linking of currency markets, globalized manufacturing, the growth of multinational corporations, the expansion of technology and communications networks, the creation of new international governing bodies—brought individual nations' economic and thus political systems into closer cooperation than they had ever been in before. To observers who thought of the Cold War in terms of containment, globalization looked liked a wholly new world system. But to those such as Bruce Cumings, who saw the Cold War in terms of international integration, the globalized world was "the anticipated consequence, the unfolding of the liberal hegemony that American internationalists like Acheson envisioned in the peculiarly American moment of 1945." During the Cold War the international structure that the U.S. had created was limited by the constraints of the Soviet Union, European imperialism, and Third World nationalism. But when the Soviet Union collapsed, "the structure continued in place and, in the 1990s, achieved the full florescence that its planners had imagined in the 1940s." For Cumings, the post-Cold War "New World Order" was "both the same old order and the ongoing fulfillment of postwar planning." At long last, the internationally integrated capitalist economy was becoming truly global in scope.[1]

Globalization and the triumph, as it was called, of market capitalism transformed much of Asia. In 1991 India decided to abandon its quasi-socialist, state-run economy and open itself up to international market forces; soon thereafter Bombay began offering telephone-operation services for American corporations, and Bangalore developed into South Asia's software-engineering center. China began moving from a command to a market economy after Mao's death in 1976; in the 1980s and 1990s it had the world's fastest-growing economy, and by 1997 it was running a $44 billion trade surplus with the U.S. Economic ties between the U.S. and Asia became increasingly close: U.S. computer companies depended on chips manufactured in Taiwan, a huge proportion of Silicon Valley engineers and entrepreneurs hailed from India, Filipino nurses staffed American hospitals, and even the U.S. military ordered its berets from Chinese manufacturers. The Asian financial crisis of 1997—which originated in the Thai currency markets, swept through the economies of Taiwan, Hong Kong, Singapore, South Korea, Indonesia, and Malaysia, jumped the Pacific to destabilize markets in Latin America, and even caused tremors in American investment houses—offered terrifying proof of the interconnectedness of the world's economies. The combined effects of economic globalization and the collapse of communism led to political changes as well, as South Korea, Taiwan, and Indonesia moved from. authoritarian toward more democratic regimes. After the demise of the Soviet Union, Beijing returned to the center of American domestic and foreign policy debates for the first time since the crisis over who "lost" China in the 1950s. Critics of China, some of whose intellectual and political roots stretched back to the Republican right of the late 1940s, viewed the world's last major communist nation as a military threat to the U.S. and to neighboring Taiwan, as a brutal violator of human rights and religious freedoms, and as an illegal occupier of Tibet. They advocated limiting American ties with China as a way of pressuring Beijing to modify what they saw as its objectionable behavior. Supporters of China, many of whom had ties to the business community, focused their attention on the vast potential of the China market and its low-wage labor supply. They argued for increased ties with China on the grounds that only economic and political engagement with the rest of the world would force Beijing to make political changes.

Not surprisingly, this rush toward economic and political integration produced a distinctive culture of globalization, in the form of movies, novels, advertisements, music, and other forms of culture that grew out of and represented these new interrelationships. What is surprising, however, is the extent to which this 1990s culture reanimated that of the 1940s and 1950s. Just as the post–Cold War processes of economic globalization extended the Cold War processes of "free world" integration, so the culture of globalization resurrected the narratives, characters, concepts, and social practices that characterized the culture of Cold War Orientalism. The return of Rodgers and Hammerstein's entire Oriental trilogy is emblematic of this larger phenomenon. In addition to the 1999 film *Anna and the King,* a major revival of *The King and I* opened on Broadway in 1996 and has been touring nationally and internationally since it left New York. In 2001 *South Pacific* was remade as a television movie, in which form it was seen by sixteen million people, and revived at the Royal National Theatre in London. David Henry Hwang, the nation's foremost Asian American playwright, who made his reputation by critically engaging with *Madame Butterfly,* created a new version of *Flower Drum Song* that same year. He incorporated Rodgers and Hammerstein's songs into a new libretto that included previously unused material from C. Y. Lee's novel.[2]

In addition to the resurrection of individual texts, the 1990s also saw the return of attitudes, ideas, and social practices that figured prominently in Cold War Orientalism. The renewed political visibility of China has affected attitudes toward Asian Americans. In some prominent cases, anxieties over China have revived fears of a "yellow-peril" menace at home: the Democratic campaign finance scandal of 1997, in which the Clinton administration accepted illegal donations from Asian and Asian American contributors, led to much media breast-beating about the influence of "foreign" elements in American politics; a few years later,

the fear of Chinese espionage led to the imprisonment of scientist Wen
Ho Lee, a Taiwanese-born U.S. citizen, on flimsy charges of mishandling
atomic weapons secrets that were later dropped. In other cases, however, economic globalization generated a self-interested enthusiasm for
the growing numbers of Asians in America. Like Michener and other
advocates of Hawaiian statehood in the 1950s, some American business
leaders saw Asian Americans as mediators who could help American
businesses gain access to Asian markets. In a 1991 speech that could have
been lifted out of the pages of the *Saturday Review,* David Murdock, the
chairman and CEO of the multinational Dole Foods Company, which
employed thousands of people in the Asia-Pacific region, praised Asian
Americans as a national resource:

> We need to be more competitive. We need people who understand the lan-
> guages, cultures, the markets, the politics of this spectacular region. Many
> Asian Americans have language ability, cultural understanding, direct fam-
> ily ties, and knowledge of economic conditions and government practices
> throughout Asia. This knowledge and ability can help Americans achieve
> political and business success in the region. . . . much of their insight and
> ability can [help] in opening doors for the U.S., building a new structure
> for peace in the Pacific.

In the 1990s as in the 1950s, Asian Americans were seen as bestowing
upon the nation a set of culturally specific ties and skills that could help
the U.S. extend its reach deeper into Asia and the Pacific.[3]

The celebrators and popularizers of globalization also resurrected the
ideal of hybridity that Michener put forth in *Hawaii.* G. Pascal Zachary,
a writer for the *Wall Street Journal,* opened his 2000 book on globalization, *The Global Me: New Cosmopolitans and the Competitive Edge:
Picking Globalism's Winners and Losers,* by announcing "Mighty is the
mongrel. . . . The hybrid is hip." In this emblematic work of post–Cold
War capitalist triumphalism, he extends Michener's argument about the
Golden Men of Hawaii as a way to explain America's unchallenged political and economic power at the end of the twentieth century. Turning
the postcolonial theory of Said and his colleagues on its head, Zachary
uses their ideas of cosmopolitanism, transnationalism, flexible citizenship, diaspora, and postnational consciousness to explain how the U.S.
has become globalization's preeminent "winner." Americans' willingness to mongrelize, he argues, has generated a surge in creativity and innovation that has fueled the nation's economic growth. Zachary champions the dissolution of ethnic, racial, and cultural boundaries through
biological and cultural mixing. He cites with approval the rising rates of

interracial marriage, the emergence of dual citizenship, the growing self-identification of people of color as multiracial, the voluntary affiliation of individuals with ethnic culture not their "own," and the emergence of "rooted cosmopolitans" who combine a secure sense of ethnic identity with a cosmopolitan sensibility. Echoing and revising Pearl Buck, who saw the Amerasian children of Welcome House as future mediators who could prevent further losses to communism in Asia, Zachary celebrates the new American mongrels for their ability to smooth the workings of global capitalism. With *The Global Me* Zachary resurrects and expands the ideological justification for America's global power that was first put forth in the 1940s. America deserves to be the world's most powerful nation, he suggests, because it alone is capable of embracing the world within itself. In 2000, he claims for all of America what Michener claimed for Hawaii in the 1950s: a hybrid population that connects America to the rest of the world in ways that lead to global economic and political power.[4]

The adoption of Chinese babies became in the 1990s one of the most visible expressions of this American willingness to hybridize. The social practice of adopting Asian children had its origins in the wars that the United States waged in Asia and the Pacific. The adoption of Chinese babies after the end of the Cold War, in contrast, grew out of a very different set of conditions, namely, China's decision to integrate itself into the world economic and political system while still retaining an authoritarian, one-party state. In the early 1980s, Beijing instituted a one-child-per-family population control policy, which it enforced rigorously. When this policy resulted in large numbers of abandoned baby girls, Beijing saw a partial solution to the problem in its new openness to the West: in 1989, the year the Berlin Wall fell and a decade of Chinese reforms culminated in the Tiananmen Square demonstrations, Beijing began allowing foreigners to adopt babies from its orphanages. The United States quickly became the number-one destination for these children, and in 1995 Americans for the first time adopted more children from China than from any other foreign country. (Russia, which also began allowing foreigners to adopt children at the end of the Cold War, and Korea were the other most popular sources of orphans.) By 2000, more than twenty-four thousand Chinese children had been adopted into American families. During the 1990s, the multiracial, multinational, U.S.-Asian family formed through adoption that had first appeared in the early Cold War became one of the most visible and widely commented-upon signs of America's increasingly close ties to Asia. Appearing in everything from John Hancock insurance advertisements to football game half-time TV features, these families have become one of the ways in which Americans live globalization in their everyday lives. These adoptive families, even more than those of the 1940s and 1950s, tie Americans to China in myriad ways. In the era of multiculturalism, parents not only travel to China to pick up their child and see her country firsthand, but are encouraged by adoption professionals to maintain a connection with China by learning about Chinese history and culture, by cultivating a Chinese American cultural identity in their children, and by befriending Chinese and Chinese American people. Some parents establish an ongoing relationship with China by donating funds to orphanages; others bring their children back to visit the land of their birth as they grow older. In these and other ways, such international adoptions not only entail the flow of Chinese children into the United States but also lead to Americans' emotional, financial, and cultural investment in China.[5]

Like these adoptions, the significance of the movie *Anna and the King* might best be grasped if movie-making is considered as a social practice. What truly sets this film apart from its theatrical and cinematic predecessors is the fact that it casts an Asian actor—Hong Kong's Chow Yun-fat—as the King (Figure 25). In doing so, the film allows us to see how the imaginative bonds that middlebrow cultural producers knit between the U.S. and Asia in the late 1940s and 1950s had by the end of the century become transnational pathways that carried Asia back into the United States. It was hardly an accident that Chow Yun-fat, one of the most popular movie stars in all of Asia, chose *Anna and the King* to make his American debut as a dramatic leading man. After making his last Hong Kong film in 1995, Chow arrived in Los Angeles eager to break into Hollywood and to move beyond the gun-toting, wise-guy characters with which he had made his reputation. Hollywood was becoming more open to the idea of Asian actors starring in action movies—Jackie Chan, Jet Li—but a dramatic role was something different. Chow's agent read a steady flow of scripts looking for an acceptable role, but they tended to recycle Chow's previous characters; eventually he relented and appeared in two action films that echoed his Hong Kong work: *The Replacement Killers* (1998) and *The Corrupter* (1999). After several years, the only acceptable offer for a starring role in a dramatic movie came from the producers of *Anna and the King*. The racial bars in Hollywood were still so strong that the King of Siam was the only sympathetic, dramatic leading character that Hollywood could imagine for an Asian male

Figure 25. Chow Yun-fat, Hollywood's first Asian King of Siam, in the film *Anna and the King*, 1999. (Museum of Modern Art/Film Stills Archive)

actor. Nearly a half century after Rodgers and Hammerstein opened the show on Broadway—and despite the protestations of the new film's producers that theirs was not a remake—*The King and I* stood as the only vehicle through which Asia's most glamorous film star could gain a dramatic foothold in America. As had Oscar Hammerstein's *Carmen Jones* in 1943 and 1954 and Rodgers and Hammerstein's *Flower Drum Song* in 1958 and 1961, *Anna and the King* derived part of its significance from the way it pressed at the color barrier in the American entertainment industry.

Chow was familiar to some American viewers even before his Hollywood debut through the films of Hong Kong director John Woo. Woo is currently playing a central role in the ongoing creation of a transnational U.S.-Chinese cinema, in which people, capital, and cinematic style flow in a reciprocal fashion between Hollywood and the East Asian film capital of Hong Kong. More than any other director, Woo has drawn the attention of American viewers and Hollywood insiders to the world's third largest film industry. Woo and Chow rose to superstardom through a series of films they made together, beginning in 1986 with *A Better Tomorrow* and culminating in 1992 with *Hard Boiled*. These films generated a cult following in the U.S. and captured the attention of Hollywood director Quentin Tarantino, who appropriated elements of Woo's style into his own films and helped make Woo's work better known in America. Woo spoke to American viewers in part because his hyperviolent, highly aestheticized action films owed a substantial stylistic debt to the slow-motion violence of Sam Peckinpah and the dark urban feel of Martin Scorsese. Thematically, however, Woo's films drew their inspiration from a Chinese sensibility. Woo has described his films, which in sharp contrast to most American movies forego heterosexual romance in favor of an intense homosocial bond among men, as being imbued with the "ancient Chinese qualities of chivalry (meaning self-sacrifice), friendship, loyalty and honor"; they are melodramas for men. Woo's mixture of Chinese and American elements, combined with a touch of French New Wave style and a liberal dose of visually pleasing mayhem, have won him audiences around the world.[6]

In the autobiography that he has crafted in interviews, Woo presents himself as a man whose life and work have been profoundly shaped by the postwar intersections of China and America. Woo allows us to see how the U.S. expansion into Asia during the 1940s and 1950s created an immense contact zone in which Asians and Americans encountered one another, learned from each other, and appropriated elements of each other's cultures. John Woo is the unexpected and unpredictable product of that contact zone.

Woo's life and career have been shaped in reaction to communism. Born in Guangdong Province in 1946, Woo arrived in Hong Kong as a refugee in 1951 after his family fled the mainland's new communist government. Forty years later he fled communism again. By the early 1990s the impending return of the British colony to Chinese control in 1997 had, along with a number of other factors, begun to undermine the Hong King film industry enough to make an offer from Hollywood look irresistible. In 1992 Woo moved his family to California and started making movies within the American system.

American musicals also shaped Woo's life in decisive ways. Woo grew up extremely poor in the slums of Hong Kong, where his father contracted a fatal case of tuberculosis. In an effort to escape these grim surroundings, Woo's mother, who supported the family by working menial jobs, took her son to the movies (which admitted children free) and introduced him to the Hollywood musicals that she adored: Fred Astaire and Gene Kelly pictures, *Seven Brides for Seven Brothers* (1954), *West Side Story* (1961). The spectacles entranced Woo: "I fell in love with the dream world. Movies became my fantasy." Merely viewing this musical dream world from the outside left him unsatisfied, however; like Rodgers and Hammerstein's King of Siam when he asks to learn the polka, Woo wanted to participate in the romantic fantasy of Western dance and become a part of it. Woo learned to dance—so well, in fact, that he worked as a ballroom dance instructor for several years before becoming a director. Woo carried this love of dance into his own movies. He appropriated the Hollywood musical aesthetic, combined it with the action movie, and merged them into a distinctive hybrid form. In his most famous gun battles, some of which last twenty minutes or more, Chow Yun-fat, the future King of Siam, flies through the air in glorious slow motion, his white suit glowing amid the arcing flare of bullets and the spattering of bright red blood. Woo has said, "When I shoot action sequences I think of great dancers, Gene Kelly, Astaire. . . . In action I feel like I'm creating a ballet, a dance. That's what I like. Even though there's violence, it's a dance. I make it a dance." [7]

Woo's life was also transformed by his experience as a virtual "adoptee" of an American Christian family. Although Woo's father had been a teacher on the mainland, his family could not afford to educate him once they arrived in Hong Kong. Woo began to attend a Christian school when an American family, working through the Lutheran church, sponsored him and paid for his education. This education turned Woo into a self-described "fervent Christian" and even spurred a desire within him to become a minister as a way to repay the generosity of his sponsors. "I wanted to return the favor—to help people as I had been helped," he explained later. "I was deeply impressed with the altruism of the American family who paid for my education that my family valued but was simply unable to supply." His love of movies proved more powerful, however, and the missionary school to which he applied rejected him for being too artistic. Woo carried his Christianity into his films, just as he did the residual traces of the Hollywood musical, and he symbolically repaid his American sponsors with scenes—some of them extraordinarily violent—replete with crucifixes, doves, and exploding statues of the Virgin Mary.[8]

Woo's arrival in Hollywood challenged the industry's racial order even as it reaffirmed its cultural aesthetic. With *Hard Target* (1993), Woo became the first Asian ever to direct a major Hollywood studio production, and with *Broken Arrow* (1996) and *Face/Off* (1997), both of which performed extremely well at the box office, he approached the top of the Hollywood hierarchy. Woo's success in America has a circular logic to it: when Hollywood invited Woo in, he brought with him a Hong Kong style so heavily indebted to Hollywood that what Hollywood ultimately received was a reworked, transformed, hybridized version of itself.

Woo's latest film at this writing, *Windtalkers* (2002), resonates with the history of the U.S.-Asian contact zone and even more so with the ethno-racial politics of U.S. global expansion. Set in the Pacific during World War II, it explores the relationship between two Marines, one white and one Native American. The Native American is one of the Navajo "codetalkers" whom the Marines employed as radiomen because their language could not be deciphered by Japanese codebreakers. The white American is his ostensible protector, but his real job is to kill the Navajo if his capture by the Japanese is imminent in order to protect the code. Woo describes the film as a "story about friendship and humanity rather than war and hatred." For the first time, Woo explores the homosocial bond that forms between men of different races. Woo's description of the film sounds like nothing so much as reviews of *The King and I*: for him, the film "is all about two different kinds of people. They come from different backgrounds but they both learn how to work and live together and influence each other. At the end of the film they become friends." Given his own biography—his childhood in the contact zone of Hong Kong, his adult experiences in America—it comes as little surprise that Woo would be drawn to a story set during a period of U.S. expansion into the Pacific and featuring a nonwhite character who finds a new place within the American nation through that expansion.[9]

"I like the idea" that the foreign policies and the middlebrow culture of the United States in the 1940s and 1950s culminated not only in the Vietnam War but also in John Woo. The irony pleases me. When Dr. J. Calvitt Clarke designed the first Christian Children's Fund advertisement urging the "adoption" and sponsorship of Chinese children, could he ever have foreseen that one of those children would grow up to direct action movies in which gun-toting gangsters regularly kill hundreds of people? When Pearl Buck promoted the idea that bi-cultural children could help prevent the spread of communism in Asia, did she ever imagine that a Hong Kong boy raised on American movies would help pry open Hollywood's door to Asian actors, directors, and martial arts choreographers? Woo is a genuine product of the postwar U.S.-Asian encounter. On the one hand, he brings into America a Chinese version of the material and symbolic violence that the U.S. has exported to Asia since 1941. On the other hand, he is a Christian convert and successful product of a missionary education. He has served as a cultural bridge-builder, forging commercial and aesthetic ties between the Hollywood and Hong Kong film industries and between American and Chinese audiences. Woo has lived his whole life within the transnational flows of money, bodies, power, culture, style, and ideas that have circulated between the U.S. and Asia since the 1940s. In his life and his art he carries within him the residual traces of America's Cold War Orientalism. He is a grown-up version of the child who demands that Nellie Forbush sing "Dites Moi," an adult incarnation of the thin-limbed boy in the Christian Children's Fund advertisement, the latest in a series of powerful Asian men who encountered America while dancing a foxtrot, a square dance, a polka.

Notes

INTRODUCTION

1. Richard Stoddard Aldrich, *Gertrude Lawrence as Mrs. A.: An Intimate Biography of the Great Star* (New York: Greystone Press, 1954), 366.

2. John Hersey, *Hiroshima* (New York: Alfred A. Knopf, 1946); John Patrick, *Teahouse of the August Moon* (1952; reprint, New York: Putnam, 1954); James A. Michener, *The Bridges at Toko-Ri* (New York: Random House, 1953); Lowell Thomas Jr., *Out of This World: Across the Himalayas to Forbidden Tibet* (New York: Greystone Press, 1950); *The World of Suzy Wong,* dir. Richard Quine, Paramount, 1960; Margaret Bourke-White, *Halfway to Freedom* (New York: Simon and Schuster, 1949); Chester Bowles, *Ambassador's Report* (New York: Harper, 1954); Eleanor Roosevelt, *India and the Awakening East* (New York: Harper, 1954); David Bernstein, *The Philippine Story* (New York: Farrar, Straus, 1947); Alan Watts, *Beat Zen, Square Zen, and Zen* (San Francisco: City Lights Books, 1959); Jack Kerouac, *The Dharma Bums* (New York: Viking, 1958); Lin Yutang, *Chinatown Family* (New York: John Day, 1948); Jade Snow Wong, *Fifth Chinese Daughter* (New York: Harper, 1950); Sven A. Kirsten, *The Book of Tiki: The Cult of Polynesian Pop in Fifties America* (Cologne, Germany: Taschen, 2000).

3. On American representations of Asia and the Pacific, see Orville Schell, *Virtual Tibet: Searching for Shangri-La from the Himalayas to Hollywood* (New York: Henry Holt, 2000); John Carlos Rowe, *Literary Culture and U.S. Imperialism: From the Revolution to World War II* (Oxford: Oxford University Press, 2000); Jonathan D. Spence, *The Chan's Great Continent: China in Western Minds* (New York: W. W. Norton, 1998); Malini Johar Schueller, *U.S. Orientalisms: Race, Nation, and Gender in Literature, 1790–1890* (Ann Arbor: University of Michigan Press, 1998); Mari Yoshihara, "Women's Asia: American

Women and the Gendering of American Orientalism, 1870–World War II,"
Ph.D. diss., Brown University, 1997; T. Christopher Jespersen, *American Images of China, 1931–1949* (Stanford, Calif.: Stanford University Press, 1996); Gina Marchetti, *Romance and the "Yellow Peril": Race, Sex, and Discursive Strategies in Hollywood Fiction* (Berkeley: University of California Press, 1993); Nathan Glazer and Sulochana Raghavan Glazer, eds., *Conflicting Images: India and the United States* (Glenn Dale, Md.: Riverdale, 1990); Sheila K. Johnson, *The Japanese through American Eyes* (Stanford, Calif.: Stanford University Press, 1988); John W. Dower, *War without Mercy* (New York: Pantheon, 1986); N. Gerald Barrier, *India and America: American Publishing on India, 1939–1985* (New Delhi: American Institute of Indian Studies, 1986); Robert Rydell, *All the World's a Fair: Visions of Empire at American International Expositions, 1876–1916* (Chicago: University of Chicago Press, 1984); Daniel B. Ramsdell, "Asia Askew: U.S. Best-Sellers on Asia, 1931–1980," *Bulletin of Concerned Asian Scholars* 15 (1983): 2–25; Eugene Franklin Wong, *On Visual Media Racism: Asians in American Motion Pictures* (New York: Arno Press, 1978); Akira Iriye, ed., *Mutual Images: Essays in American-Japanese Relations* (Cambridge, Mass.: Harvard University Press, 1975); John M. Steadman, *The Myth of Asia* (New York: Simon and Schuster, 1969); Harold R. Isaacs, *Images of Asia: American Views of China and India* (1958, originally published as *Scratches on Our Minds: American Images of China and India;* reprint, New York: Capricorn, 1962); Dorothy B. Jones, *The Portrayal of China and India on the American Screen, 1896–1955* (Cambridge: Center for International Studies, Massachusetts Institute of Technology, 1955).

4. Barraclough quoted in Robert J. McMahon, *Colonialism and Cold War: The United States and the Struggle for Indonesian Independence, 1945–1949* (Ithaca, N.Y.: Cornell University Press, 1981), 11.

5. Raymond Williams, *Marxism and Literature* (Oxford: Oxford University Press, 1977).

6. For discussions of cultural hegemony, see Williams, *Marxism and Literature;* Antonio Gramsci, *Selections from the Prison Notebooks,* ed. and trans. Quentin Hoare and Geoffrey Nowell Smith (New York: International Publishers, 1971), 350; T. J. Jackson Lears, "The Concept of Cultural Hegemony: Problems and Possibilities," *American Historical Review* 90 (1985): 567–93; Michael Denning, *The Cultural Front: The Laboring of American Culture in the Twentieth Century* (New York: Verso Press, 1996), 63.

7. Richard Slotkin, *Regeneration through Violence: The Mythology of the Frontier* (Middletown, Conn.: Wesleyan University Press, 1973), *The Fatal Environment: The Myth of the Frontier in the Age of Industrialization, 1800–1890* (New York: Atheneum, 1985), and *Gunfighter Nation: The Myth of the Frontier in Twentieth-Century America* (New York: Atheneum, 1992); Richard Drinnon, *Facing West: The Metaphysics of Indian-Hating and Empire-Building* (Minneapolis: University of Minnesota Press, 1980); Amy Kaplan, "Manifest Domesticity," *American Literature* 70 (1998): 581–606; Edward Said, *Orientalism* (1978; reprint, New York: Vintage, 1979), and *Culture and Imperialism* (1993; reprint, New York: Random House, 1994), xxv.

8. Penny M. Von Eschen, *Race against Empire: Black Americans and Anti-*

colonialism, 1937–1957 (Ithaca, N.Y.: Cornell University Press, 1997); Nikhil Pal Singh, "Culture/Wars: Recoding Empire in an Age of Democracy," *American Quarterly* 50 (1998); Mary L. Dudziak, *Cold War Civil Rights: Race and the Image of American Democracy* (Princeton, N.J.: Princeton University Press, 2000).

9. Mary Louise Pratt, *Imperial Eyes: Travel Writing and Transculturation* (New York: Routledge, 1992) 7, 39, 78, 80.

10. Joanne Dobson, "Reclaiming Sentimental Literature," *American Literature* 69 (1997): 267; Pratt, *Imperial Eyes,* 75–76; Shirley Samuels, ed., *The Culture of Sentiment: Race, Gender, and Sentimentality in Nineteenth-Century America* (New York: Oxford University Press, 1992); June Howard, "What Is Sentimentality?" *American Literary History* 11 (1999): 63–81.

11. Philip Fisher, *Hard Facts: Setting and Form in the American Novel* (New York: Oxford University Press, 1987), 87–127; Stephen Greenblatt, "Improvisation and Power," in *Literature and Society,* ed. Edward Said (Baltimore, Md.: Johns Hopkins University Press, 1980); Laura Wexler, *Tender Violence: Domestic Visions in an Age of U.S. Imperialism* (Chapel Hill: University of North Carolina Press, 2000); Vicente Rafael, *White Love and Other Events in Filipino History* (Durham, N.C.: Duke University Press, 2000).

12. Lisa Lowe, *Critical Terrains: French and British Orientalisms* (Ithaca, N.Y.: Cornell University Press, 1991), 4–5; Melani McAlister, *Epic Encounters: Culture, Media, and U.S. Interests in the Middle East, 1945–2000* (Berkeley: University of California Press, 2001), 270.

13. Said, *Culture and Imperialism,* xx, xxv, 317, 336.

CHAPTER ONE: SENTIMENTAL EDUCATION

The epigraph is from "Memorandum by the Acting Assistant Secretary of State for Near Eastern, South Asian, and African Affairs ([Raymond Arthur] Hare) to the Under Secretary of State (Webb)," in U.S. Department of State, *Foreign Relations of the United States* [hereafter *FRUS*], *1950,* vol. 1 (Washington, D.C.: Government Printing Office, 1977), 221.

1. "'Anti-Americanism' Abroad," map, *Newsweek,* 10 June 1957: 52–53.

2. Francis O. Wilcox, "Foreign Policy and Some Implications for Education," *Department of State Bulletin* [hereafter *DSB*], 29 July 1957: 180, 179, 182.

3. Wilcox, "Foreign Policy," 180, 183, 182.

4. Harry S. Truman, "The Truman Doctrine," *Documents of American History,* vol. 2, *Since 1898,* ed. Henry Steele Commager, 9th ed. (Englewood Cliffs, N.J.: Prentice Hall, 1973), 527.

5. Christian Herter, "Preparing Americans for Overseas Service," *DSB,* 21 November 1960: 775.

6. Kennan quoted in John Lewis Gaddis, *Strategies of Containment: A Critical Appraisal of Postwar American National Security Policy* (Oxford: Oxford University Press, 1982), 4; and Melvyn P. Leffler, *A Preponderance of Power: National Security, the Truman Administration, and the Cold War* (Stanford, Calif.: Stanford University Press, 1992), 180.

7. Leffler, *Preponderance of Power*, 10, 12, 16–23; Thomas J. McCormick, *America's Half-Century: United States Foreign Policy in the Cold War and After*, 2nd ed. (Baltimore: Johns Hopkins University Press, 1995), xii–xvi.

8. Robert J. McMahon, *Colonialism and the Cold War: The United States and the Struggle for Indonesian Independence, 1945–1949* (Ithaca, N.Y.: Cornell University Press, 1981), 43–73, 304–28.

9. Richard M. Freeland, *The Truman Doctrine and the Origins of McCarthyism: Foreign Policy, Domestic Politics, and Internal Security, 1946–1948* (New York: Alfred A. Knopf, 1972), 201–45; Guy Oakes, *The Imaginary War: Civil Defense and American Cold War Culture* (Oxford: Oxford University Press, 1994), 10–32; Gabriel A. Almond, *The American People and Foreign Policy* (1950; reprint, New York: Praeger, 1960), 69, 85.

10. Bruce Cumings, *The Origins of the Korean War*, vol. 2 (Princeton, N.J.: Princeton University Press, 1990), 3–34.

11. Cumings, *Origins of the Korean War*, 26.

12. Paul A. Varg, *Missionaries, Chinese, and Diplomats* (Princeton, N.J.: Princeton University Press, 1958); Patricia R. Hill, *The World Their Household: The American Woman's Foreign Missionary Movement and Cultural Transformation, 1870–1920* (Ann Arbor: University of Michigan Press, 1985); Jane Hunter, *The Gospel of Gentility: American Women Missionaries in Turn-of-the-Century China* (New Haven, Conn.: Yale University Press, 1984).

13. Michael H. Hunt, *The Making of a Special Relationship: The United States and China to 1914* (New York: Columbia University Press, 1983).

14. Richard Crossman, ed., *The God That Failed* (1950; reprint, New York: Bantam Books, 1952), 141, 140.

15. Michael Denning, *The Cultural Front: The Laboring of American Culture in the Twentieth Century* (New York: Verso, 1996), 11, 12, 56; William Stott, *Documentary Expression and Thirties America* (1973; reprint, Chicago: University of Chicago Press, 1986), 135–36; Judy Kutulas, *The Long War: The Intellectual People's Front and Anti-Stalinism, 1930–1940* (Durham, N.C.: Duke University Press, 1995).

16. Cumings, *Origins of the Korean War*, 27.

17. Freeland, *Truman Doctrine and the Origins of McCarthyism*.

18. David Caute, *The Great Fear: The Anti-Communist Purge under Truman and Eisenhower* (New York: Simon and Schuster, 1978), 169; Ellen Schrecker, *The Age of McCarthyism: A Brief History with Documents* (Boston: Bedford Books, 1994), 168–72.

19. Ross Y. Koen, *The China Lobby in American Politics* (New York: Harper and Row, 1974); John N. Thomas, *The Institute of Pacific Relations: Asian Scholars and American Politics* (Seattle: University of Washington Press, 1974), 93, 115.

20. Roger Daniels, *Asian America: Chinese and Japanese in the United States since 1850* (Seattle: University of Washington Press, 1988), 304–9.

21. "World Struggle," map, *Life*, 13 March 1947, 59.

22. Elaine Tyler May, *Homeward Bound: American Families in the Cold War Era* (New York: Basic Books, 1988), 13; Stephen J. Whitfield, *The Culture of the Cold War* (Baltimore: Johns Hopkins University Press, 1991); Michael Rogin,

Ronald Reagan, the Movie: And Other Episodes in Political Demonology (Berkeley: University of California Press, 1987), 236–71; Alan Nadel, *Containment Culture: American Narratives, Postmodernism and the Atomic Age* (Durham, N.C.: Duke University Press, 1995), 4, 5. See also Elizabeth A. Wheeler, *Uncontained: Urban Fiction in Postwar America* (New Brunswick, N.J.: Rutgers University Press, 2001); and Jane Sherron De Hart, "Containment at Home: Gender, Sexuality, and National Identity in Cold War America," in *Rethinking Cold War Culture,* ed. Peter J. Kuznick and James Gilbert (Washington, D.C.: Smithsonian Institution Press, 2001), 124–55.

23. Harold R. Isaacs, *Images of Asia: Views of China and India* (1958; reprint, New York: Capricorn, 1962; originally published as *Scratches on Our Minds*), 209–38; *The Manchurian Candidate,* dir. John Frankenheimer, United Artists, 1962.

24. Fosdick quoted in Andrew J. Rotter, *The Path to Vietnam: Origins of the American Commitment to Southeast Asia* (Ithaca, N.Y.: Cornell University Press, 1987), 108.

25. Donovan quoted in Leffler, *Preponderance of Power,* 60; "Memorandum of the Conversation between the President and T. S. Repplier, August 3, 1955," DDE Confidential File, Box 99, USIA File (2), Dwight D. Eisenhower Library, Abilene, Kansas.

26. "Record of the Meeting of the State-Defense Policy Review Group," *FRUS, 1950,* vol. 1, 198; "Memorandum by the Acting Assistant Secretary of State for Near Eastern, South Asian, and African Affairs ([Raymond Arthur] Hare) to the Under Secretary of State (Webb)," *FRUS, 1950,* vol. 1, 221.

27. Harry S. Truman, "Inaugural Address, 1949," *Public Papers of the President: Harry S. Truman, 1949* (Washington, D.C.: Government Printing Office, 1950), 112–16; John Foster Dulles, "Policy for Security and Peace," *DSB,* 29 March 1954, 460; George C. Herring, *America's Longest War: The United States and Vietnam, 1950–1975,* 2nd ed. (New York: Alfred A. Knopf, 1986), 58.

28. Acheson quoted in Penny M. Von Eschen, "Commentary: Challenging Cold War Habits: African Americans, Race, and Foreign Policy," *Diplomatic History* 20, no. 4 (fall 1996): 635; Acheson quoted in Mary L. Dudziak, "Desegregation as a Cold War Imperative," *Stanford Law Review* 41 (November 1988): 111, 101; NSC 48/5, *FRUS, 1951,* vol. 6 (Washington, D.C.: Government Printing Office, 1979), 44, 46; Penny M. Von Eschen, *Race against Empire: Black Americans and Anticolonialism, 1937–1957* (Ithaca, N.Y.: Cornell University Press, 1997); on U.S. race relations and Cold War foreign relations, see also Mary L. Dudziak, *Cold War Civil Rights: Race and the Image of American Democracy* (Princeton, N.J.: Princeton University Press, 2000); Thomas Borstelmann, *The Cold War and the Color Line: American Race Relations in the Global Arena* (Cambridge, Mass.: Harvard University Press, 2001); Brenda Gayle Plummer, *Rising Wind: Black Americans and Foreign Policy, 1935–1960* (Chapel Hill: University of North Carolina Press, 1996); "Symposium: African Americans and U.S. Foreign Relations," *Diplomatic History* 20, no. 4 (fall 1996), especially Michael L. Kren, "'Unfinished Business': Segregation and U.S. Diplomacy at the 1958 World's Fair," 591–612; and Von Eschen, "Commentary: Challenging Cold War Habits," 627–38.

29. Mary L. Dudziak, "Desegregation as a Cold War Imperative," and "The Little Rock Crisis and Foreign Affairs," *Southern California Law Review* 70 (September 1997): 1715.

30. Quoted in Caute, *Great Fear*, 168; Dudziak, "Desegregation as a Cold War Imperative."

31. Dwight D. Eisenhower, "State of the Union Address," *DSB*, 9 February 1953, 208; John Foster Dulles, "Challenge and Response in United States Policy," *DSB*, 7 October 1957, 571; Eisenhower, "Principles of U.S. Foreign Policy," *DSB*, 13 September 1954, 360.

32. Alexander Bloom, *Prodigal Sons: The New York Intellectuals and Their World* (New York: Oxford University Press, 1986), 179–80; John Daniel, "Ready to Be Radical," *Saturday Review*, 10 September 1949, 12.

33. Arthur M. Schlesinger Jr., *The Vital Center* (1949; reprint, New York: Da Silva, 1988), 37, 36.

34. Ibid., 52, 54, 189, 251, 248.

35. Ibid., 120–21, 230, 190, 235, 252.

36. McCormick, *America's Half-Century*, 99–124.

37. "United States Collective Defense Arrangements," map, *DSB*, 21 March 1955, 478–79.

38. Walter LaFeber, *America, Russia, and the Cold War*, 8th ed. (New York: McGraw-Hill, 1997), 132.

39. Dwight D. Eisenhower, "Special Message to the Congress on Foreign Economic Policy," *Public Papers of the President: Dwight David Eisenhower* [hereafter *PPP: DDE*], *1954* (Washington, D.C.: Government Printing Office, 1955), 363–64; Eisenhower quoted in Gaddis, *Strategies of Containment*, 132; Blanche Wiesen Cook, *The Declassified Eisenhower* (Garden City, N.Y.: Doubleday, 1981), 293–346.

40. Dwight D. Eisenhower, "Proclaiming Our Faith Anew," *DSB*, 2 February 1953, 167–70.

41. Eisenhower, "Special Message to the Congress on Foreign Economic Policy," 352–54; Dulles, "Challenge and Response in United States Policy," 575–76.

42. Dulles, "Challenge and Response in United States Policy," 574–78.

43. Burton I. Kaufman, *Trade and Aid: Eisenhower's Foreign Economic Policy, 1953–1961* (Baltimore: Johns Hopkins University Press, 1982); George M. Guess, *The Politics of United States Foreign Aid* (London: Croom, Helm, 1987); Eisenhower quoted in Stephen E. Ambrose, *Eisenhower*, vol. 2 (New York: Simon and Schuster, 1984), 381.

44. John E. Juergensmeyer, *The President, the Foundations, and the People-to-People Program* (Indianapolis: Bobbs-Merrill, 1965).

45. Frances Stonor Saunders, *The Cultural Cold War: The CIA and the World of Arts and Letters* (New York: New Press, 1999); Walter L. Hixson, *Parting the Curtain: Propaganda, Culture, and the Cold War, 1945–1961* (New York: St. Martin's, 1997); Eric J. Sandeen, *Picturing an Exhibition: The Family of Man and 1950s America* (Albuquerque: University of New Mexico Press, 1995); Reinhold Wagnleitner, *Coca-Colonization and the Cold War: The Cultural Mission of the United States in Austria after the Second World War*

(Chapel Hill: University of North Carolina Press, 1994); Frank A. Ninkovich, *The Diplomacy of Ideas: U.S. Foreign Policy and Cultural Relations, 1938–1950* (Cambridge: Cambridge University Press, 1981); Francis J. Colligan and Walter Johnson, *The Fulbright Program: A History* (Chicago: University of Chicago Press, 1965); Von Eschen, *Race against Empire*.

46. "Oral History Interview with Mr. and Mrs. Abbott Washburn, #2 of 2, on January 5, 1968 by Ed Edwin," Dwight D. Eisenhower Library, Abilene, Kansas, 75; "Memorandum from Abbot Washburn, USIA to James C. Hagerty, White House, May 29, 1956. Subject: June 12th People-to-People Partnership," Box 930, File 325–2, Dwight D. Eisenhower Library, Abilene, Kansas; Juergensmeyer, *The President, the Foundations, and the People-to-People Program*, 4.

47. John E. Juergensmeyer, "Democracy's Diplomacy: The People-to-People Program," Ph.D. diss., Princeton University, 1960, 409–10, 428; "'Status Report on Project HOPE,' December 15, 1960, from Abbott Washburn, USIA to Members of the Operations Coordinating Board," Dwight D. Eisenhower Library, Abilene, Kansas, Box 934, 325-F (w1), 4.

48. Dwight D. Eisenhower, "Commencement Address at Baylor University, May 1956," *PPP: DDE, 1956,* 530, 531, 533; "Project HOPE," pamphlet published by The People to People Health Foundation, Inc., n. d., Dwight D. Eisenhower Library, Box 934, 325-F (W1–1).

49. Dwight D. Eisenhower, "Remarks at the People-to-People Conference," *PPP: DDE, 1956,* 750; Liz Chilsen and Sheldon Rampton, *Friends in Deed: The Story of U.S.-Nicaragua Sister Cities* (Madison: Wisconsin Coordinating Council on Nicaragua, 1988), 18.

50. Eisenhower, "Commencement Address at Baylor University," 533, 537, 529. Dwight Eisenhower, "Remarks to the National 4-H Conference, June 19, 1958," *PPP: DDE, 1958* (Washington, D.C.: Government Printing Office, 1959), 489.

51. Arthur Larson, *What We Are For* (New York: Harper, 1959), 4–5, 2, 168.

52. Members of the Eisenhower administration often spoke positively about missionaries as models of engaged internationalism. See John Foster Dulles, "A Report on Asia," *DSB*, 2 April 1956, 541; Richard Nixon, "A Peaceful Crusade for Freedom," *DSB*, 25 June 1956, 1045.

53. "An Appraisal of U.S. Government People to People Activities," U.S. President's Committee on Information Activities Abroad (Sprague Committee), Records 1959–1961, Box 9, File 29 (1), Dwight D. Eisenhower Library, Abilene, Kansas.

54. Juergensmeyer, "Democracy's Diplomacy," 1–5, 413, 559.

55. Ibid., 579.

56. John Foster Dulles, "U.S. Responsibility—A Society of Consent," *DSB*, 2 November 1953, 587, 589.

57. Fredric Jameson, *The Political Unconscious: Narrative as Socially Symbolic Act* (Ithaca, N.Y.: Cornell University Press, 1981), 296; and "Reification and Utopian in Mass Culture," *Social Text* 1 (winter 1979): 144.

58. Chilsen and Rampton, *Friends in Deed,* 1–36.

CHAPTER TWO: *READER'S DIGEST, SATURDAY REVIEW,*
AND THE MIDDLEBROW AESTHETIC OF COMMITMENT

The epigraph is from Norman Cousins, "Tom Dooley and His Mission," *Saturday Review* [hereafter cited as *SR*], 4 February 1961, 34.

1. Cousins, "Tom Dooley and His Mission," 24; Norman Cousins, "Report from Laos," *SR*, 18 February 1961, 46–47; James T. Fisher, *Dr. America: The Lives of Dr. Thomas Dooley* (Amherst: University of Massachusetts Press, 1997), 260.
2. NSC 48/5, "United States Objectives, Policies, and Courses of Action in Asia," U.S. Department of State, in *Foreign Relations of the United States* [hereafter cited as *FRUS*], *1951*, vol. 6 (Washington, D.C.: Government Printing Office, 1979), 45–46.
3. Thomas A. Bailey, *The Man in the Street: The Impact of American Public Opinion on Foreign Policy* (New York: Macmillan, 1948), 134. Robert A. McCaughey, *International Studies and Academic Enterprise: A Chapter in the Enclosure of American Learning* (New York: Columbia University Press, 1984); Alice M. Rivlin, *The Role of the Federal Government in Financing Higher Education* (Washington, D.C.: Brookings Institution, 1961).
4. Martin Kriesberg, "Dark Areas of Ignorance," in *Public Opinion and Foreign Policy,* ed. Lester Markel (New York: Harper, 1949), 63; "Record of the Meeting of the State-Defense Policy Review Group, Department of State, Thursday, March 16, 1950," *FRUS, 1950,* vol. 1: 199; "Record of the Meeting of the State-Defense Policy Review Group, Department of State, Friday, March 10, 1950," *FRUS, 1950,* vol. 1: 192.
5. On the idea of a cultural formation, see Raymond Williams, *Marxism and Literature* (Oxford: Oxford University Press, 1977), 118–20; and Michael Denning, *The Cultural Front: The Laboring of American Culture in the Twentieth Century* (New York: Verso, 1996), 202.
6. Joseph Horowitz, *Understanding Toscanini: How He Became an American Culture-God and Helped Create a New Audience for Old Music* (Minneapolis: University of Minnesota Press, 1987); Joan Shelley Rubin, *The Making of Middlebrow Culture* (Chapel Hill: University of North Carolina Press, 1992); Janice A. Radway, *A Feeling for Books: The Book-of-the-Month Club, Literary Taste, and Middle-Class Desire* (Chapel Hill: University of North Carolina Press, 1997).
7. Radway, *Feeling for Books,* 283–84.
8. Leslie A. Fiedler, "The Middle against Both Ends," in *Mass Culture: The Popular Arts in America,* ed. Bernard Rosenberg and David Manning White (Glencoe, Ill.: Free Press, 1957), 544, 546; Dwight Macdonald, "Masscult & Midcult," in *Against the American Grain* (New York: Random House, 1962), 51, 54.
9. Macdonald, "Masscult & Midcult," 39, 46; Robert Warshow, *The Immediate Experience* (New York: Doubleday, 1962), 35; Irving Howe and Lewis Coser, *The American Communist Party: A Critical History, 1919–1957* (Boston: Beacon, 1957), 366.

10. Andrew Ross, *No Respect: Intellectuals and Popular Culture* (New York: Routledge, 1989), 15–64.

11. Dwight Macdonald, "Norman Cousins' Flat *World*," in *Discriminations: Essays and Afterthoughts, 1938–1974* (New York: Grossman, 1974), 175; Irving Howe, "This Age of Conformity," *Partisan Review,* January–February 1954, 32; Fiedler, "The Middle against Both Ends," 541.

12. Numerous scholars have used Henry R. Luce and his magazines as windows onto twentieth-century American society, politics, and attitudes toward Asia. See, for example, Robert E. Herzstein, *Henry R. Luce: A Political Portrait of the Man Who Created the American Century* (New York: Charles Scribner's Sons, 1994); T. Christopher Jespersen, *American Images of China, 1931–1949* (Stanford, Calif.: Stanford University Press, 1996); Wendy Kozol, *Life's America: Family and Nation in Postwar Photojournalism* (Philadelphia: Temple University Press, 1994); Patricia Neils, *China Images in the Life and Times of Henry Luce* (Savage, Md.: Rowman and Littlefield, 1990).

13. John Heidenry, *Theirs Was the Kingdom: Lila and DeWitt Wallace and the Story of the Reader's Digest* (New York: W. W. Norton, 1993), 22–40, 241.

14. James Playsted Wood, *Of Lasting Interest: The Story of the Reader's Digest* (1958; reprint, New York: Doubleday, 1967), 40, 266.

15. Wood, *Of Lasting Interest* 40; Heidenry, *Theirs Was the Kingdom,* passim.

16. Wood, *Of Lasting Interest* 257, 16, 15, 254.

17. Samuel Schreiner Jr., *The Condensed World of the Reader's Digest* (New York: Stein and Day, 1977), 16; Wood, *Of Lasting Interest* 29; Heidenry, *Theirs Was the Kingdom,* 170–71.

18. John Bainbridge, *Little Wonder, or, The Reader's Digest and How It Grew* (New York: Reynal and Hitchcock, 1946), 134, 113; Wood, *Of Lasting Interest,* 155–57; Heidenry, *Theirs Was the Kingdom,* 164, 262, 299; Schreiner, *Condensed World,* 11.

19. Bainbridge, *Little Wonder,* 89; Wood, *Of Lasting Interest,* 17–21; Heidenry, *Theirs Was the Kingdom,* 44–45, 48; *Reader's Digest* [hereafter cited as *RD*], January, February, March, May, October 1947, inside front covers.

20. David Halberstam, *The Fifties* (New York: Villard Books, 1993), 229; Heidenry, *Theirs Was the Kingdom,* 257, passim.

21. Schreiner, *Condensed World,* 65; Heidenry, *Theirs Was the Kingdom,* 474.

22. Schreiner, *Condensed World,* 143; see Frances Stonor Saunders, *The Cultural Cold War: The CIA and the World of Arts and Letters* (New York: New Press, 1999), 88.

23. Hannah Arendt, "The Ex-Communists," *Commonweal,* 20 March 1953, 595–99 (thanks to David Engerman for bringing this article to my attention); Schreiner, *Condensed World,* 150.

24. Norman Cousins, "Life Begins at Twenty-Five," *SR,* 24 April 1965, 26–28; Edward E. Chielens, ed., *American Literary Magazines: The Twentieth Century* (Westport, Conn.: Greenwood, 1992), 303; Sherilynn Cox Bennion, "The *Saturday Review:* From Literature to Life," Ph.D. diss., Syracuse University, 1968, 2; Norman Cousins, "A Postmortem of the *Saturday Review,*" *Center*

Magazine, May/June 1983, 33, and "A New World for 'SR,'" *SR,* 11 September 1973, 5.

25. Bennion, "The *Saturday Review,*" 312; W. R. Simmons, *Selective Markets and the Media Reaching Them* (New York: Simmons Media Studies, 1966).

26. Henry Seidel Canby, "Timely and Timeless," *SR,* 2 August 1924, 2; Joseph Wood Krutch, "Introduction," in *The Saturday Review Treasury,* ed. John Haverstick and the editors of the *Saturday Review* (New York: Simon and Schuster, 1957), xx; Bennion, "The *Saturday Review,*" 49.

27. Norman Cousins, "Confessions of a Universalist: One Man's Re-Education," *SR,* 6 August 1949, 74; Norman Cousins, "Notes on SRL," *SR,* 5 August 1944, 44–45; Krutch, "Introduction," xxii–xxiii.

28. Bennion, "The *Saturday Review,*" 72, 141, 134.

29. Norman Cousins, "The Paralysis of Conscience," *SR,* 6 October 1945, 14; Harry J. Carman, "Setting Our Sights for Tomorrow," *SR,* 15 September 1945, 16; Norman Cousins, "Modern Man Is Obsolete," *SR,* 15 August 1945, 8.

30. Robert Okin, "Asia, One or Divisible," review of *The Revolt of Asia,* by Robert Payne, *SR,* 11 October 1947, 40; Gary Wills, "Introduction," in *Scoundrel Time,* by Lillian Hellman (New York: Bantam, 1976), 24–25.

31. Paul S. Boyer, *By the Bomb's Early Light: American Thought and Culture at the Dawn of the Atomic Age* (1985; reprint, Chapel Hill: University of North Carolina Press, 1994), 27–45.

32. Heidenry, *Theirs Was the Kingdom,* 208; Boyer, *Bomb's Early Light,* 43; Arthur M. Schlesinger Jr., *The Vital Center: The Politics of Freedom* (1949; reprint, New York: Da Capo Press, 1988), 240.

33. Bradford Smith, "Directing and Evolution," review of *MacArthur's Japan,* by Russell Brines, *SR,* 15 October 1948, 15; W. D. Patterson, "America and the Challenge of Asia," *SR,* 14 August 1951, 4; Harrison Smith, "The World Knocks at Our Door," *SR,* 10 November 1945, 24.

34. Max Eastman and J. B. Powell, "The Fate of World Is at Stake in China," *RD,* June 1945, 13–20; Bishop J. Sheil, "Message to America," *RD,* May 1946, back cover; Hanson W. Baldwin, "The United States at the Crossroads of History," *RD,* May 1947, 24–26; Harrison Smith, "Our Conscience and the War," *SR,* 12 August 1950, 22; Norman Cousins, "The Grand Commitment," *SR,* 26 May 1956, 22; John T. Flynn, "Uncle Sam's Imperialistic Jag," *RD,* June 1949, 102.

35. Christopher Shannon, "A World Made Safe for Differences: Ruth Benedict's *The Chrysanthemum and the Sword,*" *American Quarterly* 47 (1995): 659–80.

36. Norman Cousins, "Confessions of a Miseducated Man," *SR,* 10 May 1952, 22.

37. Norman Cousins, "Science Will Not Save Us," *SR,* 14 December 1957, 20; Wood, *Of Lasting Interest,* 165.

38. Norman Cousins, *Human Options: An American Editor's Odyssey* (New York: W. W. Norton, 1981), 34; Charles Malik, "Is It Too Late to Win against Communism?" *RD,* September 1960, 37–43.

39. Wood, *Of Lasting Interest,* 142–46.

40. *RD,* February 1947, insert between 96–97.

41. Norman Cousins, "Disconnected Man," in *Present Tense,* 272; Cousins, "Life Begins at Twenty-Five," *SR,* 24 April 1965, 28.

42. Wood, *Of Lasting Interest,* 250.

43. Norman Cousins, "Bankrupt Realism," *SR,* 8 March 1947, 22, and "The Incomplete Power," *SR,* 1 December 1951, 28; Harrison Smith, "Themes for a New Day," *SR,* 26 April 1947, 18; "Fiction," *SR,* 6 September 1947, 16; "Literature for Survival," *SR,* 20 September 1947, 18; "End of a Year," *SR,* 27 December 1947, 20; and "A New World for Writers," *SR,* 2 June 1945, 16.

44. Letter from Lederer to Edward Lansdale, 28 October 1957, in William J. Lederer Papers, Special Collections and Archives, W. E. B. Du Bois Library, University of Massachusetts, Amherst. Thanks to Jim Fisher for sharing this with me.

45. George Herring, *America's Longest War: The United States and Vietnam, 1950–1975,* 2nd ed. (New York: Alfred A. Knopf, 1986), 43–72.

46. Herring, *America's Longest War,* 71; Norman Cousins, "What We Don't Know Can Kill Us," *SR,* 14 January 1961, 24, and "Report from Laos," *SR,* 18 February 1961, 12–14, 46–47, condensed in *RD,* May 1961, 96–101.

47. Fisher, *Dr. America,* 69–75.

48. "Eugene Burdick," in *Contemporary Authors,* vols. 5–8 (Detroit: Gale Research, 1969), 171; William J. Lederer and Eugene Burdick, authors' note, *The Ugly American* (1958; reprint, New York: Fawcett Crest Ballantine, 1983).

49. John Hellman, *American Myth and the Legacy of Vietnam* (New York: Columbia University Press, 1986), 15–18; William J. Fulbright, "'The Ugly American' and State Department Policies," *Congressional Record* [hereafter cited as *CR*], 19 May 1959, 8445–48; "'The Ugly American,'" *CR,* 7 September 1959, 18332–35; "How to Make a Movie out of 'The Ugly American,'" *CR,* 14 September 1959, 19577–79; and "Proposed Filming of 'The Ugly American,'" *CR,* 24 August 1959, 16752; Russell B. Long, "Nomination of C. Douglas Dillon to be Under Secretary of State," *CR,* 15 May 1959, 8238–40; Stuart Symington, "Foreign Service Academy," *CR,* 16 January 1959, 237; *New York Times,* 23 January 1959, L-23.

50. Lederer and Burdick, *Ugly American,* 233.

51. William J. Lederer and Eugene Burdick, "Salute to Deeds of Non-Ugly Americans," *Life,* 7 December 1959, 148–63; Fisher, *Dr. America,* 1.

52. Fisher, *Dr. America,* passim; "Pick of the Paperbacks," *SR,* 17 October 1959, 20.

53. Thomas A. Dooley, *The Night They Burned the Mountain* (1960; reprint, New York: Signet, 1961), 23; Thomas A. Dooley, *The Edge of Tomorrow* (New York: Farrar, Straus and Cudahy, 1958), 193; Fisher, *Dr. America,* 149–50, 224.

54. James T. Fisher, "A World Made Safe for Diversity: The Vietnam Lobby and the Politics of Pluralism, 1945–1963," in *Cold War Constructions: The Political Culture of United States Imperialism, 1945–1966,* ed. Christian G. Appy (Amherst: University of Massachusetts Press, 2000); Fisher, *Dr. America,* passim.

55. Dooley, *Edge of Tomorrow,* v, 98.

56. Ibid., 136, 199, 203, 198.

57. Dooley, *Night They Burned the Mountain,* 46–47.

58. Dooley, *Edge of Tomorrow,* caption of photograph following p. 80, 68, 40.

59. Ibid., 2; Barbara Ehrenreich, *The Hearts of Men: American Dreams and the Flight from Commitment* (New York: Anchor Doubleday, 1983).

60. Fisher, *Dr. America,* 69–78; Heidenry, *Theirs Was the Kingdom,* 323.

61. Ferdinand Kuhn, "A Candle for the Jungle's Dark," review of *The Night They Burned the Mountain,* by Thomas A. Dooley, *SR,* 18 June 1960, 21; Cousins, "Tom Dooley and His Mission," 34; MEDICO letterhead from 2 February 1961; thanks to Jim Fisher for sharing this with me.

62. James Sloan Allen, *The Romance of Commerce and Culture* (Chicago: University of Chicago Press, 1983), 164–67; Norman Cousins, *Dr. Schweitzer of Lambaréné* (New York: Harper, 1960).

63. George Kennan, "The Long Telegram," in *Containment: Documents on American Policy and Strategy, 1945–1950,* ed. Thomas H. Etzold and John Lewis Gaddis (New York: Columbia University Press, 1978), 63, 62; Hanson W. Baldwin, "The United States at the Crossroads of History," *RD,* May 1947, 24; Max Eastman and J. B. Powell, "The Fate of the World Is at Stake in China," *RD,* June 1945, 13; Harrison Smith, "The Die Is Cast," *SR,* 5 April 1947, 22; Kate Holliday, "Japan Discovers Modern Medicine," *RD,* April 1951, 110–12; Geoffrey S. Smith, "National Security and Personal Isolation: Sex, Gender, and Disease in the Cold War United States," *International History Review,* May 1992, 307–37.

64. Dooley, *Edge of Tomorrow,* 200–201.

65. June Howard, "What Is Sentimentality?" *American Literary History* 11 (1999): 74.

CHAPTER THREE: HOW TO BE AN AMERICAN ABROAD

The epigraph is from William Harlan Hale, "Millions of Ambassadors," *Saturday Review* [hereafter cited as *SR*], 10 January 1959, 10.

1. "Mobs Sack Hotels in Saigon, 60 Hurt," *New York Times,* 21 July 1955, 1.

2. Michener, quoted in John P. Hayes, *James A. Michener: A Biography* (Indianapolis: Bobbs-Merrill, 1984), 111–12.

3. A. Grove Day, *James A. Michener* (New York: Twayne, 1964), 32.

4. Hale, "Millions of Ambassadors," 10.

5. Mary Louise Pratt, *Imperial Eyes: Travel Writing and Transculturation in the Contact Zone* (New York: Routledge, 1992), 81, 84.

6. Foster Rhea Dulles, *Americans Abroad: Two Centuries of European Travel* (Ann Arbor: University of Michigan Press, 1964), 169; Eric Leed, *The Mind of the Traveler: From Gilgamesh to Global Tourism* (New York: Basic Books, 1991), 2. See also Louis Turner and John Ash, *The Golden Hordes: International Tourism and the Pleasure Periphery* (London: Constable, 1975).

7. Norman Cousins, *Present Tense: An American Editor's Odyssey* (New York: McGraw-Hill, 1967), 38; William D. Patterson, "E Pluribus Unum," *SR,* 2 January 1954, 16; Dulles, *Americans Abroad,* 170; "World Travel Issue," *SR,*

7 January 1961, 37; Horace Sutton, *Travelers: The American Tourist from Stage-coach to Space Shuttle* (New York: William Morrow, 1980), 258; William J. Lederer, "Western Pacific," *SR,* 17 October 1959, 29, and "Points East," *SR,* 9 December 1961, 31.

8. Preston Hotchkiss, "Increasing International Travel," *Department of State Bulletin* [hereafter cited as *DSB*], 2 May 1955, 743; Dulles, *Americans Abroad,* 169; "Anti-Americanism Abroad," *Newsweek,* 10 June 1957, 52–53; Stanley High, "They Bring the Bread of Life," *Reader's Digest* [hereafter cited as *RD*], June 1959, 218; Hale, "Millions of Ambassadors," 9.

9. Emily S. Rosenberg, *Spreading the American Dream: American Economic and Cultural Expansion, 1890–1945* (New York: Hill and Wang, 1982), 105–7, 198–99; Melvyn P. Leffler, *A Preponderance of Power* (Stanford, Calif.: Stanford University Press, 1992), 56–58.

10. Horace Sutton, "Larkism or Overseasmanship?" *SR,* 9 January 1960, 25; Hale, "Millions of Ambassadors," 9; Dwight D. Eisenhower, *The White House Years: Mandate for Change, 1953–1956* (Garden City, N.Y.: Doubleday, 1963), 141; Robert L. Branyan and Lawrence H. Larsen, *The Eisenhower Administration, 1953–1961: A Documentary History* (New York: Random House, 1971), 1198–99.

11. Patterson, "E Pluribus Unum," 16; Dulles, *Americans Abroad,* 173; Juan Trippe, "Now You Can Take That Trip Abroad," *RD,* January 1949, 70; Somerset R. Waters, "Importance of International Travel to the Foreign Trade of the United States," *DSB,* 17 October 1955, 621; Sutton, *Travelers,* 262; Dwight D. Eisenhower, "U.S. Dependence on Foreign Trade," *DSB,* 26 October 1953, 540–41.

12. Clarence B. Randall, Chair, "Report of the Commission on Foreign Economic Policy to the President and Congress," *DSB,* 8 February 1954, 194; Dwight D. Eisenhower, "Special Message to Congress on Foreign Economic Policy," *Public Papers of the President: Dwight D. Eisenhower, 1954* (Washington, D.C.: Government Printing Office, 1955), 360–61; "Development of International Travel, Its Present Increasing Volume and Future Prospects," *DSB,* 21 March 1955, 491–95; Preston Hotchkiss, "Increasing International Travel," *DSB,* 2 May 1955, 741–45; Waters, "Importance of International Travel," 621; Sinclair Weeks, "Importance of International Travel in Advancing World Peace," *DSB,* 18 July 1955, 106.

13. Hale, "Millions of Ambassadors," 11.

14. William D. Patterson, "In Defense of the Tourist," *SR,* 12 January 1957, 16, and "History and the Tourist," *SR,* 14 March 1959, 28.

15. State Dept. pamphlet quoted in Francis J. Colligan, "Americans Abroad," *DSB,* 3 May 1954, 664; "Letter of President to Be Included in U.S. Passports," *DSB,* 12 August 1957, 275.

16. Colligan, "Americans Abroad," 663–68.

17. George Kent, "How to Be an American Abroad," *RD,* June 1949, 118; Leland Stowe, "The Knack of Intelligent Travel," *RD,* September 1952, 103–6.

18. Harrison Smith, "A New World for Writers," *SR,* 2 June 1945, 16; Brenda Gayle Plummer, *Rising Wind: Black Americans and Foreign Policy,*

1935–1960 (Chapel Hill: University of North Carolina Press, 1996), 222; Richard M. Nixon, "Meeting the People of Asia," *DSB,* 4 January 1954, 14.

19. Stowe, "Knack of Intelligent Travel," 105; Norman Cousins, "Twenty Questions," *SR,* 15 December 1951, 22; Lyndon B. Johnson, "What Foreigners Want to Know about the United States," *RD,* December 1961, 47.

20. Norman Cousins, "Everyman as Reporter," *SR,* 20 October 1956, 28.

21. *Newsweek,* "James Michener: Again the Warm Voice of Asia," 24 January 1954, 92.

22. Gene Wise, " 'Paradigm Dramas' in American Studies: A Cultural and Institutional History of the Movement," *American Quarterly* 31, no. 3 (1979): 293–337; Day, *James A. Michener,* 18–22; Hayes, *James A. Michener,* 11–58.

23. James A. Michener, "When Does Education Stop?" *RD,* December 1963, 153–56; Hayes, *James A. Michener,* 61.

24. Hayes, *James A. Michener,* 100, 107; David A. Groseclose, *James A. Michener: A Bibliography* (Austin: State House Press, 1996), xvi; George Becker, *James A. Michener* (New York: Frederick Ungar, 1983), 44–47.

25. Hayes, *James A. Michener,* 89; James A. Michener, *The World Is My Home: A Memoir* (1992; reprint, New York: Ballantine, 1998), 464.

26. Lewis Nichol, "Talk with Mr. Michener," *New York Times Book Review,* 12 July 1953, 16; "James Michener: Again the Warm Voice of Asia," *Newsweek,* 92; Day, *James A. Michener,* 148, 150.

27. Harvey Breit, "Talk with Mr. Michener," *New York Times Book Review,* 22 May 1949, 26; James A. Michener, "The Conscience of the Novel," in *The Arts in Renewal,* ed. Sculley Bradley (Philadelphia: University of Pennsylvania Press, 1951), 118, 116–17, 123, 125, 140; Phyllis Meras, "A Desire to Inform," *SR,* 4 May 1968, 29.

28. Meras, "A Desire to Inform," 29; Day, *James A. Michener,* 146; "New Heads Named for Asia Institute," *New York Times,* 2 April 1953, 29; Hayes, *James A. Michener,* 9, 3.

29. Janice R. MacKinnon and Stephen R. MacKinnon, *Agnes Smedley: The Life and Times of an American Radical* (Berkeley: University of California Press, 1988); John Maxwell Hamilton, *Edgar Snow: A Biography* (Bloomington: Indiana University Press, 1988).

30. Peter Conn, *Pearl S. Buck: A Cultural Biography* (New York: Cambridge University Press, 1996).

31. Michener, *World Is My Home,* 243–47; David Caute, *The Great Fear: The Anti-Communist Purge under Truman and Eisenhower* (New York: Simon and Schuster, 1978), 284.

32. Michener, *World Is My Home,* 180–83, 198–201, 210–11; Hayes, *James A. Michener,* 110–11, 171; Daniel K. Inouye, "James A. Michener," *Congressional Record—House,* 17 September 1962, 19683; Stanley Ellin and John Baker, eds., *Conversations with Writers II* (Detroit, Mich.: Gale Research, 1978), 150–51; Conn, *Pearl S. Buck,* 373.

33. Hayes, *James A. Michener,* 108, 110–11, 158; Michener, *World Is My Home,* 129; Inouye, "James A. Michener," 19683.

34. NSC 48/5, *Foreign Relations of the United States, 1951,* vol. 6 (Wash-

ington, D.C.: Government Printing Office, 1979), 33; Michael Schaller, *The American Occupation of Japan: The Origins of the Cold War in Asia* (New York: Oxford University Press, 1985), 195–211.

35. NSC 48/5, *Foreign Relations of the United States,* 36, 35, 39, 41, 49, 55, 59, 61, 62; NSC 48/1, United States Department of Defense, *United States-Vietnam Relations, 1945–1967, Book 8* (Washington, D.C.: Government Printing Office, 1971), 244, 252.

36. James A. Michener, *The Voice of Asia* (New York: Random House, 1951), 8, 9, 64.

37. Ibid., 173, 11, 28, 334, 29, 118, 55.

38. Ibid., 230.

39. Ibid., 131–32, 11.

40. James A. Michener, "Blunt Truths about Asia," *Life,* 4 June 1951, 96; "Foreword," in *Selected Writings of James A. Michener* (New York: Modern Library, 1957), xi; and *Voice of Asia,* 11.

41. Michener, *Voice of Asia,* 9, 135, 196.

42. Ibid., 290–92.

43. Ibid., 292.

44. Michener, "Foreword," x.

45. Acheson quoted in Caute, *Great Fear,* 245.

46. Caute, *Great Fear,* 251–63.

47. Quoted in Martin Bauml Duberman, *Paul Robeson* (New York: Alfred A. Knopf, 1988), 433.

48. J. Saunders Redding, *An American in India* (Indianapolis: Bobbs-Merrill, 1954), 42, 11, 27.

49. Ibid., 172, 37, 40, 60, 148, 146.

50. Ibid., 10, 18–19, 114.

51. Carey McWilliams, "Anti-Americanism Updated," *Nation,* 31 May 1958, 489; "The U.S. Tourist: Good or Ill-Will Envoys?" *New York Times,* 1 September 1957, 8.

52. "The Reds' War of Riots," *U.S. News and World Report,* 20 June 1960, 61.

CHAPTER FOUR: FAMILY TIES AS POLITICAL OBLIGATION

The epigraph is from Philip J. Philbin, "Oscar Hammerstein II," *Congressional Record,* 2 September 1960, A6650.

1. Hugh Fordin, *Getting to Know Him: A Biography of Oscar Hammerstein II* (New York: Random House, 1977), 284–85; Peter Conn, *Pearl S. Buck: A Cultural Biography* (Cambridge: Cambridge University Press, 1996), 312–14; Pearl S. Buck International, "The Pearl S. Buck Foundation, Welcome House Adoption Program, Historical Fact Sheet," 1996.

2. Rochelle Girson, "Welcome House," *Saturday Review* [hereafter cited as *SR*], July 1952, 21.

3. Loy Henderson, "The United States and Asia," *Vital Speeches,* March

1950, 460; James A. Michener, "Foreword," *Selected Writings* (New York: Random House, 1957), ix–x; Harold Isaacs, *Images of Asia: American Views of China and India* (1958; reprint, New York: Capricorn, 1962), 37.

4. Gina Marchetti, *Romance and the "Yellow Peril": Race, Sex, and Discursive Strategies in Hollywood Fiction* (Berkeley: University of California Press, 1993); see also Robert Lee, *Orientals: Asian Americans in Popular Culture* (Philadelphia: Temple University Press, 1999), 161–79; and Caroline Chung Simpson, "'Out of an Obscure Place': Japanese War Brides and Cultural Pluralism in the 1950s," *Differences* 10 (1998): 47–81.

5. Stephanie Coontz, *The Way We Never Were: American Families and the Nostalgia Trap* (New York: Basic Books, 1992).

6. Norman Cousins, *Present Tense: An American Editor's Odyssey* (New York: McGraw-Hill, 1967), 324–52; Rodney Barker, *The Hiroshima Maidens: A Story of Courage, Compassion, and Survival* (New York: Viking, 1985); Caroline Chung Simpson, *An Absent Presence: Japanese Americans in Postwar American Culture, 1945–1960* (Durham, N.C.: Duke University Press, 2001), 113–48.

7. John W. Dower, *War without Mercy: Race and Power in the Pacific War* (New York: Pantheon Books, 1986); Andrew J. Rotter, *The Path to Vietnam: Origins of American Commitment to Southeast Asia* (Ithaca, N.Y.: Cornell University Press, 1987).

8. Norman Cousins, "Tomoko Nakabayashi of the Maidens," *Saturday Review,* 9 June 1956; John W. Dower, *Embracing Defeat: Japan in the Wake of World War II* (New York: W. W. Norton, 1999), 552–53.

9. Philip Fisher, *Hard Facts: Setting and Form in the American Novel* (New York: Oxford University Press, 1987), 101–3.

10. Bradford Smith, "We're Selling America Short," *RD,* December 1952, 6.

11. Barker, *Hiroshima Maidens,* 95–98.

12. Norman Cousins, "Hiroshima—Four Years Later," *SR,* 17 September 1949, 8–10, 30–31; Mrs. John N. Snoddy, letter to the editor, *SR,* 8 October 1949, 26.

13. Larry E. Tise, *A Book about Children: The World of Christian Children's Fund, 1938–1991* (Falls Church, Va.: Hartland, 1993), 64.

14. Tise, *Book about Children,* 50; Edmund W. Janss, *Yankee Si! The Story of Dr. J. Calvitt Clarke and His 36,000 Children* (New York: William Morrow, 1961), 182, 126; John C. Caldwell, *Children of Calamity* (New York: John Day, 1957), 1.

15. Caldwell, *Children of Calamity,* 29.

16. Ibid., 187; Christian Children's Fund, "Person-to-Person Giving," n.d.

17. Deems Taylor, *Some Enchanted Evenings: The Story of Rodgers and Hammerstein* (New York: Harper, 1953), 217.

18. Arthur Gelb, "Happy Talk," *New York Times,* 28 August 1960, 2-1; "Oscar Hammerstein 2nd," *New York Times,* 24 August 1960, 28; David Ewen, *Richard Rodgers* (New York: Henry Holt, 1957), 223–25; "R&H Shows are Pushing $8 Million," *Business Week,* 11 August 1951, 99; Walter L. Hixson, *Parting the Curtain: Propaganda, Culture, and the Cold War, 1945–1961* (New York: St. Martin's Press, 1997), 155; Stephen Citron, *The Wordsmiths: Oscar*

Hammerstein 2nd and Alan Jay Lerner (New York: Oxford University Press, 1995), 232; Marshall quoted in Eric Johnston, "Messengers from a Free Country," *SR*, 4 March 1950, 10.

19. Philip D. Beidler, "*South Pacific* and American Remembering; or, 'Josh, We're Going to Buy This Son of a Bitch!'" *Journal of American Studies* 27 (1993): 207, 217, 216, 218; Frederick W. Nolan, *The Sound of Their Music: The Story of Rodgers and Hammerstein* (New York: Walker, 1978), 160–63; Stanley Green, ed., *The Rodgers and Hammerstein Fact Book* (New York: Lynn Farnol Group, 1980), 560–78.

20. Richard Rodgers and Oscar Hammerstein II, *Six Plays by Rodgers and Hammerstein* (New York: Random House, 1955), 276; James A. Michener, *Tales of the South Pacific* (New York: Macmillan, 1947), 112.

21. Rodgers and Hammerstein, *Six Plays*, 346–47.

22. Michener quoted in John P. Hayes, *James A. Michener: A Biography* (Indianapolis: Bobbs-Merrill, 1984), 66.

23. John W. Dower, "Occupied Japan and the American Lake, 1945–1950," in *America's Asia*, ed. Mark Selden and Edward Friedman (New York: Vintage, 1971), 146–206; James A. Michener, "When Does Education Stop?" *RD*, December 1963, 156.

24. Arthur M. Schlesinger Jr., *The Vital Center* (1949; reprint, New York: Da Silva, 1988), 190.

25. Rodgers and Hammerstein, *Six Plays*, 276, 365.

26. Caption for photograph of Joshua Logan and children in unidentified newspaper, 13 March 1949; Richard H. Brodhead, *Cultures of Letters: Scenes of Reading and Writing in Nineteenth-Century America* (Chicago: University of Chicago Press, 1993), 13–47.

27. George C. Herring, *America's Longest War: The United States and Vietnam, 1950–1975* (New York: Alfred A. Knopf, 1986), 16, 39; Norman Cousins, "The Lukewarm Peace," *SR*, 25 June 1955, 22.

28. James A. Michener, letter to the editor, *New York Times*, 1 September 1991, 2-2, and *The World Is My Home: A Memoir* (1992; reprint, New York: Ballantine, 1998), 149.

29. Michael Rogin, *Ronald Reagan, the Movie* (Berkeley: University of California Press, 1987), 236–71; Philip Wylie, *The Innocent Ambassadors* (1957; reprint, New York: Cardinal, 1958), 13.

30. Cleveland Amory, "The Antic Arts," *Holiday*, February 1959, 91; Gelb, "Happy Talk," 2-1; Ewen, *Richard Rodgers*, 252–53; J. Anthony Lukas, *Common Ground: A Turbulent Decade in the Lives of Three American Families* (New York: Vintage, 1986), 286.

31. Eisenhower quoted in Mary L. Dudziak, "The Little Rock Crisis and Foreign Affairs: Race, Resistance, and the Image of American Democracy," *Southern California Law Review* 7 (1997): 1663; Robert H. Haddow, *Pavilions of Plenty: Exhibiting American Culture Abroad in the 1950s* (Washington, D.C.: Smithsonian, 1997), 169–200; Michael L. Krenn, "'Unfinished Business': Segregation and U.S. Diplomacy at the 1958 World's Fair," *Diplomatic History* 20 (1996): 591–612.

32. "Juanita Hall, as Bloody Mary, she helps make 'South Pacific' biggest hit

in Broadway's history," *Ebony,* July 1950, 29–32; "South Pacific: Lavish Film Scores Racial Hate among U.S. Troops," *Ebony,* June 1958, 76–79.

33. Audience member quoted in Michener, *The World Is My Home,* 294–95; Georgia state legislators quoted in Fordin, *Getting to Know Him,* 270; South African government statement quoted in A. Grove Day, *James A. Michener* (New York: Twayne, 1964), 53.

34. Fordin, *Getting to Know Him,* 115, 284; Pearl S. Buck International, "The Pearl S. Buck Foundation, Welcome House Adoption Program, Historical Fact Sheet," 1996; Conn, *Pearl S. Buck,* 338; Ewen, *Richard Rodgers,* 308; Hayes, *James A. Michener,* 241; Norman Cousins, "Earle Reynolds and His *Phoenix,*" *SR,* 11 October 1958, 26; Charles Michener, "Long Live the King," *Newsweek,* 16 May 1977, 103.

35. Robert C. Matthews, "The Littlest Immigrants: The Immigration and Adoption of Foreign Orphans," Ph.D. diss., Virginia Polytechnic Institute and State University, 1986; Howard Altstein and Rita J. Simon, eds., *Intercountry Adoption: A Multinational Perspective* (New York: Praeger, 1991); Richard H. Weil, "International Migrations: The Quiet Migration," *International Migration Review* 18 (1984): 276–93; Ron Moxness, "Harry Holt and a Heartful of Children," *RD,* October 1956, 67–70; Shaila K. Dewan, "Bertha Holt, 96, a Leader in International Adoptions," *New York Times,* 2 August 2000, C21; Pearl S. Buck International, "The Pearl S. Buck Foundation, Welcome House Adoption Program, Historical Fact Sheet," 1996.

36. Michael Hunt, *Ideology and U.S. Foreign Policy* (New Haven: Yale University Press, 1987); Stuart Creighton Miller, *The Unwelcome Immigrant: The American Image of the Chinese, 1785–1882* (Berkeley: University of California Press, 1969); Dower, *War without Mercy,* 147–80; Julie Berebitsky, "Rescue a Child and Save the Nation: The Social Construction of Adoption in the *Delineator,* 1907–1911," paper presented at American Studies Association annual meeting, 1995, Pittsburgh, Penn.

37. Isaacs, *Images of Asia,* 127; Jane Hunter, *The Gospel of Gentility: American Women Missionaries in Turn-of-the-Century China* (New Haven, Conn.: Yale University Press, 1984), 191–93; Patricia R. Hill, *The World Their Household: The American Woman's Foreign Mission Movement and Cultural Transformation, 1870–1920* (Ann Arbor: University of Michigan Press, 1985), 95–100.

38. T. Christopher Jespersen, *American Images of China, 1931–1949* (Stanford, Calif.: Stanford University Press, 1996); Isaacs, *Images of Asia,* 195; on Asian orphans and adoption in American TV during the 1960s and after, see Darrell Y. Hamamoto, *Monitored Peril: Asian Americans and the Politics of TV Representation* (Minneapolis: University of Minnesota Press, 1994), 100–154.

39. Helen Doss, *The Family Nobody Wanted* (1954; reprint, Boston: Northeastern University Press, 2001).

40. Pearl S. Buck, "The 1957 Anisfield-Wolf Awards," *SR,* 28 June 1958, 22.

41. Mary Dudziak, "Josephine Baker, Racial Protest, and the Cold War," *Journal of American History* 81 (1994): 543–70.

42. Taylor, *Some Enchanted Evenings,* 232; Stanley Green, *The Rodgers and Hammerstein Story* (London: W. H. Allen, 1963), 153.

43. Gelb, "Happy Talk," 2-1; Gerald Weales, "Oh What an Endlessly Beautiful Morning!" *South Atlantic Quarterly* 61 (1957): 204; Ethan Mordden, *Rodgers and Hammerstein* (New York: Harry N. Abrams, 1992), 85; Hammerstein quoted in Amory, "Antic Arts," 91.

44. Green, *Rodgers and Hammerstein Story*, 51–52.

45. Citron, *Wordsmiths*, 70; Martin Bauml Duberman, *Paul Robeson* (New York: Alfred A. Knopf, 1988), 196–97, 228; Michael Denning, *The Cultural Front: The Laboring of American Culture* (New York: Verso, 1996), 396; Fordin, *Getting to Know Him*, 160.

46. Larry Ceplund and Steven Englund, *The Inquisition in Hollywood: Politics in the Film Community, 1930–1960* (New York: Anchor, 1980), 104; Fordin, *Getting to Know Him*, 143; California Legislature, *Fourth Report of the Senate Fact-Finding Committee on Un-American Activities [Tenney Committee], 1948*, 262–63, 255–56, 239–40; Schlesinger, *Vital Center,* 121; California Legislature, *Fifth Report of the Senate Fact-Finding Committee on Un-American Activities [Tenney Committee], 1949*, 542–44. Thanks to Michael Denning for telling me about the Tenney Committee references.

47. Fordin, *Getting to Know Him*, 211; David Caute, *The Great Fear: The Anti-Communist Purge under Truman and Eisenhower* (New York: Simon and Schuster, 1978), 168.

48. Fordin, *Getting to Know Him*, 235, 183; Citron, *Wordsmiths*, 71.

49. Denning, *Cultural Front*, 309–10; Citron, *Wordsmiths*, 10; Taylor, *Some Enchanted Evenings*, 144.

50. Denning, *Cultural Front*, 371.

51. Richard Maney, "Billy Rose and Carmen Jones," *New York Times*, n.d.; Harvard University Theatre Collection, *Carmen Jones* playbill, 1943. The preceding are from the Schomburg Center for Research in Black Culture, Schomburg clipping file. Thanks to Richard Newman of Harvard's W. E. B. Du Bois Center for telling me about this collection.

52. Harry Taylor, "Meet Carmen Jones," *New Masses*, 21 December 1943; Ralph Warner, "New Plays," *Daily Worker*, 6 December 1943; Ralph Warner, "On Broadway," *Worker*, 12 December 1943; advertisement, *New York Times*, 24 March 1946; Louis Kronenberger, " 'Carmen Jones' Is a Fine Exciting Show," *PM*, 3 December 1943. The preceding are from the Schomburg Center for Research in Black Culture, Schomburg clipping file.

53. Miles M. Jefferson, "The Negro on Broadway—1944," *Phylon* 6 (1945): 47–48; James Baldwin, "Carmen Jones: The Dark Is Light Enough," in *Collected Essays* (New York: Library of America, 1998), 35; James Agee, "Pseudo-Folk," *Partisan Review* 11 (1944): 219–23.

54. Fordin, *Getting to Know Him*, 290, 313; Amory, "Antic Arts," 99.

55. "Rodgers, Hammerstein Reply to Lee Newton on 'Show Boat,' " *Daily Worker*, 25 October 1948, 13. The preceding is from the Schomburg Center for Research in Black Culture, Schomburg clipping file.

56. Hammerstein quoted in Fordin, *Getting to Know Him*, 312.

57. Steichen quoted in Eric J. Sandeen, *Picturing an Exhibition: The Family of Man and 1950s America* (Albuquerque: University of New Mexico Press, 1995), 3.

58. Sandeen, *Picturing an Exhibition,* 95; "Family of Man" files at the Museum of Modern Art, New York.

59. Sandeen, *Picturing an Exhibition,* 58, 64–68.

60. Herring, *America's Longest War,* 60–62; John F. Kennedy, "America's Stake in Vietnam," *Vital Speeches,* 1 August 1956, 618.

61. On the masculinization of the Cold War, see Geoffrey S. Smith, "National Security and Personal Isolation: Sex, Gender, and Disease in the Cold-War United States," *International History Review* 14 (1992): 307–35; Frank Costigliola, "'Unceasing Pressure for Penetration': Gender, Pathology, and Emotion in George Kennan's Formation of the Cold War," *Journal of American History* 83 (1997): 1309–39; Robert Dean, "Masculinity as Ideology: John F. Kennedy and the Domestic Politics of Foreign Policy," *Diplomatic History* 22 (1998): 29–62. On domestic ideology as a restrictive force, see Betty Friedan, *The Feminine Mystique* (New York: W. W. Norton, 1963); Elaine Tyler May, *Homeward Bound: American Families in the Cold War Era* (New York: Basic Books, 1988); Brett Harvey, *The Fifties: A Woman's Oral History* (New York: HarperCollins, 1993). Many of the essays in Joanne Meyerowitz's edited collection, *Not June Cleaver: Women and Gender in Postwar America, 1945–1960* (Philadelphia: Temple University Press, 1994) challenge the idea of domestic ideology as an essentially conservative force, but none of them explore it as discourse that supported U.S. global expansion.

CHAPTER FIVE: MUSICALS AND MODERNIZATION

The epigraph is from John Lahr, "The Lemon-Drop Kid," *New Yorker,* 30 September 1996, 68–74.

1. Michael E. Latham, *Modernization as Ideology: American Social Science and "Nation Building" in the Kennedy Era* (Chapel Hill: University of North Carolina Press, 2000).

2. Richard Slotkin, *Regeneration through Violence: The Mythology of the Frontier* (Middletown, Conn.: Wesleyan University Press, 1973); *The Fatal Environment: The Myth of the Frontier in the Age of Industrialization, 1800–1890* (New York: Atheneum, 1985); *Gunfighter Nation: The Myth of the Frontier in Twentieth-Century America* (New York: Atheneum, 1992), 441–86.

3. Thomas Schatz, *Hollywood Genres: Formulas, Filmmaking, and the Studio System* (New York: McGraw-Hill, 1981), 34–35; Rick Altman, *The American Film Musical* (1987; Bloomington: Indiana University Press, 1989).

4. Lahr, "Lemon-Drop Kid," 74; Donal Henahan, "As Corny as Kansas in August," *New York Times,* 15 March 1987, 2:25.

5. Stanley Green, ed., *Rodgers and Hammerstein Fact Book* (New York: Lynn Farnol Group, 1980), 579–97; David Foil, liner notes, Broadway Classics recording of *The King and I.*

6. Susan Morgan, "Introduction," in *The Romance of the Harem,* by Anna Leonowens (Charlottesville: University of Virginia Press, 1991). For discussions of factual inaccuracies in Leonowens's books, see A. B. Griswold, *King Mongkut of Siam* (New York: Asia Society, 1961); W. S. Bristowe, *Louis and the King of*

Siam (New York: Thai-American Publishers, 1976); William Warren, "Anna and the King: A Case of Libel," *Asia*, March/April 1980, 42–45.

7. Hugh Fordin, *Getting to Know Him: A Biography of Oscar Hammerstein II* (New York: Random House, 1977), 283–84; Oscar Hammerstein II, "Getting off the Pyramid," *Saturday Review* [hereafter cited as *SR*], 23 December 1950, 22–23, "Should the U.S. Support a Federal Union of All Nations?" *Congressional Digest*, 31 (August–September 1952): 212, 214, and "Inertia . . . ," address in Boston, 29 April 1959, New York Public Library Theater Collection; Cousins quoted in Green, ed., *Rodgers and Hammerstein Fact Book*, 737.

8. Richard Rodgers and Oscar Hammerstein II, *Six Plays by Rodgers and Hammerstein* (New York: Random House, 1955), 388.

9. Dulles quoted in Frank C. Darling, *Thailand and the United States* (Washington, D.C.: Public Affairs Press, 1965), 133.

10. Darling, *Thailand and the United States*, 79–80.

11. Latham, *Modernization as Ideology;* Frederick Cooper and Randall Packard, eds., *International Development and the Social Sciences* (Berkeley: University of California Press, 1997); W. W. Rostow, *The Stages of Economic Growth: A Non-Communist Manifesto* (Cambridge: Cambridge University Press, 1960).

12. Michael H. Hunt, *Ideology and U.S. Foreign Policy* (New Haven, Conn.: Yale University Press, 1987), 160; Emily S. Rosenberg, *Spreading the American Dream: American Economic and Cultural Expansion, 1890–1945* (New York: Hill and Wang, 1982), 7–13.

13. Walter L. Hixson, *Parting the Curtain: Propaganda, Culture, and the Cold War, 1945–1961* (New York: St. Martin's Press, 1997); Frank A. Ninkovich, *The Diplomacy of Ideas: U.S. Foreign Policy and Cultural Relations, 1938–1950* (Cambridge: Cambridge University Press, 1981); Frances Stonor Saunders, *The Cultural Cold War: The CIA and the World of Arts and Letters* (New York: New Press, 1999); Walter Johnson and Francis J. Colligan, *The Fulbright Program* (Chicago: University of Chicago Press, 1965).

14. Streibert quoted in John W. Henderson, *The United States Information Agency* (New York: Praeger, 1969), 65; Reinhold Wagnleitner, *Coca-Colonization and the Cold War: The Cultural Mission of the United States in Austria after the Cold War* (Chapel Hill: University of North Carolina Press, 1994).

15. Vicente L. Rafael, "Colonial Domesticity: White Women and United States Rule in the Philippines," *American Literature* 67 (1995): 639–66.

16. Margaret Landon, *Anna and the King of Siam* (New York: John Day, 1944), 86–87.

17. Rodgers and Hammerstein, *Six Plays*, 374.

18. Ernest R. May, ed., *American Cold War Strategy: Interpreting NSC 68* (Boston: Bedford Books, 1993), 27; Kennedy quoted in Gary Wills, "Introduction," in *Scoundrel Time*, by Lillian Hellman (1976; reprint, New York: Bantam 1977), 18.

19. Harry Truman, "Communist Attack on North Korea a Violation of UN Charter," *Vital Speeches*, 1 August 1950, 612; Hixson, *Parting the Curtain*, 14; George Kennan, "Long Telegram," in *Containment: Documents on American*

Policy and Strategy, 1945–1950, ed. Thomas H. Etzold and John Lewis Gaddis (New York: Columbia University Press, 1978), 55.

20. Rodgers and Hammerstein, *Six Plays,* 439.

21. Ibid., 440.

22. Ibid., 449.

23. Ibid., 448; United States Department of Defense, *United States–Vietnam Relations, 1945–1967,* book 8 (Washington, D.C.: Government Printing Office, 1971), 249.

24. Rodgers and Hammerstein, *Six Plays,* 446–47.

25. Wendell L. Wilkie, *One World* (New York: Simon and Schuster, 1943), 33–34.

26. MacKinnon and MacKinnon, *Agnes Smedley,* 187.

27. Ibid., 188, 191.

28. "New Empire of the American Musical," *Newsweek,* 7 May 1956, 63; Joseph Wechsberg, "The American Musical Conquers Europe," *SR,* 29 December 1956, 37; Wagnleitner, *Coca-Colonization,* 200.

29. Rudolph Elie, "King and I—But Who Is the King in This?" (no source); Elliot Norton, "King and I Triumphant New Musical Play," *Boston Sunday Post,* 11 March 1951; "After Hours," *Harper's,* September 1951; Brooks Atkinson, *New York Times,* 8 April 1951, II:1:1; *Punch,* 14 October 1953; Ed Baker, "Rodgers, Hammerstein Score again with King and I," *Seattle Times,* 17 August 1954; Robert Coleman, "King and I Has Heart, Comedy, Lyrics," *New York Daily Mirror,* 30 March 1951; Brooks Atkinson, "Theatre: London Trio," *New York Times,* 17 May 1955, 33–34; Thomas R. Dash, review, *Women's Wear Daily,* 19 April 1956. All of the preceding are from New York Public Library Theater Collection clipping files. The last quotation is from Richard Rodgers, *Musical Stages,* 270–71.

30. "Do the Reds Stop Here?" *Newsweek,* 26 July 1954, 30.

31. Lee Hills, "Elizabeth and the Crown Prince of Japan," *Reader's Digest* [hereafter cited as *RD*], January 1948, 129–31; Erika Leuchtag, "Erika and the King of Nepal," *RD,* February 1957, 94–97.

32. "Getting to Know You," *RD,* March 1958, inside front cover; Project Hope pamphlet, no date, Dwight D. Eisenhower Library, Abilene, Kansas; Christopher Isherwood, *Diaries, Volume I: 1939–1960* (London: Methuen, 1996), 624; Kennan quoted in Priscilla Clapp and Morton Halperin, "U.S. Elite Images of Japan: The Postwar Period," in *Mutual Images: Essays in American-Japanese Relations,* ed. Akira Iriye (Cambridge, Mass.: Harvard University Press, 1975), 213.

33. William Warren, *Jim Thompson: The Legendary American of Thailand* (1970; reprint, Bangkok: Asia Books, 1979), 70–71.

34. Warren, *Jim Thompson,* 101–3, 178; James T. Fisher, *Dr. America: The Lives of Thomas A. Dooley, 1927–1961* (Amherst: University of Massachusetts Press, 1997), 131.

35. Francis and Katherine Drake, "Jim Thompson and the Busy Weavers of Bangkok," *RD,* October 1959, 231–36; Horace Sutton, "Jet Trails around the World—8: Babes in Thailand," *SR,* 11 April 1959, 29.

36. Landon, *Anna and the King of Siam,* 388; Warren, "Anna and the King,"

42; Bristowe, *Louis and the King of Siam,* 31; "No Music for the King," *New York Herald Tribune,* 24 August 1962, n.p.; James Marnell, "Newsmakers," *Los Angeles Times,* 17 March 1985, n.p. All of the preceding are from the New York Public Library Theater Collection clipping file.

CHAPTER SIX: ASIANS IN AMERICA

The epigraph is from "Enchanting 'State,'" *Newsweek,* 23 February 1959, 29.

1. Michener quoted in A. Grove Day, *James A. Michener* (New York: Twayne, 1964), 25.

2. Michael Omi and Howard Winant, *Racial Formation in the United States: From the 1960s to the 1990s,* 2nd ed. (New York: Routledge, 1994); Ronald Takaki, *Strangers from a Different Shore: A History of Asian Americans* (New York: Penguin, 1989); Sucheng Chan, *Asian Americans: An Interpretive History* (New York: Twayne, 1991).

3. William Petersen, Michael Novak, Philip Gleason, *Concepts of Ethnicity* (Cambridge, Mass.: Harvard University Press, 1982); Myrdal and McWilliams quoted in Nikhil Pal Singh, "Culture/Wars: Recoding Empire in an Age of Democracy," *American Quarterly* 50 (1998): 486, 475.

4. Gunnar Myrdal, *An American Dilemma: The Negro Problem and Modern Democracy* (New York: Harper, 1944); Roger Daniels, *Asian America: Chinese and Japanese in the United States since 1850* (Seattle: University of Washington Press, 1988).

5. Daniels, *Asian America,* 306–7; Neil Gotanda, "Towards a Repeal of Asian Exclusion," and William R. Tamayo, "Asian Americans and the McCarran-Walter Act," in *Asian Americans and Congress: A Documentary History,* ed. Hyung-chan Kim (Westport, Conn.: Greenwood, 1996), 318.

6. Lisa See, "C. Y. Lee," *Publisher's Weekly,* 14 August 1987, 84–85; Jim Henry, "C. Y. Lee," *Notable Asian Americans,* ed. Helen Zia and Susan B. Gall (New York: Gale Research, 1995), 190–91.

7. Elaine H. Kim, *Asian American Literature: An Introduction to the Writings and Their Social Context* (Philadelphia: Temple University Press 1982), 45, 156.

8. Ibid., 59.

9. Ivan Light, "From Vice District to Tourist Attraction: The Moral Career of American Chinatowns, 1880–1940," *Pacific Historical Review* 43 (1974): 367–94.

10. Edward Skillin Jr., review of *Father and Glorious Descendant,* by Pardee Lowe, *Commonweal,* 23 April 1943, 18.

11. Deems Taylor, *Some Enchanted Evenings: The Story of Rodgers and Hammerstein* (New York: Harper, 1953), 8; Andrea Most, "'We Know We Belong to the Land': The Theatricality of Assimilation in Rodgers and Hammerstein's *Oklahoma!*" *PMLA* 113 (1998): 77–87.

12. Robert Berry White, "Back in Lights," *Newsweek,* 1 December 1958, 53.

13. Bosley Crowther, *New York Times,* 10 November 1961, 40; Brendan Gill, "The Current Cinema: Paper Problems," *New Yorker,* 16 November 1961,

207; Unidentified review; Patrick Dennis, "Broadway in Bloom," *New Republic,* 22 December 1958, 23; Kenneth Tynan, "Tiny Chinese Minds," *New Yorker,* 13 December 1958, 104; Guy, review of *Flower Drum Song, Variety,* n.d.; "No Tickee, No Worry," *Time,* 24 November 1961. All of the preceding are from the clipping files of the New York Public Library Theater Collection.

14. Yuan-kwan Chan, "An Old Song Resung," *A. Magazine,* August–September 1996, 76–77; "*Flower Drum Song* Blooms Again," *Happy Talk: News of the Rodgers and Hammerstein Organization* 9, no. 2, (winter 2002): 1; Karen Wada, "A Different Song," *Los Angeles,* September 2001, 69.

15. "The Girls on Grant Avenue," *Time,* 22 December 1958, 42; Asian American Arts Foundation, Golden Ring Awards brochure, "Special Tribute to the Original Cast and Author of *Flower Drum Song,*" 1997; Yuan-kwan Chan, "Old Song Resung," 76–77; Holland Carter, "Dong Kingman, 89, Whimsical Watercolorist," *New York Times,* 16 May 2000, 23; Dong Kingman, *Paint the Yellow Tiger* (New York: Sterling, 1991), and *Portraits of Cities* (New York: Twenty-second Century Film, 1997).

16. "Broadway 'Oriental,'" *Ebony,* March 1959, 128.

17. Richard Rodgers and Oscar Hammerstein II, *Flower Drum Song: A Musical Play* (New York: Farrar, Straus and Cudahy, 1959), 34.

18. Ibid., 26.

19. Frank Chin et al., eds., "Introduction: Fifty Years of Our Whole Voice," in *Aiiieeeee! An Anthology of Asian American Writers* (1974; reprint, New York: Meridian, 1991). On Asian Americans as permanent foreigners, see Lisa Lowe, *Immigrant Acts: On Asian American Cultural Politics* (Durham, N.C.: Duke University Press, 1996); and Robert G. Lee, *Orientals: Asian Americans in Popular Culture* (Philadelphia: Temple University Press, 1999).

20. Todd S. Purdum, "Code Talkers' Story Pops Up Everywhere," *New York Times,* 11 October 1999, A14; Max Corvo, *The O.S.S. in Italy, 1942–1945: A Personal Memoir* (New York: Praeger, 1990); Wendy L. Wall, "America's 'Best Propagandists': Italian Americans and the 1948 'Letters to Italy' Campaign," in *Cold War Constructions: The Political Culture of United States Imperialism, 1945–1963,* ed. Christian G. Appy (Amherst: University of Massachusetts Press, 2000).

21. "C. Y. Lee," *Contemporary Authors,* vols. 9–12 (Detroit: Gale Research, 1974), 498; *Flower Drum Song* theater program, 1959; Carter, "Dong Kingman"; Kingman, *Paint the Yellow Tiger,* 114; Kingman, *Portraits of Cities,* 74, 79–83; "Official Dispatch: Artist Records His Mission on Forty-Foot Painted Scroll," *Life,* 14 February 1955, 66–70.

22. Jade Snow Wong, *No Chinese Stranger* (New York: Harper and Row, 1975), 54–55, 82.

23. Penny M. Von Eschen, "Who's the Real Ambassador? Exploding the Cold War Racial Ideology," in *Cold War Constructions: The Political Culture of United States Imperialism, 1945–1966,* ed. Christian G. Appy (Amherst: University of Massachusetts Press, 2000).

24. Gavan Daws, *Shoal of Time: A History of the Hawaiian Islands* (New York: Macmillan, 1968).

25. Noel J. Kent, *Hawaii: Islands under the Influence* (New York: Monthly

Review Press, 1983), 99, 146; Lawrence H. Fuchs, *Hawaii Pono: An Ethnic and Political History* (1961; Honolulu: Bess Press, 1983), 379; Horace Sutton, "Where the Twain *Will* Meet," *SR,* 12 November 1960, 44; Norman Cousins, "Life Begins at Twenty-Five," *SR,* 24 April 1965, 28.

26. Fuchs, *Hawaii Pono,* 380.

27. Michener, "'Aloha' for the Fiftieth State," *New York Times Magazine,* 19 April 1959, 14.

28. Joseph R. Farrington, *Vital Speeches,* 15 February 1949, 274.

29. Thurmond quoted in Daws, *Shoal of Time,* 388.

30. Pillion quoted in Daws, *Shoal of Time,* 387–88, 369.

31. Jonathan Y. Okamura, "The Illusion of Paradise: Privileging Multiculturalism in Hawai'i," in *Making Majorities: Constituting the Nation in Japan, Korea, China, Malaysia, Fiji, Turkey, and the United States,*" ed. Dru C. Gladney (Stanford, Calif.: Stanford University Press, 1998); Paul F. Hooper, *Elusive Destiny: The Internationalist Movement in Modern Hawaii* (Honolulu: University of Hawaii Press, 1980), 26; "Hawaii: A Melting Pot," *Life,* 26 November 1945, 103–4.

32. James A. Michener, "The Case for Our Fiftieth State," *RD,* December 1958, 168.

33. James A. Michener, "'Aloha' for the Fiftieth State," *New York Times Magazine,* 19 April 1959, 94.

34. James A. Michener, "Hawaii's Statehood Urged," letter to the editor, *New York Times,* 1 January 1959, 30; "Hawaii—A Bridge to Asia," *Businessweek,* 13 May 1950, 128; Elsa and Don Mayer, "49 Stars and Hawaii," *Paradise of the Pacific,* December 1959, 103.

35. "Hawaii—A Bridge to Asia," 128. "Enchanting 'State,'" *Newsweek,* 23 February 1959, 29; "Hawaii: The New Breed," *Time,* 23 March 1959, 16.

36. Daws, *Shoal of Time,* 384.

37. James A. Michener, *Hawaii* (1959; reprint, New York: Fawcett Crest, 1973); Stanley Ellin and John Baker, eds., *Conversations with Writers II* (Detroit: Gale Research, 1978), 162; Stephen H. Sumida, *And the View from the Shore: Literary Traditions of Hawai'i* (Seattle: University of Washington Press, 1991), 68; Daniel K. Inouye, *Congressional Record—House,* 17 September 1962, 19682.

38. *Library Journal,* 15 December 1959, 3870; Maxwell Geismer, "Gods, Missionaries, and the Golden Men," *New York Times Book Review,* 22 November 1959, 4–5.

39. Michener, *Hawaii,* 629, 986; Fanny Butcher, "Major Chronicle of Hawaii and Its People," *Chicago Sunday Tribune,* 22 November 1959, 1.

40. Michener, *Hawaii,* 910, 921, 848.

41. Ibid., 973.

42. Ibid., 977, 980, 986; Peter Conn, *Pearl S. Buck: A Cultural Biography* (Cambridge: Cambridge University Press, 1996), 313.

43. Michener, *Hawaii,* 633, 1090.

44. Takaki, *Strangers from a Different Shore,* 382.

45. Caroline Chung Simpson, *An Absent Presence: Japanese Americans in Postwar American Culture, 1945–1960* (Durham, N.C.: Duke University

Press, 2001); "Broadway: The Girls on Grant Avenue," *Time,* 22 December 1958, 44.

46. On the need to integrate the study of the foreign and domestic spheres of American history, see Amy Kaplan, "'Left Alone with America': The Absence of Empire in the Study of American Culture," in *Cultures of United States Imperialism,* ed. Amy Kaplan and Donald Pease (Durham, N.C.: Duke University Press, 1993) 3–21. A number of scholars whose work I have cited earlier, including Mary Dudziak, Penny Von Eschen, Melani McAlister, Thomas Borstelmann, and Nikhil Singh, are doing precisely this work.

CONCLUSION

1. Bruce Cumings, "The American Ascendency: Imposing a New World Order," *The Nation,* 8 May 2000, 20.

2. Diane Haithman, "Cover Story: A Different Drummer," *Los Angeles Times,* 14 October 2001, calendar, part 6, p. 4.

3. Murdock quoted in Aihwa Ong, "Flexible Citizenship among Chinese Cosmopolitans," in *Cosmopolitics,* ed. Pheng Cheah and Bruce Robbins (Minneapolis: University of Minnesota Press, 1998), 154.

4. G. Pascal Zachary, *The Global Me: New Cosmopolitans and the Competitive Edge: Picking Globalism's Winners and Losers* (New York: Public Affairs Press, 2000), ix, 198.

5. State Department statistics on immigrant visas granted to orphans: <http://travel.state.gov/orphan_numbers.html>.

6. Lisa Odham Stokes and Michael Hoover, *City on Fire: Hong Kong Cinema* (New York: Verso, 1999), 40.

7. Woo quoted in Bernard Weinraub, "Ballet with Bullets," *New York Times,* 22 February 1996, C4; Francis Dass, "Woo's Mission of Success," *New Straits Times* (Malaysia), 24 June 2000, 6; the *Economist* played on the familiarity of these 1950s musicals in its coverage of China: its 19 December 1998 issue included a story about unbalanced male-to-female ratios produced by the one-child family policy under the headline "6.3 Brides for Seven Brothers."

8. Woo quoted in Stephen Teo, *Hong Kong Cinema: The Extra Dimensions* (London: British Film Institute, 1997), 174.

9. Woo quoted in Kenneth M. Chanko, "Tom Cruise Gets Woo'd," *Boston Globe,* 28 May 2000, P7.

Index

Page numbers in italics refer to illustrations.

doctor and, 93–94, 98; modernization and, 193–94, 198, 211; musicals and, 193, 210; people-to-people narratives and, 84–85, 88, 99; resistance to, 26–27; tourism and, 107–10; universalism and, 80

International Educational Exchange Service, 110, 138

internationalism, 22, 28, 32, 33, 42, 49, 56, 58–59, 62, 63, 113, 215–16, 219, 224, 243; of Dooley, 90–91, 95, 119; of Hammerstein, 196; humanitarian, 74, 148; left-liberal, 29–33, 41, 54–55, 56, 58–59, 60, 63, 76, 78, 91, 124, 137, 215–16; of Michener, 124; of People-to-People program, 50, 51, 54–55, 219; of Popular Front, 31, 58, 137; racial solidarity and, 139–40; of *Reader's Digest*, 69–71, 74, 78; right, 29–30, 32, 33, 34, 41, 54, 56, 58–59, 63, 71, 124, 178; of *Saturday Review*, 74–76, 78; touristic, 109

International Rescue Committee (IRC), 91, 100, 171

Iran, 44, 57, 81, 188

I Remember Mama (Van Druten), 230

Isaacs, Harold, 75, 145, 176

Isaacson, Leo, 136

Isherwood, Christopher, 219

isolationism, 9, 20, 22, 28, 29, 33, 46, 69, 75

Israel, 114

Italy, 47, 177, 241

James, C. L. R., 181

Jameson, Fredric, 58

Janss, Edmund, 153

Japan, 5, 27, 19, 25, 241, 242, 275; adoption of children from, 175, 177; anti-American riots in, 141–42, 142; atomic bombing of, 75, 76, 83, 113, 151; Christian Children's Fund in, 153, 154; educational exchanges with, 199; "Family of Man" exhibit in, 188; Hawaii and, 250; immigration from, 224, 226, 255, 256; invasion of China by, 31, 152; Michener in, 125–27, 131, 132; missionaries in, 4, 30; modernization of, 198; occupation and reconstruction of, 26, 77, 98, 122, 149, 150, 163, 218–19, 244; opening to Western trade of, 24; *Reader's Digest* and, 70, 77, 82, 218; *Saturday Review* and, 80; sister-city affiliations with, 51; treaties with, 150

Japanese Americans: in Hawaii, 246; in *Hawaii*, 253–60; internment of, 123,

182, 227, 235, 261–62; *see also* Asian Americans

Jefferson, Miles, 184

Jen, Gish, 168–69

Jhabvala, Ruth Prawer, 80

John Henry (play), 181

Johnson, Lyndon B., 6

Joy Luck Club, The (film), 232

Judd, Walter, 32, 78

Juergensmeyer, John, 51, 56

Julin, Captain Donald D., 117

jungle-doctor narratives, 59, 89–99, 161

Kataki (play), 232

Kelly, Gene, 274

Kennan, George, 24, 98, 111, 219

Kennedy, John F., 6, 88, 124, 125, 189, 191, 206

Kern, Jerome, 180

Kerouac, Jack, 4

Kerr, Deborah, 2, 3, 194, 209

Khrushchev, Nikita, 44, 188

King and I, The (Rodgers and Hammerstein), 1–2, 2, 3, 8, 10, 11–14, 17, 160, 191–97, 209, 230, 273–75; banned in Thailand, 221; Brynner in, 174, 191, 222; London production of, 186; modernization in, 192–94, 197, 200–15, 217–19, 222; revivals and adaptations of, 265–66, 268; source material for, 9, 194–95

Kingman, Dong, 233, 241

Kipling, Rudyard, 115, 231, 247, 248

Kiss Me Deadly (film), 36

Kon Tiki (Heyerdahl), 102

Korea, 5, 21, 71, 84, 116, 117, 125, 126; adoption of children from, 175, 177, 270; U.S. bases in, 163; *see also* North Korea; South Korea

Korean War, 26, 37, 57, 78, 79, 82, 126, 136, 154, 159, 244; and adoption of Asian children, 175, 270; Chinese intervention in, 143; Eisenhower and, 44, 47; end of, 27, 248; films about, 139, 153; Michener and, 2–3, 119, 125, 132

Kraft, Hy, 185

Kriesberg, Martin, 62

Krutch, Joseph Wood, 74

Kuomintang, 26, 33, 78

Kurahashi, Mutsumi, 82

Kurosawa, Akira, 80

Kwan, Nancy, 233, 236, 238, 239

Ladejinsky, Wolf, 75

Lahr, John, 191

Library of Congress Cataloging-in-Publication Data

Klein, Christina
    Cold war orientalism : Asia in the middlebrow imag-
ination, 1945–1961 / Christina Klein.
        p.   cm.
    Includes index.
    ISBN 0–520–22469–8 (cloth : alk. paper)—
    ISBN 0–520–23230–5 (paper : alk. paper)
    1. Asia—Foreign public opinion, American.
2. Orientalism—United States—History—20th century. 3. Public opinion—United States. 4. Asians
in mass media. 5. United States—Foreign relations—
1945–1989. 6. United States—Relations—Asia.
7. Asia—Relations—United States. 8. Cold War—
Social aspects—United States. 9. Popular culture—
United States—History—20th century. 10. United
States—Civilization—1945- . I. Title.
DS33.4.U6K55   2003
950.4′24—dc21   2002013310

             Indexer: Ruth Elwell
          Compositor: G & S Typesetters, Inc.
                Text: 10/13 Sabon
             Display: Sabon
  Printer and Binder: Thomson-Shore